SHUT UP HE EXPLAINED

Shut Up He Explained

A LITERARY MEMOIR

VOL. II

JOHN METCALF

BIBLIOASIS

FIRST EDITION

Library and Archives Canada Cataloguing in Publication

Metcalf, John, 1938-
Shut up he explained : a literary memoir / John Metcalf.

Includes bibliographical references.
ISBN 978-1-897231-32-6

1. Metcalf, John, 1938- 2. Criticism. 3. Canadian literature—History and criticism. I. Title.

PS8576.E83Z477 2007 C818'.5409 C2007-904543-X

Jacket photo by Brenda Schmidt
Copyedited by Michael Carbert
Readied for the press by Dan Wells

Canada Council for the Arts / Conseil des Arts du Canada

ONTARIO ARTS COUNCIL
CONSEIL DES ARTS DE L'ONTARIO

We gratefully acknowledge the support of the Canada Council for the Arts and the Ontario Arts Council for our publishing program.

John Metcalf gratefully acknowledges the financial support of the City of Ottawa.

PRINTED AND BOUND IN CANADA

For

MYRNA

as always

and in their ink-stained glory

for

Tim and Elke Inkster

and

Daniel and Alexis Wells

CONTENTS

TITLES

Book titles are quirky creatures and provoke odd emotional responses. Friends have *begged* me not to entitle this book *Shut Up He Explained.* They have said the title is "negative," "dismissive," "minatory," "contemptuous;" it will turn readers away from the book, they say. It will, they say, confirm readers in their impression of my being cantankerous and curmudgeonly, a charge which has been levelled against me for forty years. Some of my friends *do* find the title funny but feel that as I lack academic qualifications I should present myself with greater gravity; being funny, they seem to be saying, makes it easier for readers to dismiss my opinions and conclusions as being slight.

Their responses astonish me but I have to admit that humour in titles is a rather subjective matter. I remember being at Hugh Hood's house one day in 1978 after Alice Munro had published *Something I've Been Meaning to Tell You* and *Who Do You Think You Are?* In generally playful mood, we were composing other conversational and colloquial titles that Alice might use on future books. Our minds seemed to be running on admonitions to children. Hugh's best Alice title was *Just You Wait Till I Get You Home.* Mine was *You Should Have Gone Before We Left.* In collegial spirit, we passed them on to Alice who was *very* unamused.

Some titles seem almost magical to me. They crowd in upon me from the years: *The Tale of a Fierce Bad Rabbit, King Solomon's Mines, The White Company, The Pickwick Papers, The Constant Nymph, From an Abandoned Work,* Amos Tutuola's *The Palm-Wine Drinkard, Fair Stood the Wind for France.*

The problem, though, is that what is gold to one reader is dross to another. The complicatedly funny short story writer Bruce Jay Friedman tells a story about a phone call from his friend Mario Puzo. He has just finished a novel and is considering calling it *The Godfather.* What does Bruce think?

"The worst!" says Bruce. "Terrible! You'll sink it. Use that as a title and you'll have a disaster on your hands."

I spend a week every year teaching at the Humber School for Writers. Part of the lure of the job is Bruce's endless gentle anecdotes. Here's Bruce's lunch with Isaac Bashevis Singer.

The setting was a literary luncheon in New York where speeches were to be made and awards presented. Bruce was seated at a long table opposite Singer. He was considerably in awe of this sage, this giant of Yiddish culture, this repository of *shtetl* experience and wisdom, this Chagall of literature, author of *Gimpel the Fool and Other Stories* and *The Magician of Lublin*, recipient of the Nobel Prize.

The old man sat silent. He looked about him, nodding occasionally as if in grave and considering thought. Bruce sat waiting to hear what profundities he might utter. Joyce Carol Oates got up and made her way to the podium, stood there rustling papers.

Isaac Bashevis Singer crooked a finger to draw Bruce closer across the table.

"Tell me . . ."

"Yes, Mr. Singer."

"Tell me, Mr. Friedman."

"Yes?"

Singer turned from his inspection of Joyce Carol Oates.

"Tell me Mr. Friedman, why is that girl's skirt so little?"

However.

Titles.

* * *

H.E. Bates' *Fair Stood the Wind for France* has always struck me as a title packed with magic and allure. The novel itself is a rather dull potboiler about the escape through Nazi-occupied France of the crew of a downed Wellington bomber. I suppose part of the appeal of the title is the nautical usage "stood" and the slight archaism of "Fair." It is a title which promises the heroic and hints at a traditional British pleasure – giving the dastardly French a severe duffing-up. Moonlight on canvas, thrumming in the cordage, guns run out. Hornblower high jinks these, or Bolitho, or Jack Aubrey, those creations of C.S. Forester, Alexander Kent, and Patrick O'Brian. Though the line is actually, of course, from an earlier era, not the eighteenth century wars against France, but from Michael Drayton's poem "Agincourt."

I suppose I remain sufficiently English to have a visceral distrust of France; something in me responds to Noel Coward's remark in *Conversation Piece*: "There's always something fishy about the French." Sir Edward March in *Ambrosia and Small Beer* recorded Coward's fellow actor and director Ivor Novello as topping this by his even more memorable:

"There's something Vichy about the French."

How elegantly Coward's best plays stand up: *Private Lives*, *Blithe Spirit*, *Present Laughter*, witty, stylish, and unashamedly sophisticated.

I feel nostalgic for the world of Olivier, Ralph Richardson, Binkie Beaumont, Gertrude Lawrence, Prince Littler, and John Gielgud though it's a world known to me only through diaries, autobiographies, and memoirs. One of those memoirs records Noel Coward and friends crossing Piccadilly Circus. Above them is a huge hoarding advertising a film of naval derring-do featuring Michael Redgrave and Dirk Bogarde. One of Coward's entourage intoned the film's title: *The Sea Shall Not Have Them*.

"I don't see why not," sniffed Coward. "Everyone else has."

Homosexuality seems to be an unsurprising constant in the theatrical world. In 1953, John Gielgud was knighted for his services to the theatre. In the same year, he was arrested for what is known in the British demi-monde as "cottaging," importuning in a public lavatory. He appeared in court where he described himself as "employed as a clerk." He was fined a tenner.

The strange word "cottaging" according to *Cassell's Dictionary of Slang*, derives from "the published particulars of an eccentrically worded will in which the testator left a large fortune to be laid out in building 'cottages of convenience.'" I'd heard the word used by the late Harry Hill, actor and raconteur, in one of his scabrous anecdotes involving a power failure in the lavatories of the Montreal Voyageur Bus terminal at Berri-de Montigny and the loss of his partial plate.

Nigel Hawthorne who played Sir Humphrey in the *Yes, Minister* TV series described the aftermath of Gielgud's arrest in his autobiography *Straight Face*.

"When he reported for rehearsal the following day, he was advised to enter via the front rather than through the stage door where there were reporters. The cast working on stage in his absence paused mid-sentence as he made his awkward way down the aisle. It was Sybil Thorndike who broke the tension, stepping forward and wagging her finger with a 'Who's been a naughty boy, then?'"

Another memoir records a *Hamlet* rehearsal. Actor-managers, like Olivier and Gielgud, hired a company of actors and actresses for a season of plays, rented theatres, took the profits, and, of course, played the juiciest roles. On this occasion one of the actors was musing rather academically about whether Hamlet sleeps with Ophelia.

"In this company," said the actor-manager, "always."

In *Gielgud: An Actor and His Times: A Memoir,* Gielgud reminisces about Ralph Richardson: "We were both in *Henry IV Part I* with which the 1930 season opened. Ralph hated the fighting and I did not like it much either. During the battle of Shrewsbury Ralph used to shout 'Left . . . right . . . now you hit me, Cocky . . . now I hit you' – I was sure the audience could hear him. He was not particularly happy as Prince Hal, but absolutely superb as Caliban and, later in the same season, as Enobarbus and Kent. In fact, I cannot imagine anybody playing them so well. He always took great care with his make-up, for which he would make elaborate drawings beforehand. He and Olivier vied with each other in the construction of putty noses."

What comes across in most of these memoirs is not so much the wit and warmth – though they glitter and glow everywhere – but rather the consuming dedication to craft. The construction of putty noses! This is particularly evident in the *Noel Coward Diaries* published in 1982. It is a dedication I find intensely moving. Here is an example.

Donald Spoto describes Laurence Olivier preparing to play Othello:

> Finally, after a preliminary week in Birmingham, *Othello* opened at the Old Vic on April 21, 1964. Olivier spent the morning at the gymnasium, dispatched company business, and had an early luncheon of steak and half a bottle of red wine . . . Then he answered letters and telephone calls and rested for three hours – this was his schedule whenever he played the Moor that season. At five he began the arduous, nearly three-hour process of applying the makeup he had designed: he shaved the hair from his chest, arms and legs and then applied Max Factor number 2880, a black liquid stain, over his entire body. When that had dried, he added a lighter brown and then a third coat to give a mahogany sheen. He and his dresser then used yards of chiffon to polish his skin until he shone (pancake powder would run under perspiration). Then he painted his fingernails with a pale-blue

varnish, coated the inside of his mouth with gentian violet, put on a tightly curled black wig, and with a pinkish hue polished his palms and the soles of his feet; four hours later, after the performance, almost two hours were required to remove the make-up . . .

Olivier stepped onstage to a collective gasp from the audience. Moving like a panther . . .

In this season Sir Laurence Olivier was fifty-six years old.

Kingsley Amis records – and "records" is the exact word to capture Amis' habitual mimicry – records a conversation about this very performance. He was teaching at Vanderbilt University in Nashville, a racist institution he had come to loathe. What follows is from *Memoirs*.

> There was a do at the house of the Professor of Iberian Languages. Of my host I remember nothing, of my hostess among other things that she had the biggest pair of knockers I had ever seen in the flesh and still unequalled. When you stood at an ordinary conversational distance from her, you found you were standing too close to her. I know it sounds puzzling.
>
> 'Did you happen to see,' she said in her no more than averagely unbelievable tones, 'the movie Surr Laurence Oh-livyay made of Shakespeare's *Oh-thello?'* – lately shown in the States.
>
> 'Yes,' I said, fighting for concentration on more than one front.
>
> 'And what did you think of it? – I don't mean so much the movie itself, I mean *him*.'
>
> 'Well . . . I thought he was very good.'
>
> 'You mean the way they made him up to look?'
>
> 'Well, yes, that too.' There was by now general silence. In my mind's or memory's eye a hundred Western barkeeps reached for the shotgun.
>
> 'But they made him look like a black mayun!'
>
> 'Yes, they did, didn't they?'
>
> 'But he even toked like a black mayun!'
>
> 'Yes, perhaps a bit –'
>
> 'But he even *woked* like a black mayun!'
>
> 'Yes,' I said, lying in a good cause, 'I thought that was the most brilliant part of his whole performance.'

> They had not allowed for anything like that, which went down like the appearance of a U.S. marshal. Only Mrs. Iberian Languages said in melancholy defiance, 'But how could a real lady fall in love with a man like that?' . . .

Amis describes such pronunciations as "hayyut" for "hat" and "bawun" for "born" as polyphthongs, a useful arrow for one's quiver.

Stop meandering!

Get to the *point.*

Yes.
Yes, of course.
I'm sorry.

But I ought just to add that not everyone was adulatory about Olivier. Dramatist Peter Nichols in *Diaries 1969-1977* expresses a more socialist view. Olivier was known to the actors as "Sir." Nichols refers to Michael Blakemore, Kenneth Tynan, and Olivier at the National Theatre as "the régime" and calls Olivier "Sir Larynx Delivery."

Nigel Hawthorne in *Straight Face* alludes to Olivier's general disdain for actors and tells of opening in a new John Mortimer play and enduring from the front row Olivier's "reptilian gaze."

Nichols gives us a charming vignette of "the regime" casting his play *The National Health.*

> Olivier liked *The National Health* more on his second reading. Doesn't care for the rude jokes and wants the best one cut out. Mike [Blakemore] went to see him to discuss actors and designers.
>
> 'Close the door, Michael. I don't want the gentleman doing the garden to hear what we're saying. Much as I admire the negro races, I'm no great admirer of their histrionic abilities. This play has a number of coloured characters. D'you think the regular girls in the company should black up? Joan, for instance?'
>
> . . . We went through the cast of 22 characters, matching them to the available actors. His opinions of his company were unimpressed, even brutal. 'No, he can't play Foster because he's not staying.' This was evidently news to Tynan. 'No. Boring man. Drinks too much and

is always slapping me on the back and asking me to supper with his family. No.'

Discussing the negro contingent of nurses, chaplain, etc., Michael raised the name of Cy Grant [handsome actor and popular calypso singer of the time.] 'Cy Grant,' said Olivier, 'so large and strong! When Vivien and I were managing the St. James', now alas! vanished, we took a boat party for the whole numerous company, down the river. I, as befits the manager, held aloof, though seeming to join the fun and games. My lovely prop-men and carpenters, strong as oxen every manjack, carried off the drunks on stretchers. Cy was seen disappearing in the direction of the Bishop's Palace of Lambeth. At a word from me, off went the boys and down went Grant in a great flurry of arms and legs . . .' – here he used the swirling movements with snake hands from the opening soliloquy of *Richard III* – ' . . . when suddenly from under this hefty scrimmage Grant's voice rang across the fore-court "FUCK Sir Lawrence Oh-liv-ee-ay" –' and this was with all the stops out and one hand flung across his forehead. Then the sudden diminuendo on – 'I never worked with him again but followed his career with in-ter-est and was happy at his success.'

Please!
Yes. Meandering. Sorry again.
Titles.

Titles, in general, are difficult but the titles of autobiographies and memoirs offer special problems. The writer is presenting to the public a version of himself and events. The title ideally should suggest something of how the writer wants to be seen. Immodesty must be avoided. The writer wishes to ingratiate himself but without being ingratiating. Charm must be used to disarm. Humour needs to be deployed. Self-deprecation is probably called for.

Niggling away for both writer and reader is the suspicion that autobiography itself, the very genre, is tinged with self-importance, with mild pomposity, with deception.

Malcolm Bradbury dealt with this problem in his witty book *Unsent Letters* which is an autobiography of sorts by comically deflating both writer and genre:

> One of the problems of middle age, I find, is that one is constantly tempted into reminiscence, there being little else to do with oneself. For the fact is that I have evidently reached that time in my life when the present, by some peculiar process that I do not understand, has become the past, and the is has somehow through no fault of my own become the was.
>
> . . . Somehow, once the idea of writing an autobiography arises, one grows a little more sententious in all one says and does. One starts sitting up very straight in the car, talks differently to one's children, in a tone of nostalgia and reminiscence, and looks at one's old friends in a quite new way, wondering whether they are more page 17 or page 120. At the same time one begins to lose panache. One breathes harder when chasing the wives of one's friends up the stairs, and the past somehow grows more patchy and luminous, filled with glimpses of summers when the sun always shone, and of perfect British Rail kippers.

I remember, in the days when the sun always shone, the delight of Bradbury's first novel *Eating People Is Wrong*, the vile comedy of *The History Man*, and the deeply imagined *Rates of Exchange*.

Autobiography titles do seem to fall into groups or classes. There is the simply descriptive, declarative title. *My Father and Myself* by J.R. Ackerley, author also of *Hindoo Holiday*. *Memoirs of an Aesthete* by Sir Harold Acton. *A Little Learning* by Evelyn Waugh, the title, of course, a quotation from Pope's *An Essay on Criticism.*

> A little learning is a dangerous thing;
> Drink deep, or taste not the Pierian spring.

Learning to Look by John Pope-Hennessy, ex-Director of the British Museum, whose brother, the biographer James Pope-Hennessy, wrote of Wallis Simpson, wife of Edward VIII, that she was "an American woman *par excellence* [except for] the suspicion that she is not a woman at all."

I return to Evelyn Waugh again and again; his work has always been one of the central delights of my life. At the risk of meandering again, here from *A Little Learning* is Waugh's factual account of the boarding school and the original of "Captain Grimes" who was brought to fictional life in *Decline and Fall.*

> After a week or two a whole holiday was ordained in honour of Mr. Vanhomrigh's birthday. It was no holiday for the assistant masters. The whole school was packed into charabancs in the early morning and driven to the slopes of Snowdon, where games were played and a picnic luncheon devoured and scrupulously cleared up. Great licence was allowed; boys and masters chased one another and scuffled on the turf. At length at nightfall we returned wearily singing. When it was all over and the boys in bed we sat in the common-room deploring the miseries of the day. Grimes alone sat with the complacent smile of an Etruscan funerary effigy.
>
> 'I confess *I* enjoyed myself greatly,' he said as we groused.
>
> We regarded him incredulously. '*Enjoyed* yourself, Grimes? What did you find to enjoy?'
>
> 'Knox minor,' he said with radiant simplicity. 'I felt the games a little too boisterous, so I took Knox minor away behind some rocks. I removed his boot and stocking, opened my trousers, put his dear little foot there and experienced a most satisfying emission.'

The original of "Captain Grimes" later in life donated to the Ashmolean Museum a large collection of European porcelain; I never see it without smiling.

(Evelyn's much-abused son Auberon is now largely forgotten as a novelist but I would still recommend *The Foxglove Saga* and *Consider the Lilies.* Also highly recommended, Auberon Waugh's autobiography entitled *Will This Do?* While a Cornet in the Royal Horse Guards (The Blues) on National Service in Cyprus, he managed to shoot himself with his own armoured car taking five Browning .300 machine gun shells through the chest, shoulder, and arm.)

Another type of title threatens or suggests a certain belligerence. *Borstal Boy* by Brendan Behan. *A Better Class of Person* by John Osborne. *The Air-Conditioned Nightmare* by Henry Miller. *Light on a Dark Horse* by Roy Campbell. *Down and Out in Paris and London* by George Orwell with those unforgettable *plongeurs.*

Some titles are boisterous or melodramatic. *It's Me, O Lord!* by A.E. Coppard. *Leftover Life to Kill* by Dylan's tiresome relict, Caitlin Thomas.

Many titles are oblique and slightly enigmatic and suggest the revelation to come of a life, a world. *A Cab at the Door* and *Midnight Oil* by V.S.

Pritchett. *Lions and Shadows* by Christopher Isherwood. *The Military Orchid* by Jocelyn Brooke. *As I Was Going Down Sackville Street* by Oliver St. John Gogarty, the lively original of Joyce's "stately plump Buck Mulligan" in *Ulysses.*

Other titles, presumably attempting to be charming, overreach themselves and sound coy or cute. *Dear Me* by Peter Ustinov. *Me All Over: Memoirs of a Misfit* by James Kirkup. *Here Lies Eric Ambler* by, of course, Eric Ambler. It's strange to detect cuteness in a writer as brilliant as Ambler. Few novelists can have begun a novel with such élan as Ambler did in *Dirty Story.* Here are the opening two sentences:

> Write it on the walls.
> *H. Carter Gavin, Her Britannic Majesty's Vice-Consul in Athens, is a shit.*

Some writers seem to feel no need to charm or ingratiate and use titles which seem to seek or proclaim grandeur. *Speak, Memory* by Vladimir Nabokov. *Summoned by Bells* by John Betjeman. *Memory Hold the Door* by John Buchan. *World within World* by Stephen Spender.

This last autobiography was memorably reviewed by Evelyn Waugh. Waugh considered Spender a literary functionary rather than a real writer and took the opportunity to savage him.

". . . to see him fumbling with our rich and delicate language is to experience all the horror of seeing a Sèvres vase in the hands of a chimpanzee."

I have a fondness for the light elegiac quality of Betjeman, elegy not for the warrior borne on his shield but for the quotidian, the decline of the crumpet, the retreat of the cummerbund. The Betjeman *tone* is exquisitely captured in a parody by Alan Bennett called "Place Names of China," a poem about the brand names on British toilets. "Harpic" is the brand name of a toilet cleanser.

The last stanza runs:

> Here I sit, alone and sixty,
> Bald, and fat, and full of sin,
> Cold the seat and loud the cistern,
> As I read the Harpic tin.

And finally there is the category of autobiography title to which, I hope, *Shut Up He Explained* belongs: the comic. There aren't many titles in this category. There is the account of Spike Milligan's military service, mainly as a lance-corporal, entitled, magnificently, *Hitler: My Part in His Downfall.* And perhaps my favourite title of all, the autobiography of Peter Nichols which recounts – splendidly eccentric father – his growing up in Bristol.

He achieved great success with his first stage play, the dark comedy *A Day in the Death of Joe Egg.* His satiric comedy *The National Health* played to great critical success at the National Theatre in 1969. Ken Tynan had brought in Michael Blakemore to direct. He went on writing for the stage and for film and television. The movie *Privates on Parade* in 1977 was a feisty Nichols frolic. I used to teach at what in my fiction I call Bluebell Secondary Modern School with Peter's brother Geoff who played trumpet in the Avon Cities Jazz Band. To this day, I can see his face gaunt and grey with fatigue as he appeared in school by 8 A.M. after having played half the night in clubs and pubs as far afield as Birmingham.

Peter's autobiography was entitled *Feeling You're Behind.*

Although the *titles* of Australian writer Clive James' three volumes of autobiography aren't funny – *Unreliable Memoirs, Falling Towards England,* and *May Week Was in June* – the books themselves are *snortingly* funny and . . .

Oh, God! Not *another* digression!
Just a brief . . .
Quickly then!
A brief quotation from Falling Towards England.

> [Bruce] Jennings left you in doubt of his brilliance, though in some fear that his monologues might never end. A career drinker, he would stand balefully in the middle of a party, the only man present in a Turnbull & Asser shirt, antique Chavet tie, pin-stripe double-breasted Savile Row suit, Lobb shoes, black fedora and a monocle. 'Des is the name,' he would loudly confide to an invisible interlocutor, 'Des Esseintes.' And indeed he was the hero of *A Rebours* to the life, a Count Robert de Montesquieu *de nos jours,* creating himself as a work of art. He didn't have the living tortoise inset with turquoises but no doubt it was on order. Meanwhile he had everything else, and I was wide-eyed even as he stood there swaying. When he fell to the floor he would usually take a couple of people with him. Laid to rest on a sofa, he would sleep until the party thinned out. Then, with just the right-sized audience, he

would start a closed-eyed, resonant muttering which might consist of nothing but brand-names and radio jingles from the far Australian past. 'Rosella Tomato Sauce . . . Twice As Nice If Kept On Ice . . . Sydney Flour is our flour, we use it every day . . . I like Aeroplane Jelly, Aeroplane Jelly for me . . . You'll sleep tight 'cause you'll sleep right, on a Lotusland inner-spring mattress . . .'

Years later I was to realize that this was the most original side of his mind talking. He was rediscovering and reordering an Australian language which had never had any pretensions beyond the useful and had thus retained an inviolable purity. It was the language written on bottles of cough medicine and packets of junket powder: a vocabulary without any value beyond common currency, and therefore undiluted by aesthetic pretension. With a sure instinct reinforced by his dandyish collector's erudition, he had realized that not all the ephemeral was evanescent – that there was such a thing as a poetry of trivia, uniquely evocative for a country whose art was hag-ridden by a self-conscious striving towards autonomous respectability.

Those advertisements remind me of Keith Waterhouse's autobiography *City Lights: A Street Life.* Waterhouse claims to remember advertisements from the World War II years. One read: "Forward to Victory! And Regular Supplies of Bassett's Liquorice All-Sorts." Another even more memorable, read: "Cadbury's Chocolate: Rich and Dark Like the Aga Khan."

What?

Oh, sorry. Yes. Back, then, on track.

In *An Aesthetic Underground* I described the course I gave myself in getting acquainted with the short story form and mentioned Ring Lardner and his marvellous baseball stories *You Know Me, Al.* These stories are letters by Jack Keefe, White Sox rookie, to "Friend Al" and represent a vital stage in the invention of a literary American vernacular. This truth was noted, astonishingly, by Virginia Woolf.

As a high school student Ernest Hemingway was reading Lardner closely and later admitted that Lardner had been an influence on *In Our Time*, arguably one of the most important books of the twentieth century.

Although many of Lardner's stories are too slick or formulaic others hold their place in world short story writing. I remember still the immense pleasure and insight into craft given me by such stories as "Some Like them Cold," and "I Can't Breathe," "Alibi Ike" and "Mr. and Mrs. Fix-It."

Some books are written in response to others, are provoked by them. One of my favourite books – and titles – is Stella Gibbons' *Cold Comfort Farm* which was published in 1932 in response to the rural tedium of Mary Webb's *Precious Bane* which appeared in 1925. *Precious Bane* is described in the *Reader's Encyclopedia* as "a story of fierce, morose country people, in which Prudence Sarn, the narrator, finds a husband who appreciates her in spite of her harelip." Stella Gibbons' parody is extremely funny and her loving play with language always leaves me envious. Ring Lardner responded to Daisy Ashford in exactly the way Stella Gibbons had responded to Mary Webb.

In 1919 in England, Daisy Ashford, as an adult, published a book she had written when she was nine. It is called *The Young Visiters* and is so unconsciously funny that it has never been out of print. With all its misspellings and its child's view of upper class society –"It was a sumpshous spot all done up in gold with plenty of looking glasses" and dukes and earls having "levies" in "Crystall Pallace" and poor Mr. Salteena who is "not quite a gentleman" – the book was immediately popular. There was controversy at the time about the book's authenticity – though it is now accepted as totally genuine – and Lardner was persuaded the book was a fraud. As a spoof of *The Young Visiters* Lardner published in 1920 "The Young Immigrunts," the purported recounting of a journey by Bill Lardner, aged four, with his father, Ring. The story contains the following masterly lines to which the title of this book is both thanks and homage.

> The lease said about me and my father's trip from the Bureau of Manhattan to our new home the soonest mended. In some way ether I or he got balled up on the grand concorpse and next thing you know we was thretning to swoop down on Pittsfield.
>
> Are you lost daddy I arsked tenderly.
>
> Shut up he explained.

GOODBYE TO ALL THAT

The sound in my study was changing. As the three men from the moving company emptied the bookshelves and boxed the books, the sound in the room became higher, sharper, hollow. Six hours later the moving truck pulled away with over 5000 books and the archives of the Porcupine's Quill from 1989 onwards, archives of more than a hundred books in all their various states, many with extensive editing, hundreds of photographs of readings and launches, reviews, financial records, metre after metre of correspondence – all of it heading for the Rare Book Room at McGill University.

This July day in 2003 was one more day in a year which seemed marked by change and upheaval, a year of conclusions, terminations, summations. In December of this year John Newlove died. He was exactly my age. His work and life were accorded two column inches in the *Globe and Mail.* Friends were variously diagnosed this year with cancer, heart conditions, subdural haematoma. In December again, I received my first Old Age Security cheque. Time's wingèd chariot . . .

In March of this year *An Aesthetic Underground: A Literary Memoir* had appeared. Writing the book had exhausted me. There had been one morning towards the end when I felt so weak I could not get up; I lay in bed wondering if I was dying. It was not simply the writing that had exhausted me. It was a cumulative exhaustion, the exhaustion of years. I was feeling deeply weary of swimming against the tide, deeply weary of living embattled.

The centre of *An Aesthetic Underground* for me had been the two chapters concerning the deliberate re-shaping of the story form in Canada but only one review mentioned the topic. Most reviews took the "gadfly" or "curmudgeon" angle, that being simpler than having to think about language.

There was a certain uniformity to the reviews:

". . . pompous, self-aggrandizing . . . ," "sophomoric boosterism," "boastful . . . unnecessary self-advertisement . . . ," "relentlessly negative . . . ," "critical muggers who try to strengthen their own scrawny reputations by throwing punches at literary heavyweights . . . ," "vitriol . . . combatively unfair . . . ," "vociferous complainer," "Crank Emeritus."

Change and upheaval, too, on the family front. My brother, Michael, retired from the Ashmolean Museum, finally sold his vast pile in North Oxford, bought a *pied à terre* on North Parade in Oxford and returned to end his days in the landscape of his childhood buying a house in Leyburn in the North Riding of Yorkshire. The house is on the limestone escarpment called The Shawl overlooking Wensleydale. Legend claims that Mary Queen of Scots in 1569, in attempted escape from nearby Bolton Castle, travelled along the escarpment path and there dropped her shawl. Less romantically, "shawl" probably comes from "shalle," a local derivation of the Viking "scali" meaning huts or dwellings. Excavations have turned up skeletons and Roman pottery.

It was to this house that we headed in August 2003 to celebrate my mother's one hundredth birthday. Shortly before this Michael had written to tell me that he had been diagnosed as having cancer, a fact he did not want revealed or raised. He had arranged a luncheon in a small hotel in Reeth, a village on the hillside where Arkengarthdale and Swaledale join. Many family members arrived from Yorkshire and from what I still insist on calling Cumberland and Westmoreland.

Michael and I had prepared brief speeches and my mother gave a reply completely extempore and in perfect paragraphs, without faltering, reviewing what had been her aims in life.

It was a day of blue skies, warm sunshine, the fells purple with heather. In the hotel's rose garden which looked out over the village green, sundry little Metcalfs threw their toys at each other and ran and shouted. The day was idyllic and made more so perhaps by our knowledge of the frosts to come.

When a child I'd thought the three Ridings of Yorkshire were something to do with horses, with how far one could ride in a day, but the word comes from the Danish "treding" meaning "a third part." Most place names in England derive from Old English but in the northeast, in the lands of the Danelaw, the place names derive from Old Scandinavian.

akr "plot of cultivated or arable land," *askr* "ash tree." *bekkr* "stream," *by* "farmstead, village," *dalr* "valley," *eski* "place growing with ash trees," *garth* "enclosure," *gil, kirkja, thorp.*

Leyburn itself is Old English *burna* "stream," possibly with *hleg* "shelter" but the nearby towns and villages are largely Scandinavian.

Aysgarth meaning "Gap or open place where oak trees grow."

Askrigg meaning "Ash tree ridge."

Spennithorne meaning "Thorn tree by the fence or enclosure."

Bellerby meaning "Farmstead or village of a man called Belgr."

Bedale meaning "Nook of land of a man called Bēda."

The soft chime of this history charms me, allures me. I was tempted to stay in Leyburn or Witton or Middleham where as a youth the future Richard III lived in Richard Neville's castle and there learned courtly manners and the arts of war.

I was tempted to relax back into the embrace of England and shake the dust of Canada from off my feet. No doubt that this was country of the heart, the Metcalfe name everywhere – on trucks and vans, on shopfronts, on farm gates. I was in the centre of my history. We drove one day to have lunch in a local seventeenth-century pub and passed through the hamlet of Bainbridge, for centuries a Metcalfe stronghold where Metcalfes held hereditary office. Just minutes drive from my brother's house on The Shawl stands Nappa Hall, a fortified manor house below the village of Nappa Scar built by James Metcalfe in 1416. The land was given him by Lord Richard le Scrope as reward for leading the Wensleydale men against the French armour at Agincourt in 1415.

Thinking of this English victory reminded me of Michael Drayton's poem about the battle. In the verse that came to mind, King Harry is rallying his men.

> Poitiers and Crécy tell,
> When most their pride did swell,
> Under our swords they fell;
> No less our skill is
> Than when our grandsire great,
> Claiming the regal seat
> By many a warlike feat
> Lopped the French lilies.

I was tempted by the photographs in the windows of estate agents in every small town, photos of listed limestone houses none younger than the eighteenth century. Daily, *The Times*. Country walking. Grouse whirring low over dry-stone walls, heather and bracken on the high fells, stiles, the scuts of running rabbits. On the butcher's window a whitewash sign: Put British Pork Upon Your Fork. The nursery comfort of cheese straws, Cumberland sausage, soft-boiled eggs with marmite soldiers. At night the nightly pints of Theakston's Old Peculiar.

I found myself thinking of Tom Wilcher's words in Joyce Cary's *To Be a Pilgrim,* the second novel in the trilogy of *Herself Surprised* and *The Horse's Mouth.*

> The English summer weighs upon me with its richness. I know why Robert ran away from so much history to the new lands where the weather is as stupid as the trees, chance dropped, are meaningless. Where earth is only new dirt, and corn, food for animals two and four-footed. I must go, too, for life's sake. This place is so doused in memory that only to breathe makes me dream like an opium eater. Like one who has taken a narcotic, I have lived among fantastic loves and purposes. The shape of a field, the turn of a lane, have had the power to move me as if they were my children, and I had made them. I have wished immortal life for them though they were even more transient appearances than human beings.

My impulse was quite the reverse of Wilcher's; *my* impulse was not to escape but to return.

Wensleydale is a landscape so beautiful that the pagan feeling for *numina,* presiding spirits, is never really far from even the most rational of minds. Sir Kenneth Clark wrote in the first volume of his autobiography *Another Part of the Wood* ". . . searching in my mind for the first moments in which I seemed to be lifted out of my immediate childish preoccupations, the first emotions that could be described as religious, they seem to have been inspired by the trunks and roots of trees."

Instinctively, I know he is thinking of beech trees.

Insofar as I believe in immanence at all, I would have to admit that brambles and blackberries have something of that trunk-and-root effect on me. Seeing the briers in the hedgerows gives me intense aesthetic pleasure, the shine of the blackberries, the plump glinting weight of them. I remember an afternoon a quarter of a century ago picking just over 13 pounds of blackberries with my mother on Shotover Common on the edge of Oxford. Thinking of her great age and frailty, of her deepening blindness, of my brother's illness, and my own aches and twinges made me recall Seamus Heaney's sturdy poem about blackberries and mortality.

Blackberry Picking

Late August, given heavy rain and sun
For a full week, the blackberries would ripen.
At first, just one, a glossy purple clot
Among others, red, green, hard as a knot.
You ate that first one and its flesh was sweet
Like thickened wine: summers' blood was in it
Leaving stains upon the tongue and lust for
Picking. Then red ones inked up and that hunger
Sent us out with milk-cans, pea-tins, jam-pots
Where briars scratched and wet grass bleached our boots,
Round hayfields, cornfields and potato-drills
We trekked and picked until the cans were full,
Until the tinkling bottom had been covered
With green ones, and on top big dark blobs burned
Like a plate of eyes. Our hands were peppered
With thorn pricks, our palms sticky as Bluebeard's.
We hoarded the fresh berries in the byre.
But when the bath was filled we found a fur,
A rat-grey fungus, glutting on our cache.
The juice was stinking too. Once off the bush
The fruit fermented, the sweet flesh would turn sour.
I always felt like crying. It wasn't fair
That all the lovely canfuls smelt of rot.
Each year I hoped they'd keep, knew they would not.

I was very conscious in 2003 of time squandered. I was very conscious of how little time was left. I was tired of years of teaching ABC. Tired of having to assert and defend the blindingly obvious. Tired of proclaiming the best, tired of defending the best, tired of all the numb nihilist minds who crow that "best" is a meaningless concept, tired in many ways by a world in which the Dodo's words – "*Everybody* has won, and *all* must have prizes" – are no longer understood as funny.

A return to Canada would mean a resumption of the role of "gadfly" or "curmudgeon," a tired resumption of opposition to our continually embarrassing literary judgements. I feel little connection to Canada's literary establishment whose fundamental interest is not in literature but in nationalism.

Recent comments of Hélène Chalifour Scherrer, newly appointed Minister of Heritage, reveal the uncomprehending coarseness of institutional establishment view . . . "what I repeat to people is that Heritage Canada isn't necessarily about knowing a lot about culture, but rather taking care of its Canadian identity. Culture is a tool. And you need a vision to be the guardian of the Canadian identity. You don't necessarily have to know what books were published last week."

Some of us would think that was *precisely* what you have to know.

We laud Margaret Laurence's truly appalling novel *The Diviners,* the national book-trade magazine *Quill and Quire* declares Carol Shields to be "Our Jane Austen," Rudy Wiebe's ponderous historical novels garner the nation's highest literary honour. Has no one read Sir Walter Scott, Mary Stewart, Mary Renault, or Alfred Duggan? Margaret Atwood's dystopias plod glumly on to universal admiration. Has no one read Russell Hoban's *Riddley Walker* or Thomas Berger's *Regiment of Women,* or Kurt Vonnegut's *The Sirens of Titan* and *Cat's Cradle* or Walter M. Miller's *A Canticle for Liebowitz?*

Historical novels and dystopias are subgenres but we should not be unaware of gradations of attainment.

We do not compare.

We do not weigh.

We seem utterly deaf to language.

We embrace and honour stodge. We honour plodding writers like Marian Engel whose mindless book *Bear* won the Governor General's Award in 1976. *Bear* started out as a contribution to what was called the Trolley project, an anthology of pornography to be published as a fund-raiser for the Writers' Union of Canada, but metastasized.

I offer this brief synopsis because *Bear* is not much more inadequate than most of what stirs Canadian literary fervour and devotion and garners accolades.

Bear, according to Margaret Laurence, speaks of a "moving journey toward inner freedom and strength, and ultimately toward a sense of communion with all living creatures."

Robertson Davies in full flatulence blurbed the book as showing "the necessity . . . to ally ourselves with the spirit of one of the most ancient lands in the world. In our search for this spirit, we are indeed in search of ourselves."

This uplifting dust-jacket guff should have warned of the *longueurs* within.

Bear tells the story of Lou, an Ontario archivist, sent north to catalogue a donated library. The house itself is on a remote island and boasts in an out-house a large pet bear which exudes "a scent of musk as shrill as the high, sweet note of a shepherd's flute" and which has, we are informed more than once, a tongue that is "vertically ridged."

The bear is made to carry much pseudo-mystical weight. (See Robertson Davies above; Spirit of the Land.)

Lou falls in love with the bear.

"'Bear,' she whispered to it, 'who and what are you?'"

The affair deepens.

"'Oh, bear,' she laughed. 'We're a funny pair.' He turned around and quite definitely grinned."

The affair continues.

"'Bear, I cannot command you to love me, but I think you love me. What I want is for you to continue to be, and to be something to me. No more. Bear.'"

The affair, on Lou's part, takes on even more significance.

"One morning she got on her hands and knees, and they shared their cornflakes and powdered milk and raspberries. Their strange tongues met and she shuddered."

The bear beavers away with his "assiduous" and "vertically ridged" tongue but increasingly becomes bored and seems to Lou less committed.

"'Eat me, bear,' she pleaded, but he turned his head wearily to her and fell asleep."

Lou was driven to drizzling her nether parts with honey to sweeten the pot.

But the affair sputters out.

Lou, however, is not defeated.

"Through acceptance of herself in such a bizarre affair," writes critic John Moss in his low-wattage compendium *A Reader's Guide to the Canadian Novel,* "Lou comes to accept herself as a woman."

Huh?

This high-minded smut – and it is the high-mindedness which is appalling – was seized on by academics from coast to coast who pontificated about sex, feminism, power, the Spirit of the Land, and "the need to be at one with nature"!

Christ!

A literary prize for Female Writers at Mid-Career was established by the Writers' Development Trust in Marian Engel's name.

We honour posturing windbags like Robertson Davies. We embrace the mildly hysterical writings of Timothy Findley. We luxuriate in the flowery and the florid, the imprecise, the incomprehensible. We declare the work of a journeyman to be "classic." Canada's literary elite refers to Matt Cohen's "classic Kingston trilogy;" when I first read the books I thought they might be intended as parodies in the manner of Stella Gibbons' *Cold Comfort Farm.* Cohen's best work was in the story form; I published the best of the best in *Lives of the Mind Slaves.* Here's a paragraph from the opening pages of *The Sweet Second Summer of Kitty Malone.*

> It seemed that he never slept any more. Ever since the winter had started to melt into spring he had been waking in the middle of the night to discover himself breathing the dark air, slow and careful, drawing it through places in his body that had slept for decades. The air sifted through him until it turned his life transparent, until he felt himself turned into the boy he had once been, felt his whole young body green and reedy, the force of the spring earth pushing through it, making him tingle like a seed ready to explode.

Blithely we read on.

When we reached *drawing it through places in his body that had slept for decades* we *should* have exclaimed *Whoa, boy! Whoa!* and kept on saying it until the paragraph ended.

This book is, according to Dennis Lee, "a work of joy and mastery."

What astonishing crapola!

A literary prize was established in Matt Cohen's name.

The Giller Prize in 2003 was awarded for the *second* time to M.G. Vassanji. The writing reads like a translation into English. And a creaking fustian English at that. Here is the second paragraph of *The In-Between World of Vikram Lall*:

> I call forth for you here my beginning, the world of my childhood, in that fateful year of our friendships. It was a world of innocence and play, under a guileless constant sun; as well, of barbarous cruelty and terror

> lurking in darkest night; a colonial world of repressive, undignified subjecthood, as also of seductive order and security – so that long afterwards we would be tempted to wonder if we did not hurry forth too fast straight into the morass that is now our malformed freedom.

The Giller Prize jury in its citation described this as "inspiring prose." *Christ!*

The machine rolls on with a national tour of ten cities and a national print advertising campaign and representation in *Books for Everybody.*

In the year 2000 W.J. Keith, Professor Emeritus of the University of Toronto, wrote an essay entitled "Blight in the Bush Garden: Twenty Years of 'CanLit.'" The title of the essay refers to Northrop Frye's essay collection on Canadian literature *The Bush Garden.*

> As anyone who has taught through this period knows, students in arts subjects are even less prepared now than they were a quarter of a century ago. Up to the end, I tried to draw attention to some of the subtler 'pleasures of the text' – the sheer beauty of Ethel Wilson's prose, the intricate texture of a P.K. Page poem, the control of cadence in Jack Hodgins' *The Invention of the World* – but I knew that I was losing the battle. Why bother when high grades were being received elsewhere by students who merely spotted racist implications in one author or applauded politically correct sentiments in another? When I began teaching, I saw my function as conveying my intense enjoyment of CanLit to others. But I remember, even then, a colleague remarking that '– is a good text to teach – it raises so many problems.' Enjoyment! The word itself sounds trivial as well as irrelevant in a discipline that, when not dominated by barren aesthetics, concentrates on the sociological, the political, the ideological. The 'literary' appears to be extinct.
>
> Is CanLit nowadays anything more than an excuse for politically correct indoctrination? Should I have called this article 'Brain-washing in the Bush Garden'? It was a brave crusade while it lasted. But it failed.

The University of Toronto at the time of writing is offering a course entitled *The Poetics of Haunting in Canadian Fiction.* The course description reads:

> This course will focus on the spectral effects in contemporary Canadian fiction. Questions to be considered include: how does living with ghosts entails [sic] a politics of memory, of inheritance, and of mourning that continues to shape Canadian literature? As well, if ghosts signal the return of a secret, something repressed, then what types of secrets (ranging from familial to national) are encrypted in the texts under consideration? What is the impact of haunting on textual production; for instance, to what extent is abjection (understood textually as an impulse toward decomposition, disintegration and the break-up of language) the structuring principle of haunting? To address these questions, the course will draw on psychoanalytic, feminist, post-colonial, and post-structuralist theory.

This course description induces gloom but the accompanying list of "texts" to be read provokes something closer to apoplexy as it includes Anne-Marie MacDonald's *Fall on Your Knees.*

"There is no resisting this story" wrote the *Globe and Mail,* Canada's National Newspaper. The book was shortlisted for the Giller Prize, Winner of the Commonwealth Prize for Best First Novel, Winner of the CAA Harlequin Literary Award for Fiction, shortlisted for the Trillium Award, the Chapters/Books in Canada First Novel Award and was a selection of Oprah's Book Club. "Stunning" wrote the *Toronto Star.* "Brilliant," wrote the Vancouver Sun. "Captivating," wrote the *Winnipeg Free Press.* "Extraordinary," wrote *Books in Canada.* The *Globe and Mail* selected it as Editor's Choice and Notable Book of the Year.

What a barrage of ignorance! What a gross clamour of commerce!

Not that Canada was alone in its bizarre enthusiasm. The book sold in huge numbers all over the world. The translation into Dutch is reputed to have sold an amazing 150,000 copies.

When I realized the book was a family saga concerning Gaelic-speaking Lebanese in late nineteenth century Cape Breton I admit I thought it all rather unlikely and bizarre. But immediately realized I was being unfair. I have in my own lifetime in Montreal known ancient Cantonese waiters at Ruby Foo's who spoke Yiddish.

Fall on Your Knees is 566 pages of Maritime Grand Guignol. The characters are cardboard, the plot soap-operatic, the dialogue often emetic. The writing is completely artless and derives, at a guess, from old movies, possibly black and white ones. This sort of thing:

> When Kathleen steps onto Pier 54, she starts writing the book of her life in her head: *And then she arrived in the New World. She heard the heels of her sensible shoes ring out on the gangplank, and resolved never to be sensible.*
>
> There are a bewildering number of uniformed porters and un-uniformed scamps ready to seize her trunk and make off with it, but Kathleen hauls it to the centre of the terminal and sits on it beneath the big clock, an eye out for her distant cousin, not minding the wait, serenaded by the crowds. It's clear: the whole world comes to New York City.

How many times have we seen this ingénue-arriving-scene at the Port Authority or Grand Central Station?

And who is playing her? Doris Day? Audrey Hepburn?

What *happens* in this ghastly book?

James Piper elopes with a Lebanese girl called Materia Mahmoud on her thirteenth birthday. They produce a daughter, Kathleen, who is gifted with perfect pitch. They decide she will have an operatic career.

In the Cape Breton mining town the miners go on strike. James works as a scab to earn enough to pay for Kathleen's career. He realizes he is Sexually Attracted to His Own Daughter.

Materia now conceives Mercedes. Followed by Frances.

James enlists to Avoid Possessing Kathleen.

While he is away Materia produces Lily who suffers a Crib Death.

At Passchendaele one of James' Toes Falls Off.

He returns to the Halifax Explosion.

He builds a shed in the back yard and for thirteen years makes boots, apparently in sufficient number to support five people. No details are given.

Kathleen returns from New York Pregnant.

It is a Breech Birth.

Kathleen Dies.

Materia Opens Her Up With the Kitchen Scissors.

There are Twins.

Frances Baptizes the Twins that night in the back yard Stream but Drops One in Which Drowns.

The Twin, Lily, survives But Later Gets Polio.

Two days after the Caesarian, Materia, for Complicated Catholic Theological Reasons, Puts Her Head in the Gas Oven and Commits Suicide.

James next Sexually Abuses Frances.

To Make Ends Meet He Gives Up Boot-Making and Takes Up Bootlegging.

Frances Becomes a Whore.

She Becomes Impregnated by a West Indian Maker of Ginger Beer.

The Ginger Beer Maker's Wife Shoots Frances in the Abdomen.

James Suffers a Stroke when his Still Blows Up and He Becomes Senile.

Frances Gives Birth but the Baby Promptly Dies.

I can't go on.

The climax of the book is the revelation that Kathleen's twins were the result of her father raping her after he walked in on her while she was grappling with her lesbian (and African-American) lover, Rose. Thus Lily is his daughter with his daughter. Which might explain why Lily with the Leg-Iron is mildly Retarded and given to Religious Visions.

Kathleen's Diary ("O Diary. My loyal friend.") is discovered later and records in barely comprehensible similes the progress of her lesbian conquest.

> She kissed me again and we didn't stop for a long time, except to lean out of the light when we heard horses coming. We slipped into an alley and I pulled her shirt out from her pants. I pressed my centre into her and she sighed. It made me flood from inside, the sweetest music. We were finally dancing. I slid my hands under and up her smooth sides, I wanted to be slow to savour but we couldn't, she gripped me and moved under me. I felt her nipples under my palms and I think I died. Rose gasped as though I'd stabbed her and I felt like a savage robbing a sacred tree, her thigh between my legs. I found her hand and led it to a place I know, I kissed it with the mouth that I keep hidden, then took her inside and sucked her like the greedy tide that can't decide to swallow or disgorge. I lost track of everything. And even after I finally could stop, I knew that I would never be finished.
>
> Oh Rose, it's not enough until I have all of you inside me, then give you back to the world fresh and new from my belly. She just said softly 'Oh' for the longest time.

Anne-Marie MacDonald!
Fall On Your Knees!
As literature!
At the University of Toronto!
Oy vey!

* * *

Pilots-in-training thundered low-flying fighter jets up and down Wensleydale morning and afternoon. The planes were flying out of the RAF station at nearby Leeming, named from Leeming Beck, an Old English river name meaning "bright stream." During the Second World War the station had been home to two RCAF squadrons of Lancaster bombers. Norman Levine was stationed there flying night and day raids over Germany into the flak from the ack-ack guns. "Small puffs of light purple appearing just ahead of us" was how he described it. Mordecai Richler told me how after the war all his artistic crowd in London had looked up to this handsome ex-officer as a figure of considerable glamour.

Norman and I remain in fairly close contact. I have long admired the integrity and courage of his artistic life. I once said to him that we had both left our countries of origin and that I thought he had made the right decision and that I had probably made the wrong one. He replied that we had both made decisions that suited our personalities.

After a brief stint in London, Norman moved to St. Ives – "silence, exile, cunning" – and began forging his style, the main preoccupation of most modernist writers. Norman's mature work is marked by its fragmentation, unorthodox grammar, and denial of cadence. We can imagine the effect upon his youthful work of daily contact with such blossoming abstract painters as Peter Lanyon, Terry Frost, Patrick Heron, Roger Hilton, and Bryan Wynter all with their own preoccupation with technical innovation.

Norman wrote: "If it hadn't been for St. Ives, and especially the painters I grew up with, I wouldn't be the writer I am."

Alison Oldham in an article on Norman's St. Ives years wrote: "I was visiting him on a research inquiry, to ask how painters he knew in St. Ives had influenced him. The impact of 'Ringa Ringa Rosie' may derive from two ways he believed they did – by sharpening his awareness of the visual world and by making him want to give his writing the same immediacy as a painting had when seen in a studio: 'And there it was. At a glance. Through the eyes. Onto the nervous system.'"

In a special Levine issue of *Canadian Notes & Queries* Cynthia Flood wrote brilliantly on the evolution of Levine's style. She entitled her piece "All the Heart Is in the Things;" what follows is an excerpt.

> Like a painter himself, Levine lays down colour, line, mass, dimension, angle.
>
> > 'All vegetation was killed by the sulphur that the wind carried from the Sinter Plant. You could see the direction of the wind. It was like a scar in the landscape. In the distance, on either side, I could see more hills with the blue-black outline of growing trees on them. But here everything was dead. The rocks the colour of ashes and the burned-out remnants of trees sticking up like a field of gibbets.'
>
> That was 1958. An older Levine would peel out 'You could see, It was like, I could see, on them' and 'sticking up like a field of gibbets' (he is not a simile fan), but the simple diction and spatial clarity continue.
>
> > 'She had kept everything neat and clean. Now a thin layer of dust was on the furniture and on the wooden floor, and on the leaves of the plants in the front room. The earth was dry. I watered the plants. Looked in the fridge. A few potatoes were sprouting. The pears were bruised . . .'
>
> That's 1991 . . .
>
> We must see the images singly, if we're to read Levine.
>
> > 'Past Bytown Museum that always seemed shut. Past the jail with its high, small greystone walls. Up Laurier Bridge. The horse straining.'
>
> So precise. To reach this plainness, Levine abandons plain sentences.
>
> > 'The glare from the snow. Washing hanging out. The long winter underwear. Then by an open crossing with the red arm flashing in and out like a heartbeat, the cars waiting on either side. Why can't I settle for this?'
>
> To strip out all that plugs up prose: that is Levine's aim. Articles, linking verbs, clause-breeding relative pronouns, wordy modifiers –

dangerous. They draw attention to themselves. Worse, they smother energy. Readers, rolling along the shiny habitual rails of subject and predicate, enter the familiar sentence-tunnel knowing when the verb will arrive and the terminal light appear. We read to reach an expected end. That habit Levine wants to break. We are to *look.* Outside the train.

Norman and I had arranged to spend a day together but his flat in Barnard Castle in County Durham is difficult to reach by bus from Leyburn so we agreed to meet at the Market Cross in Richmond, a little town dominated by the vast keep built by Count Alan Rufus, nephew of William the Conqueror. Norman's friend Moira Dale drove him over and after lunch at the King's Arms Hotel took us to Fountains Abbey where we strolled through the remains of the abbey, bare ruined choirs, and through the eighteenth century landscaping of John and William Aislabie.

When Norman had sought a washroom I asked Moira how he was really; he is so spry that I find it difficult to remember that he is eighty.

She gave a slight shake of her head.

"What?"

"He gets confused," she said. "He's forgetting things. Not just . . ."

"Me, too," said Myrna. "Names. The dentist. If I don't write it . . ."

"No," said Moira. "No. Not that. If I put him down at a shop and park," she said, "he can't find the car when he comes out."

"Is he writing?"

"We're arranging for a scan to see if it's a tumour."

"And if it isn't?"

"I've had him examined by a psychologist," she said.

"And if it isn't?"

She pursed her lips.

"His father had Alzheimer's," she said.

We were standing looking down onto the water gardens when Norman started telling me a story about Robert Weaver. When Weaver ran the CBC "Anthology" programme he commissioned story after story from Norman and was one of Norman's main financial supports so the story Norman was telling me with great bitterness was extremely peculiar and on the face of it unlikely. But what possible reason could he have for inventing it? And who could *imagine* such a remark?

In the eighties when Norman was back living in Toronto the French literary critic Simone Vauthier was active in interviewing writers and writing articles on Canadian short fiction. She published an entertaining collection of these called *Reverberations: Explorations in the Canadian Short Story.* According to Norman, Weaver proposed to Simone Vauthier the idea of recording for the CBC a conversation with a writer of her choice. She chose Norman and the conversation was duly taped. Then nothing happened. Some weeks later Norman bumped into Weaver on the street and asked him when the conversation would be broadcast. Norman said that Weaver replied, "It won't be broadcast."

"Why not?" asked Norman.

"Because," said Weaver, "she was too enthusiastic about your work."

I expressed astonishment at this story.

Norman said with great intensity, "I have not spoken with him since that day. And will not."

I came to realize that afternoon with Norman at Fountains Abbey that dreams of returning to England were merely dreams. A return to England would be, as it were, deserting the field of battle. A return would dishonour both of us. We sat on a bench by the lake warm in the late afternoon sun watching the burly Canada geese, Norman telling a meandering story about St. Ives painter Roger Hilton, and I understood again that his life had been touched by greatness and wondered anew why others couldn't seem to see it.

As we strolled back towards the sandstone ruins of the abbey Norman said, "How is that woman who writes short stories?"

"Who do you mean?"

"Oh, you know."

"Alice, do you mean? Alice Munro?"

"No, no. Not her."

Struggling with it, he stared at me.

"She . . ."

"Give me a title," I said.

He frowned.

"She lives in France. In Paris."

"Oh, you mean Mavis Gallant."

"Mavis Gallant, Mavis Gallant," he said. "Yes. Mavis Gallant. I'll remember that."

SOMETHING HAPPENED HERE

[When my library and the Porcupine's Quill archives were bought by McGill University I was asked to mark the occasion by delivering the annual Hugh MacLennan Memorial Lecture. I prefer to think of what I had to say as a talk rather than a lecture and give it here preserving its relative informality.]

I am honoured this evening to be giving the Hugh MacLennan Memorial lecture which I have entitled "Something Happened Here." A couple of months ago I received a letter from Robert T. Robinson who used to work before retirement for the Maclean-Hunter publishing company. He asked me if I would be interested in publishing in *Canadian Notes & Queries* an account of a magazine he'd edited called *Books in Review.* His magazine had aimed to be a Canadian version of *The New York Times Review of Books.* The first issue appeared in 1949 and the magazine lasted for three more issues before its inevitable collapse. Bob Robinson sent me a copy of Volume 1 Number 1 and the lead article was entitled "Why I Choose to Live and Write in Canada." It was by Hugh MacLennan.

MacLennan wrote in part:

> There are many signs that our period of transition is nearly over. Canadians have at last reached the point where they find their own country more interesting than any other. Some Canadian magazines have doubled their circulations by dealing more and more with Canadian material. Canada as a nation has so greatly increased in stature that each year that passes makes her more familiar to the rest of the world.
>
> Some day, perhaps some day fairly soon, a Canadian novel will be published which will be true and accurate without any of our old and necessary self-consciousness. If such a book achieves success abroad, our growing pains will be over and the flood gates will be opened wide. Canadian books will be accepted then as part of the literature of the world, not as regional curiosities or the tentative gropings of a people

> still colonial. It is because I have real hope that this time will soon arrive that I find it exciting to be a writer in Canada during these days of pioneering.

The flood gates certainly were opened wide though not as quickly as MacLennan had predicted and not in the manner he'd imagined. Old prejudices, lethargies, and stylistic inadequacies were to reign for 20 more years. And the identification of literature with nationalism which MacLennan asserts in his article bedevils us to this day.

MacLennan also looks for "success abroad." This, he claims, will validate Canadian books. This is another attitude which has bedevilled us. I tire of repeating that we must look not to others but to ourselves. We cannot recognize or elect books as important because we have not educated ourselves sufficiently to be a discerning audience.

Ten years after MacLennan's 1949 article something happened here at McGill which perhaps more accurately mirrored Canadian literary life than MacLennan's optimistic yearnings do. I would characterize that literary life then as intensely old-fashioned and parochial, intensely nationalistic, and intensely mediocre. Its sad flavour can be tasted in *William Arther Deacon: A Canadian Literary Life* by Clara Thomas and John Lennox.

Some of you, I'm sure, recognize *Something Happened Here* as the title of a Norman Levine story collection. After graduating from McGill, Levine went to live in England. In 1958 he returned and travelled across Canada and wrote a less-than-boosterish account of his experiences.

I quote from the book's penultimate paragraph: "I wondered why I felt so bitter about Canada. After all, it was all part of a dream, an experiment that could not come off. It was foolish to believe that you can take the throwouts, the rejects, the human kickabouts from Europe and tell them: Here you have a second chance. Here you can start a new life. But no one ever mentioned the price one had to pay, how much of oneself you had to betray."

Canada Made Me was published in London by Putnam and Jack McClelland took 500 copies for Canada but refused to put his name on the book and refused to take more copies when the 500 quickly sold out.

Levine said, "I had to accept that Canadian publishing was closed to my work."

In 1959, while on a promotional tour of Canada, Levine offered the manuscript of *Canada Made Me* as a gift to his alma mater. The Director of Libraries at that date, Richard Pennington, said:

"McGill does not have room for this manuscript."

Bitterly insulted, Levine took the manuscript back with him to London and put it into the hands of Bertram Rota, then one of England's most distinguished booksellers. Rota promptly sold the manuscript to the University of Texas at Austin.

Since those dreadful days of boosterism and Babbitry there have been extraordinary changes in Canadian writing; the last 40 years have seen a flowering – especially in the story form – that is unprecedented. As a writer, teacher, editor, and anthologizer I found myself heavily involved in this rather amazing efflorescence and, given my nature, it was inevitable I would document what was unfolding.

I would defend almost any collection of anything because I believe that collections provide new information and prompt new ways of thinking – though I was slightly shaken last year on a visit to an English stately home whose noble owner had amassed an astonishing array of dog collars. Although collections *are* accumulations of things, important collections are concerned with much more than simple acquisition. Important collections usually spring from ideas and, as the collection evolves, explore ideas. I can trace the genesis of my own collection to an idea that came to me one afternoon in an English bookshop in 1957.

In the fall of 2001, Patrick Crean, publisher at Thomas Allen Publishers, asked me if I'd be interested in writing an autobiography. The book, entitled *An Aesthetic Underground,* was published in 2003. In it I explain how the idea behind my collection came to me that afternoon in 1957.

> My real initiation into the world of books happened just before I went to university. My father had been transferred from Beckenham to Leicester, an unlovely city. Although it had been an important Roman administrative centre little of any antiquity had been spared. The factories were brutal, the streets and housing mean. Guide books describe the city as: 'Noted for its bulk manufacture of boots and shoes.'
>
> I fell into the habit of walking every day to the museum. They had on display a small collection of oils and watercolours by Edward Ardizzone whose work as an illustrator I'd been drawn to some years earlier when

I'd seen his cramped and spiky drawings in H.E. Bates' two story collections *My Uncle Silas* and *Sugar for the Horse.*

Strolling back home one afternoon along New Walk, trees and shrubbery on one side, small houses on the other, I saw a sign in a window: Books. I opened the front door and found myself in a small hallway which was stacked with books on either side. Books almost blocked the staircase to the second floor. I edged along the hall until it opened onto what must once have been a sitting room. It was now a cave of books. Shelved floor to ceiling but most of the floor stacked perilously with thousands more books. Most of them were leather bound.

Sitting at a desk in the middle of the room was a Dickensian figure in rumpled cardigan, *muffler*, pipe ash and dottle. Behind thick glasses his eyes were swimmy as raw oysters. He wore woolen gloves with the fingers cut off. There was a strong suggestion about him of a Peter Sellers character. I asked if I might look round. Although it was full summer the gas fire burbled and popped in the room's silence. On the desk top were a packet of Chocolate Wholewheat Digestives and a large magnifying glass.

Most of the books were eighteenth century and early nineteenth bound in full calf but here and there standing out because of their lighter colour earlier books bound in vellum. I had not had the opportunity before to handle so many old books. On the bottom shelves massive leather-bound folios. I was mesmerized. I felt excited and in some way upset. I was unable to take it all in. *Flustered* is perhaps the word. Titles appeared out of the blur of leather and cloth. Dugdale's *Antiquities of Warwickshire,* William Camden's *Britannia*, Layard's *Nineveh and its Remains*, Surtees' *Jorrock's Jaunts and Jollities*, Thomas Love Peacock's *Headlong Hall.*

It felt to me like uncovering a treasure trove, a Sutton Hoo of books, one glittering marvel after another. The room was very hot and the smell of leather heavy. I felt almost as if I were sinking into the books, swooning. I found a three-volume leather-bound edition of *The History of Tom Jones, a Foundling* and asked how much it was. He opened the first volume and peered through the magnifying glass at the title page.

'Are you a local boy?'

'No, we've just moved here.'

'I don't get many boys in here local *or* otherwise.'

'The books are beautiful.'

He looked up at me with swimmy eyes.

'Beautiful,' he repeated. 'Hmm. Well, well. You're a rum one and no mistake.'

'Why rum?'

'And what will you do with our Mr. Jones?'

'Well, I like the story,' I said and then shy and blushing but somehow compelled, rushed on, 'But I'd like to own a book that someone held and read in the eighteenth century.'

He twisted his head round and up and opened his mouth and made a caricature of astonishment.

''Pon my soul!' he said. *'Upon my soul!* Ten bob.'

I was soon going to see Bernard Halliday nearly every day. It was a fortunate conjunction for both of us as I was eager to learn and he was lonely and longing to teach. He instructed me to buy John Carter's *ABC for Book Collectors* and his *Taste and Technique in Book Collecting.* Then I was to read Lownde's *Bibliographer's Manual of English Literature.* Later he guided me through the gruelling terrain of Ronald McKerrow's *An Introduction to Bibliography for Literary Students.* He taught me to read catalogues and gave me old catalogues from Maggs and Quaritch.

'Always read catalogues,' he'd say. 'Catalogues are where all the knowledge sifts down to.'

If I made mistakes he would say sternly, 'It behooves you to know what's o'clock.' The tea I brewed for us he dismissed as 'maiden's water.' Modern first editions were anathema. 'No different from gambling.' And then with shaking shoulders he forced out 'Some bloody pillocks collect . . . *detective stories!'*

I soaked up Mr. Halliday's outpouring of information. How to clean dust-soiled vellum bindings. Better than any gum or rubber eraser was white sliced bread. How to straighten bowed boards. Leather soap. Neat's foot oil. The uses of lighter fluid.

I wallowed in bindings and leathers and fonts, in all the lovely jargon of the trade, half-titles, colophons, blind stamping, foxing, black letter, washed leaves, cancels . . . I came to believe that there were few things in the world more beautiful than the deep burning black of Baskerville type on crisp rag paper.

The best part of this education, however, was simply handling the books in their hundreds, coming to an understanding of the meaning of condition. I would take volumes to him excavated from the filthy piles and he would say,

'So *that's* where that went. Well! Well! Interesting old book that. Russian. St. John Chrysostom. Know what that means? "Golden Mouth." Homilies, these are. Parchment and written in a nice hand. How much? Oh, I don't know. I could let you have it for nine thousand . . .'

He would then break down in rheumy mirth and mop at his eyes with his grubby handkerchief.

He did give me what are called 'reading' or 'working' copies of various of the well-known eighteenth century novels. Both terms mean 'damaged' or 'in non-collectible condition.' I remember taking to Canada Mackenzie's *The Man of Feeling,* Graves' *The Spiritual Quixote* (much appreciated because it is a satire on Methodism) and Smollett's *Roderick Random.* He also gave me 'reading' copies of anonymous eighteenth-century novels typically written 'By a Lady.'

Anonymous novels are catalogued, incompletely, in a work by Halkett and Laing entitled *A Dictionary of the Anonymous and Pseudonymous Literature of Great Britain.* I've never read any kind of survey which talks about them *as literature.* During those visits to that filthy house with the musty smell of old leather and old paper in my nostrils, I imagined reading those novels in Halkett and Laing and writing about them as the matrix, as it were, from which rose the peaks of Richardson, Fielding, Smollett, Sterne . . .

The idea, then, behind the collection McGill has acquired, is to record the Canadian short story as completely as possible to provide a context for study of the genre. The collection is both peaks and matrix. This means that the volumes range from the sublime to the semi-literate. They enable a student to watch the development of the genre from the late nineteenth century to the present.

The collection is not limited to Canadian story writers. I have included British and American writers for two reason. Our own writers are inevitably deeply influenced by American writers and the story is an international form. I think it is entirely appropriate to consider Canadian writing as North

American writing. I also have resisted for my entire career the nationalist notion that a native Canadian tradition exists or should exist. If a Canadian writer has not read, say, Raymond Carver, then he or she is the poorer for it.

As for those dim scholars who claim that we all derive from Duncan Campbell Scott's *In the Village of Viger* . . . words fail me.

In 1958 Robert Weaver edited for *The World's Classics* series from Oxford University Press a volume entitled *Canadian Short Stories.* In the Introduction he wrote: "There have been so few collections of Canadian short stories that there is no tradition which an editor is required either to follow or to explain away . . ."

Later in the Introduction he wrote: "Knister and Callaghan published abroad in the 1920s because there were almost no outlets in Canada for serious and experimental short fiction. This fugitive existence of the short story has continued until today in this country."

That was written in 1958.

In 2003 – only 45 years after Weaver's "fugitive existence" this collection offers over 260 anthologies of Canadian short stories and well over 700 individual collections.

The reasons for this sudden efflorescence are fairly obvious. The House of Anansi was founded in 1967 and the small press movement got under way. The movement was heavily funded by the government which saw in it an instrument to nourish and express Canadian identity and nationalism. The short story in Canada cannot be understood outside the context of the subsidized literary presses and this remains true to this day.

Roy McSkimming writes in his just-published *The Perilous Trade*:

> It's a cliché to portray small presses as the farm teams of the industry. In reality, they represent the heartland of Canadian literature. They not only inhabit every region but live among the people in a manner not possible for a Toronto-based multinational like Random House of Canada or a large Canadian-owned company like M&S or Key Porter. Small presses occupy the front lines, spotting new talent before it surfaces elsewhere, egging on and launching new writers.

Hugh MacLennan's "flood gates" were opened, then, not by the publication of an unselfconscious novel in Britain or the States but by government gold and the raging nationalism of Dave Godfrey and Dennis Lee.

This collection offers within itself a complete collection of the Porcupine's Quill Press and a close to complete collection of Oberon Press. These press collections enable students to understand the shape of a press over time and to understand something of the press' editorial quirks and preferences.

Of equal importance are the literary magazines where most beginning writers get their first publication. I am just completing a run of the New Brunswick magazine *The Fiddlehead.* Students can have no real idea of a literary period unless they have actually handled the magazines and read the matrix. Without doing so they will have no idea of how energetically awful most writing is and how rare writing which is accomplished. *The Fiddlehead* has been published since 1945, the early issues under the aegis of the Bliss Carman Society of Fredericton. Words to drive dread into any poetic soul.

The completed collection will also contain complete runs of *The Malahat Review, Prism, Canadian Fiction Magazine, The Tamarack Review* and *The New Quarterly.*

I bought the scarce early issues of *The Fiddlehead* from the brilliant Vancouver dealer in rare books William Hoffer just before he closed shop and shipped all his stock to Peter Howard's Serendipity Books in California. Hoffer had acquired the run when UBC Library de-accessioned them after presumably transferring them to some kind of film "to save space." This criminally irresponsible practice is documented and discussed in Nicholson Baker's *Doublefold: Libraries and the Assault on Paper.* It gives me a grim satisfaction that McGill has now benefited from UBC's folly.

I have also studded the collection with copies of magazines carrying now-famous stories by such luminaries as Hugh Hood, Ray Smith, Clark Blaise, Mavis Gallant, Norman Levine, and Alice Munro.

How deeply moving it is to look upon Clark Blaise's "A Class of New Canadians" in *The Fiddlehead* (1970), "Eyes" in *The Fiddlehead* (1971) and "A North American Education" in *The Tamarack Review* (1971); Norman Levine's "Champagne Barn" in *The Tamarack Review* (1978), and Alice Munro's "Meneseteung" in *The New Yorker* (1988) and "Royal Beatings" in *The New Yorker* (1977).

These stories – and I could have cited many others – in their original magazine issues ought to be looked on and valued by us as we might gaze upon a Vincent-Jaggard copy of the 1623 First Folio in the Folger Shakespeare Library. A preposterous comparison, I know, but the *spirit* is exactly right. It is the spirit we must cultivate. These magnificent stories were written by us, in the twentieth century, in Canada. They will only *be* great, however, if we embrace them, celebrate them, make them a part of our life.

Prospects do not look good.

In the case of Alice Munro I collected – with surprising difficulty – every single *New Yorker* appearance, vitally important as in most instances the book versions differ. *The New Yorker* had a policy of sanitizing Alice's sometimes robust language. The last stubborn issues were dug out of a used book store in Back Bay, Boston.

Although the overall intention of the collection is to give students a view of the matrix it would have been foolish not to have concentrated extra attention on our very best writers. I was advised early on by William Hoffer to draw up a list of those writers I considered of most significance and then to buy at any cost. Bill used to startle me by saying oddly illuminating things such as, "If a book is being sold for under $100 that is not a 'cost' or a 'value' – it is merely a service charge." I miss his eccentric presence more than I can say and often think of his saying to an unserious-looking browser in his Gastown store, "When God invented bookshops He didn't have *you* in mind."

We all owe a large debt to those who own and run used-book stores. They are in no small way the custodians of culture. Most of them enjoy teaching and are generous with advice and knowledge. They are part of our hope for the next generation.

I still have warm memories of forty years ago listening to Mr. Heinemann in the Mansfield Book Mart as he taught a first-year McGill student how to read a Scribners alphabetical code on the reverse of the title page. Yes, said Mr. Heinemann, it *was* a first edition of *For Whom the Bell Tolls* but it bore under the date the letter "H" which meant that it was the eighth printing of the first edition and therefore to a collector of little value. And where else forty years ago could one have bought sheets of renaissance music manuscript? The people who ran shops like Mr. Heinemann's Mansfield Book Mart and Max Klein's Le Petit Musée on Sherbrooke helped give Montreal its cultural spice.

The list I drew up under Hoffer's prompting was: Leon Rooke, Hugh Hood, Alice Munro, Mavis Gallant, Audrey Thomas, Mordecai Richler, Margaret Atwood, Morley Callaghan, Carol Shields, Ray Smith, Norman Levine, Margaret Laurence, and Clark Blaise.

If any of these key figures wrote poetry, plays, essays, or novels then I collected their entire output.

Mordecai Richler isn't really a short story writer – though his book of stories and sketches *The Street* is delightful – but I included him because I enjoy him so much.

Callaghan is on the list not because I consider him an important writer but because he is widely asserted to be in Guides and Companions "The Father of the Canadian Short Story." Students coming to the field will have to grapple with this arrant nonsense.

Because my life has been lived among writers the collection is particularly rich in signed and inscribed volumes. These inscriptions are an interesting record of a network of friendships and influences. And I must confess to sheer romanticism. To hold a book inscribed to Clark Blaise by Mavis Gallant! To hold a signed copy of Eudora Welty's *The Golden Apples!* To hold a signed, limited edition of Evelyn Waugh's *Basil Seal Rides Again!*

The collection is also rich in uncorrected proofs. The National Library does not collect these but I think they are misguided. Proofs are, after all, the earliest state of the book. Many books undergo their final revisions by authors or editors after the printing of the proof copies, so proofs often show a state of the author's work, otherwise unpublished, that precedes the final version. I recently bought from the Massachusetts dealer Ken Lopez an uncorrected proof of Raymond Carver's 1981 collection *What We Talk About When We Talk About Love.* Here, in part, is Lopez's description of the proof.

"Carver's relentless paring away of the excess in his stories, which earned him the label 'minimalist' – a designation he stridently rejected throughout his career – is evident in this collection: two of the stories had been published earlier in the collection *Furious Seasons* but here are shorter and more spare (one of them also having been re-titled). [The proof] reproduces the author's holograph corrections to the text, including a number of small word changes, excisions, and in one case the addition of a line to the end of a story. A remarkable glimpse of the stories as works-in-progress, up to and even after they had been typeset for publication."

The collection also contains the rarest Alice Munro text in existence – a Macmillan proof of *Who Do You Think You Are?* It was sent out to reviewers but then recalled because Alice Munro had decided to rewrite the stories. How many copies are extant? My guess would be three or four.

Other rare oddities have floated my way because dealers and their scouts have scavenged in dumpsters and found amazing things. For example, the collection contains the Macmillan in-house typescript of Morley Callaghan's *A Time for Judas* – with all the editor's very heavy rewriting on nearly every page. An opportunity for someone to reach conclusions about Callaghan's much-debated style. The tediousness of the debate could be ended by comparing what Callaghan had actually written with what an editor had sculpted from the rough materials at hand. Another interesting oddity is a typescript of Carol Shields' *The Stone Diaries* when it was called *Monument* and before the New York editors had cut 100 pages.

The physical books can teach so much that bibliography tends not to do. A non-collector browsing the shelves might wonder perhaps why there are seemingly identical duplicate copies of, say, Mavis Gallant's *Selected Stories*. The book was published in Canada in hardcover by McClelland and Stewart in 1996. The book was available in stores for about a month and then seemed to disappear. This vast book (887 pages) was priced at $39.99. In 1997 the book was re-released by M&S as a quality paperback priced at $26.99. Not much later this paperback version, still in the first issue of the first printing, was remaindered in Chapters with a sticker on it offering it at $7.99.

What has all this to do with literature? Why would the collection contain a duplicate book simply because it bears a sale sticker? Fussy collectors actually *do* differentiate; they describe the stickered book as a later "state" of the book. But the sticker suggests something else. It suggests that Mavis Gallant books are not being bought in great numbers. It suggests that it's entirely possible that a Mavis Gallant book sells only 1,000 copies. Or even fewer. Her 1993 collection in hardcover *Across the Bridge* was later overstickered by M&S. The sticker read "Special. Hardcover Edition Now at Paperback Price." It too was still the first issue of the first edition.

Stickers, dots, remainder marks – all these tell a story and it is often not quite the story history records. The Guides and Companions may say of Morley Callaghan that he was the dominant figure in the history of his times, that Mavis Gallant is widely considered one the best short story writers in the world, that all Canadian story writers have a "gateway" ancestor in Duncan Campbell Scott and descend from his seminal collection *In the Village of Viger*. But what these authorities do not reveal is how many copies were likely sold. Such information pulls history into a different shape.

In the Village of Viger was published in Boston by Copeland and Day in 1896. It has been estimated that the print run would have been at most 1,000 copies and more likely 750. In 1899 when the publishing company was dissolved, 578 copies remained unsold. This figure means that if the print run was 1,000, 422 copies were sold. If the print run was 750 it means that 172 copies were sold. Very few would have made their way to Canada. All the dealers I have talked to have said that all the copies they have seen have come from the States. All dealers describe the book as "rare."

Such practical considerations suggest that the "seminal collection" assertion and the "gateway ancestor" assertion are desperate nationalist attempts by academics to invent Canadian ancestors and a Canadian tradition. It is always wiser to trust what the books themselves tell us. We can say with confidence *In the Village of Viger* did not circulate in Canada.

Similarly, a non-collector might wonder why there are so many copies of, say, Alice Munro's *The Love of a Good Woman* or *The Progress of Love.* Closer examination will show that the books are from Canada, England and America and that all the paperbacks are from different companies and are sometimes reprints from companies different yet again. What we are looking at here is the construction of Alice Munro's career and reputation. What we are looking at is the masterly planning and plotting of Alice Munro's agent, Virginia Barber. As I have said before, Alice Munro's career is an American construct and one managed with flair and brilliance.

The actual books show us how the job was marshalled – for it *was* a campaign – and they should leave us thoughtful about other careers, Blaise, Levine, Mavis Gallant . . . history being pulled into a different shape.

Before coming to the archives of the Porcupine's Quill I should also mention that the collection is rich also with many manuscripts and typescripts which always add a certain flair.

In *The New Quarterly* (Volume XXI, Nos. 2 and 3) the editor, Kim Jernigan, writes: "Under the editorship of John Metcalf and through the energy and dedication of its owners, Tim and Elke Inkster, the Porcupine's Quill has developed a reputation as *the* champion of the short story form in Canada, seeing many daringly innovative younger writers into print and preserving signal story collections from early on in the careers of writers more established."

I felt extremely gratified when Roy McSkimming described the Porcupine's Quill as "Canada's pre-eminent literary press."

The significance of the archive, then, is that it completely complements the books and continues the story into the next generation. It has so turned out that I published first or early story collections by writers who have gone on to become significant figures in the genre. I might cite, among others, Caroline Adderson, K.D. Miller, Michael Winter, Steven Heighton, Mike Barnes, Libby Creelman, Terry Griggs, Elise Levine, Mary Borsky, Sharon English, and Annabel Lyon.

The archive allows the student to see the very process of publishing, to see the emergence of the book as the writer struggles towards the finish line. The archive shows us the various states of the book, the editing, the correspondence. Newspaper clippings record the book's contemporary reception. Financial records tell us of the grim reality of sales. Hundreds of photographs record launches, readings, festivals and friendships. This huge archive records the Porcupine's Quill since 1989 when I started to work with Tim and Elke Inkster.

I began this evening by deploring the loss to Canada of the manuscript of Norman Levine's *Canada Made Me*. That national treasure still sits in Austin, Texas. But I will be conveying into McGill the second earliest state of the book.

A couple of years ago Steven Temple, the Toronto dealer in antiquarian and rare books, phoned me saying, "I've got one with your name written all over it."

"What's that, Steve?"

"One of my scouts turned up the advance proof of *Canada Made Me*."

Later, I talked to Norman about it. In 1958 in England, proofs to be distributed outside the house were still a fairly new-fangled idea and very few copies would have been produced. Twenty copies would probably be a generous estimate. Norman said he had no doubt this copy would have been the one sent by Putnam in England to Jack McClelland at McClelland and Stewart.

So some part of our history has been saved.

I feel honoured that this collection of books and archives has found a home in McGill. I have had a long connection with the university. More years ago than I really care to remember I taught here with, and for, Bharati Mukherjee. And years earlier than that I had attained a kind of distinction here. I wrote an exam in educational statistics and achieved what the professor described as the lowest score he had ever given in a lifetime of teaching.

In closing I would like to thank five very important McGill people.

I would like to thank Eric Ormsby not only for the deep pleasure his brilliant poems give me but also for standing in my study doorway and looking at the shelves and saying, "This would be of interest to my wife."

I would like to thank Eric's wife, Irena Murray, curator of McGill's Rare Book Room for standing in my study doorway and saying, "If McGill acquired this library it would immediately become the leading university in Canada for the study of the short story."

I would also like to thank David McKnight of the Rare Book Room who laboured to make a digest of the catalogue.

My particular thanks to Professor Robert Lecker of McGill's English Department. Robert has been a friend for many years and I have admired for many years his endless commitment to Canadian literary culture. As publisher, writer, editor, and teacher he has given himself more than generously. Robert wrote a letter to Frances Groen, Director of Libraries, urging the merits of the collection.

And finally I would like to thank Frances Groen herself who confirmed the acquisition and facilitated it and who has shown exuberant enthusiasm ever since.

WINNER TAKE ALL

The October 1990 issue of *Quill and Quire* featured an obituary of Morley Callaghan written by Professor David Staines of the University of Ottawa. Professor Staines was chairman of the university's English department and is now Dean of Arts. He is also the general editor of McClelland and Stewart's *New Canadian Library* series.

Professor Staines quoted approvingly Callaghan's literary creed as outlined by Callaghan in *That Summer in Paris*:

> 'The trouble with writing was that poets and story-writers used language to evade, to skip away from the object, because they could never bear to face the thing freshly for what it was in itself.' Writing should be 'the right relationship between the words and the things or the person being described: the words should be as transparent as glass, and every time a writer used a brilliant phrase to prove himself witty or clever he merely took the mind of the reader away from the object and devoted it to himself.'

His taste and judgement possibly distorted by personal grief, Professor Staines then went on to say:

> Readers of *That Summer in Paris* remember a boxing match where Callaghan knocked down Hemingway, while Fitzgerald, as time-keeper, looked on. When will we realize that Callaghan was, more importantly, a better writer than Hemingway?

"When will we realize that Callaghan was, more importantly, a better writer than Hemingway?" It's a question that makes one think. It made *me* think about the hundreds of hapless students infected by Professor Staines' flabby chauvinism. How many *more* years will it now take to root out such ludicrously deformed judgements?

Perhaps it's something in the Ottawa air. Downtown at the University of Ottawa, Professor Staines is elevating Callaghan to giddy heights in the hierarchy of Canadian and world literature, while a couple of miles away at

Carleton University, Professor Mathews, whose literary insights are about as scintillating as those of Professor Staines, for years denied Callaghan any place in Canadian literature whatsoever on the grounds that Callaghan embraced the example of Hemingway and in so doing rejected "the Canadian dialectic" and bowed to "the New Colonialism" (see Mathews). Both of these academic arbiters of elegance put me in mind of hamburger franchises whose slip-in-the-slot lettering proclaims them: Proudly Canadian.

And think of the money they earn!

Some days after reading Professor Staines' astounding question I found myself in Books Canada on Sparks Street in Ottawa. Among the new books was a reprint of Morley Callaghan's *No Man's Meat.* The book had first been published in 1931 in Paris when Callaghan was presumably at the height of his powers. The dust jacket carried critical commendations by William French (*Globe and Mail*) and Ken Adachi (*Toronto Star*), who, at one time, were Canada's two most influential reviewers.

French had written: "Callaghan is the wily old pro, skillfully weaving a plot from his own experiences and geography and from his fanciful imagination." Adachi had written: "His plain style is in splendid evidence, always laconic and suggestive and imposed on true feeling." Had I in the past, I wondered, been too cranky about Callaghan? I opened the book at random and read a series of Dick-and-Jane-ish sentences and the following wildly improbable and silly dialogue. It was not encouraging.

> 'I thought I ought to come back here and tell you about it,' she said. 'It's amusing, but it's seriously interesting.'
>
> 'What was the matter with Jean? How can it be amusing?'
>
> 'She's so lovely, so gentle in her own nature, it's hard to help loving her. And here she's come to this hard bright lake and its rocks and now so unhappy.'
>
> 'She's too softly feminine for this sterile country.'

And so on. But determined to grapple with the merits of the question Professor Staines had put, I plunked down the exorbitant $14.95 for the forty-two-page novella and took it home to read. The first two sentences are as follows:

> Rays of morning light filtering through leaves on trees on the hill shone through the window to the bed. Beddoes, sitting up, looked out of the

opposite window over the dark lake which was never blue from the cottage window in the morning sun, even without a shadow from the big rock across the water.

And that, I must confess, was as far as I could get.

Critical commentary on Callaghan is extensive. Academic balls rumble down the lanes towards the pins of justice, Christian personalism, Christian dualism, allegory, symbolism, moral parabolism, Jacques Maritain and the redemptive power of love. On and on they rumble but not one of the commentaries that I've read attempts to come to grips with the fact that we are dealing with a writer whose language plods and who has an indifferent command of literary technique.

Put succinctly, not one of the critics I've read seems at all perturbed about reading in Callaghan's stories such lines as: "She stood on the corner of Bloor and Yonge, an impressive build of a woman, tall, stout, good-looking for forty-two, and watched the traffic signal." (*Morley Callaghan's Stories*, 116)

* * *

Hemingway and Callaghan have from the start been compared in Canadian criticism and commentary. Outside Canada, of course, such comparison or identification rarely if ever occurs. Outside Canada Callaghan is a spear-carrier and has no speaking part.

The following comparisons of the two writers are almost comic in their wrongheadedness as they seek to denigrate one of the most important writers of the twentieth century and elevate the comfortable mediocrity of a compatriot.

In 1931, Charles G.D. Roberts in full Major Hoople mode, wrote of Callaghan in "A Note on Modernism":

> Mr. Morley Callaghan is reported as having declared himself a humble disciple of Mr. Hemingway – as having learned his art from Mr. Hemingway. If this be so, the disciple has on many counts excelled the master. Compare the two novels, *Strange Fugitive*, and *The Sun Also Rises*. The latter is marred by eccentricities in the vogue of the moment. You find yourself skipping whole pages of conversation whose only purpose is to display the reiterant vacuities of the drunken mind. Able as it is in

> many respects, the book will hardly, I think, survive a change of fashion. It carries too great a burden of mere words. Mr. Callaghan's story, on the other hand, carries no such burden. There is not a superfluous word in it. The style is clear, bare, efficient. It is modernism – the subject matter is very 'modern.' But it has sanely avoided the modern fault of striving after effect. It does not date itself; and it may well appear as readable a hundred years hence as it does today.

In 1942, Wyndham Lewis (stranded in Canada during the war) wrote about *Now That April's Here* for *Saturday Night,* sounding, most uncharacteristically, like a smarmy vicar:

> These are tales very full of human sympathy – a blending of all the events of life into a pattern of tolerance and of mercy; there is no sultry misanthropic phobia lurking anywhere in it . . . Apart from the literary merit of the stories it contains, this book is beautifully replete with a message of human tolerance and love. Every one – or almost all – of these discrete miniature dramas ends softly and gently. At the end of some anguish there is peace; at the end of some bitter dispute there is reconciliation.
>
> All of these creatures are dimly aware that the parts they play – for all the sound and fury into which they may be led by the malice of nature, by the demands of the instinct for animal survival, or by our terrible heritage of original sin – the roles they are called upon to take are played according to some great law, within the bounds of a rational order.
>
> The plot, however tragic, is *not* some diabolic and meaningless phantasy, in other words – which is the fatal conclusion that we are required to draw from the perusal of a story, say of Mr. Hemingway's. There is good and evil – not merely *good luck* and *bad luck.* And if they end in a witty sally . . . or in a comic deflation . . . the wit and the comic deflation are full of a robust benevolence.

In 1965, Desmond Pacey wrote on Callaghan in the *Literary History of Canada:*

> His association with Hemingway, which had begun in Toronto when the American writer was temporarily on the staff of the *Daily Star,* was

> particularly influential: his early stories and novels are very similar to those of Hemingway, both in style and in subject-matter. In style, he began by appropriating Hemingway's spare manner of understatement and simplification . . .

In the second edition of the *Literary History of Canada* (published in 1976), Pacey wrote:

> Profiting from the example of three writers who were transforming the short story in English while he was a student at Toronto – Sherwood Anderson, Katherine Mansfield, and Ernest Hemingway – Callaghan looked closely at the people about him, and in a simple, stripped, suggestive prose style recorded the small triumphs and tragedies of their ordinary lives.

In 1985, W.J. Keith, in his survey history *Canadian Literature in English,* wrote of Callaghan: "Above all, from a purely artistic standpoint, he is known for the lucid simplicity of his style, for direct language without frills or snags. He displays, in short, a technical professionalism . . ."

In 1993, George Woodcock wrote in *George Woodcock's Introduction to Canadian Fiction:* "both the style and the characterization in some of Callaghan's early stories and in an apprentice novel like *Strange Fugitive* are largely derivative from Hemingway . . ." And so the comparisons continue.

By 1958, Callaghan had long been tired of the linking of his work with Hemingway's. That year, Robert Weaver published "A Talk with Morley Callaghan" in the *Tamarack Review:*

> WEAVER: . . . I don't want to try to label you with influences and so on, but the Canadian idea used to be that you are sort of a Canadian Hemingway. Anderson's more important in the long run, isn't he?
> CALLAGHAN: I really don't know what to do with people. You shouldn't blame this on Canadians. You see, the difficulty is that as soon as a new writer appears, you feel uncomfortable unless you can label him or link him with something. And I – unfortunately or fortunately as the case may be – was linked with Hemingway. All my early stories were appreciated by Hemingway, that's true. He really liked them, but then we both had the same editor, Max Perkins, at Scribner's.

WEAVER: Thomas Wolfe's editor.

CALLAGHAN: Yes. But the relationship was very flimsy in terms of writing, so what I would like some of these boys to do is get a collection of my stories and get a collection of the early Hemingway stories, and sit down and read them. Wyndham Lewis, the English critic, did this; and he wrote a piece about it – he was astounded by it. He said that he went on for years thinking that I was somehow or other very close to Hemingway until he read a collection of my stories. Wyndham Lewis said that he could see a very close relationship between me and Tolstoy, but he could see very little between me and Hemingway.

Callaghan is, of course, quite right; his writing is nothing like Hemingway's. Why, then, has the identification persisted? I think there are two main reasons. Firstly, Callaghan has stated that he was influenced by, and indebted to, Hemingway. Hemingway, seven years older than Callaghan, encouraged him to write. They were both published by Scribner's, both edited by Max Perkins. The advertising Scribner's issued in the early days linked their names. They were historically connected with each other in Toronto and Paris. Literary critics and historians cannot resist such facts.

Secondly, both described their literary and aesthetic intentions in similar-sounding terms. Most Canadian critics seem not to have read either writer with particular attention; most – if they pay any attention to style whatsoever – seem to have accepted Callaghan's statements about style at face value. In other words, the critics describe Callaghan's prose as "laconic," "lean," "stripped," and so on because Callaghan *said* it was. Hemingway made similar claims about *his* prose. Therefore Callaghan and Hemingway . . .

I wish to suggest that, on the evidence of the writing itself, Callaghan was not much influenced by Hemingway and did not really understand Hemingway's stylistic innovations. He certainly never attempted to use or reproduce them. Callaghan took quite literally such Hemingway dicta as the aim of writing being "to strip language clean, to lay it bare down to the bone" and to "Put down what I see and what I feel in the best and simplest way I can tell it." What he didn't seem to grasp was that "the best and simplest way" wasn't, in Hemingway's case, simple at all. Hemingway's writing has the *illusion* of simplicity; Callaghan's *was simple.*

In *That Summer in Paris,* Callaghan offered various observations about style and aesthetics. In the following two excerpts he is describing his student and cub-reporter days:

> Why did I dislike so much contemporary writing? I would wonder. The popular writers of the day like Hergesheimer, Edith Wharton, James Branch Cabell, Galsworthy, Hugh Walpole, H.G. Wells – except for *Tono Bungay* – I had rejected fiercely. Show-off writers; writers intent on proving to their readers that they could be clever and had some education, I would think. Such vanities should be beneath them if they were really concerned in revealing the object as it was. Those lines, *A primrose by a river's brim a yellow primrose was to him, and it was nothing more,* troubled me, aroused my anger. What the hell else did Wordsworth want it to be? An orange? A sunset? I would ask myself, Why does one thing have to remind you of something else? Going from hotel to hotel on my job I would brood over it.
>
> I remember deciding that the root of the trouble with writing was that poets and storywriters used language to evade, to skip away from the object, because they could never bear to face the thing freshly and see it freshly for what it was in itself. A kind of double talk; one thing always seen in terms of another thing. Criticism? A dreary metaphor. The whole academic method! Of course there were lines like *Life's but a walking shadow . . .* Just the same, I'd be damned if the glory of literature was in the metaphor. Besides, it was not a time for the decorative Renaissance flight into simile. Tell the truth cleanly.

(Why the lines about the primrose from Wordsworth's "Peter Bell" should have troubled and angered Callaghan is beyond me. He must have completely misread the poem – and such misreading raises questions about Callaghan's literary sophistication. Of course Wordsworth did not want the primrose to be anything other than a primrose. He simply meant in these lines that the beauty of the primrose did not have any spiritual significance for Peter Bell, a point on which he elaborates at considerable Wordsworthian length.)

Another anecdote from his cub-reporter days on the hotel beat:

> In the hotel one day I remember encountering a British author, a nice middle-aged gray-haired man. And in no time I was telling him firmly

> that writing had to do with the right relationship between the words and the thing or person being described: the words should be as transparent as glass, and every time a writer used a brilliant phrase to prove himself witty or clever he merely took the mind of the reader away from the object and directed it to himself; he became simply a performer. Why didn't he go on the stage? . . . I remember one time at twilight, sitting at the typewriter in the sunroom of my parents' home. I could smell the lilacs. A night bird cried. A woman's voice came from a neighbour's yard. I wanted to get it down so directly that it wouldn't feel or look like literature. I remembered too being with a girl one night, and on the way home, walking alone, I felt the world had been brought close to me; there seemed to be magic in the sound of my own footsteps, even in the noise of the streetcars – all mingled with the girl's kiss, the memory of the little run I had noticed in her stocking, the way she said good-bye to me. None of it had to be written up. There it was, beautiful in itself. A 'literary guy' would spoil it.

A third quotation relates to his time in Paris:

> But I knew what I was seeking in my Paris street walks, and in the typing hours – with Loretto waiting to retype a chapter. It was this: strip the language and make the style, the method, all the psychological ramifications, the ambience of the relationships, all the one thing, so the reader couldn't make separations. Cézanne's apples. The appleness of apples. Yet just apples.
>
> Wandering around Paris I would find myself thinking of the way Matisse looked at the world around him and find myself growing enchanted. A pumpkin, a fence, a girl, a pineapple on a tablecloth – the thing seen freshly in a pattern that was a gay celebration of things as they were. Why couldn't all people have the eyes and the heart that would give them this happy acceptance of reality? The word made flesh.

The last two quotations are of particular interest. Callaghan's insistence on facing the thing freshly and seeing it freshly for what it is in itself and his celebration of the object are strange assertions coming from one of the *least* precise and sensual of writers. Even the most casual glance at paragraphs of description any where in the stories shows Callaghan manifestly *not* seeing things "freshly;" his writing, far from engaging and celebrating the observable world, usually paints the world like a crude backdrop. His descriptive writing is typically vague, generalized, and unfocused. All too often it is unintentionally funny.

As has been my practice in writing this essay, I opened *Morley Callaghan's Stories* at this point entirely at random and found myself reading the following descriptive paragraph from "The Red Hat":

> The stairs in the apartment house were long, and on other evenings very tiring, but tonight she seemed to be breathing lightly as she opened the door. Her husband, Eric, was sitting by the table lamp, reading the paper. A black-haired man with a well-shaped nose, he seemed utterly without energy, slumped down in the chair. A slight odour of whisky came from him. For four months he had been out of work and some of the spirit had gone out of him. . . .

The word "long" in the first line is vague and the rhythm of the sentence is limply conventional. The proximity of "whiskey" to "spirit" in the last two lines is injudicious; rather than going out, the spirit seems to have been going in. But worse is the ludicrous – and pointless – description of Eric ("A black-haired man with a well-shaped nose"), a description that put me in mind of Daisy Ashford's *The Young Visiters.*

And a final quotation from *That Summer in Paris.*

> Then [Hemingway] became very talkative about writing. He talked about style, and we were in happy splendid agreement. The decorative style, the baroque based on a literary adornment of perceptions, was an affectation in our time, he said. Only the clear direct stripped statement belonged to our time. . . .

They were in "happy splendid agreement." Presumably, too, Callaghan would have agreed with other elements of the Hemingway credo, expressed repeatedly in books, letters, and interviews: "I only know what I have seen," and "A writer's job is to tell the truth." But Callaghan was not as sophisticated as Hemingway; he did not seem to grasp just how much of a "literary guy" Hemingway actually was.

One of the most interesting things revealed in *That Summer in Paris* is Callaghan himself, his conventionality and rectitude. He was made uneasy by the flow of Bohemian life and was shocked by some of the expatriates' drunken antics. He was too *decent* for this fast Paris scene. Toronto was more his speed, and he wasted little time in getting back home. There are few hints in the book, beyond the passages quoted, of a mind passionately engaged in absorbing the theory and craft of writing.

Callaghan did not seem to grasp the simple point that literature is artifice, that "the truth" and "the way it was" are created by smoke and mirrors. He learned from Hemingway – and from imagist ideas that had been in the air for years – to shun ornament, and seems to have equated "lack of ornament" with "truth," but his writing shows no evidence of his having understood the artistic complexity of what Hemingway was about. (His confusion about style and his unsophisticated thinking on the subject are rather embarrassingly revealed in the transcript of a conversation with Ray Ellenwood in 1987. This conversation was later entitled "Eternal Style" and published in the *Idler*.)

But if Callaghan, stripped and unadorned, was plodding artlessly onward, Hemingway was experimenting passionately and forging the style that was to have such a massive impact on twentieth-century prose. He learned from Gertrude Stein, who, as he puts it in *A Moveable Feast*, "discovered many truths about rhythms and the uses of words in repetition that were valid and valuable. . . ." He also learned from her the need for clarity, for a language that would allow the reader to see and feel what the writer had seen and felt. This is the core of Hemingway's achievement.

Hemingway knew how far ahead he was of the reading public. In the following extract from *A Moveable Feast* he recalls writing the early stories:

> It was a very simple story called 'Out of Season' and I had omitted the real end of it which was that the old man hanged himself. This was omitted on my new theory that you could omit anything if you knew that you omitted and the omitted part would strengthen the story and make people feel something more than they understood.
>
> Well, I thought, now I have them so they do not understand them. There cannot be much doubt about that. There is most certainly no demand for them. But they will understand the same way that they always do in painting. It only takes time and it only needs confidence.

> It is necessary to handle yourself better when you have to cut down on food so you will not get too much hunger-thinking. Hunger is good discipline and you learn from it. And as long as they do not understand it you are ahead of them. Oh sure, I thought, I'm so far ahead of them now that I can't afford to eat regularly. It would not be bad if they caught up a little.
>
> I knew I must write a novel. But it seemed an impossible thing to do when I had been trying with great difficulty to write paragraphs that would be the distillation of what made a novel.

He also recalls the artistic struggle in the following extract from *A Moveable Feast*:

> Since I had started to break down all my writing and get rid of all facility and try to make instead of describe, writing had been wonderful to do. But it was very difficult, and I did not know how I would ever write anything as long as a novel. It often took me a full morning of work to write a paragraph.

How revealing is that first sentence! I think his contrasting "make" and "describe" captures the essence of the difference between his and Callaghan's writing. Hemingway was "making" his scenes; he was using English in ways it had never been used before. Ford Madox Ford once remarked of Hemingway's writing that the words "strike you, each one, as if they were pebbles fetched fresh from a brook." This illusion of freshness was the result of a new poetics of prose, new principles of architecture.

In *Death in the Afternoon*, Hemingway wrote: "Prose is architecture, not interior decoration, and the Baroque is over." He described the new prose further in one of the campfire chats in *Green Hills of Africa*:

> 'The reason everyone now tries to avoid [literary writing], to deny that it is important, to make it seem vain to try to do it, is because it is so difficult. Too many factors must combine to make it possible.'
>
> 'What is this now?'
>
> 'The kind of writing that can be done. How far prose can be carried if any one is serious enough and has luck. There is a fourth and fifth dimension that can be gotten.'

'You believe it?'

'I know it.'

'And if a writer can get this?'

'Then nothing else matters. It is more important than anything he can do. The chances are, of course, that he will fail. But there is a chance that he succeeds.'

'But that is poetry you are talking about.'

'No. It is much more difficult than poetry. It is a prose that has never been written. But it can be written, without tricks and without cheating. With nothing that will go bad afterwards.'

'And why has it not been written?'

'Because there are too many factors. First, there must be talent, much talent. Talent such as Kipling had. Then there must be discipline. The discipline of Flaubert. Then there must be the conception of what it can be and an absolute conscience as unchanging as the standard meter in Paris, to prevent faking. Then the writer must be intelligent and disinterested and above all he must survive.'

Callaghan's working methods and vaguely expressed aesthetic views make an instructive contrast with Hemingway's. The following rather incoherent extracts are from Callaghan's 1987 conversation with Ray Ellenwood:

> . . . You see I was eliminating all style, that's what I wanted to do . . . I remember when I was twenty-five, Sinclair Lewis said in a burst of generous enthusiasm, 'How Flaubert would have loved you!' This rather surprised me, because I knew how long and arduously Flaubert worked on a page, whereas I didn't, you see. If I got into the right groove, it would be right. . . . There are a dozen writers I could think of as having been enormously influenced by Flaubert, you know, guys who really work on their work to get in that final touch, whereas I don't work that way at all. I like working at finding the right groove. But it may well be that the right groove for me has this peculiar correspondence with the Flaubertian view; it may be as simple as that. I was an admirer of Flaubert, of course – who in the world wasn't at that time? – but I don't know who shapes your point of view about language. Except to get back to one cardinal thing: I wanted language to come easily, you know? I believed in that. I believed in a kind of happy flow of language. I mean

take my book, *That Summer in Paris*: some people at the time thought that book was delightfully written, truthful, and charming. And I remember *Time* magazine, which for some reason had decided to turn thumbs down on me, and some bright wag (I can see him with the pencil stuck behind his ear, grinning) said that I was a sucker for a left bank – meaning the Left Bank in Paris, of course – the way Hemingway was a sucker for a left hook. The point was, you see, that I wrote as clumsily as Hemingway boxed. That was their view. The *Time* guy probably had a literary bug in his head. He thought he knew what fancy writing was, and there's no fancy writing in the book, because I would have despised that, you see.

Ellenwood finally pushed Callaghan to define more clearly what he meant by his claim to have "eliminated all style":

ELLENWOOD: . . . in effect what I'm saying to you is that I don't believe in non-artifice in literature. I think that literature *is* artifice. And I don't believe in the transparency of language; I believe in the *illusion* of transparency. And I believe that what you create is an illusion of transparency, because you've got to, willy nilly, select your details, select the things that you're going to talk about, and somehow those things have to have significance for you and eventually for your reader. Otherwise you're just doing a documentary, and that's certainly not what you're doing.

CALLAGHAN: Well, it's a kind of dumb style in a way. This thing I'm writing now, I write, say ten pages, and I'm trying to go over it to get it ready for the girl who's typing it. And I just go over that, changing syntax here and there, but all I'm really trying to do is get the thing so she can read it. And that's the style. I mean it sounds utterly plebeian, but that's all I'm trying to do, to get the thing so it will read naturally, you know, and throw out the phrases that are clumsy, that get in the way of the movement. That's all I'm really trying to do when I go over this thing, is try and get everything in the right place. Everything will be right if you get it in the right place. If it's in the right place it won't sound forced, won't sound calculated, you'll never think of it as a literary effect, you'll just say: Gee, this is true, it's all true, absolutely true.

All of the foregoing tends to suggest that Callaghan was not, to put it politely, a particularly rigorous theoretician. Hemingway strove to "break down" his writing to "get rid of all facility." Callaghan seems to have sought facility. Hemingway was very much one of the "guys who really work on their work;" Callaghan was not. It seems necessary at this point to examine representative samples of Hemingway's and Callaghan's writing to illustrate how profoundly they are unlike each other. I have chosen to look at the first two paragraphs of Hemingway's "In Another Country" because David Lodge has written an essay on them in his book *The Art of Fiction* (1992) that provides a lengthier analysis that I can afford here. I urge Lodge's essay, "Repetition," on all who are interested in Hemingway's style, and I warmly commend the book in general.

The narrator of "In Another Country" is a soldier who has been wounded fighting on the Italian side in World War I. He and his companions at the hospital have been variously mutilated, and although they have escaped death they are perhaps condemned to a life not worth living. "In Another Country" is a story about men coping with trauma. The maimed soldiers are cut off from other people; they live, emotionally, "in another country." Death, in this story, is always imminent. The story's title is taken from Marlowe's *The Jew of Malta*: "Thou hast committed – / Fornication? but that was in another country: and, besides, / the wench is dead." "In Another Country" was published in 1927 in *Men without Women.*

Here are the first two paragraphs:

> In the fall the war was always there, but we did not go to it any more. It was cold in the fall in Milan and the dark came very early. Then the electric lights came on, and it was pleasant along the streets looking in the windows. There was much game hanging outside the shops, and the snow powdered in the fur of the foxes and the wind blew their tails. The deer hung stiff and heavy and empty, and small birds blew in the wind and the wind turned their feathers. It was a cold fall and the wind came down from the mountains.
>
> We were all at the hospital every afternoon, and there were different ways of walking across the town through the dusk to the hospital. Two of the ways were alongside canals, but they were long. Always, though, you crossed a bridge across a canal to enter the hospital. There was a choice of three bridges. On one of them a woman sold roasted chest-

nuts. It was warm, standing in front of her charcoal fire, and the chestnuts were warm afterward in your pocket. The hospital was very old and very beautiful, and you entered through a gate and walked across a courtyard and out a gate on the other side. There were usually funerals starting from the courtyard. Beyond the old hospital were the new brick pavilions, and there we met every afternoon and were all very polite and interested in what was the matter, and sat in the machines that were to make so much difference.

David Lodge begins his essay as follows:

If you have the time and inclination, get some coloured pens or pencils and draw a ring round the words that occur more than once in the first paragraph of Hemingway's story, a different colour for each word, and join them up. You will reveal a complex pattern of verbal chains linking words of two kinds: those with referential meaning, *fall, cold, dark, wind, blew,* which we call lexical words, and articles, prepositions and conjunctions like *the, of, in, and,* which we can call grammatical words.

Hemingway rejects traditional rhetoric. "The words are simple," says Lodge, "but their arrangement is not." It is impossible not to notice the repetition of the word "and," which joins together the simple declarative statements. Good writing demands elegant variation of vocabulary and syntax, but Hemingway defies the rules to create an incantatory, elegiac rhythm, the repeated lexical words sounding again and again.

Of these words Lodge writes:

The American word for autumn, *fall,* carries in it a reminder of the death of vegetation, and echoes the conventional phrase for those who die in battle, 'the fallen.' Its juxtaposition with *cold* and *dark* in the second sentence strengthens these associations. The brightly lit shops seem to offer some distraction (an effect heightened by the fact that there is no lexical repetition in this sentence) but the narrator's attention quickly focuses on the game hanging outside the shops, further emblems of death. The description of the snow powdering in their fur, and the wind ruffling their feathers, is literal and exact, but tightens the association of *fall, cold, dark, wind, blew,* with death. Three of the

> repeated words come together for the first time in the last sentence with a poetic effect of closure: 'It was a cold fall and the wind came down from the mountains.' The mountains are where the war is going on. Wind, so often a symbol of life and spirit in religious and Romantic writing, is here associated with lifelessness. God is very dead in these early stories of Hemingway. The hero has learned from the trauma of combat to distrust metaphysics as well as rhetoric. He trusts only his senses and sees experience in starkly polarized terms: cold/warm, light/dark, life/death.

I disagree with Lodge that "The brightly lit shops seem to offer some distraction;" rather, I think the brightly lit shops are an example of what Lodge later calls an "implied simile." The shops are bright and warm while the street is dark and cold; the narrator is *outside* the shops, his being outside looking in yet another expression of his being "in another country."

The animals hanging outside the shops, emblems of death, also suggest in the detail of the description something of the indignities of death, the birds, feathers being ruffled out of place, the foxes' tails twirling in the wind, the deer, once graceful and aquiver with nervous life hanging "stiff and heavy and empty." "Empty" is a powerful but curious word to use to mean simply *gutted*, and I think its use in combination with "stiff" suggests also the emptiness of the maimed soldiers.

It's helpful to think of this first paragraph as an image in itself, the statement of the melody, the story in miniature. What might seem to the careless reader to be a comment on the weather and a description of Milanese butchers' shops is, in fact, a poetic distillation of the story's heart, an example of that prose which Hemingway described in *Green Hills of Africa* as "a prose that has never been written."

The second paragraph is also radically innovative. Here the key words are "hospital," "bridge," and "canal." Lodge suggests that the word "hospital" is repeated so inelegantly because it is the centre of the men's lives, and the repetition reinforces its emotional importance to them. The flat rehearsal of the possible ways of getting to the hospital suggests to us the unnumbered times the narrator has made the journey, the duration and tedium and ineffectiveness of the medical treatment.

Lodge wonders if the canal is intended as a "faint suggestion of the river Styx in the underworld": I would be much firmer. Crossing the bridge is a daily going into "another country." All the journeying in the paragraph carries a poetic implication; it is all a going in and out, a crossing over to "the other side." The funeral processions that start from the courtyard of the old hospital also have to cross the bridge.

Lodge says of the roasted chestnuts that they are "warm in the pocket like the promise of life – except that Hemingway doesn't use that simile, he merely implies it." Even such a superficial examination of these paragraphs illustrates what Hemingway meant by the sentence "Since I had started to break down all my writing and get rid of all facility and try to make instead of describe, writing had been wonderful to do."

As I've previously stated, I can see no evidence in Callaghan's writing that he understood anything much of Hemingway's "making." Professor W.H. New of the University of British Columbia, however, has recently claimed exactly the reverse. In an essay entitled "Tense/Present/Narrative: Reflections on English-Language Short Fiction in Canada," Professor New offers an analysis of the opening paragraphs of Callaghan's "Ancient Lineage," claiming that the setting functions as image and that there is a carefully wrought pattern of lexical words just as there is in the opening paragraphs of "In Another Country." He writes:

> It begins with a young man heading to a small Ontario town to interview an aging woman about her presumed family line; he arrives with confidence intact, his condescension toward woman, family, and small town all reinforced by his age, class, and university training in history. The story's sentences are the agency not only of establishing this impression but also of indicating the likelihood of some sort of comeuppance. Upon his arrival, the man 'hurried along the platform and jumped down on the sloping cinder path to the sidewalk.
>
> 'Trees were on the lawns alongside the walk, branches drooping low, leaves scraping occasionally against the young man's straw hat. He saw a cluster of lights, blueish-white in the dusk across a river, many lights for a small town. He crossed the lift-lock bridge and turned on to the main street. A hotel was at the corner.'
>
> Setting functions as image. The repetitive emphasis – down, slope, droop, cross, bridge, turn, and corner – suggests a point of imminent change. The rhythms, moreover (rhythms of associational as well as sequential observation), are those of unthinking security: that is, the story

> initially establishes the voice of a presumptive faith in the empirical limits of reality and, by analogy, in the certainties of genealogical history, which he has come to town to investigate.

Before commenting on this bloated analysis, I must point out that Professor New has omitted from his quotation the first two sentences of the first paragraph – a strange thing to do if one is setting out to illuminate a carefully wrought aesthetic whole. The complete passage reads as follows:

> The young man from the Historical Club with a green magazine under his arm got off the train at Clintonville. It was getting dark but the station lights were not lit. He hurried along the platform and jumped down on the sloping cinder path to the sidewalk.
>
> Trees were on the lawns alongside the walk, branches drooping low, leaves scraping occasionally against the young man's straw hat. He saw a cluster of lights, blueish-white in the dusk across a river, many lights for a small town. He crossed the lift-lock bridge and turned on to the main street. A hotel was at the corner.

Why the omission? Because the sentences don't offer lexical words that fit the pattern Professor New claims to find?

But the one thing to be said – simply, flatly – is that the Callaghan passage does not *feel* like the Hemingway passage. Hemingway's prose is intense, alive, quick to the touch, while Callaghan's is slack and lifeless.

I do not read "down," "slope," "droop," "cross," "bridge," "turn," and "corner" as having "repetitive emphasis." The description does not signal to me "a point of imminent change." It doesn't signal anything much at all; I take it as Callaghan rambling on with not much more intention than getting the young man from A to B.

The real repetition in the paragraph is of the words "lights," "lit," "dark," "dusk," "lights," and "lights," but these do not generate emotion. Callaghan merely wishes us to know that it was dark and the young man could see lights.

We might test Professor New's reading of the paragraph further by glancing at the second descriptive paragraph in the story. Is the "repetitive emphasis" still apparent? Is its purpose, if a purpose exists, any clearer?

> Mr. Flaherty sauntered out and turned to the left. It was dark and the street had the silence of small towns in the evening. Turning a corner he heard girls giggling in a doorway. He looked at the church on the hill, the steeple dark against the sky. He had forgotten whether the man had said beside the church or across the road, but could not make up his mind to ask the fellow who was watering the wide church lawn. No lights in the shuttered windows of the rough-cast house beside the church. He came down the hill and had to yell three times at the man because the water swished strongly against the grass.

One "turned," one "turning," one "corner," one "across," and one "down" – but instead of playing with academic Scrabble tiles, let us ask the question again: Does this paragraph *feel* as if it has rhetorical structure and significance? If any reader still imagines a debate is going on here, I would ask that reader to *read aloud* the paragraphs from "In Another Country" and then to *read aloud* the paragraphs from "Ancient Lineage."

Given that the story is about lineage and, ultimately, sexual feeling, one might in academic desperation invest with significance the giggling girls, the phallic steeple, and the swishing hose, but for a sensitive reader it's difficult to avoid the suspicion that it's all simply Callaghan artlessly plodding along with no particular destination in mind.

To further probe the subtlety and complexity of Callaghan's prose, let us look at the opening paragraphs of "A Wedding-Dress," a story that seems to be generally admired. It appeared in *A Native Argosy* in 1929, two years later than "In Another Country."

> For fifteen years Miss Lena Schwartz had waited for Sam Hilton to get a good job so they could get married. She lived in a quiet boarding-house on Wellesley Street, the only woman among seven men boarders. The landlady, Mrs. Mary McNab, did not want woman boarders; the house might get a bad reputation in the neighbourhood, but Miss Schwartz had been with her a long time. Miss Schwartz was thirty-two, her hair was straight, her nose turned up a little and she was thin.
>
> Sam got a good job in Windsor and she was going there to marry him. She was glad to think that Sam still wanted to marry her, because he was a Catholic and went to church every Sunday. Sam liked her so much he wrote a cramped homely letter four times a week.

> When Miss Schwartz knew definitely that she was going to Windsor, she read part of a letter to Mrs. McNab, who was a plump, tidy woman. The men heard about the letter at the table and talked as if Lena were an old maid. 'I guess it will really happen to her all right,' they said, nudging one another. 'The Lord knows she waited long enough.'
>
> Miss Schwartz quit work in the millinery shop one afternoon in the middle of February. She was to travel by night, arrive in Windsor early next morning and marry Sam as soon as possible.

I do not want to belabour the obvious – or at least what I *hope* is obvious – by examining such pedestrian prose in detail, but I will point out again that academics in Canada have almost unanimously claimed its relationship with Hemingway's prose *for sixty years*. There *is* no relationship. This prose is not "laconic," "suggestive," "spare," "sure," or "stripped": it is merely *boring*. Nor is it particularly "lucid;" what, for example, does Callaghan intend us to understand by: "She was glad to think that Sam still wanted to marry her, because he was a Catholic and went to church every Sunday"?

The four quoted paragraphs contain two more typically pointless – if not ludicrous – descriptions of people: "Miss Schwartz was thirty-two, her hair was straight, her nose turned up a little and she was thin." And, "When Miss Schwartz knew definitely that she was going to Windsor, she read part of a letter to Mrs. McNab, who was a plump, tidy woman." Callaghan is capable of these vague, unfocused "descriptions" of the people in his stories because he doesn't "see" these people; they are crudely painted puppets. Consider, too, the tone of these opening paragraphs of "A Wedding-Dress," a tone typical in his work; how like the tone it is of fairy tales or stories for children.

I wish to return to this point later, but cannot resist saying now how condescending and patronizing I find all the talk of his stories being about "little people" and "common folk." I have never met a "little person" and don't believe in them. Even the simplest human life is so complex it is beyond the abilities of the most sophisticated fiction to encompass it. "Little people" are the creation of arrogant and sentimental ideologists.

And Miss Schwartz is a strange creation indeed. She may have struck decades of Canadian critics as a example of "urban realism" (God!), but what I want to know is what sort of girl of seventeen meets a man and waits fifteen years for him to get a good job? If it's possible to answer that question –

which I doubt – then there are other things I must know about this Miss Schwartz to whom Sam writes "homely" letters. What about friends and family? The furnishings of her room, her faith and pastimes, her friends and enemies in the millinery shop, the texture of her daily life? Miss Schwartz is only a "little person" because Callaghan made her so; she is less a person than sentimentality exploited.

It is, of course, perfectly possible to create characters on the margins of society without condescension. The example of Miss Brill springs to mind. I can remember to this day where I first read "Miss Brill;" I was sixteen years old and sitting in the library in Beckenham Grammar School in Kent. I can still remember the hair rising on my nape. The thrill was an aesthetic one; the way Katherine Mansfield had suggested the rhythms of Miss Brill's speaking voice while writing in the third person seemed to me then an almost miraculous legerdemain.

Callaghan, according to Desmond Pacey (in the 1965 edition of *Literary History of Canada*), profited from the example of Katherine Mansfield (no evidence provided) and "looked closely at the people about him, and in a simple, stripped, suggestive prose style recorded the small triumphs and tragedies of their ordinary lives." Here is the first paragraph of "Miss Brill," published in *The Garden Party and Other Stories*. The story, with its opening evocation of the beginning of fall, concerns Miss Brill's realization that she is too old and set in her ways for life to offer her any possibility of a romantic relationship. What a relief to move from Callaghan's bumbling to Mansfield's exquisite performance:

> Although it was so brilliantly fine – the blue sky powdered with gold and great spots of light like white wine splashed over the Jardins Publiques – Miss Brill was glad that she had decided on her fur. The air was motionless, but when you opened your mouth there was just a faint chill, like a chill from a glass of iced water before you sip, and now and again a leaf came drifting – from nowhere, from the sky.

Now *that* is setting functioning as image.

Katherine Mansfield toppled into damaging sentimentality in "Miss Brill," but she had dared new kinds of writing and left a legacy for writers who succeeded her. After prose such as that what a wrench it is to return to the Callaghan who wrote in "Ancient Lineage" – the book is open on my desk and my eye lights on the sentences – "He stood in the hall while the large woman lit the gas in the front room. The gas flared up, popped, showing fat hips and heavy lines on her face."

Michael Darling, a critic writing outside the universities and one of the keenest and funniest literary minds in Canada, skewered Callaghan's lumpen prose in the following merciless unpublished parody:

If Morley Callaghan Had Written Ernest Hemingway's 'A Clean, Well-Lighted Place'

For years Johnny Wilson had been a regular customer at Al Smith's café. Johnny was an old man with thinning grey hair and a wrinkled red face. He liked to sit in one corner of the café where it was neither light nor dark but partly both, and think despairingly about his need for identity and a sense of self-worth.

On this particular night, two waiters stood watching him. Bill Jones was a burly old man with white hair and a shiny red face. Fred Brown was a thin young man with straight black hair and a smooth red face. He was engaged to Molly Smith, Al Smith's niece, a tall blonde girl with really swell legs. Fred rubbed the end of his smooth red nose and grinned as he thought of Molly's swell legs. Molly was a really fine girl and they were going to get married as soon as they could.

'Last week Johnny tried to commit suicide,' said Bill Jones in his deep but slightly cracked voice, brimming with sorrow and compassion. He took out his handkerchief and wiped his shiny red face, thinking to himself, 'I could be Johnny, sitting there and drinking, and wishing I could stay in this clean and well-lighted café.'

The look on Bill's face brought a strange feeling to Fred Brown, who suddenly looked at Johnny Wilson with a puzzled, shy, wondering look on his face, feeling that there was something about the old man that might someday be important to him, something that went beyond Molly Smith's swell legs. It seemed to him that this was the first time he had ever looked upon Johnny Wilson.

'Maybe he just has insomnia,' suggested Bill Jones gently, hoping to spare Fred Brown the painful realization of his own mortality. 'Many have it.'

Fred Brown nodded sadly, his smooth red face suddenly becoming

> wrinkled and old. Now when he tried to think of Molly Smith's swell legs, all he could visualize was Johnny Wilson's thinning grey hair. He stood beside Bill Jones in the shadows of Al Smith's café and thought to himself, 'Golly, a clean, well-lighted place might be fine too.'

* * *

It is almost a commonplace in Callaghan criticism that his strongest work is in the story form. Desmond Pacey writes in the introduction to *A Book of Canadian Stories* (1952) that Callaghan had "done most of his work, and achieved his greatest success, in the short story form." Donald Stephens wrote of him in 1969 in *The Sixties*: "The master of the short story in Canada – and still the best – [is] Morley Callaghan. . . ." In 1981, Stephens reiterated this view in *The Callaghan Symposium*: ". . . the greatest of Callaghan's achievements is the simple fact that he is a good storyteller and he is at his best in his short stories." Robert Weaver and William Toye wrote of him in *The Oxford Anthology of Canadian Literature* (1973): "Morley Callaghan is Canada's most distinguished novelist and short-story writer . . . Today he is admired by most younger writers of fiction in Canada as their only true predecessor in this country . . ."

Some critics, however, have had reservations about the stories, most notably Fraser Sutherland in his book on Hemingway and Callaghan, *The Style of Innocence* (1972):

> It is unlikely that Callaghan ever set out to write a formula story of the kind one finds in women's magazines. But there is a sameness about much of his work. In such stories, events start out badly for the main character, get a little better, and then deteriorate. Or, alternatively, they begin well, turn a little worse, and then improve somewhat. In both cases the tone is compassionate and 'poignant,' and there is a sort of 'Aw gee' ending. The last line of 'A Cap for Steve' is typical: 'The wonderful generosity of childhood – the price a boy was willing to pay to be able to count on his father's admiration and approval – made him feel humble, then strangely exalted.'

More recently, W.J. Keith, in his survey history *Canadian Literature in English* (1985), has expressed an uneasiness about Callaghan's stories:

> The discussion of length in Callaghan's later novels reminds us that he has a further reputation as a short story writer. Indeed, it has sometimes been argued that this represents his finest achievement. There can be no doubt that his example helped to establish the short story as an important genre within modern Canadian literature. His virtues of directness, economy, and clarity all show themselves to advantage in this concentrated form. Callaghan is a master at creating small situations that generate profound meanings: a plain woman is caught stealing a dress in which to get married; a priest gives absolution to a dying woman against the wishes of her husband; a woman is both distressed and ecstatic when her sister's fiancé displays his covert feelings for her. These are simple situations, but they are intensely human and Callaghan tells them cleanly, without pretentiousness or sentimentality or any attempt to exalt them into a weakening generality. Story by story, they are excellent; yet if we read them in bulk, in the volume entitled *Morley Callaghan's Stories* (1959), which contains all the short pieces he wished to preserve and from which the above examples are taken, it has to be admitted that a certain monotony becomes evident. Callaghan's consistent skill suggests a formula. We know a story will end appropriately but without undue sensationalism; we know that, perfect in itself, it will stay within the bounds of its expectations.

Desmond Pacey, in the revised *Creative Writing in Canada* (1961), also expressed reservations:

> One feels the lack, in Callaghan's novels and stories, of any definite standards by which his characters are to be judged. He succeeds admirably in revealing the shoddiness of most of the prevailing standards, but when it is a matter of suggesting alternatives he can only offer vague words like simplicity, tenderness and compassion. The result is that all of Callaghan's work has a certain moral flabbiness. This is much less obvious in the short stories than in the novels, because the short story can be made out of a moment of insight, a compassionate glimpse of suffering humanity.

Fraser Sutherland in *The Style of Innocence* commented on the stories being fashioned from what Pacey calls "a moment of insight":

> Can a moment of mercy or wonder be enough to sustain a story? Obviously it can – if the mercy or wonder is profound enough. But in many of the stories this profundity never has a chance to occur. Instead, it is kept within the bounds of a formula. Basically, the formula is this: an object, event or third person comes between the principal characters in the story and acts as an agent either to unite the main characters emotionally, if they are divided; or, to divide them if they were united at the start. Often, the agent does both. In 'Mr. and Mrs. Fairbanks,' a young couple are walking in the park when the wife decides to give a quarter to an old man sitting on a bench. When the 'tramp' turns her down she feels humiliated, which in turn unsettles her husband, until the old man smiles at them and makes it all better.

But these reservations, demurrals, and outright criticisms have not really had much impact on the general perception of Callaghan's work. Most standard works of reference continue to assign him a central place in our literature. Hugo McPherson, writing in *The Canadian Encyclopedia*, might be said to be representative: "Possibly because of his speculations about time and eternity, Canadians have not always been friendly to Callaghan, but in the larger world of literature he remains a classic."

What fascinates me about all this criticism is the way the critics – with the honourable exception of Fraser Sutherland – avoid grappling with the dogged awfulness of Callaghan's prose. It genuinely seems not to matter to them. They seem oblivious to aesthetic concerns, to art itself. Those critics who point out Callaghan's clumsiness, implausible characters, wooden dialogue, moral flabbiness, and formulaic constructions yet urge us to read him are surely analogous to music critics urging us to appreciate the playing of a pianist with maimed hands.

And think of the money they earn!

Critics such as John Moss, in his dumb compendium *A Reader's Guide to the Canadian Novel* (1981), baffle and confound me. Of Callaghan's novel *More Joy in Heaven* he wrote:

> This novel, as much as any, shows why Callaghan is a significant writer in the Canadian tradition without necessarily being an accomplished artist. [WHAT?] The prose is awkwardly simplistic, but forceful and direct [WHAT?] . . . He is probably the best example we have of the serious artist as entertainer. [WHAT?]

Again, of *The Loved and the Lost*, Moss writes:

> It contains some of his least successful writing – and at his worst, Callaghan is capable of atrocious prose, violently forced symbolism, and turgid dramatics. It shows only a superficial understanding of the subject materials: of women, blacks, Montreal society, and the nuances of human personality. Throughout all this, however, it displays the ambiguities, anomalies, and ironies of real life without cloying explanation – indeed, with a compassion and tolerance his other fiction lacks.

"*Throughout all this, however. . . .*"

Dear God!

The critics may whiffle on as they wish but I for one refuse to hang on my wall a painting about which I have to say: "It's actually very good when you take into account that he painted it with his foot."

* * *

If I had the patience to write a detailed study of Callaghan's stories I might well approach the task by writing an introductory chapter examining the beginnings and endings of the stories. Even a quick canter through some beginnings and endings is revealing.

First, some beginnings.

> Dave Diamond, a poor man, a carpenter's assistant, was a small, wiry, quick-tempered individual who had learned how to make every dollar count in his home. His wife, Anna, had been sick a lot, and his twelve-year-old son, Steve, had to be kept in school. Steve, a big-eyed, shy kid ought to have known the value of money as well as Dave did. It had been ground into him. ('A Cap for Steve')

*

> Mary Slater was a slim-bodied, dark-haired, nervous girl, with big brown eyes, who dressed very plainly because she felt that the men in the neighbourhood were no longer interested in her.
>
> She was accustomed to doing the housework for her father, talking in the afternoon with the women on the street who had been married a long time, and waiting on her young sister, Peg, and on Peg's sweetheart, Stevenson, whenever he came to the house. He came almost every night

to the old house on Grove Street and sat in the front room with the plump, fair-haired, rosy-cheeked Peg; and Mary passed back and forth from the front room to the kitchen carrying coffee and sandwiches. Most of the evening Mary remained in the kitchen, talking with her father, a quick-tempered, devout, hard-working man in the trucking business. It never occurred to Mary that Stevenson ever noticed her at all. ('Guilty Woman')

*

Ever since he had been a kid Fred Sloane had wanted to be a cook, not just a cook in a beanery but a man who might some day be called an important chef. For two years he had done the cooking for the O'Neils, who owned a small quick-lunch.

Mrs. O'Neil, who sometimes helped him in the kitchen, was a heavy, hard-working woman, always a little afraid of her husband, whom she obeyed from a strong sense of religious duty. ('Lunch Counter')

*

The first time Mrs. Jerry Austin's husband went away she cried a good deal and wrote a long letter home, but in two months' time he came back. They had a big dinner and agreed never to quarrel again and he promised not to feel restless any more. The second time he left her she didn't even bother looking for a job. She told the landlady, Mrs. Oddy, that Mr. Austin had gone travelling and was doing well. Mrs. Oddy, who had red hair, a toothy accent and a loud voice, said that whenever Mr. Oddy did any travelling she liked to keep him company, but after all, it was none of her business. ('A Regret for Youth')

*

Although they were both out of work, Timothy Harshaw and his wife were the happiest people in the Barrow Street house. Timothy was a round, smooth-faced, very fair young fellow who never thought of wearing a coat with trousers to match, and yet somehow looked neat and distinguished. ('Timothy Harshaw's Flute')

*

Mrs. Massey, a stout, kindly woman of sixty, full of energy for her age, and red-faced and healthy except for an occasional pain in her left leg which she watched very carefully, had come from Chicago to see her son

> who was a doctor. The doctor's family made a great fuss over her, and she felt in such good humour that she suddenly said one night: 'I declare, I'll go and see Mary Woolens. I wonder what's happened to her? Find out where she lives for me.'
>
> She had grown up with Mary Woolens. Thirty years ago they had quarrelled, she had married and gone West, and they had not seen each other since. ('An Old Quarrel')

What do these openings reveal? Certainly not cunningly contrived patterns of lexical words; not even Professor New could discover artifice here. And naughty as the suggestion may be, if we can't find such patterns here perhaps it's logical to suspect that "Ancient Lineage" is innocent of such patterning too.

These openings reveal that Callaghan's approach to his material and to his readers is dictatorial. He is always completely external to the stories he is telling. The reader is not invited to participate in any way; we are not allowed to experience events in a Callaghan story and neither are we allowed to draw our own conclusions. Rather, Callaghan relentlessly tells and explains.

His characters are simple puppets, and that is precisely why he describes them so endlessly; such descriptions are hopeless attempts to cover up the wood with heavy paint. His characters are awkwardly invented "little people" who exist simply to perform the plot. Similarly, because Callaghan is not particularly interested in the physical world, the worlds of his stories are perfunctory and nebulous. There is nothing in Callaghan – despite his assertion to the contrary – of facing the thing freshly and seeing it freshly for what it is. There is never a loving dwelling on texture as there is in, say, Alice Munro, because these people and their worlds have not been lovingly and passionately observed and invented. Callaghan's characters and the worlds they are supposed to inhabit are subordinate to the author's didactic purpose, and for that reason they never come to life.

These beginnings also have a tone in common. It is the tone of "Once upon a time . . ." or "There once lived in a distant country a prince who . . . ." To attempt to disguise this fairy-tale tone, Callaghan would have written: "There once lived in a distant country called Neutralia a tall, dark-haired, handsome prince with a well-shaped nose . . ." – but well-shaped nose or not, it's obvious that we are dealing here with something quite different from the modernist short story.

These beginnings also suggest that Callaghan lacked a sense of humour and suffered from a tin ear. The unintentionally funny sentences – "Most of the evening Mary remained in the kitchen, talking with her father, a quick-tempered, devout, hard-working man in the trucking business" – bring to mind the mighty lines of William McGonagall.

And now to look at some endings.

> He got up restlessly, realizing that neither Mike's wisdom nor his brother's anguish could teach him anything tonight. Standing at the open window, he looked out over the lighted streets where he walked a little while ago, looking over toward Jessie's place, stirred with a longing for more and more of whatever she would be able to give him. It had started now for them and it would keep going on. And then he was filled with awe, for it seemed like the beginning of a voyage out, with not much he had learned on that night to guide him. ('The Voyage Out')
>
> *
>
> When the shoes, now dyed black were returned to Mary the next day she put them on slowly, and then she put her feet together and looked at the shoes a long time. They were no longer the beautiful red shoes, and yet as she stared at them, solemn-faced, she suddenly felt a strange kind of secret joy, a feeling of certainty that her mother had got the shoes so that she might understand at this time that she still had her special blessing and protection. ('Very Special Shoes')
>
> *
>
> But when they came home from church and she heard Peg laughing and talking cheerfully, she knew that Stevenson hadn't mentioned her at all. She wondered why he was so sure she wouldn't tell, and then she felt sorry for him, for he seemed so young, and he didn't know how to have her when he really wanted her. As she began to think of the few moments she had had with him, his smooth face and his damp curly hair pressed down against her breast, she said softly, 'Maybe he didn't know the way it was with me,' and part of a world that nobody else could ever touch seemed to belong to her alone. ('Guilty Woman')

*

'I feel very contented now, that's all,' she said simply. 'Tonight everything is so still on the street outside and in the dark here. I was so very happy while Joe was with me,' she whispered. 'It was as though I had never been alive before. It's so sweetly peaceful tonight, waiting, and feeling so much stirring within me, so lovely and still.'

'What are you waiting for?' he asked.

'It seems now he'll come back again,' she said.

'When Ellen?'

'I don't know. I just feel that he will.' She smiled patiently, with such a depth of certainty and peace that he dared not speak. For many minutes he sat beside her, stirred and wondering. Deep within him was a pain that seemed to be a part of all the years of his own life, but he could really feel nothing but her contentment now. Nothing that had ever happened to him seemed as important as this secret gladness Ellen was sharing with him.

He got up at last and said quietly, 'I'll go now, Ellen. Good night.'

'Good night, Dad,' she said, and he felt that she was smiling. ('Ellen')

*

And as Frances thought of the way the hat had looked on the mannequin head in the window she hoped vaguely that something would turn up so that she could get it back from Mrs. Foley by the end of the week. And just thinking of it, sitting there, she felt an eagerness and a faint elation; it was a plain little red hat, the kind of hat she had wanted for months, elegant and expensive, a plain felt hat, but so very distinctive. ('The Red Hat')

*

In the cold, early-morning light, with heavy trucks rumbling on the street, he felt terribly tense and nervous. He could hardly remember anything that had happened. Inside him there was a wide, frightening emptiness. He wanted to reach out desperately and hold that swift, ardent, yielding joy that had been so close to him. For a while he could not think at all. And then he felt that slow unfolding coming in him again, making him quick with wonder. ('One Spring Night')

What do these endings reveal? Wyndham Lewis' oily review of *Now That April's Here* described the stories as "beautifully replete with a message of human tolerance and love" and as "full of a robust benevolence." Professor Victor Hoar, in the Studies in Canadian Literature series, wrote on *Now That April's Here*: "The one theme recited again and again . . . is the promise of growth inherent in human beings. . . . Again and again, Callaghan's protagonists are left enriched and excited by the new vision of themselves and of the world around them."

These endings do not offer me "a message of human tolerance and love," nor do they reveal to me a "new vision" or a "promise of growth;" overwhelmingly, they reveal sloppy, gooey sentimentality. Consider the sheer vagueness of the words Callaghan uses to describe this "new vision": "stirred," "longing," "awe," "secret joy," "lovely," "still," sweetly peaceful," "stirred and wondering," "secret gladness," "faint elation," "yielding joy," "slow unfolding," "quick with wonder."

Where Callaghan is not unintentionally funny, as in "Ellen," with its preposterous dialogue, he is simply embarrassing. One cannot take seriously the work of a writer who produces lines of alleged dialogue such as: "It's so sweetly peaceful tonight, waiting, and feeling so much stirring within me, so lovely and still." Desmond Pacey wrote of a "certain moral flabbiness" in Callaghan's work; I wish he had pressed through into seeing that "moral flabbiness" is exactly the same thing as verbal flabbiness.

Twenty years or so ago I wrote an essay called "The Curate's Egg" wherein I suggested that Callaghan was not really in the modernist tradition at all, that his major impulse was moralistic and didactic and that this impulse was constantly at war within his work against what little artistry he possessed. This brief glance at beginnings and endings tends to confirm for me that suggestion. The forced openings, the fairy-tale tone, the puppet characters, and the cloying endings with their "message of human tolerance and love" – surely this smacks more of Sunday school than it does of the great modernist tradition of Anderson, Hemingway, Joyce and Mansfield?

* * *

Some academics have suggested that my criticism of such writers as Callaghan is an effort to "kill the father," to demolish what went before me in order to assert the greater value of my own writing. I had not heard of Morley

Callaghan until I was twenty-five. The writers who shaped my taste and style had worked their magic long before I had read a word of Callaghan. Callaghan was in no way a father or an example to me. My literary fathers were Ernest Hemingway and Evelyn Waugh, and far from wanting to kill them I continue to revere their work. I am basically indifferent to Callaghan. This essay was provoked by far more serious concerns than the desire to attack an inept writer of sentimental religiosity.

I wrote this essay in my lean, sure, stripped, laconic, professional, spare style for three reasons. Firstly, I was depressed that Professor Staines' Callaghan obituary didn't provoke even one letter of derisive protest to *Quill and Quire*, not a single letter from this vast, illiterate land suggesting that Staines had gone off his chump.

Secondly, to revert to boxing, I think it is *wicked* to teach students that stumblebum writing is great writing.

It is not an argument to hail Callaghan as a great writer simply because Ernest Hemingway and Scott Fitzgerald said he was good, simply because he was edited, as they were, by Maxwell Perkins, simply because he was published by Scribners and Macmillan, simply because Edmund Wilson said of him that he was "unjustly neglected" and compared him with Chekhov and Turgenev. None of these aberrant judgements can stand against the saccharine sentimentality, the *unthinking* quality of the writing, the sheer sad *sound* of the entirely typical sentences I've quoted.

If readers are deaf to the *ridiculousness* of: "She stood on the corner of Bloor and Yonge, an impressive build of a woman, tall, stout, good-looking for forty-two, and watched the traffic signal" then prose in all its infinite beauty will remain for them a closed book.

Thirdly, I wrote this essay so that I could end it with questions I want to ask of the entire CanLit apparatus: If Morley Callaghan, as *The Canadian Encyclopedia* states, is "a classic," what can we meaningfully say of Alice Munro? What can we meaningfully say of Mavis Gallant? Of Leon Rooke? Of Clark Blaise? Of Norman Levine? What can we meaningfully say of a dozen or more younger writers we continue to ignore?

CASTING SAD SPELLS

Alice Munro's "Walker Brothers Cowboy"

Most of the fifteen stories collected in *Dance of the Happy Shades* had been previously published in magazines. Two or three of the stories, however, were specially written to enlarge and complete the volume and among these later stories were "Images" and "Walker Brothers Cowboy."

Both stories are interestingly different from most of the other stories in the book and represent a stylistic change. These two stories are more highly wrought than previous stories, the rhetoric at a higher pitch, the images more intense, the painting of detail more vibrant.

While some of the stories in *Dance of the Happy Shades* were first published in such literary magazines as *The Fiddlehead* and *The Canadian Forum,* others were first published in *The Montrealer* and *Chatelaine.* None of the stories was "commercial" but all were traditional in form and one or two might be criticized for being overly explicit. The two stories written especially for the book, on the other hand, seem more consciously "literary;" they are more complex than the other stories not only in language but in form and they make no concessions to popular expectation.

That one of these stories is *called* "Images" directs us to the nature of the change in Alice Munro's work at this time; she is beginning to relinquish conventional plot and is beginning to work in what is essentially a poetic manner letting images and the accumulation of detail carry the story's line and emotional weight. She withdraws in these stories far more than she usually does as commentator or explicator and allows the reader to come into more unmediated contact with the imagery.

Not surprisingly, "Images" and "Walker Brothers Cowboy" also exhibit a concomitant change in form. The structures of the stories are unlike anything she had attempted before and they emphasize and enhance the primacy of the image. "Walker Brothers Cowboy" is divided into three sections; the first is introductory, the second is amplification and extension of the essential melody in the first, and the third concludes and returns us to the opening section by way of allusion and repetition. The important thing to realize about the first section is that it is, in itself, an image. It cannot be read conventionally as an aspect of plot for read in that way it makes little sense. If we approach it looking for the "story," looking for the "what happens," we will prevent ourselves from seeing what *is* there; we must give ourselves up to language and to image. The first section is the whole story in miniature; it contains in essence all that is to come in sections two and three. It might not be entirely fanciful to suggest that there is about the story something almost sonata-like but however one wishes to think about the structure of "Walker Brothers Cowboy" some sort of analogy with music seems inevitable.

Before considering this opening section, however, it is important to pay attention to the narrating voice because the pleasure we should take in Alice Munro's skilled handling of the narrative conventions is a rich part of the story's larger pleasures. Both "Images" and "Walker Brothers Cowboy" are initiation stories, stories about the gaining of knowledge, and so the effectiveness of the stories depends to a certain extent on our sharing the child's innocence and on our growing with the child towards understanding. Although the narrator of "Walker Brothers Cowboy" is actually the Jordan girl grown up and looking back at her childhood, the writing is intended to suggest a young girl's voice and sensibility. The use of the present tense in narration – a device which in the hands of a lesser writer could have induced numbing monotony – is varied here with subtle craft and goes a long way in itself towards suggesting youth and simplicity.

Consider again the following passage:

> He has a song about it, with these two lines:
>
> And have all liniments and oils,
> For everything from corns to boils . . .
>
> Not a very funny song, in my mother's opinion. A pedlar's song, and that is what he is, a pedlar knocking at backwoods kitchens. Up until last winter we had our own business, a fox farm. My father raised silver foxes and sold their pelts to the people who make them into capes and coats and muffs. Prices fell, my father hung on hoping they would get better next year, and they fell again, and he hung on one more year and one more and finally it was not possible to hang on any more, we owed everything to the feed company. I have heard my mother explain

> this, several times, to Mrs. Oliphant who is the only neighbour she talks to. (Mrs. Oliphant also has come down in the world, being a schoolteacher who married the janitor.) We poured all we had into it, my mother says, and we came out with nothing. Many people could say the same thing, these days, but my mother has no time for the national calamity, only ours. Fate has flung us onto a street of poor people (it does not matter that we were poor before, that was a different sort of poverty), and the only way to take this, as she sees it, is with dignity, with bitterness, with no reconciliation. No bathroom with a claw-footed tub and a flush toilet is going to comfort her, no water on tap and sidewalks past the house and milk in bottles, not even the two movie theatres and the Venus Restaurant and Woolworths so marvellous it has live birds singing in its fancooled corners and fish as tiny as fingernails, as bright as moons, swimming in its green tanks. My mother does not care.

In the lines, "Not a very funny song, in my mother's opinion. A pedlar's song, and that is what he is, a pedlar knocking at backwoods kitchens," I think we are hearing in the repetition of "pedlar" and the implied "that's what you are" the child echoing something of the mother – though sharing none of her bitterness.

The next two sentences present the girl's voice; notice how the voice is suggested by "the people who make them into capes and coats and muffs" instead of, say, "furriers." The sentence following these, however, with its succession of "ands" and its final comma-spliced conclusion represents not so much the girl's voice as the girl reproducing the oft-heard monotony of her mother's litany of complaint.

Next, the mother is quoted directly though without quotation marks – an omission perhaps meant to suggest that this remark is made often and always in the same words, a suggestion that the remark has become ritual. The words in the next sentence, "but my mother has no time for the national calamity, only ours," sounds rather sophisticated for the girl but we are meant to take them, I think, as her perception because of the words "these days." Perhaps such a phrase as "national calamity" was current on the radio or in newspapers. Had Alice Munro intended us to read this sentence as if spoken by the adult looking back, she would have used different tenses and "those" days as opposed to "these."

Note in the following sentence that in "Fate has flung us . . ." we are again intended to hear, at a remove, the mother's vocabulary and histrionics. The long concluding sentence which also suggests the mothers' voice with its *No, nor, not* then modulates back into the simulation of the voice of the child, a voice suggested not merely by subject matter but by the rhythm of the "ands" and by the syntax of "Woolworths so marvellous . . ." and by the sentence's rhythmically awkward conclusion.

It's important to remember that in a writer like Alice Munro we are reading prose which is more subtle than much of what now passes for poetry; it's necessary to be alert to the play of voice because it is only by paying close attention that we can savour the story's fullness.

The first paragraph of the first section is a beautifully compressed piece of writing which suggests the girl's voice, gives us information about the family's straitened circumstances and sketches the relationships within the family. The particular love the girl has for her father is established.

The description of the walk down to the lake is the presentation of a physical and emotional landscape. Alice Munro has rightly always resisted symbol-seekers and reductive reading insisting that a spade is indeed and always a spade but the accumulation of physical detail in this opening section obviously functions as more than topographical survey.

The evening games of the children they pass are "ragged, dissolving." The children "draw apart, separate into islands of two or one . . . occupying themselves in . . . solitary ways."

The sidewalks are "cracked and heaved;" father and daughter walk past a factory with "boarded-up windows." And then the town "falls away in a defeated jumble of sheds and small junkyards . . . we enter a vacant lot . . . and there is one bench with a slat missing on the back . . ."

Father and daughter sit and look at the lake – "Which is generally grey in the evening, under a lightly overcast sky, no sunsets, the horizon dim." Further along is a lifeguard's "rickety throne" and further off still are the docks where the grain boats load, boats that are "ancient, rusty, wallowing."

This landscape, then, is a suitable background to the Jordans' descent into urban poverty and it suggests something of the defeat and bleakness of Ben Jordan's emotional life.

The third paragraph of this opening section is rather curious. Why is it there? What does it contribute? Tramps wander up from the "dwindling" beach and climb the "shifting, precarious path." Such meetings are, we learn, not infrequent but they always frighten the girl. The paragraph tells us directly that the father is "hard up" and his actions suggest that he has sympathy for the tramps, perhaps even a fellow-feeling for he, too, has come down in the world.

The incident described is obviously important. The paragraph contains only the third sentence of the section actually spoken. It concludes with a sentence whose rhythms and word placements are deliberate: "My father also rolls and lights and smokes one cigarette of his own."

The use of the word "one" suggests that the father does not smoke a great deal, perhaps cannot afford much tobacco. The deliberateness of the sentence echoes the deliberateness of the act; the rhythm tells us that it is a *rationed* ritual and pleasure. We are meant to assume that the manufacture and smoking of a cigarette are something of a performance, something done deliberately and at significant junctures.

The story will return us to this incident.

The final paragraph contains the fourth line of actual speech in this first section: "Well, the old ice cap had a lot more power behind it than this hand has." There is, perhaps, in this a faint suggestion of the ineffectual, of the father's powerlessness against the indignities of poverty. The section concludes with the child trying to think about Time and change and wishing that everything would always remain the same and safe. This passage obviously looks forward to the concluding two paragraphs of the entire story and thus links beginning and end.

The body of the story, the second section, now amplifies what we've already been given in concentrated form in the first section. We learn the history of the family's decline into poverty and we learn in greater detail how the girl feels about her parents.

The girl is humiliated by the mother's pretensions to gentility and resists recruitment to her views: "I pretend to remember far less than I do, wary of being trapped into sympathy or any unwanted emotion."

The mother uses her various ailments as a weapon against the father and as a means of holding onto him.

"He goes back once again, probably to say goodbye to my mother, to ask her if she is sure she doesn't want to come, and hear her say, 'No. No thanks, I'm better just to lie here with my eyes closed.'"

The girl doesn't actually hear these words spoken on this occasion; she doesn't have to; she's heard them many times before. The girl's sympathies and feelings are entirely for the father.

It's probably important at this point to say something about those sympathies and feelings and about Alice Munro's young female narrators in general. At the end of "Walker Brothers Cowboy," the girl has begun to grasp something of the complexities of her father's life, about its sadness, about paths not taken; she has sensed the meaning of mysteries and has begun to learn things about herself as a female. Exactly *what* she has learned is neither described nor articulated but "Walker Brothers Cowboy" is charged with a sexuality we should not ignore.

The same is true of "Images." Too many readers, I think, have assumed too firmly that "Images" is concerned with the child's learning simply about death; they seem to have given insufficient weight to the story's sexual concerns. They seem to have overlooked the fact that Mary McQuade, Death's harbinger, has come to the house to deliver the girl's mother of another baby, that the girl is making a connection between death and birth and sex and being female, that Mary McQuade is always being teased about possible husbands. The child watches the shadows cast by her father and the flirtatious Mary Mcquade and tries "to understand the danger, to read the signs of invasion."

The narrator in "Images" is slightly younger than the narrator in "Walker Brothers Cowboy" but in both cases the stories are richer for us if we realize that they are narrated by a girl who is very sensitive to the sexual currents around her, who is hungry for sexual knowledge, and who is eager to learn how this sexuality will affect *her* life. Both stories are in a way as much about sexuality and the female role as is the far more explicit "Boys and Girls."

(Adolescent sexuality is, of course, the main subject and focus of *Lives of Girls and Women*, the next book Alice Munro was to write.)

The girl, then, rejects her mother's embittered gentility and cleaves to her father. The father deals with their poverty and with their having come down in the world by maintaining a façade of jollity. He amuses the children with his improvised songs, with his patter, jokes, and comic self-mockery. There is even a suggestion of the father as artist turning his trials into "the song." Father knows the short cut out of town; he represents for his children the "hope of adventure."

He bears the weight of the family on his shoulders.

He attempts to coax his wife into laughter by performing for her amusingly "rude" sales routines. The daughter says: ". . . and she would laugh finally, unwillingly."

The father's territory is a desolate landscape, "flat, scorched, empty" with dust hanging over the dirt roads and with "falling-down sheds and unturning windmills" on the decaying farms; all this forms the background for, and is the counterpart of, the father's emotional life.

The event which is the turning point of the story is the emptying of the chamber pot out of the window. He is not actually hit: "The window is not directly above my father's head, so only a stray splash would catch him."

But splashed or not, the event is the final degradation, the final straw. He picks up the suitcases "with no particular hurry" and walks back to the car "no longer whistling." He sits in the car which is raucous with the laughter of his son and daughter exulting in the naughtiness of *pee* and in the exquisite pleasure of pee having been poured out of a window. He sits there and does not start the car until he has rolled and lighted a cigarette. And it is this at the pivotal point of the story which should return us, if only for a moment in memory, to the scene in section one with the tramp.

Sitting there, smoking that deliberate cigarette, Ben Jordan reaches a decision. He starts to drive. He tells his son not to tell his mother about the pee because she wouldn't see the joke. In other words, her sympathies would not be for Ben's humiliation; her anger would be directed against him for working at such an "ungentlemanly" job. The boy wants to know if the incident is in the "song." Ben says that he'll try to work it in. But he isn't singing.

The conversation with the daughter is both naturalistic and yet full of significance: "'Are we still in your territory?' He shakes his head."

He is heading *out* of his territory, both physical and emotional, and he is neither singing nor being amusing. He is heading towards the house of a woman he *might* have married, a woman who would not have suffered headaches. He is driving so fast over the pot-holed roads that all the bottles clink and gurgle and are in danger of being broken, the bottles that are the source of his livelihood. He is driving in full flight both away from the scene of his humiliation and towards someone who can offer comfort.

Nora, not recognizing him at first, says: "Have you lost your way?"

A poignant question for us as readers for by now we've realized that he'd lost it years before. This sudden appearance of Ben Jordan is an immense shock to Nora: "'Oh, my Lord God,' she says harshly, 'it's you.'"

The heavy stresses fall on every word.

When asked if she's got a husband hiding in the woodshed, her laugh is "abrupt and somewhat angry." (Though we get the impression that Ben knows full well that she's unmarried.) When she is reintroducing Ben to her mother and explaining that he is now married, she speaks "cheerfully and aggressively" as though challenging her mother to comment. The blind old mother has not spoken to Ben for many years yet recognizes his voice instantly. We are to assume, then, that at one time Ben and Nora were extremely close.

We are told little about their past relationship. Like the daughter, we must try to piece things together. It would not be unseemly to guess that one strong reason for the failure of their relationship was that Ben Jordan was Protestant and Nora Catholic. The bigotry in Ontario in the twenties and thirties was virulent. Nora *digs with the wrong foot* – a Protestant Irish expression meaning, "She's Catholic – she's not one of us," "She's not our sort."

Whatever the reasons for the collapse of the relationship, Nora is the sister who has remained unmarried at home to care for her blind mother. One sister is married with children, the other is a teacher in western Canada, financially independent, who hasn't been back to the farm in five years. The "faint sour smell" that the girl smells in the kitchen is metaphorically the smell of frustration and disappointment.

When Nora reappears, washed, scented,changed into a flowered dress and more "sociable and youthful," Ben says of the flowers on the material that he'd never known there were green poppies. Nora's reply is both flirtatious and blunt: "You'd be surprised all the things you never knew."

Nora and Ben drink whisky together. Nora's having a bottle other than for "medicinal purposes" marks her as a woman out of the ordinary, a woman morally suspect. The girl is fascinated by the fact that her father is drinking because her mother has gone out of her way to tell the girl that he never does. We are to assume from this, I think, that Ben once drank more than the occasional nip but has been weaned from it – and from other enjoyable bad habits. His drinking days were those he spent with Nora. The implied background here is the puritanical connection between nonconformist protestantism and the temperance movement. Ben's wife in her "good dress, navy blue with little flowers, sheer, worn over a navy-blue slip. Also a summer hat of white straw, pushed down on the side of the head, and white shoes I have just whitened on a newspaper on the back steps" is the embodiment of arid respectability and Protestant religiosity.

It is at this point that Alice Munro starts to tinge Nora's speech with Irish syntax and rhythms.

(Implied social, religious, and historical backgrounds are precisely what give Alice Munro's stories their dense, textured feel. A single line of dialogue such as Ben's "Keep it in case of sickness?" vibrates with meanings that soon will have to be explained to a young and urban readership.

How should we read Ben's enquiry? Is it serious? Is it seeking an answer to questions not being directly asked? Is it jocular?)

Ben next performs for Nora a version of the chamber pot incident. His daughter remarks on the discrepancy between what she'd seen happen and his account of it. As usual, Ben is turning his disappointments and humiliations into entertainment for others. There is a sense, too, that it is only by refashioning reality that he is able to bear it; in his created version of the incident he emerges a "hero in the ranks of Walker Brothers" even if his heroism is Chaplinesque.

Nora laughs "almost as loud as my brother did at the time" – the brother who's been told not to mention the incident at home because his mother wouldn't be "liable to see the joke." Ben then entertains Nora with his sales spiel and his song.

We are reading a scene which is parallel to the scenes alluded to earlier where Ben tries to coax his disapproving wife into laughter, where her laughter finally is "unwilling;" in this scene, then, she and Nora are being compared and contrasted. Ben's clowning is, in both cases, a kind of offering, a kind of courtship.

The scene immediately following, the scene where Nora dances with Ben's daughter, is curious; this, we feel, is no ordinary dancing lesson; it is uncomfortable, faintly disquieting. The girl is aware of sexual currents even if she doesn't understand them; we the readers, however, understand the girl as a surrogate.

What is faintly disturbing about this scene – and the child's presence in it – is Nora's unladylike heat and arousal, an excitement which is conveyed through the child's registering of "her strange gaiety, her smell of whisky, cologne, and sweat. Under the arms her dress is damp, and little drops form along her upper lip, hang in the soft black hairs at the corners of her mouth."

Nora waltzes the girl to a stop in front of Ben and says:

"Dance with me, Ben."

"I'm the world's worst dancer, Nora, and you know it."

She stands there in front of him "her breasts . . . rising and falling under her loose flowered dress, her face shining with the exercise, and delight."

She asks him again.

"'Ben.'

"My father drops his head and says quietly, 'Not me, Nora.'"

The whole of this dancing passage is a masterly piece of writing. The second time that Nora asks Ben she is not asking him to dance. She does not say "Ben?" She says, "Ben." She is both offering and claiming.

(And is Ben's "Not me, Nora" simply negative, or does "Not me" imply someone else perhaps? Another or others who helped Nora drink half the whisky because she doesn't care for drinking alone? Or are we to accept her statement, "I can drink alone but I can't dance alone"?)

Ben's declining the invitation is a sad acceptance on his part of duty, of the choices he has made in life. The scene peters out in painful conversational small-change and ends in silence. Nora stands close to the car in her "soft, brilliant dress," a dress which is flamboyant, possibly even slightly vulgar – and so very different from the dress described earlier, Ben's wife's dress, which is "navy blue with little flowers."

The third and last section of the story restates and returns us to the story's first section; the story's last sentence – a reference to the Lake – returns us to the story's opening sentence.

The father does not behave on this afternoon as he usually does. He does not buy the usual pop or ice cream. He buys licorice. We realize that this is to mask the smell of the whisky when he gets home but the girl does not. She does, however, feel and share her father's sadness although she is unable to articulate its nature. She has caught some of the heated sexuality and sadness in Nora's front room and without understanding why, knows instinctively that these are matters not to be mentioned to her mother. Alice Munro – not, of course, for the first time in the story – uses the girl's innocence and naivety to twist the emotional screws. The daughter, utterly devoted to her father, resolves that the mother will learn nothing of the afternoon from *her*. She guesses that the most serious material to be kept from the mother must be the dancing lesson and the whisky. This loyal innocence on her part somehow intensifies the sadness of what it really is that her father wants kept secret – the desolation that his life has become.

The girl feels confident that her little brother won't betray anything because "he does not notice enough." The most he might remember would be "the blind lady, the picture of Mary." With these two references, Alice Munro turns us back into the story before opening the throttle, as it were, for the story's conclusion.

The two flat references suggest again the sadness of Nora's life and its mystery for the narrator. The picture of Mary would only be found in the homes of Roman Catholics, those who *dig with the wrong foot,* words which now seem "sad to me as never before, dark, perverse." The "blind lady," Nora's mother, is recalled for us sitting in the faintly sour-smelling kitchen with a drop of silver liquid welling from the sunken eye, "a medicine, or a miraculous tear."

This is an example of the command of odd detail which makes Alice Munro's prose so rich and persuasive. It is so *peculiar* yet so real that we are persuaded it could never have been invented. At the same time, it renders the scene almost iconic, as though the old lady's silver tear is a tear for all human sadness and suffering.

The penultimate paragraph of "Walker Brothers Cowboy" has always troubled me. It feels as if Alice Munro is straining for rhetorical effect and impact. While it is true that the girl's feeling about her father's life is expressed in terms of fairy tale and enchantment, the syntax seems far less the girl's than the author's. I have never been quite sure what Alice Munro *meant* by this paragraph; usually she writes with precision and economy but the writing here is vague and ambiguous. I am tempted to say that it is slightly pretentious.

Clark Blaise in a brief essay entitled "On Ending Stories" describes two basic kinds of endings in modern stories:

> There are only two kinds of endings: those that lead you back into the story, and those that lead you – gently or violently – away. I associate the first kind of ending with de Maupassant and Chekhov, and with modernists who adapted those stories for their own purposes – Hemingway, Joyce, James. Of authors who lead away from the story, who

wish to emphasize the artifice of the story, or wish to address the reader directly, I associate dozens of our contemporaries. Impatience with art is as old as faith in art; the choice of ending is the battlefield for those particular feelings.

You are aware of stories that end with a let-down. 'That's it? It's over?' you ask yourself. There's a Hemingway story (there are many Hemingway stories like it) that ends, 'Bill selected a sandwich from the lunch basket and walked over to have a look at the rods.' That's an ending? Norman Levine can fade out in the same way. It's subversive of course, a subversion of the expected neatness of closure, the gathering up of narrative and thematic threads, the welling-up of music, the frozen gesture that summarizes *the whole meaning of the story* . . . We realize that the short story initially paid its debts to theatre, or to fable; audiences expected a big pay-off at the end. When it didn't happen, it was revolution, it was art.

I think of these endings as the most disturbing. They hit a glancing blow at the reader but generally ignore him. By approximating the most casual of voices, they manage (in the hands of masters) to sound most urgent. By ignoring us, they speak to us directly . . .

Endings that lead us away from the story can do so gently or abruptly. The most traditional kind of ending is the one that serves as a prose equivalent to the theatrical last scene, the rising of music and receding of the camera as lights go out, one by one, and characters fade off together in a figurative sunset. Such endings announce a faith in continuity, order, harmony – no matter what particular horrors may have been investigated in the story. They are sophisticated and traditional ways of updating the old 'happily ever after' ending so familiar from fables. Even if the endings are thematically 'sad,' they are formally (or cosmically) 'happy;' they lead away from the specific exemplum (the story) to a generalized harmony. They are religious in form, if not in content.

How can you detect such an ending? Well, they *sound* like endings. From Eudora Welty (a prime influence on Alice Munro) we get,

'Outside the redbirds were flying and criss-crossing, the sun was in all the bottles on the prisoned trees, and the young peach was shining in the middle of them with the bursting light of spring . . .'

From Margaret Laurence's first collection, 'The sea spray was bitter and salt, but to them it was warm, too. They watched on the sand their

> exaggerated shadows, one squat and bulbous, the other bone-slight and clumsily elongated, pigeon and crane. The shadows walked with hands entwined like children who walk through the dark.'

Let's look more closely now at the penultimate paragraph of "Walker Brothers Cowboy." It is too "literary," too wrought. It strives for the second kind of ending that Blaise talks about, the symphonic ending. What Blaise didn't mention in his essay but which is typical of "symphonic" endings is that the writers consciously or unconsciously heighten their language. Elevated rhythms and archaic syntax tend to creep in. We may well hear biblical echoes in grammatical constructions or in repetitions. Sense sometimes capitulates to incantation.

What is meant *exactly* by "my father's life"? What does the word "life" mean? Why would that life be "flowing back from our car"? Back to where? To Nora? Or is it "flowing" in the sense of, say blood from a wound? Or are we to understand "flowing" as meaning something like "diminishing, emptying" in the manner of a deflating balloon?

Is it "life" which is "darkening and turning strange" or is it "the last of the afternoon?" In what way can we really compare a "landscape" and a "life"?

Is this language believable in the girl's mouth? Are these apprehensions totally credible in this child?

These confusions are compounded because in the final paragraph Alice Munro produces a *second* ending – an ending of the *first* type described by Blaise, the "let-down" ending. Thus the story ends symphonically and then ends in deflation. The result is somewhat of a mess.

Alice Munro made interesting comment on the endings of her stories in an interview with J.R. (Tim) Struthers. The interview was published in Louis MacKendrick's *Probable Fictions: Alice Munro's Narrative Acts*.

> TS: . . . Something that interests me is your sense of the fashions of fiction-writing at certain periods.
>
> AM: Well, when you've been writing for a while, you can't help but be aware of this. You may flatter yourself that you're not influenced by fashions, but I certainly am. That is, I don't adopt a fashion in order to get published somewhere or in order to win critical acclaim. It's just that there is a current way of saying things which seems effective, and so one

begins to experiment with that way and to use it. And then later on, it seems possible to say things in another way. And these are actually fashions.

TS: Could you identify a number of the fashions – magazine fashions, perhaps – that . . .
AM: Oh, I wouldn't get that definite. I don't mean this thing . . . you know the way you used to be advised to read about the market [laughter] and then write stories for the market. I don't mean at all that kind of thing because I was never interested in it. But, for instance, when I read over my stories of the '50s . . . and I've never been an innovator or an experimental writer. I'm not very clever that way. I'm never ahead of what's being done at the time. So in those stories in *Dance of the Happy Shades* there's an awful lot of meaningful final sentences. There's an awful lot of very, very important words in each last little paragraph. And that's something that I felt was necessary at the time for the stories to work. It must have been a prevalent fashion. That's the idea I got that it was necessary. But it wasn't something any market was demanding or any critic was demanding. It was the way I felt that you made a story most effective. And now, I would go back, if I could rewrite most of those stories, and I would chop out a lot of those words and final sentences. And I would just let each story stand without bothering to do the summing up, because that's really what it amounts to.

TS: I remember when you read 'Postcard' at Western in the mid-'70s.
AM: I know I often chopped . . .
TS: You dropped the last paragraph when you read the story.
AM: And if I ever do a final edition of all those things, I'll drop the last paragraphs. God knows if I'm right or not. That is just the way I feel now. Isn't it true that Henry James went through and made a lot of his early stuff more difficult and obscure later on? And I believe that Frank O'Connor continued writing stories over and over even after they'd been published. I haven't seen the different versions, but the point I'm making is just that it's not even that you are necessarily improving the story. You are telling it the way you see it now. And you have no idea what improvement means. You're just telling it the way it seems to work now. And I could go on and on doing my stuff over and over that way. I

> wouldn't do any of the stories in *Dance* quite the same. And that's why the rewriting after a while gets to be such a strange thing. I rewrite stories now, and my editors don't like them as well as earlier versions. And sometimes they may be right. There's a point after which you're not sure what you're doing with the rewrites.

It is gross impertinence to rewrite a writer but I've often thought "Walker Brothers Cowboy" could be improved by cutting most of the last section so that with the necessary adjustments the story could have ended with the father saying: "I don't know. I seem to be fresh out of songs. You watch the road and let me know if you see any rabbits."

Or – even better – it could well have ended with Nora in her brilliant dress making an unintelligible mark in the dust of the car.

I suspect that's precisely where the story *did* end and that the final four paragraphs were added later. On the other hand, it must be remembered that this story appeared in Alice Munro's first book. Her writing since then has grown ever more dazzling. Few short story writers in Canada even now would be capable of matching the opening paragraph of "Walker Brothers Cowboy" for precision, economy, and grace.

> After supper my father says, 'Want to go down and see if the Lake's still there?' We leave my mother sewing under the dining room light, making clothes for me against the opening of school. She has ripped up for this purpose an old suit and an old plaid wool dress of hers, and she has to cut and match very cleverly and also make me stand and turn for endless fittings, sweaty, itching from the hot wool, ungrateful. We leave my brother in bed in the little screened porch at the end of the front veranda, and sometimes he kneels on his bed and presses his face against the screen and calls mournfully, 'Bring me an ice-cream cone!' but I call back, 'You will be asleep,' and do not even turn my head.

THE SHAPES WE'LL BE

The years 2003 and 2004 were a blur of work. Running the editorial side of the Porcupine's Quill involves endless phone calls, five to six hundred letters a year, manuscript reading, literary magazine reading, proofreading, shaping story collections by culling weaker work, interviews, speeches, letters of support for people applying for jobs and residencies, photocopying and mailing, and in these two particular years work on twenty-two new titles.

Among all the new titles I was relieved to get into place the third volume – of four – of Clark Blaise's *Collected Stories*. This volume, *Montreal Stories* was important to me in a personal way as I'd been there when he wrote them and had grown up learning from them and comforted by them. I was also pleased to be delivered of *Writers Talking*, a book I'd edited for far too long with Burning Rock writer Claire Wilkshire. It was a book of interviews with eight younger writers we wanted to promote – Michael Winter, Lisa Moore, Steven Heighton, Mary Borsky, K.D. Miller, Terry Griggs, Elise Levine, and Annabel Lyon. The book seemed necessary as none of these writers was receiving attention or recognition and they seemed to be writing in limbo.

Some titles from these years required next to no work – Mary Swan's delicate collection *Emma's Hands*, Mike Barnes' *Contrary Angel*, David Helwig's *Duet*. Others required struggle – Lorna Jackson's *A Game to Play on the Tracks*, Royston Tester's *Summat Else*. Ray Smith came to stay with us as we grappled with the final section of *The Man Who Hated Emily Brontë*.

The first twelve pages or so of Lorna Jackson's book are a profound pleasure, so gorgeously written, so complex, so rich in detail, in rhythm, so subtle in exposition, that a neophyte writer could profitably study them for weeks. I so much enjoy writers who raise the bar.

The critical series was reinforced by two bracing new works, David Solway's *Director's Cut* and Carmine Starnino's *A Lover's Quarrel*. Four more issues of *Canadian Notes & Queries* added to the critical assault, an assault aimed at sloppy thinking and feeling manifesting themselves in sloppy language.

I also managed in the magazine to record some history and bibliography concerning House of Anansi. We put out special issues on Norman Levine, Richard Outram, and George Johnston. David O'Rourke and Carmine Starnino considered Irving Layton's achievement and David O'Meara celebrated the glittering talent of Eric Ormsby.

Circulation figures for *Canadian Notes & Queries* are quaint but I feel it essential to use the magazine to keep on asserting the central importance of such slighted writers as Ormsby, Outram, Blaise, and Levine. The magazine also offers a necessary pulpit to younger critics such as Michael Carbert, David O'Meara, Amanda Jernigan, and Carmine Starnino. Michael Darling commissions abrasive book reviews and writes some himself which are exemplary; his reviews of *The Ash Garden* by Dennis Bock and of Mordecai Richler's *Barney's Version* teach with a vigour and intelligence rarely found in Canada's literary play-pens.

Carmine Starnino's depth-charge essay "Canadian Poetry as a Busted Flush or, I'll See Your Anne Szumigalski and Raise You a David Donnel" went unremarked. Carmine had demonstrated that E.D. Blodgett's poem "Autumn Air," from a collection that won the Governor General's Award, could be written backwards without noticeable difference. That this shattering essay went unremarked did not surprise me; in the seven years I've been editing *Canadian Notes & Queries* the magazine has received one letter.

Eric Ormsby has published five volumes of poetry: *Bavarian Shrine and Other Poems*, *Coastlines*, *For a Modest God*, *Araby*, and *Daybreak at the Straits*. John Updike has written of his work: "He is a most excellent poet, resonant and delicately exact with words and objects. Ormsby's reverent attention to things as they are, lights up his every page with a glow."

Neither *The Cambridge Companion to Canadian Literature* edited by Eva-Marie Kröller nor W.H. New's numbing second edition of *A History of Canadian Literature* (McGill-Queens) so much as *mention* Eric Ormsby so *Canadian Notes & Queries* must and will. I find it unsurprising, inevitable almost, that the writers I consider among our best are precisely the ones consigned to oblivion by media and academe.

(The only benefit I've derived from the distilled dullness of W.H. New's literary criticism over *so* many years is that it conjures up John Dryden's *Mac Flecknoe,* a spirited attack on the wit and dramatist Thomas Shadwell.

All human things are subject to decay
And, when Fate summons, monarchs must obey.
This Flecknoe found, who, like Augustus, young
Was called to empire and had governed long,
In prose and verse was owned without dispute
Through all the realms of Nonsense absolute.
This aged prince, now flourishing in peace
And blest with issue of a large increase,
Worn out with business, did at length debate
To settle the succession of the state;
And pondering which of all his sons was fit
To reign and wage immortal war with wit,
Cried, 'Tis resolved, for Nature pleads that he
Should only rule who most resembles me.
Shadwell alone my perfect image bears,
Mature in dulness from his tender years;
Shadwell alone of all my sons is he
Who stands confirmed in full stupidity.
The rest to some faint meaning make pretence,
But Shadwell never deviates into sense.
Some beams of wit on other souls may fall,
Strike through and make a lucid interval;
But Shadwell's genuine night admits no ray,
His rising fogs prevail upon the day.

Dryden not a good man up whose nose to get.)

Somewhere in all this I found time to write an essay for Branko Gorjup's book *White Gloves of the Doorman: The Works of Leon Rooke* and an essay for the catalogue of Andrea Bolley's retrospective exhibition at the Thames Art Gallery.

I was also working on building what is to be an addendum to the McGill University short story collection so I was constantly reading catalogues, contacting dealers, cataloguing, chasing down desirable titles in Canada, England, and the U.S.A. Among hundreds of other first editions, I was particularly pleased to get my hands on fine copies of Mark Helprin's first book *A Dove of the East and Other Stories*, *Airships* by Barry Hannah, *Days* by Mary Robison, an advance proof of *Emperor of the Air* by Ethan

Canin, and a copy of Richard Yates' *Liars in Love* warmly inscribed to his agent Andrew Wylie. We drove down to Massachusetts one month to pick up a run of the annual *Best American Stories.* Rare book dealer Ken Lopez had been building it for me for nearly three years. The first volume had appeared in 1915. Only two volumes are missing now and a complete run will be, I imagine, decidedly rare and immensely useful.

By the fall of 2003 I was feeling somewhat jaded if not mildly hysterical with overwork and so Myrna and I decided on a Swan Hellenic cruise. Swan Hellenic is a British company with a focus on history and archaeology. It hires for its cruises lecturers from British universities and museums and retired clerics steeped in knowledge of the classics, men from another era, the Very Revd. this, Bishop of that, Canon, Prebendary, Rt. Revd., Dean Emeritus . . . all deliciously British in an Agatha Christie kind of way. The ship, *Minerva II,* has a library of history, archaeology, and biography and a commodious bar named the Wheeler Bar after that jaunty archaeologist Sir Mortimer Wheeler who looked rather like the British comedian Terry Thomas. He was known in the archaeological fraternity as "Flash Harry."

(I noticed in an old Swan Hellenic brochure that Colin Renfrew had been one of the lecturers. Renfrew is the author of *Before Civilization*, the most scintillating study of ancient cultures I have ever read.)

We had decided on a tour of the major Greek bronze age sites and joined the *Minerva* at Heraklion in Crete. The next day we explored the palace at Knossos. Then to Souda Bay where the German parachute assault on Crete centered in World War II. Then Piraeus for Athens. The ship then sailed to Nauplion and we visited Agamemnon's Mycenae and the theatre at Epidauros. Followed by Byzantine Mistra north of Sparta, Nestor's palace at Englianos, the Venetian Methone Castle, Olympia, the shrine of Apollo at Delphi, Butrint in ghastly Albania, Dubrovnik, Split and Diocletian's Palace, and finally Venice, the ship approaching in sunlight across the lagoon and turning into the Grand Canal, past the Bridge of Sighs, the Doge's Palace, St. Mark's Square . . . the most beautiful city in the world, Serenissima.

As usual, the most vivid things for me were not the major attractions, palaces, theatres, stadia but tiny details glowing now in my memory. In the museum in Heraklion I was very taken with clay coffins shaped much like Edwardian hip-baths in childhood attics. At Delphi I was gripped by the names of manumitted slaves scored into the temple's base wall. At Diocletian's Palace I loved a little vegetable market outside the gates selling produce from garden plots. One old man was selling olive oil from his trees in corked Coca-Cola bottles. At Epidaurus, the shrine of the god of healing, Asclepius, I was touched less by the magnificent theatre and stadium than by little bronze scalpels, paper-thin and shaped like willow leaves.

But equally interesting were the passengers. Most were British, most were middle-aged or older and all were middle class. Some had walkers. Many had strange gaits, wayward feet, the legacy of strokes.

Foot-flop *slap*.
Foot-flop *slap*.

Many backs were humped by osteoporosis. Hearing-aids whined off into silence like ricocheting bullets. Conversations were at considerable volume and reminded me of Lady Constance at Blandings trying to extract information from her brother, Lord Emsworth.

"What is this chap saying?"

"I don't believe you're switched on, dear."

"What say?"

"You're to give him the TICKETS."

"What was that?"

"TICKETS."

"It's no use speaking on my right side. You of all people ought to know that, old girl. I think this chappie probably wants the tickets."

The ship provided a British doctor who accompanied the more strenuous expeditions carrying a bulging rucksack of medicines presumably to deal with strokes, heart attacks, grievous falls. The sight of this straggling band of ancients with canes and walkers tackling the mountain fastnesses of Mycenae was both funny and touching.

The spectacle reminded me of a long-cherished shot from Tony Richardson's film *Tom Jones*, a ragged file of army recruits marching along the crest of a hill, comically uncoordinated figures black against the sky line.

Just as strange were the things that people said, remarks beyond invention. As we were walking into the great Tholos tomb at Mycenae called the Treasury of Atreus a jolly lady said to Myrna, prompted perhaps by the tomb itself, "I've cremated three husbands." She laughed. "So far." And then glancing about her in the gloom said, "I've got them upstairs in the airing cupboard."

Exploring the Venetian site of Methone Castle, formerly held by the Ottoman Turks, walking through the ruins I came upon one of our party sunning herself on a wall, having taken off her blouse.

"Oops!" she said. "I'm just greedy greedy for the sun."

Later I went into the ruins of a Turkish *hamam*. When I came out again into the field she was lying on a knoll blouse *and* bra discarded.

"Oh, dear!" she said, scooping the clothing against her. "Don't see my ta-tas."

That evening we dressed for dinner and went to the elevator. As the door slid open she said, "Oops! *Whatever* will you think of me!"

The dining room offered a feast of eccentricity.

Every night sat a woman dressed in a man's suit and wearing a tie. She looked like a creature from *Cabaret* but sadly raddled. Her hair was an improbable ginger colour and heavily brylcreemed. Every night she drank a martini. One evening when it was slow in arriving she struck the Philippino waiter across the shins with her ebony stick saying, "Tardy."

To me she said, "What are *you* staring at?"

"Oh," I said, "nothing, no."

"It doesn't do," she said, "to be soft on these Asian laggards."

Many of the ladies carried little evening bags made of fine metal mesh or glittering with sequins. There swam up into my mind from the linguistic depths the word: *reticule*. The whole trip was rather like that.

We spent the last two days of the holiday in Venice. Did the usual tourist things, even the Doge's Palace again but tired quickly of its gilt grandeur which, like Blenheim Palace, soon seems overwhelmingly vulgar. The only art in the Palace I really like is the statues of the Tetrarches in red porphyry. So we sloped off to the Hotel Danieli and had a martini each for the astonishing price of thirty euros.

* * *

Days later I was flying to Windsor to read at an event called the Windsor Festival of the Book. This festival was being run by a young bookseller called Dan Wells who owned a used book store called Biblioasis. He picked me up at the airport, drove me to my hotel, and presented me with a bottle of

Glenlivet. The literary life, I thought, was looking up.

Among other writers in Windsor were Judith McCormack, David O'Meara, Robert Adams, George Bowering, Joy Kogawa, Michael Redhill, and a weary and drawn Leon Rooke just recovering from an attack of gout.

Joy Kogawa read some of the worst prose I've heard in years, prose that was sentimental and what some would doubtless call "sensitive." A pleasant woman, though. We had breakfast together one morning.

Robert Adams, the hammy book critic, put on his usual, pompous performance, his voice throbbing with creamy Welsh emotion, his delivery a mixture of non-conformist pulpit and the bombast of a Donald Wolfit. There are Welsh voices I enjoy more. I've always been strongly moved by R.S. Thomas' austere poetry in *Song at the Year's Turning*, by Caradoc Evans' impeccably managed satire in *My People*, a story collection that weathers the years in a way most don't, and by the sprightly Gwyn Thomas who wrote: "There are still parts of Wales where the only concession to gaiety is a striped shroud." And there's always Dylan Thomas with *Portrait of the Artist as a Young Dog* and that shimmering fragment *Adventures in the Skin Trade*. But I'm doubtless in a minority on Adams as people actually pay money to listen to these fruity extravaganzas of his.

Kingsley Amis disliked the uproar and ranting rhetoric of Dylan Thomas' poetry and disliked also Thomas' Roaring Boy persona – though he more than once announced his appreciation of *A Portrait of the Artist as a Young Dog*. In his second novel, *That Uncertain Feeling*, still a lively read more than fifty years on, Amis draws a wildly pretentious dramatist called Gareth Probert, a character which has been widely read as a rendering of Thomas.

Reviewing a posthumous collection of Dylan's early prose pieces, *A Prospect of the Sea*, Amis wrote ". . . it can be asserted with utter finality that here is a volume which every admirer of Thomas' poems will want to possess, for most of the qualities of the poems are to be found in it. In spite of this, the book seems to me worth having."

Always pleasing to hear steel clear scabbard.

Amis was not happy teaching at the university College of Swansea. The intellectual atmosphere was unsparkling, the town unrelievedly mild-and-bitter. Amis was provoked by what he felt as Welsh provinciality and irritatedly amused by the earnest nationalism of the revival of the Welsh language. In constant letters, Amis invented a mock-Welsh orthography to amuse Philip Larkin:

> 'Llgo andw ghet stwft, iu stwpydd olld swd.'
> (Go and get stuffed, you stupid old sod.)

and

> 'Scwrr offw, iu blwddy wyatt-eddyd chwmp-an-si ffaced maas-tyr-batwr.'
> (I *take* this to be . . . white-headed chimpanzee-faced masturbator.)

In one letter to Larkin from Swansea he wrote what is among the most plaintive sentences I've read:

"Altogether here I feel like a swordsman in a country where dueling is unknown."

Taking a respite, I read standing up in the festival bookstore George Bowering's *His Life: A Poem*. Page after page of hobbling doggerel. I remembered Bill Hoffer's cataloguing Bowering's *Autobiology* in these words: "Because I like George I have refrained from reading much that he has written." And I remembered Hoffer's later cataloguing of Bowering's *The Concrete Island*. He described the book as inscribed on the half title, "for Wm. Hoffer, signed so he can't sell it yet, George Bowering 1977." Followed by Hoffer's notation: "Well, George, the time has come."

Possibly the Poet Laureateship of Canada was a suitably clownish cap to a long career subservient to dreary theory.

Standing in that festival bookstore amid all those books I didn't want to read I felt a welling sadness that Bill Hoffer had died. How much I miss his splenetic eruptions in his catalogues.

Of bp Nichol: "At best he was a meagre punster; he was seldom at his best."

Of Al Purdy: "I have never been convinced that he is entirely literate . . ."

His contempt for so much of what passed for literature was, I think, entirely justified. Some people dismissed him as destructively negative but they miss the point which was that Bill insisted that our lodestar should be greatness.

He wrote in "The Tanks Campaign": "For many years I have ridiculed the absurd spectacle of apparently grown men and women pretending to have succeeded at the very difficult tasks of art."

Bill also knew that he was not alone in his low opinion of most Canadian writing; it was shared by nearly all Canadians. There seem to be few book collectors in Canada and even fewer collectors of Canadian books. The lack of a first edition market for Canadian books is a rather extraordinary fact. It means that there aren't enough people who love a book to buy it competitively.

I was talking to poet and book dealer Michael Harris recently in Montreal who said that on the net he can sell Seamus Heaney or Ted Hughes or Philip Larkin because they are constantly sought after but that he had had some early inscribed Layton on offer for over a year without a single nibble. No one, he said, wants Canadian books. Even books that once were valued are now a drug in the market, their "value" tumbling.

"I cannot believe after many years of writing, editing, and collecting experience," Michael Harris said, "that there will ever be a Canadian literature."

Hoffer, again in "The Tanks Campaign," wrote: "As a rare book dealer I have had an unusual perspective. As a major dealer in Canadian literature I have been aware that no one actually buys most of the books that are supposed to be, or have been important. The invention of Canadian culture has resulted in the creation of a few thousand academic jobs, and the necessity of an infrastructure of library collections and a critical literature."

Toronto dealer Steven Temple said to me a couple of years ago that if I offered him Irving Layton's first book *Here and Now* – conventionally priced at about $3000.00 – for $300.00 he wouldn't buy it because there is no one to whom he could sell it.

These gloomy thoughts were reinforced by the size of the festival audience. Dan Wells was upset and embarrassed at the low turn out and I attempted to console and fortify him, knowing how he was feeling, having spent so much time myself in that particular trench. As we talked, it emerged that Dan had a passionate interest in expanding his bookshop, Biblioasis, into a press. I was attracted by his enthusiasm and seriousness and said I'd be willing to help him.

I thought that he should work from his strengths which in his case were his experience as a book dealer and his familiarity with the net. I also thought he should not, at first, attempt the mainstream model.

The problem would be that established writers would not want to publish with an unknown press and something of the same might well be felt by beginners. My name and reputation would help but wouldn't be enough to persuade. So he needed a way to attract names to his list which was not detrimental to their careers. I suggested to him that I act as editor for him and that we publish a series of limited edition chapbooks of individual stories. These would, of course, be cheaper to produce than books and so he would be better protected financially. We would keep the print-run small – 50 or 60 copies – each copy numbered and signed by the author.

To sell into the market we had in mind the books had to be well-designed and printed on good paper. We soon decided on Gaspereau Press in Nova Scotia as printer. Copyright would, of course, remain with the authors, meaning that they would be free to republish the story in a subsequent collection. The writers would get from this deal a painless publication which in no way impinged on their dealings with their regular publishers or agents. They would be paid. They would have a desireable "A" item for their bibliographies. And they would have the cachet of private press publication.

Over the next weeks and months I acquired for Dan and edited new stories from Leon Rooke (*Balduchi's Who's Who*), Caroline Adderson (*Mr. Justice*), Annabel Lyon (*Saturday Night Function*), Clark Blaise (*The Sociology of Love*), and Judith McCormack (*A Theory of Probability*). I also lined up stories by Terry Griggs and Patricia Robertson to follow.

In December of 2004, a year after the Windsor festival, the first of these Biblioasis books appeared, chaste, austere, dark blue wrappers, red Japanese endpapers, *Balduchi's Who's Who* by Leon Rooke.

The book was typeset by Dan's friend Dennis Priebe in Adobe Garamond and printed on Strathmore Laid at Gaspereau Press. The cover was printed on letterpress on a Vandercook 219 from photopolymer plates. A very pretty production.

Dan had his names and the foundation stone of a press.

I had the fun of organizing the venture but I also had a serious purpose beyond helping Dan. I wanted to get well-crafted and beautiful books into the hands of collectors and dealers. I wanted to encourage a love of books. I wanted people to want the books and value them not only as artifacts but as rare things signed and handled by remarkable and distinguished writers. I own a signed and numbered copy of Evelyn Waugh's *Basil Seal Rides Again*.

I feel a kind of reverence towards it. It was a sense of reverence I was trying to spread with Dan's chapbooks.

(The first five pages of *Basil Seal Rides Again* are not only a comic delight but could teach an aspiring writer more than a month of Sundays at the Humber School for Writers.)

A month after the Windsor festival Tim Inkster phoned from Porcupine's Quill and said that he and Elke had decided to sell *Canadian Notes & Queries* because printing it in addition to the books had become burdensome. I suggested to Dan Wells that he buy it and offered to keep on editing. The magazine would give him access to more names and if it were published four times a year instead of twice would take on a greater weight and momentum. It would also give him a ready-made national presence.

Some tentative negotiations began.

At about the same time Clark Blaise asked me to give the keynote speech at the Eighth International Conference on the short story in English. Clark was the Director of the conference which was to take place in October of 2004 at the University of Alcalá in Alcalá de Henares just outside Madrid. He wanted me to talk about editing and anthologizing and the way we had set out to create a national literature in the 60s, 70s, and 80s. He also asked me to bring three other short story writers to represent both Canada and the genre. I asked Leon Rooke, Terry Griggs, and Annabel Lyon.

I mentioned to my brother that I would be going to Alcalá and he wrote back sending me five offprints of articles he had written on Spanish coinage. The five offprints were entitled:

"Some Geographical Aspects of Early Medieval Monetary Circulation in the Iberian Peninsula."

"Where Were Suevic Coins Minted?"

"A Parcel of Coins of Alfonso VI of Leon (1073-1109)"

"A Note on the 'Suevic' Triens Bought in Santarem."

"Sixth-Century Visigoth Metrology, Some Evidence from Portugal."

His letter suggested the offprints would come in handy "to read during the tea-breaks." With *my* crew it would more likely be Rioja-breaks. Or in the case of Terry Griggs, a dedicated single maltiste, Laphroig-breaks.

In the summer of 2004 McGill University conferred an honorary doctorate on Clark Blaise. The degree was awarded by Dick Pound, McGill's Chancellor, and Clark's hood was bestowed by Eric Ormsby. Myrna and I drove to Montreal and sat with Bharati Mukherjee, Clark's wife, as convocation dragged on. Clark gave the commencement address. As the graduates – all nine hundred of them – crossed the stage one by one, Dick Pound in his black and gold robes sat looking with moody interest at girls' legs. He put me in mind of a Dorothy Parker anecdote. At a similar event at a girls' college in the States she said: "If all these young girls were laid end to end . . . I wouldn't be at all surprised."

The next evening we all went to Ray Smith's apartment for a party to launch his just-released *The Man Who Hated Emily Brontë*. Noreen Hood was there and we were all keenly aware Hugh wasn't. But I was immensely pleased that Clark was getting recognition at last. As writer, as teacher, as founder of Concordia's creative writing department, as missionary for Iowa – but principally as writer – Clark's contribution to literary life has been heroic. I was saying something of this to Ray who interrupted with, "No Canadian institution'll ever honour *you* – unless it's an Institute for the Criminally Insane."

Just seven days later a courier handed me an envelope which I assumed was another damned manuscript. Rather irritably I ripped open the top and found inside, along with pamphlets and a history, an invitation to become a member of the Order of Canada. I have no idea how this came about and remain rather astonished.

At about this time my selected stories, *Standing Stones*, appeared. The book received one review. The lady reviewer described the voice in the stories as "irrevocably male" – apparently not a good thing. "Irrevocably" reminded me of a recording of the last music hall appearance of Max Miller, the Cheeky Chappie, a man whose timing and inflections I've studied for years. After some banter with the pit-band leader Maxie says of him mock-admiringly, "He's a boy, isn't he!" He pauses. "Well, I hope so. No," he protests against the laughter, "no, you can change overnight."

As the date drew nearer for the speech in Alcalá the year seemed to go into overdrive. I was working on the speech itself and on the essay about Andrea Bolley's paintings entitled "Uneasy Beauty." A friend of Tony Calzetta's, Linda Corbett, was making a video about him and came to the house to film and interview dropping the bombshell that she'd like her next film to be about me. I organized a hectic issue of *Canadian Notes & Queries*, a tribute to George Johnston and his poetry, hectic because Norman Levine at the last moment refused permission for quotation from his

York University archives in an article by Alison Oldham. We had to pull the article and desperately plug the gap.

I was also cataloguing a complete run of *Fiddlehead* magazine, working on Joan Alexander's first story collection *Lines of Truth and Conversation*, proofreading Biblioasis books, editing Carmine Starnino's *A Lover's Quarrel*, organizing the next issue of *Canadian Notes & Queries*, a special issue on Clark Blaise, and reading and rejecting submissions to the Porcupine's Quill.

Visitors at home were also adding some stress at this particular time. Noreen Hood came to stay after the sad death of her son Dwight; Royston Tester came to discuss a new book; Marius Kociejowski came over from London visiting family; Tony Calzetta and Gabrielle de Montmollin visited and we gallivanted off to Montreal to see a Riopelle show of late works on paper. And ate. And drank.

I attended the Eden Mills Writers' Festival, talking to writers until I was hoarse. I was reading and re-reading the typescripts of David Helwig's autobiography *The Names of Things* and Paul Glennon's second story collection *Dodecahedron*. I was organizing future Biblioasis chapbooks from Michael Winter, Steven Heighton, Sharon English, Lisa Moore, and Russell Smith. But the speech for Alcalá was beginning to hagride me. The comforting story I had set out to tell was, I realized in the telling, simply not true. I was forced to face some unhappy facts and forced by these facts to rethink the speech's shape.

Alcalá de Henares is chiefly famous as the birthplace of Miguel de Cervantes. The house where Cervantes was born is now a small museum furnished in mid-16th-century style. An upstairs room displays a collection of Cervantes editions and translations and illustrations of the melancholy knight on Rosinante squired by Sancho Panza.

The University of Alcalá is now largely housed in the Colegio Mayor de San Ildefonso. Within the Colegio is the great hall, once the examination room where Lope de Vega and St. Ignatius of Loyola defended their degrees. In this beautiful room every April the King and Queen award Spain's highest literary honour, the Cervantes Prize.

I delivered the speech under that gorgeous Mudéjar carved-panel ceiling.

The second I'd finished an aged Spanish Canadianist shot up and denounced me and all my works. He seemed almost to vibrate with rage. He rabbited on for what felt an age as I stood at the lectern. "Your speech," he concluded curtly, "was a disappointment."

"Thank you," I said.

I add the speech here in the interests of cultural history and entertainment.

The Shapes We'll Be

The short story in Canada effectively began in the late sixties. There had been isolated outbreaks earlier but they were not of much significance. *Hugh Garner's Best Stories* won a Governor General's Award in 1963 and Garner's unsubtle, if not crude, command of his craft can stand for the general low level of achievement and appreciation. In 1963 there were, to the best of my knowledge, only three or four Canadian story collections in print.

In 1960 Robert Weaver published the anthology *Canadian Short Stories* in the Oxford World's Classics series; prior to that, the most widely circulated anthology had been Raymond Knister's *Canadian Short Stories* published in 1928.

Knister's anthology represents the end of a tradition of magazine writing, stories that were more "yarn" or "tale" than anything we would understand as being in the modernist tradition. Knister himself had made stumbling attempts at more vital short fiction but his stories are now only of interest as literary history.

What explains this arid literary moonscape? I have often borrowed the science fiction idea of a time warp. Canada seemed to exist many years behind the rest of the English-speaking world and seemed impervious to innovation. It was a country largely indifferent to art or literature. The National Gallery of Canada was not founded until 1913 and the National Library of Canada was founded as recently as 1953.

Canada had few magazines and a publishing industry which was comatose and which existed to import British and American books. What few Canadian books did get published appeared usually from the Ryerson Press which was owned by the United Church of Canada and administered by a gentleman known as The Book Steward, a figure I imagine as a male counterpart to *Saturday Night Live's* The Church Lady. The press' most famous editor was the Methodist minister Lorne Pierce, an ardent booster of stupefying books by the likes of Bliss Carman, Sir Charles G.D. Roberts, and Frederick Philip Grove.

The decades dragged on. The literary flame flickered in such little magazines as *Contemporary Verse, The Fiddlehead, Preview, First Statement, Northern Review*, and the three issues of *Here and Now*. The Ryerson Press Chapbooks and Fiddlehead Poetry Books published endless twee verse. Amateur theatre groups put on amateur plays which competed for the Dominion Drama Festival Award.

But this dreary scene was soon to change. Canada was about to enter into one of its nationalist cycles. It celebrated the country's centennial year with a world's fair in Montreal, Expo 67, in a state of euphoria. The Liberal Government, suffering from its habitual delusion that the arts could define and unify the country, started to pour money into the burgeoning small press movement and into the universities to fuel studies of the literature that was being produced. From the beginning, then, there was a deeply unhealthy connection between literature and nationalist politics. Literature was quickly subsidized, institutionalized, and bureaucratized through federal and provincial government agencies. As our uncomprehending Liberal Minister of Heritage informed us this year, "Culture is a tool."

Margaret Atwood's book on Canadian literature, *Survival*, published in 1972 by the small press House of Anansi, and sadly to be soon reprinted, reputedly sold 80,000 copies. It was a prime example of the confusion of literature with politics. The book is less literary criticism than it is nationalist manifesto and with its anti-aesthetic, non-evaluative stance has done untold damage to any real appreciation of Canadian writing.

In an essay about *Survival* called "Mathews and Misrepresentation" published in *Second Words* she writes: "It [*Survival*] is not evaluative . . . Though I try not to include any books I myself find tedious, it isn't 'good writing' or 'good style' or 'literary excellence' I'm talking about here. I make it clear also that I'm concerned with patterns, not authors, and I don't find this concern invalid. It's quite true that some literature written in Canada, which I happen to enjoy and find 'good' – got left out; things like George Jonas' poetry, Michael Ondaatje's poetry, Malcolm Lowry's prose, a lot of Brian Moore; nor do I pay as much attention to Grove as some might like. Why? It seems to me dangerous to talk about 'Canadian' patterns of sensibility in the work of people who entered and/or entered-and-left the country at a developmentally late stage of their lives."

The Quebec-based critic Professor Ronald Sutherland in his book *The New Hero* (1970) published the following thoughts about a national literature:

> . . . a sphere of consciousness which is uniquely Canadian does exist in this country, and from within this sphere the mainstream of Canadian literature is rapidly emerging.
>
> The distinguishing feature of the sphere of consciousness which governs the mainstream of Canadian literature is, understandably enough the same feature which principally distinguishes the Canadian nation – the co-existence in this country of two major ethnic or language groups . . .
>
> May I repeat once again that the mainstream of Canadian literature has nothing to do with literary merit; it is a matter of sphere of consciousness, an author's awareness of and sensitivity to fundamental aspects of both language groups in Canada, and of the inter-relationships between these two groups.

This tenured twaddle is more than dotty; it is *exaltedly* dotty.

Poor old Professor Sutherland excluded with such vigour that he was left with a Canadian "mainstream" composed of only seven writers. The "mainstream" was Hugh MacLennan, Hugh Hood, Margaret Atwood, Leonard Cohen, Dave Godfrey, Ralph Gustafson, and a book by Jim Bacque called *Big Lonely.*

Professor Robin Mathews, homespun thinker and demagogue, in his astounding book *Canadian Literature: Surrender or Revolution* asserts that MacLennan is a Canadian writer but Mordecai Richler is not. Nor is Irving Layton. Nor is Morley Callaghan. Callaghan is in fact a traitor to "Canadianness" because he openly admitted to having been influenced by Ernest Hemingway.

Some years later when Callaghan died the ubiquitous and All-Purpose Professor David Staines proclaimed in print that Callaghan was not only a better boxer than Ernest Hemingway but also a better writer. Staines was not fired; he was promoted.

It was not long before Professor Mathews had descended to decrying the "imperial centres" and braying the virtues of "birthright Canadians." It was an extraordinary period to have lived through. We all believed at the time that we were taking part in the creation of a literature. Much of what passed for literary criticism and much of the editing and anthologizing was in fact the statement of differing political visions.

The political implications of these literary judgements I have quoted are, needless to say, deeply distasteful. What have all these exclusionists in common? The answer is undeniable: they will not accept immigrants as Canadian. They are hostile to the internationalism of Jews. They disallow any heritage other than French or English.

George Jonas (Hungary), Michael Ondaatje (Sri Lanka, England), Malcolm Lowry (England), Brian Moore (Northern Ireland), Frederick Philip Grove (Germany).

My position in this not very intelligent squabbling was that writing-in-English is a world activity, that Canadian writing is a current within a broad river, that Canadian writers should emulate the best writing in the world which is written in what is, inevitably, an international style. I also put forward the simple idea that a Canadian is someone who holds Canadian citizenship and that Canadian literature is what is written by Canadians. Cultural nationalists, of course, detested such views.

Professor Sam Solecki of the University of Toronto wrote in rebuttal:

". . . by characterizing the best work of the past twenty-five years as modern or international in style Metcalf, consciously or unconsciously, leaves the Canadian writer and critic without a Canadian tradition."

In all this talk of a national literature and of who ought to be included and who ought to be excluded you will notice that artistry is never mentioned except to be rejected or denigrated. The same notes are sounded again and again. Says Professor Sutherland, "the mainstream of Canadian literature has nothing to do with literary merit." Says Margaret Atwood, ". . . it isn't 'good writing' or 'good style' or 'literary excellence' I'm talking about here."

How sadly true.

In *Between Europe and America: The Canadian Tradition in Fiction* (1988) T.D. MacLulich praises Canadian literature's conservatism of form because it has "contributed to its distinctiveness from American literature." The central tradition, he says proudly, does not "rely on superficial treatments of trendy subjects nor on clever tricks played with narrative point of view."

MacLulich exhibits here a very Canadian mistrust of style and elegance. He is not the last of these critics to absolutely cherish lumpishness.

Rabid anti-Americanism turned Canadian writing in on itself so that it became ever more parochial. Writers like Mordecai Richler, Clark Blaise, Norman Levine, and Mavis Gallant who had left Canada were ostracized, Mavis Gallant being particularly disliked for living in Paris rather than in, say, Moncton, New Brunswick.

Concurrent with this turning inward, style and craft were decried as suspect, un-Canadian attributes. Thematic criticism dominated and obviously had nothing whatever to say about style or language. A refusal to evaluate accommodated the mediocre. The nascent literature turned not only inward but also looked to the rural past. Terry Rigelhof wrote recently of "the hostility many Canadian cultural nationalists showed toward the urban and urbane in art through much of the second half of the twentieth century . . ." Russell Smith put it more pithily when he said that Canadian literature was about "angst on farms."

It is almost comic that Canadian writers who gave their books non-Canadian settings were regarded by many reviewers as having committed treasonable acts. In 1982 I published an anthology of stories by seven writers I then considered the country's best. There was an outcry from reviewers. Three of the seven had been born outside of Canada and two had lived away from Canada for many years. Seven of the fourteen stories were *set* outside Canada – one of them in Budapest, a locale which seemed to particularly enrage one reviewer.

The Montreal *Gazette* headlined its review: "Short and Sweet, but Hardly Canadian."

In the seventies and eighties chauvinist academics fabricated Canadian ancestors and a Canadian literary tradition. They claimed that all Canadian story writers were descended from Duncan Campbell Scott's *In the Village of Viger*, a piffling collection of tales published in Boston in 1896 and not circulated in Canada. This spurious claim anchored Canadian writing in this genre to a Victorian confection very much setting the tone for what, academically, was to come.

It was against this background that I inherited in 1976 the editorship of Oberon Press' *New Canadian Stories*, the only annual anthology of short stories in the country. I also inherited a co-editor, Joan Harcourt. Joan and I edited the anthology for two years. During 1977 I realized I wanted as co-editor someone tougher and harsher in judgement. I settled on Clark Blaise. Joan wrote a farewell introduction to the 1978 volume in which she said: "I think I learned that there is little real fiction in Canada. What we have instead are personal histories with the names changed and the facts slightly bent . . . The large run of the stories we received presented carefully crafted reliquaries, little boxes in which were enshrined little memories. Some of these reliquaries were elaborately enamelled, but mostly they were simple sturdy constructions."

Mavis Gallant, in a personal letter, disdainfully described them as "pallid little 'I' stories."

Looking back at that time, it seems to me now that those aspiring writers simply had not read widely, had not educated themselves, had not studied the necessary writers. Alice Munro has talked about the influence on her of Anderson's *Winesburg, Ohio* and of Eudora Welty's *The Golden Apples* but most stories we were reading seemed utterly innocent of the great American sophistication in the genre.

One way of avoiding Joan's "little boxes" was to change the anthology's emphasis. I wanted to stop publishing new work and instead republish the best stories from the literary magazines. I wanted a Canadian version of Martha Foley's *Best American Stories.* Clark and I made the title change with the 1978 volume though Michael Macklem, Oberon's publisher, insisted that we continue to read new writing. We worked around this by inviting new work from writers we could trust to be moving in the direction we wanted.

When Clark left Canada to work in the States I co-opted a new voice, Leon Rooke. Leon and I went on to edit together *Best Canadian Stories, The New Press Anthologies* and *The Macmillan Anthologies.*

It was important that Leon, Clark, and I were writers rather than academics, important because it meant that our reading was up to date. Academics as editors at this period would have been theme-mongering and encouraging writing which was "teachable." We, on the other hand, were all interested in language and rhetoric and the ways in which stories performed themselves. We wanted stories whose language was on fire. Because we were writers ourselves we were able to hear, to recognize new voices.

It was also important to what evolved that Clark and Leon were American born and raised and that I came from England, important because we were not marked by the extreme nationalist prejudices of the time. Important, too, that our yardstick was not Canadian.

We were all aware of the fact that we were building a Canadian literature but we were all more interested in literature than in its Canadianness. Perhaps because of our backgrounds we were more interested in including people than in excluding them. We all believed that our first allegiance was to language and form rather than to nation.

Indeed, so uncaring were we about nationalistic narrowness that when Clark and I edited a 1977 anthology called *Here and Now: Best Canadian Stories* we included a story by Russell Banks on the grounds that we liked it. No one seemed to notice.

Margaret Atwood in an essay entitled "An End to Audience?" expresses almost exactly the opposite of what I take literature to be and how to make it. She writes: "I believe that fiction writing is the guardian of the moral and ethical sense of the community. Especially now that organized religion is scattered and in disarray, and politicians have, Lord knows, lost their credibility, fiction is one of the few forms left through which we may examine our society not in its particular but in its typical aspects; through which we can see ourselves and the ways in which we behave towards each other, through which we can see others and judge them and ourselves."

This is incredible enough in itself.

But then she goes on: "Writing is a craft, true, and discussions of the position of colons and the rhyming of *plastic* and *spastic* have some place in it . . ."

"some place in it"!

We saw craft as our salvation. We used it to celebrate the particular. We evaluated without even a nag of doubt. By the eighties the literary world in Canada was considerably changed from the sixties. Writing was generally much more sophisticated and I would put some part of that change down to the insistence we had all placed on the position of colons and the rhyming of *plastic* and *spastic*. We taught technique. We had firmly suppressed Joan Harcourt's "little boxes in which were enshrined little memories." We opened boxes and let language loose. We insistently anthologized the best of our older writers – Clark Blaise, Alice Munro, Mavis Gallant, Norman Levine, Hugh Hood, Elizabeth Spencer, Audrey Thomas – and we cheered on talented new voices – among them Keath Fraser, Caroline Adderson, Linda Svendsen, Terry Griggs, Diane Schoemperlen, Douglas Glover, Mary

Borsky, Steven Heighton, Sharon English, Michael Winter, Libby Creelman, K.D. Miller, Mike Barnes, Elise Levine, Mary Swan, Annabel Lyon.

My expectations of a national literature evolving, however, were dashed for two reasons. The first was the lack of audience. The second was the fact that the influence of American writers was far stronger than collegial influence.

Philip Marchand, literary columnist for the *Toronto Star* wrote recently:

> There is something both heartening and disheartening about the fact that so much of the strength of Canadian literary culture lies in the short story form. It is heartening because there are now many Canadian writers who are truly proficient in the art – so much so that whatever is enduring in our literature will be more likely found in their work than in over-stuffed prose epics such as [Rohinton Mistry's] *A Fine Balance* or [Timothy Findley's] *The Piano Man's Daughter*.
>
> The situation is in some respects similar to Elizabethan and Jacobean England, where a cultural climate favoured the production of an enormous amount of good lyric verse, sonnets, and so on. Most of this good verse has since been classified by academic critics as 'minor' but it was wonderful minor stuff and it has remained undimmed by time.
>
> Something similar may be said about Canadian short fiction in the late twentieth century. The disheartening element in the situation, of course, is that few people actually read it.

I edit *Canadian Notes & Queries* and I asked Annabel Lyon to write a piece for me about her experience of the University of British Columbia's writing department. Annabel is a particularly brilliant young writer now working on a third book. Her first was a story collection entitled *Oxygen*. Her second was three novellas called *The Best Thing for You*. I was particularly interested to learn who she read.

Here, in part, is what she wrote:

> Alice Munro, Robertson Davies, George Orwell, Ernest Hemingway, Evelyn Waugh, Oscar Wilde, T.S. Eliot, and Margaret Laurence were the kinds of writers I was reading before I entered the program, reading driven by a sense of duty (the Canadians) and an admiration for conventional elegance (Waugh, Wilde, Eliot). Richard Ford, Joy

> Williams, Denis Johnston, Mary Robison, Lorrie Moore, Amy Hempel, and Barry Hannah were just some of the writers I encountered for the first time in my two years at UBC, many of them recommended by fellow students. These – and there is no other word for them – *Americans* rang the bells and shot out the lights and wrote so rightly, to my ear, that I couldn't (can't) escape their influence. John Metcalf asks me, from time to time, (with the unhappy curiosity of an anthropologist asking his native host what is in the soup, only half-wanting to know), why there were no Canadians on this list. I can only answer that at that time I was unaware of any Canadian writers who wrote with such simultaneous jazzy abandon and emotional subtlety.

She goes on to conclude that "Canadians are still playing cultural catch-up . . ."

Annabel's experience and the influences upon her would be echoed I think by a large majority of the young Canadian writers I work with. This leads me to believe that over time – and I have been talking only about forty-five years – Canadian writing will come to be seen as North American writing and this more and more likely as publishers merge and agents place manuscripts in American and international markets.

Whatever the future holds, we can say that writing in Canada has changed from Joan Harcourt's "personal histories with the names changed and the facts slightly bent" to a sparkling sophistication which is concerned above all else with language. Academic and institutional views still lumber about far in the rear.

The division between writers and critics is, unfortunately, almost absolute. In a recent review, James Wood wrote: "There is no greater mark of the gap that separates writers and English departments than the question of value. The very thing that most matters to writers, the first question they ask of a work – is it any good? – is often largely irrelevant to university teachers. Writers are intensely interested in what might be called aesthetic success: they have to be, because in order to create something successful one must learn about other people's successful creations."

Criticism is further bedeviled in Canada by academic and popular obsessions with nationality. Because critics are locked into the desire for a native tradition they persist in celebrating, for example, the work of Morley

Callaghan and claim him to be formative. This claim deforms taste and warps judgement. Indeed, it denies us the possibility of a literature.

If all authorities conspire in this celebration of Callaghan's work it is a judgement which makes nonsense of any other judgements we make. If we celebrate such writing as "classic" what can we meaningfully say of the writing of Alice Munro or Clark Blaise or Leon Rooke?

Robert Weaver of the CBC and William Toye of the Oxford University Press wrote of Morley Callaghan in *The Oxford Anthology of Canadian Literature:* "Today he is admired by most younger writers of fiction in Canada as their only true predecessor in this country . . ." Here again sound the notes of fantasy and longing typical of their generation and mine, fantasy that Callaghan had been accomplished, longing for a literature that never came to fruition. Bitter truths for Toye and Weaver after their years of toil on that splendid magazine *The Tamarack Review.*

The truth would appear to be that many young writers of fiction in Canada have never read Callaghan at all. If they had, they'd have found prose so inept and ungainly that they'd have turned away either embarrassed or amused.

Callaghan is typically capable of an opening like this:

> Mrs. Massey, a stout, kindly woman of sixty, full of energy for her age, and red-faced and healthy except for an occasional pain in her left leg which she watched very carefully, had come from Chicago to see her son who was a doctor. The doctor's family made a great fuss over her, and she felt in such good humour that she suddenly said one night: 'I declare, I'll go and see Mary Woolens. I wonder what's happened to her? Find out where she lives for me.'

When Clark Blaise invited me here he asked me to choose three other writers representative of great achievement in story writing in Canada. I asked my old friend and co-editor Leon Rooke, one of the dominant voices. Then I wanted someone who could represent writers at mid-career and chose the madly inventive Terry Griggs. And then to represent emerging writers the wonderfully fizzy Annabel Lyon.

We've just heard the opening of a story by Morley Callaghan, a writer of whom *The Canadian Encyclopedia* says, ". . . he remains a classic." We have moved in the last forty years to a prose more finely tuned, to a prose that dances. In conclusion then, and to showcase, as it were, the changes in our writing I'd like to ask Annabel Lyon to read the opening of her story "Watch Me" and Terry Griggs to read the opening of her story "Suddenly."

Watch Me

Marie's brother called to tell her the junkies were gone.

"Since when?" she asked.

"Two days," Steven said. "But mum has their babies."

"Oh, surprise."

"I know, Marie, but two days. She says she's running out of activities."

"Someone should report those people."

"Someone did. Mum reported them to me and now I'm reporting them to you."

"You know what I mean."

"I know I'm going this afternoon and you're coming. Pick you up in an hour."

"Oh, Steven." She cut him off with the tip of her finger and poked her mother's number.

"Beth?" Laura, her mother answered. Beth was the woman junkie.

"No."

"Oh, Marie," said her mother. "Now, I wish you had been here for lunch. I made this pesto salad such that the curtains smell of garlic."

"How are things?"

"Well," Laura said. "I'm surprised you can't smell it down the phone, it's that strong."

"I can't smell it," Marie said.

*

Laura lived out in Langley, farm country a good two hours' drive from Vancouver. As they left the city behind the land opened up and flattened out. Marie sensed large animals, furtive cows and horses, fading in and out of the waning day.

"She just wants to talk," she said.

"I know what she wants," Steven said.

Laura was in her front yard, playing with the twins from next door. They had jagged translucent teeth and hot sweet eyes, like fudge oozing. They wore plastic boots, quilted space-suit overalls and miniature turtlenecks. Laura wore jeans, black rubber boots and their dead father's shirt. Her grey hair was stuffed up attractively under a baseball cap.

"You're just in time," she said. "We're going to shellac some gourds."

The twins belonged to a couple of gentle junkies, Beth and Morty, for whom basic excursions – to the gas station or the supermarket – were perplexing epics. Often Laura found herself putting Natalie and Dylan to bed and getting them up again in the morning because their parents had run out of postage stamps.

Suddenly

Away we go.

Went, I mean.

Snowflakes streaking past our eyes, stars jiggling up there in the sky.

Foop, into the snowbank.

Buck was laughing to split a gut, and he said, "Marsha, you're a kook," and I suppose he was right, considering. "*Exhilarator!* Haw, haw." He was smacking his hand on the dashboard. Did I say that? I expect I did. You know, words zip out of my mouth assbackwards half the time. Like then, when I hit the, excuse me, *accelerator* instead of the brakes and couldn't even get the swearing right. Probably because I was trying to pray at the same time, "Holy Shitface Mother of Bob, not the fender, please not the headlights." What we're talking about here is Daddy's brand new Comet GT with the Luxury Decor Option – cut-pile carpeting, colour-keyed vinyl roof and wheel covers, reclining contoured bucket seats – all the spiffy features Daddy couldn't stop jawing about that I'd just parked in a huge fucking snowbank.

"Shut up, Buck!" Though I shouldn't have said that, either. Way to impress a guy, eh?

I'd been working on it, too. "It" being Buck and me, somewhere alone. Not in a snowbank, I'll admit. That wasn't exactly what I was after. Getting my mitts on Daddy's car hadn't been easy. Getting Buck *in it* hadn't been easy. He's had his mind, such as it is, on other things lately. *Two* things,

Trudy's, and they keep changing sizes, that's the joke. I nearly had to run him over. "Hey, Buckaroo, wanna go for a ride?"

What I wanted from Buck was simple. I wanted his undying love, his thrashing gushing heart in my hand (no matter it was likely cold and blue as a ball of ice), and I wanted to sing in his band, the Tomcats, New Year's Eve at the Lantern.

"Annabel Lyon.
Terry Griggs.
Thank You."

THE PORCUPINE'S QUILL: A RETROSPECTIVE

After the oddities of Antoni Gaudí in Barcelona, the warm glories of the Alhambra in Grenada and the Alcazar in Seville, and the dignity of Madrid, we returned home to a three-foot high mound of mail, snow, and a telephone call from Tim Inkster. He announced that he was winding down the Porcupine's Quill with the intention of closing it in 2007. He would publish in 2005 what we had agreed on, but in 2006 and 2007 he was cutting the number of titles by 50% and putting out the books in the fall season only. This meant that my work with the press was more or less finished. With a cut of 50% over two years, every available publishing slot was already filled as I had been working two years ahead of where we currently were.

In my speech in Alcalá I had said that my expectations of a national literature evolving were dashed because of a lack of audience and a lack of collegial interaction. Tim's decision to wind down the press was based on the first of these points, declining sales, lack of audience.

On November 20, 2004, Tim sent the following e-mail to Gordon Platt, Acting Director, Book Publishing Policy and Programmes, Department of Canadian Heritage.

(The word "Chindigo" in his e-mail stands for Chapters/Indigo. BPIDP is a Canadian Heritage Initiative to fund publishing and stands for Book and Periodical Industry Development Programme. It is pronounced in the trade generally as "Bippydip.")

> Gordon, I have received a copy of 'Printed Matters' in which a BPIDP priority seems to be 'the development of a strategy for small and medium-sized cultural enterprises.' I attach, for your interest, a paper written for the Rotman School of Management Studies at the University of Toronto subtitled 'The Future of the Small Publisher in the Canadian Context.'
>
> The reality is, of course, grim.
>
> PQL net sales to Chindigo peaked in the 24 months ended 31 Dec. 1998 at $130,000.

For the 24 months ended 31 Oct. 2004 PQL net sales to Chindigo have dropped to $58,000.

In the five months of our fiscal ytd (to 31 Oct 04) we are seeing a FURTHER 50% reduction in Chindigo orders, from the comparable period a year earlier coupled with a DOUBLING of returns levels, back up to 56%.

We are also seeing Chindigo refusing to stock ANY (i.e. not one) copies of some of our frontlist titles.

PQL has been described (as you know) as Canada's 'pre-eminent' literary press . . . by Roy MacSkimming in *The Perilous Trade: Publishing Canada's Writers.*

My response to the challenges facing my company is that I have cancelled our Spring 2006 list.

We intend to fulfill many of our commitments for 2005, though we have dropped four titles from the Fall 2005 list.

I do have a BPIDP-funded intern (Jack Illingworth) whose internship expires in July, 2005. I have informed Mr. Illingworth that he is currently earning three times what I make, as publisher, with thirty years experience.

Mr. Illingworth will be terminated at the end of his internship and PQL will no longer publish in any Spring season from 1 Jan. 06 forward. Our book publishing programme will be cut from 11 titles a year to 5, and I will sell (or scrap) one of the two literary magazines I publish.

I am not crying wolf.

I am not asking for assistance.

I am simply telling you what I intend to do, to survive.

Gordon Platt's response to the demise of Canada's "pre-eminent literary press," a press described in the *Globe and Mail* as "one of the country's treasures," was filled with that urgency, energy, and cultural concern typical of Ottawa: "Thanks for this – it is disturbing . . . There are no easy solutions."

On Nov. 27, 2004 Tim again e-mailed Gordon Platt.

You may have noticed that PQL placed two titles on the *Globe and Mail* 100 List [Best Books of the Year] released just today. This is a considerable achievement when you consider that 68 of the 100 titles

With Terry Griggs and Annabel Lyon in the great hall of the Colegio Mayor de San Ildefonso. Professor Carmen Flys above. About to deliver "The Shapes We'll Be." (MYRNA METCALF)

The Canadian Contingent. John Metcalf, Connie Rooke, Leon Rooke, Terry Griggs, Carmen Flys, Annabel Lyon. (MYRNA METCALF)

Above: Leon Rooke with Terry Griggs. (MYRNA METCALF)

Right: Leon and Connie Rooke. (MYRNA METCALF)

Below: With Clark Blaise in the courtyard of the Colegio. What dubious proposal was this? (MYRNA METCALF)

With Bharati Mukherjee. On the left, Allan Weiss, compiler of *A Comprehensive Bibliography of English Canadian Short Stories.* (MYRNA METCALF)

Clark Blaise. (MYRNA METCALF)

Some enchanted evening at the Magnum/Opus readings. (MICHELINE ROCHETTE)

Left: In Ottawa 1996 with Leo Simpson. The real work of literature; lugging books about in boxes. The launch of *Sailor Man*. (MYRNA METCALF)
Right: Diane Schoemperlen reading at the Fire Station in Ottawa in 1996. (MYRNA METCALF)

Above: Clark Blaise, Ray Smith, Noreen Hood, at the Montreal launch of Ray's *The Man Who Hated Emily Brontë*, 2004. (MYRNA METCALF)

Right: James Reaney launching *The Box Social* at the Fire Station in Ottawa, 1996. (AUTHOR)

Below: Humber School for Writers, 2003. In a stretch limo with Alistair and Anita MacLeod. Photo by Isabel Huggan who is crouched some fifty feet further down the car.

Above: In Montreal, 2001. Carmine Starnino, Eric Ormsby, David Solway, and Michael Harris. Myrna said with frightening logic, "Either this is out of focus or you were all drunk." (IRENA MURRAY)

Right: Carmine Starnino and David O'Meara at the Manx in Ottawa, 2003, for the launch of *An Aesthetic Underground*. (AUTHOR)

Below: The launch of Leon Rooke's *The Painted Dog* in 2001 at the Manx in Ottawa. Chris Swail, Melanie Little, Leon Rooke. Chris and David O'Meara run the Manx's esteemed reading series. (DAVID O'MEARA)

Above: Sam Tata in 1991 surveying his *Portraits of Canadian Writers* show at the National Library. (MICHELINE ROCHETTE)

Right: Tony Calzetta in his studio in 2004. I'm soon to start a book on his work entitled *Marigold Mumble.* (AUTHOR)

Below: In Andrea Bolley's studio in 2004 before writing the catalogue *Uneasy Beauty* for her retrospective at the Thames Art Gallery. (MYRNA METCALF)

Above: With John Mills in 1992 at Magnum/ Opus. John is author of *Thank Your Mother for the Rabbits*, Canada's finest essay collection. (MICHELINE ROCHETTE)

Right: Under the watchful eye of Terry Rigelhof, author of *This Is Our Writing*. Concordia 2002. (AUTHOR)

Below: With editor Patrick Crean in the Chateau Laurier in 2006 in sober discussion of matters literary. (MYRNA METCALF)

A Flash from the Past: Geoff Hancock, editor of *Canadian Fiction Magazine*, and Clark Blaise in 1997 at York University at the Hugh Hood Symposium. (DAVID O'ROURKE)

Left: A literary samurai: Mark Anthony Jarman at Eden Mills in 2002. (AUTHOR)
Right: Irene Murray, Eric Ormsby's wife and currently librarian of the Royal Institute of British Architects in London. (AUTHOR)

Richard Shue (Port Colborne) Alphabet Book Shop. (AUTHOR)

Richard Spafford (Regina) Richard Spafford Books. (AUTHOR)

Steven Temple (Toronto) Steven Temple Books. (AUTHOR)

Janet Inksetter (Toronto) Annex Books. (AUTHOR)

Adrian King-Edwards (Montreal) The Word Bookstore. (AUTHOR)

Mordy Bubis (Ottawa) Benjamin Books. (AUTHOR)

Bjarne Tokerud (Victoria) Bjarne Tokerud – Bookseller. (AUTHOR)

Richard Peterson (Kingston, Ontario) Berry and Peterson, Booksellers. (AUTHOR)

Cameron Treleaven (Calgary) Aquila Books. (AUTHOR)

John Rush (Hamilton) John Rush Books. (AUTHOR)

Robert Wright (Tamworth, Ontario) Robert Wright Books. (AUTHOR)

Marty Avenhaus (Toronto) The Village Book Store.

Hugh Anson-Cartwright (Toronto) Hugh Anson-Cartwright Books. (AUTHOR)

Rhys Knott (Merrickville, Ontario).

David Mason (Toronto) David Mason Books. (AUTHOR)

David Bergen and Mike Barnes, Wild Writers We Have Known, Stratford, 1998. (JOHN HANEY)

Veronica Ross, Libby Creelman. (JOHN HANEY)

Sandra Sabatini, K.D. Miller. (JOHN HANEY)

Douglas Glover, Mark Anthony Jarman. (JOHN HANEY)

With Peter Hinchcliffe, Kim Jernigan, Alice Quinn (Alice Munro's editor at *The New Yorker*). (JOHN HANEY)

Andrew Pyper, Michael Crummey. (JOHN HANEY)

Elise Levine. (JOHN HANEY)

Terry Griggs. (JOHN HANEY)

Robyn Sarah, Steven Heighton. (JOHN HANEY)

Diane Schoemperlen, Annabel Lyon. (JOHN HANEY)

Keath Fraser. (JOHN HANEY)

Russell Smith, Michael Winter. (JOHN HANEY)

Lorna Jackson, Tim Inkster, Jack Illingworth at Eden Mills in 2004. Between them flies the PQL colophon. (AUTHOR)

Left: Russell Smith in 1994 at Eden Mills in the days before he dispensed sartorial advice in the *Globe and Mail.* The launch of *How Insensitive*. (AUTHOR)
Right: Barbara Howard and Richard Outram at Eden Mills in 1999. (AUTHOR)

Above: Amanda Jernigan with Sharon English at Eden Mills. (AUTHOR)

Right: Elke and Tim manning the PQL Booth at Eden Mills, 2005. (AUTHOR)

Below: Myrna with Stephen Henighan at Eden Mills in 2004. (AUTHOR)

on the list were published by foreign-owned companies, and a further 20 titles were published by large Canadian trade houses.

Of the twelve titles published by smaller publishers on the list, only one publisher (other than PQL) placed more than one title. In this case it might be worth noting that Scott Griffin (at Anansi) has access to several tens of millions of dollars more capital than Tim Inkster at PQL.

All of which means that we can, and do, compete with the very best in the world.

BUT . . .

The two titles PQL placed on the list this year are both first collections of stories – *So Beautiful* by Ramona Dearing and *Emma's Hands* by Mary Swan. In both cases, the authors have already signed with literary agents who will ensure that PQL shares in no way in the future success of these authors.

And what can we expect in the way of added sales from placing a first collection of stories on the *Globe and Mail*'s Top 100?

Last year we had three titles on the list, one of which (*The Rule of Last Clear Chance* by Judith McCormack) was a first collection of stories.

In the twelve months since 30 Nov. 03 we have sold 73 copies of *The Rule of Last Clear Chance*. That's about it, I'm afraid. The very best we can hope for . . . 73 copies.

The implications of such numbers for the establishment of a literature are profound. When, over the years, I've described Canadian literature as being in crisis, I've been shouted down as "cynical" or "negative" and decried as being a "curmudgeon" or a "gadfly." Nationalist boosters point to the sales of Margaret Atwood, Michael Ondaatje, and Jane Urquhart, to movies, to vast advances paid to some writers.

These numbers point to success in commerce, not in literature. When we turn from commerce to literature we are confronted by different numbers. And to face the truth is not to be "cynical" or "negative." Bill Hoffer used to quote a Yiddish saying, "The worst truth is better than the best lie." We have been living a lie for years. Here is more of the truth, a quotation from an embattled Inkster e-mail in 2005 to a university professor who had written requesting him to reprint Hugh Hood's "important" *Flying a Red Kite*.

> . . . John Newlove's selected poems *Apology for Absence* might be considered by some to be an 'important' Canadian book . . . which has sold an average of six (6) copies a year over the past four years.
>
> George Johnston's *Endeared by Dark* is another book that some might consider 'important.' There was a flurry of interest when George died. A 'flurry' can consist of as little as two dozen 'flakes,' which, in this case, it did.

With such numbers, with such sales, to reprint a work would be financial suicide. Yet out-of-print books are usually out-of-mind. As we move forward, our past, and with it, our literature, disappear like the froth of a ship's wake.

Some readers will protest that I am citing mainly the titles of poetry books, traditionally a minority interest. I want to make very clear that I am talking about Canadian literature in the broadest terms. To drive home the extent and nature of the crisis in readership I am going to take the unusual step of citing actual sales figures. *The Oxford Companion to Canadian Literature* (Second Edition) states, "The list of the Porcupine's Quill includes some of the finest stories of the 1990s." Reference books generally agree that among the "finest" are Clark Blaise, Keath Fraser, and Norman Levine. What follows are titles, authors, dates of publication, and cumulative sales figures since publication to 2005.

> *Southern Stories.* Clark Blaise. (2000) 711 copies over 5 years.
> *Pittsburgh Stories.* Clark Blaise. (2001) 609 copies over 4 years.
> *Montreal Stories.* Clark Blaise. (2003) 558 copies over 2 years.
> *Telling My Love Lies.* Keath Fraser. (1996) 430 copies over 9 years.
> *Canada Made Me.* Norman Levine. (1993) 553 copies over 12 years.

And now for some sales figures for outstanding younger writers, writers whose work is obviously (obviously to *me*, that is) going to feature in reference books in the future.

> *Uncomfortably Numb.* Sharon English (2002) 501 copies over 3 years.
> *Aquarium.* Mike Barnes (1999) 274 copies over 6 years.
> *Give Me Your Answer.* K.D. Miller (1999) 380 copies over 6 years.
> *One Last Good Look.* Michael Winter (1999) 915 copies over 6 years.
> *Emma's Hands.* Mary Swan. (2003) 527 copies over 2 years.

These figures are pretty much typical for all our literary titles.

Poetry is, of course, worse, a typical title selling 200 copies or fewer.

In the 1960s the print run of a Contact Press title was 300 copies, 250 in paper, 50 bound. The Press, conducted by Layton, Dudek, Souster, and Peter Miller was private and unsubsidized. Now, hundreds of millions of dollars later, with Canadian Literature taught in schools and universities, with vast Arts Bureaucracies, with Publishing Centres in universities, with Creative Writing Departments, with Oxford and Cambridge *Companions* – with all this vast apparatus, sales figures have not dramatically increased from Contact Press days.

The Globe and Mail wrote in an article on the Press' demise ("Literary Gem to Cut Staff, Book List"):

> One of the first books the press ever printed, the poetry collection *Letters of State* by Montreal poet and lawyer Lazar Sarna, sold 410 copies when it was released in the late seventies, despite the then-nascent company not having professional sales representation or distribution deals. Now, The Porcupine's Quill plans on releasing the latest book of poetry by Sarna this fall, *He Claims He Is the Direct Heir*, with projected sales of 250 copies.

Sales for literary titles, always few in number, have tumbled even further with the advent of Heather Reisman's Chapters and Indigo stores, stores which represent nearly 70% of the market.

In an article for *CNQ: Canadian Notes & Queries* entitled "Heavy Weather: The Porcupine's Quill at Thirty" Tim Inkster wrote:

> At one time I was optimistic that Chapters, and then Indigo, would be advantageous for small presses, and literary presses, in Canada.
>
> It is certainly true that historically we never did do much business at all with Coles or even W.H. Smith, largely because the mall store formats were too small to include shelf space to stock anything other than high-turnover bestsellers and profitable remainders.
>
> My thinking was that the big box stores would have to put *something* on the shelves at the back of the last aisle on the top floor, and that would be *my* books, and I wanted to buy into David Peterson's argument that Chapters was going to 'grow the market' for Canadian books.

(Mr. Peterson, at the time, was chairman of the board of Chapters.)

For a while, that's exactly what happened . . .

1) In 1998 Chapters and Indigo ordered 13,293 copies of PQL books. And they returned 4,052 – less than 30%, which was somewhat higher than industry standards, but not excessively so, and left us with a net sale of 9,241, which was worth about $90,000 in business for PQL, which was not bad at all.

2) In 2004 (six years later) Chapters ordered 2,797 copies of PQL books. And returned 1,415 – more than 50%; which left us with a net sale of 1,382 – which means we have lost 85% of our business with Chapters over the past six years.

3) In the current year-to-date [Oct. 2005] Chapters has ordered 3,877 copies of PQL books. And returned 2,640 – a net sale of 1,237 books and a return rate of 68%.

Inkster goes on to quote from a paper written by Jamie Glover for the Rotman School of Management at the University of Toronto:

All in, the emergence of the big-box bookseller as market leader changed the dynamics of the retail front for all publishers, but the least capable of absorbing the deleterious effects of this market shift were the small presses. Without the cash flow to pay for minimum required inventory or a place on the chain's 'power tables,' and without the attentive sales people at the retail level to encourage readers to experiment with small publishers' works, the already small Canadian market became considerably smaller . . .

Small publishers have historically had strong relationships with independent booksellers. The fit was good: earnest, reliable small press agents forged long-term relationships with booksellers, and a low requirement of copies of new works for each store limited the pressure on cash flow for both the producer and the seller. Beginning in the early 90s, however, the emergence of Chapters/Indigo as the market leader in the retailing of books in Canada had disastrous consequences for the small publisher. Despite the increased sales seen across the board for publishers in Canada, the format of the stores worked against the small press; unless a publisher was willing to place ten or more copies of a book in each store, no book would get more than 'spine placement' on

> the shelves, meaning that only the spine would be visible to the eye of the shopper. Larger publishers with more working capital could afford to stack books ten-deep in order to get front-cover placement, a key trigger for increased sales. This problem for the small publisher was compounded by Chapters/Indigo's business model of requiring publishers to pay for strategic placement throughout the stores. Even if the cost of producing a book was the same for a small and a large publisher, these added inventory demands and cash requirements served as a structural disadvantage for the cash-poor small publisher.

To have a book displayed face-out at the end of an aisle in Chapters costs $5000 a month. To have a book displayed on a "power table" – what puerile language! – costs a publisher $10,000 a month. It is even rumoured that "Heather's Picks" are not favours freely bestowed.

The effect of all this is to distort the shape of our literature. We are allowing a chain to dictate to us what we read, which books we know about, which books we don't know about, and which books we are expected to value. The result is Anne-Marie MacDonald's *Fall on Your Knees* rather than, say, Caroline Adderson's *A History of Forgetting* or Leon Rooke's *The Fall of Gravity*. We live in a world where books displayed spine-out are granted an existence of 90 days and are then automatically returned. Chapers does not stock "backlist," a writer's earlier titles; Chapters places "product." It does, however, stock candles and coffee-mugs.

In 2006 sales seemed likely to plummet further. The Literary Press Group (LPG), the group of sales representatives who present small press books to the trade, for the first time projected shipments for each press. (It is important to notice the word "shipments;" these are not concluded sales. Unsold books, "returns," can be sent back to the press.) The following figures represent what the LPG realistically hopes to accomplish.

Tim Inkster sent an e-mail on the subject to the Canada Council. Here, in part, is what he said:

> . . . And what am I going to do with the 3512 books that Chindigo returned last year, other than to pulp most of them. Pulping is free, but still . . . now that we no longer can afford staff, I really don't think Elke and I want to spend the hundreds of hours it takes us to (personally) manufacture 3512 books, only to see them pulped a year later.

> For this reason we have instructed the LPG to avoid 'presenting' PQL titles to Chapters for Spring 06 . . . That leaves what's left of the independents. You will be interested to learn that the LPG sales force is projecting that shipments (before returns) of the PQL Spring 06 list will be 648 books.
>
> That's an average of 162 copies each of four titles.
>
> The four authors in question are P.K. Page, David Helwig, Clark Blaise, and Gerard Brender à Brandis, a wood engraver from Stratford.

The first three are widely considered to be among Canada's most important writers.

In his article for *CNQ: Canadian Notes & Queries* entitled "Heavy Weather: The Porcupine's Quill at Thirty," Tim Inkster pursued the topic of projected sales.

> LPG sales manager Margaret Bryant has recently reported that our Spring 2006 list has been received with enthusiasm across the country.
>
> *Hand Luggage* by P.K. Page, for example, 'is selling well' as a result of 'a lot of bookseller interest' in 'quantities that range from 1 to 4.' *A gathering of Flowers* is also 'selling quite well,' 'in quantities from 1 to 4.' And 'wholesalers are also very interested' in *World Body* by Clark Blaise. But what does this mean in terms of orders at the University of Toronto Press? [UTP is the actual distributor of the books for which the LPG secures orders.] The LPG sales force has been presenting our Spring list for over three months now. Orders for *World Body* are 29 copies, ordered by a total of 13 stores. David Helwig's *The Names of Things* has attracted orders for 66 copies, from 19 stores. *A Gathering of Flowers* has 98 orders, from 30 stores. And *Hand Luggage* by P.K. Page has 190 orders, from 37 stores. On average then, the four spring titles have attracted advance orders of 95 copies each, from an average of 25 retail stores, nationally, which pretty much characterizes the extent of what remains of the trade market for literary titles in Canada.

Further aggravating this depressing state of affairs is the hostility towards art and literature so evident now on university campuses. Students infected by "Theory" would have nothing but contempt for the radiant simplicity of that splendid painter David Milne when he wrote:

> Feeling is the power that drives art. There doesn't seem to be a more understandable word for it, though there are others that give something of the idea: aesthetic emotion, quickening, bringing to life. Or call it love; not love of man or woman or home or country or any material thing, but love without an object . . . intransitive love.

Those whose traditional role was to foster the arts and reveal ways in which students might experience more pleasure in them now grub after sociology and the politics of race and gender. Students are now taught that judgements are meaningless, that distinctions are elitist self-delusion, that Barbara Cartland is no better or no worse than Jane Austen. Both are "texts" to be "deconstructed." Of all this farcical inanity Robert Hughes wrote in *Culture of Complaint: The Fraying of America*:

> It is in the nature of human beings to discriminate. We make choices and judgements every day. These choices are part of real experience. They are influenced by others, of course, but they are not fundamentally the result of a passive reaction to authority. And we know that one of the realist experiences in cultural life is that of inequality between books and musical performances and paintings and other works of art. Some things do strike us as better than others – more articulate, more radiant with consciousness. We may have difficulty saying why, but the experience remains. The pleasure principle is enormously important in art, and those who would like to see it downgraded in favour of ideological utterance remind me of the English Puritans who opposed bear-baiting, not because it gave pain to the bear, but because it gave pleasure to the spectators.

Sir Kenneth Clark in his autobiography *Another Part of the Wood* also asserts the primacy of pleasure. When he was about ten or eleven he was allowed to look at and to handle a collection of Japanese prints.

> These Sunday afternoons with Mr. Macdonald's Japanese prints were among the happiest and most formative in my life. They confirmed my belief that nothing could destroy me as long as I could enjoy works of art, and for 'enjoy' read 'enjoy': not codify or classify, or purge my spirit or arouse my social consciousness, just enjoy. From

this hedonist, or at best epicurean, position I have never departed. It is true that I have tried to communicate my pleasure to other people, but that is not because I feel it my duty to do so, but simply because I cannot contain myself.

When I read in critical journals the obscurantist language, the flap-doodle of deconstruction, hermeneutics, *parole, langue,* binary oppositions, analytico-referential discourse, heteroglossia, signified and signifier, I tend to think of Ben Jonson's *The Alchemist.* I think of Subtle, Face, and the strumpet Dol Common softening up the puritan dupe, Ananias.

Subtle: Can you sublime and dulcify? Calcine?
Know you the sapor pontic? Sapor stiptic?
Or what is homogene, or heterogene?
Ananias: I understand no heathen language, truly.
Subtle: Heathen! you Knipperdoling! Is *ars sacra,*
Or chrysopoeia, or spagyrica,
Or the pamphysic, or panarchic knowledge,
A heathen language?

And Subtle in an aside to Face:

Take away the recipient,
And rectify your menstrue from the phlegma.
Then pour it o' the Sol, in the cucurbite,
And let 'em macerate together.

But Subtle, Face and Dol were confidence tricksters, cozeners out to gull. Today's sad "theorists" are far worse. They are true believers.

W.J. Keith, Professor Emeritus at the University of Toronto, in his recent book *Canadian Literature in English: Revised and Expanded Edition* concludes, "It is no exaggeration to claim that we have witnessed a massive contemporary *trahison des clercs.*"

I feel so hopeless about our universities and so disconnected from the theory behind their literary concerns that I am too numb to write. Instead I'll quote from a *New Yorker* article on Philip Roth (May 8, 2000) wherein Roth says what I would say had I his grace and humour.

Roth, who learned to read at Bucknell and the University of Chicago a half century ago, was dumbstruck as he was pressed on the significance of his characters' names: Seymour (Swede) Levov, it means 'love'? Lev? Lion? And, Seymour. It means See-more? See-*more*, yes? And what about Merry? Is she the Mary? Christ's Mary? There were questions about numerology, about the 'tripartite nature' of *American Pastoral*: its three generations, its three parts, its three family members. Then the subject turned to the Talmud and Hebrew philology (Roth's Jewish learning is modest, and he speaks Catskills Yiddish and no Hebrew). On all these matters, Roth suggested to the French students that perhaps they were reading with a 'subtlety that is misplaced.' He hoped instead that they would begin to think of *American Pastoral* as a book less about the mysteries of its names than as one about the costs of a revolutionary period in American life, about 'the uncontrollability of real things,' the inability to explain random events and catastrophes in a good man's life.

Later, when I asked Roth about such readings, he laughed, and said, 'It's like baseball. Suppose you and I went up to the ballpark together, and there's a guy next to us with his kid. And he was saying, "Now, what I want you to do is watch the scoreboard. Stop watching the field. Just watch what happens when the numbers change on the scoreboard. Isn't that great? Now, do you see what just happened up there? Did you see what happened? Why did that happen?" And you say, "That guy is crazy." But the kid imbibes it and he goes home and he's asked, "How was the game?" And he says, "Great! The scoreboard changed thirty-two times and Daddy said last game it changed only fourteen times and the home team last time changed more times than the other team. It was really great! We had hot dogs and we stood up at one point to stretch and we went home." Is that politicizing the baseball game? Is that theorizing the baseball game? No, it's having not the foggiest idea in the world what baseball is.'

Probably enough said.

For the 2005 Eden Mills Writers' Festival, Leon and Connie Rooke had organized a retrospective tribute to Tim and Elke Inkster and to the Porcupine's Quill. Leon had gathered encomiums and had produced a booklet, a bouquet of praise. It was a rather doleful occasion, the demise of the press a reminder of Canadian cultural realities. Yet the kindness of our colleagues' comments reminded us that not all was loss and defeat. We had over the years accumulated victories.

Alice Munro wrote:

> I would like to send a message of gratitude to Porcupine's Quill and to John Metcalf who has given so much energy to writing over the years. The result has been a certain brightness, a liveliness and severity, a commitment to what is not fake in writing, that has entered our literature and that I hope will stay there.

Philip Marchand wrote:

> In my sixteen years of reviewing Canadian literature for the *Toronto Star*, I have found that the Porcupine's Quill has upheld the most consistently high level of excellence in writing and publishing of any of the literary presses in this country. Its output alone would put Canada on a firm international footing in contemporary world literature.

Amanda Jernigan, the Press' first intern, contributed an occasional poem which touched and moved even the most ink-stained and hardbitten among us.

ROUTINE
for Tim and Elke

'The world of publishing,' you told
me on my first day on the job, 'is mad.
Well – what did you expect?
There is no money in it: what we've sold
this summer wouldn't buy you lunch:
which is what editors are out to – in both senses.
Authors? Unavoidable expenses.
Printers? An eccentric bunch,
but mostly daft (myself excepted).
One more thing: the public doesn't read.

All this no doubt intended to dissuade.
Instead, intrigued (and obstinate) I stayed –
and saw, against the fickle post,
which might bring money or disaster,
there was coffee at exactly ten o'clock,
the local gossip at the dairy, toasted
sandwiches in paper bags, and last
year's bulbs reliably emerging. And though
we were behind, the press would slow
unfailingly at four, for Simba's walk.
You've been typecast (excuse the pun)
quixotically: on pressback, Zephyr
Antique laying waste forever
to shoddy bindings, box-stores, bills.
Yet I have seen this battle done
with neither swords nor slings – nor quills.

On Friday nights you swept the shopfloor clean.
Against the wrack of publishing, the sanity of routine.

THE PORCUPINE'S QUILL: THE AESTHETIC AIMS

What were the achievements of the Porcupine's Quill Press in the nineteen years I worked with Tim and Elke? On a very personal level I feel pleasure in the emotional richness of the life I've been able to live. When Roy MacSkimming was writing *The Perilous Trade: Publishing Canada's Writers* he taped an interview with me during which I apparently said about working gratis for the press: "I get paid as an editor in that a succession of extraordinary young people allow me to share in the passion of their lives." In retrospect, that may sound rather like a statement to the police by an apprehended choirmaster but it remains the absolute truth.

The central achievement of the Press was to fight for and establish an aesthetic approach to literature. I was pushing all the time to find and encourage work where the words mattered. I was looking for new rhetoric, new artifice. I wanted formal skill, play, verbal mastery. The reader may think there's nothing much out of the way in that but very few readers actually read words. They read themes, characters, and plots and so are deaf to the blandishments and subtleties of our better writers.

Kicking Against the Pricks, *What Is a Canadian Literature?*, *Volleys*, and *Freedom from Culture* were all part of a critical effort to direct attention to language. I was trying to propose very simple ideas. That writing is artificial. That it is made of words. That it pursues its ends by the use of rhetoric. That it is a game that the reader must learn to play. That writing is more about *the way of looking* than it is about *what is being looked at.* That said, that the ends of art are emotional. That artifice creates emotion which locks us to the real.

Maurice Denis, the principal theorist of Les Nabis, wrote near the beginnings of modernism in 1890, "Remember that a picture, before being a battle horse or a nude, or some anecdote – is essentially a flat surface covered with colours assembled in a certain order."

Writers – and readers who want aesthetic pleasure – take the battle horse more or less for granted – it is something obvious – the interest lies in that "certain order."

Here is much the same sort of thing being said by John Updike in his *Self-Consciousness: Memoirs*:

> . . . every day, I groped for the exact terms I knew were there but could not find, pawed through the thesaurus in search of them and through the dictionary in search of their correct spelling. My English language had been early bent by the Germanic locutions of my environment, and, as my prose came to be edited by experts, I had to arbitrate between how I in my head heard a sentence go and how, evidently, it should correctly go. My own style seemed to me a groping and elemental attempt to approximate the complexity of envisioned phenomena and it surprised me to have it called luxuriant and self-indulgent; self-indulgent, surely, is exactly what it wasn't – *other*-indulgent, rather. My models were the styles of Proust and Henry Green as I read them (one in translation): styles of tender exploration that tried to wrap themselves around the things, the tints and voices and perfumes, of the apprehended real. *In this entwining and gently relentless effort there is no hiding that the effort is being made in language: all professorial or critical talk of inconspicuous or invisible language struck me as vapid and quite mistaken, for surely language, printed language, is what we all know we are reading and writing, just as a person looking at a painting knows he is not looking out of a window.* [Italic added]

And now here is much the same sort of thing being said by Sir Kenneth Clark in the second volume of his autobiography, *The Other Half: A Self Portrait.* He is describing a visit to Picasso's studio in 1945.

> He lived in a large, empty studio, furnished only by two green park benches. Around the wall were (literally) hundreds of canvasses, neatly stacked and all dated on the back. Among them was a number of the worst landscapes I have ever seen. Nature, in the Claudian sense, had no appeal to Picasso whatsoever. He was extremely perceptive, and saw at once what I thought of them. He then produced a large portfolio of drawings of a Cupid and Psyche motive – in most of them the man asleep and the girl looking down at him, which were amongst his most beautiful drawings. What on earth has happened to them! He did not show me the hideous, but powerful, pictures of children with distorted

> faces, which were exhibited in England a few years later, and were supposed to express his mental anguish at the thought of the German occupation. This is the kind of nonsense that makes a critic 'feel good.' *In fact, great artists seldom take any interest in the events of the outside world. They are occupied in realising their own images and achieving formal necessities.* As is well known, the images that are the basis of *Guernica* occur in drawings that antedate by over a year the bombing of the Basque town. [Italic added.]

And now here is Alice Munro saying much the same sort of thing in an interview with Geoff Hancock in *Canadian Fiction Magazine:*

> What happens as event doesn't really much matter. When the event becomes the thing that matters, the story isn't working too well. There has to be a feeling in the story.

And here in an interview with the Australian literary magazine *Meanjin* is Alice digging in:

> MEANJIN: How does a story get started?
>
> ALICE: Story telling is continuous. Story doesn't stop, at least the sort of stories I'm interested in writing. There are certain types of stories which do, in fact, end. Which do come to a conclusion. Political stories conclude. Because they have some purpose to fulfil which is separate from telling a story. Such stories want to engage and challenge us with the issues they present, usually in the hope of satisfying some political or social agenda. The problem with issue-driven fiction is that it doesn't arouse feelings or disturb us in the way I think good fiction should. The message becomes more important than the questions or puzzles nurtured by human experience or behaviour . . .
>
> . . . Why invent characters if they simply embody some polemical goal? I don't like messages attached to my reading. This is why I'm not too fond of Tolstoy or D.H. Lawrence. While some of the writing in both writers is beautiful, I'm not at all interested in the sermons attached to their stories. On the other hand, Eudora Welty makes a southern American town feel absolutely magical, but she may be – in fact, often is – politically incorrect. The experience she relates, though,

> is both accurate and authentic. And emotionally and intellectually disturbing. Her book, *The Golden Apples,* is one of my favourite books. But I guess if I were black and had grown up in the South, I would have felt excluded from that book.
>
> By contrast, I was annoyed with the dialogue in a novel I read recently because the exchange between the characters appeared to be little more than a political debate. I think my response here has something to do with the fact that I proceed from induction rather than deduction. I also think that writing about 'current issues' dates very quickly.

And then there's my old writer in the story "The Years in Exile" sitting in the garden and dreaming his childhood.

> What will the young man say to me this evening? And what can I say to him? It is difficult to talk to these young college men whose minds no longer move in pictures. Had he been here this morning I could, like some Zen sage, have pointed to the Monarchs about the apple leaves and preserved my silence.
>
> Particular life. Particular life.
>
> All else is tricks of the trade or inexpressible.

In essence, then, my emphasis in editing was to ignore as much as possible the "battle horse" or "anecdote" and concentrate rather on "colours assembled in a certain order." Such an emphasis led me inevitably to Caroline Adderson, Mike Barnes, Annabel Lyon, Elise Levine, Russell Smith, Michael Winter, Libby Creelman, Terry Griggs, Mary Swan, Joan Alexander, Sharon English, Keath Fraser, Mary Borsky, K.D. Miller . . . the list is happily long.

In order to talk more about editing and to illustrate "colours assembled in a certain order" I want to present ten extracts from nine writers and then attempt a conclusion. Not one of these writers is Canadian as I will be discussing Canadian writing in a subsequent chapter. The writers are: Katherine Mansfield, Evelyn Waugh, Sylvia Townsend-Warner, John Banville, Ronald Firbank, Simon Raven, Raymond Carver, Beryl Bainbridge, and Samuel Beckett.

* * *

Katherine Mansfield was ill most of her life and dead at thirty-five, most probably from the complications of sexually transmitted disease. This is explored in Claire Tomalin's 1987 book *Katherine Mansfield: A Secret Life*. On what was to be her final journey, a journey to the Institute for the Harmonious Development of Man run by the disgusting Gurdjieff, glutton, fornicator, dipsomaniac, ex-carpet-salesman, suspected spy, Katherine wrote to the Hon. Dorothy Brett:

> We had a divine crossing, very still silvery sea with gulls moving on the waves like the lights in a pearl. It was fiery hot in Calais – Whoof! It was blazing. And there were old women with pears to sell wherever you looked . . . old hands holding up satiny baskets. So beautiful. English ladies trying to eat them through their veils. So awful. The way to Paris was lovely too. All the country just brushed over with light gold, and white oxen ploughing and a man riding a horse into a big dark pond. Paris too very warm and shadowy . . .
>
> (From *The Letters of Katherine Mansfield* Volume II. Ed. John Middleton Murray.)

For those curious about the monstrous guru, an American disciple, Fritz Peters, has written entertainingly about the Institute at Le Prieuré in his 1976 *Gurdjieff*. Peters' job at the Institute was to clean the master's filth from his bathroom and bedroom walls.

* * *

In the 1970s I taught at Loyola of Montreal with Erika Ritter. She went on to write some successful plays, most notably *Automatic Pilot*, and gravitated to Toronto where she eventually ran a jolly, comfy talk-show for CBC Radio. One segment of the show often featured a writer who had been asked to select a favourite passage from literature's range, read it, and then comment on its felicities. I was in Toronto to promote my story collection *Adult Entertainment* and Erika phoned me asking if I'd like to do the programme. Usually the passage to be read was vetted and the reader was rehearsed because the show went out live.

"Well, probably something from Evelyn Waugh," I said.

"Oh, just come in and do it," said Erika.

And so it was that I got to deliver on national radio – live and unstoppable – Dr. Fagan's judicious anatomizing of the Welsh race. It was when I reached, "From the earliest times the Welsh have been looked upon as an unclean people" that I secured Erika's incredulous attention.

As I launched into Dr. Fagan's catalogue of Welsh shortcomings – habitual incest, bestiality, the sodomizing of sheep – Erika was becoming visibly agitated, grew pale, paler.

The technicians on the other side of the glass were rolling about and punching each other on the arms in laughter.

I regard this broadcast as one of the highpoints of my literary career.

From *Decline and Fall* then, Dr. Fagan's speech to Paul Pennyfeather at the Llanabba Castle School Sports Day.

> 'The Welsh character is an interesting study,' said Dr. Fagan. 'I have often considered writing a little monograph on the subject, but I was afraid it might make me unpopular in the village. The ignorant speak of them as Celts, which is of course wholly erroneous. They are of pure Iberian stock – the aboriginal inhabitants of Europe who survive only in Portugal and the Basque district. Celts readily intermarry with their neighbours and absorb them. From the earliest times the Welsh have been looked upon as an unclean people. It is thus that they have preserved their racial integrity. Their sons and daughters mate freely with the sheep but not with human kind except their own blood relations. In Wales there was no need for legislation to prevent the conquering people intermarrying with the conquered. In Ireland that was necessary, for there inter-marriage was a political matter. In Wales it was moral. I hope, by the way, you have no Welsh blood?'
>
> 'None whatever,' said Paul.
>
> 'I was sure you had not, but one cannot be too careful. I once spoke of this subject to the sixth form and learned later that one of them had a Welsh grandmother. I am afraid it hurt his feelings terribly, poor little chap. She came from Pembrokeshire, too, which is of course quite a different matter. I often think,' he continued, 'that we can trace almost all the disasters of English history to the influence of Wales. Think of Edward of Caernarvon, the first Prince of Wales, a perverse life, Pennyfeather, and an unseemly death, then the Tudors and the disso-

lution of the Church, then Lloyd George, the temperance movement, Nonconformity and lust stalking hand in hand through the country, wasting and ravaging. But perhaps you think I exaggerate? I have a certain rhetorical tendency, I admit.'

'No, no,' said Paul.

'The Welsh,' said the doctor, 'are the only nation in the world that has produced no graphic or plastic art, no architecture, no drama. They just sing,' he said with disgust, 'sing and blow down wind instruments of plated silver. They are deceitful because they cannot discern truth from falsehood, depraved because they cannot discern the consequences of their indulgence. Let us consider,' he continued, 'the etymological derivations of the Welsh language . . .'

But here he was interrupted by a breathless little boy who panted down the drive to meet them.

* * *

Sylvia Townsend Warner was born on December 6, 1893, at Harrow-on-the-Hill, where her father was a housemaster and taught history. What emerged from her infancy was a charming, preternaturally intelligent child. When she was old enough for kindergarten she disrupted the class by mimicking the teachers – meaning no offence – and her parents were asked to withdraw her. They then decided to educate her at home. Her mother taught her to read, from the Bible, and other basic subjects, and her father taught her history informally when they were on vacation in Wales or Switzerland. By the time she was ten she had read halfway through *Vanity Fair*.

This is drawn from the Foreword by William Maxwell to *The Music at Long Verney*, twenty stories by Sylvia Townsend Warner published posthumously. During her life she published 14 collections of short stories. Between 1936 and 1977 she published over 150 stories in *The New Yorker*. William Maxwell was her editor for nearly forty years. Even aficionados of the story form are sometimes unaware that William Maxwell is one of the elect. His stories are disgracefully scanted. They are collected in *All the Days and Nights* (1995).

What follows is the opening of a story called "Maternal Devotion."

'I was taught how to make tea by Professor Abernethy in Dresden. He always used an egg cup. Not that his name was Abernethy, or anything like it,' Mrs. Finch said to the young man who had come to call on her daughter. 'It was more like Euston or Thompson.'

As kittens bring in the mice that are too much for them to be finished off by the cat, Cordelia Finch had a habit of depositing any inconvenient suitors with her mother and leaving the rest to nature. When the Finches moved from London to Kent and their new neighbours hastened to call on them, the number of deposited suitors rose sharply. This one was a Mr. Weatherby, who was locally expected to become a Member of Parliament when he had matured. Mrs. Finch had told him that Cordelia was not at home, adding with equal mendacity, that she had hoped he would stay and have tea.

'I can't think why I should so persistently call him Abernathy,' she continued. 'He wasn't in the least like a biscuit.'

'Some association of ideas, perhaps,' Mr. Weatherby suggested.

'I don't see how it can be, for I detest Abernethy biscuits, and he was such a kind old man. He used to be followed about by a cab.'

After a slight pause, Mr. Weatherby said, 'Really?'

* * *

Sir Anthony Blunt was an art historian and a Soviet spy. He was an accomplice of Guy Burgess, Donald Maclean, and Kim Philby and abetted Burgess and Maclean's escape to Moscow. In 1964 a confession was obtained in return for immunity from prosecution. He continued as Director of the Courtauld Institute of Art and as Surveyor of the Queen's pictures. Only in 1979 was his full involvement in espionage revealed. His knighthood was immediately annulled.

John Banville's brilliant novel *The Untouchable* bases itself on Blunt's career, the "Blunt" character being called Victor Maskell. In what follows Maskell is writing in his journal. He refers to a painting by Nicholas Poussin entitled *Et in Arcadia Ego*. This 1647 painting represents four Arcadians, in a meditative and melancholy mood, symetrically arranged on either side of a tomb. A kneeling shepherd reads the inscription on the tomb: *Et in Arcadia Ego* which can be translated "And I too am in Arcadia," "I" meaning Death. Or as "I [the person in the tomb] also used to live in Arcadia." The second shepherd seems to be discussing the inscription with the beautiful girl standing near him. The third shepherd stands pensively aside. Arcadian pastoral is given a tinge of melancholy by Death's intrusion.

> Public disgrace is a strange thing. Fluttery feeling in the region of the diaphragm and a sort of racing sensation all over, as of the blood like mercury slithering along heavily just under the skin. Excitement mixed with fear makes for a heady brew. At first I could not think what this state reminded me of, then it came to me: those first nights on the prowl after I had finally admitted to myself it was my own kind that I wanted. The same hot shiver of mingled anticipation and fear, the same desperate grin trying not to break out. Wanting to be caught. To be set upon. To be manhandled. Well, past all that now. Past everything, really. There is a particular bit of blue sky in *Et in Arcadia Ego*, where the clouds are broken in the shape of a bird in flight, which is the true, clandestine centre-point, the pinnacle of the picture, for me. When I contemplate death, and I contemplate it with an ever-diminishing sense of implausibility in these latter days, I see myself swaddled in zinc-white cerements, more a figure out of El Greco than Poussin, ascending in a transport of erotic agony amid alleluias and lip-farts through a swirl of clouds the colour of golden tea head-first into just such a patch of pellucid bleu céleste.

Wow!

What a piece of perfected pizzaz.

(And if it *was* a figure more out of El Greco than Poussin, I'm almost certain that what's in Banville's mind is *The Burial of the Count of Orgaz* in the Iglesia de Santo Tomé in Toledo.)

* * *

Ronald Firbank's novels are unlike any other. With one exception, he paid to have them published and for many years they were known only to a small circle of fellow-writers and aesthetes. Some claim that "he did more to liberate the novel from 19th-century concepts of realism than Joyce himself." (*The Oxford Companion to English Literature*. Edited by Margaret Drabble. Sixth Edition.)

Firbank more or less banished plot and his intense concentration of language and image still seem massively innovative. His oblique and mercurial dialogue must have spoken deeply to Evelyn Waugh and Anthony Powell. I fancy I can hear Firbank quite clearly in Anthony Powell's *Afternoon Men.* Some of the novels seem to proceed almost – almost – by verbal free-association – particularly true of *The Flower beneath the Foot.* His last finished novel *Concerning the Eccentricities of Cardinal Pirelli* was published posthumously in 1926. Brigid Brophy in her rather wooden study of Firbank, *Prancing Novelist,* flatly claims *Concerning the Eccentricities of Cardinal Pirelli* as among the greatest books of the twentieth century.

In a later essay collection *Brigid Brophy Reads* she writes:

> The three greatest novels of the twentieth century are *The Golden Bowl* by Henry James, *A la Recherche du Temps Perdu* by Marcel Proust and *Concerning the Eccentricities of Cardinal Pirelli* by Ronald Firbank.
>
> . . . Not only the styles but the mental attitudes of all three writers have been formed by the aesthete's practice of continual refinement. Both James and Proust, however, when they think of another stroke that would bring them yet closer to their precise meaning, *add* it – a method which makes, at the same time, for solidity. Only Firbank, perhaps the most ruthless, does not build up to strength but excises to it. . . . The Firbank technique is that of mosaic in a glittering material. The more ruthless and masterly he became, the more spaces were left deliberately unfilled by anything except his immense power of suggesting whole characters *in absentia.* The later books are discoveries of fragmentary mosaic pavements, like the discovery of a Sappho fragment in *Vainglory.*

Concerning the Eccentricities of Cardinal Pirelli opens with an unforgettable baptism.

> Huddled up in a cope of gold wrought silk he peered around. Society had rallied in force. A christening – and not a child's.
>
> Rarely had he witnessed, before the font, so many brilliant people. Were it an heir to the DunEden acres (instead of what it *was*) the ceremony could have hardly drawn together a more distinguished throng.
>
> Monsignor Silex moved a finger from forehead to chin, and from ear

to ear. The Duquesa DunEden's escapades, if continued, would certainly cost the Cardinal his hat.

'And ease my heart by splashing fountains.'

From the choir-loft a boy's young voice was evoking Heaven.

'His hat!' Monsignor Silex exclaimed aloud, blinking a little at the immemorial font of black Macael marble that had provoked the screams of pale numberless babies.

Here Saints and Kings had been baptized, and royal Infantas, and sweet Poets, whose high names thrilled the heart.

Monsignor Silex crossed his breast. He must gather force to look about him. Frame a close report. The Pontiff, in far-off Italy, would expect precision.

Beneath the state baldequin, or Grand Xaymaca, his Eminence sat enthroned ogled by the wives of a dozen grandees. The Altamissals, the Villarasas (their grandee-ships' approving glances, indeed, almost eclipsed their wives'), and Catherine, Countess of Constantine, the most talked-of beauty in the realm, looking like some wild limb of Astaroth in a little crushed 'toreador' hat round as an athlete's coif with hanging silken balls, while beside her a stout, dumpish dame, of enormous persuasion, was joggling, solicitously, an object that was of the liveliest interest to all.

Head archly bent, her fine arms divined through darkling laces, the Duquesa stood, clasping closely a week-old police-dog in the ripple of her gown.

'Mother's pet!' she cooed, as the imperious creature passed his tongue across the splendid uncertainty of her chin.

Monsignor Silex's large, livid face grew grim.

What – disquieting doubt – if it were her Grace's offspring after all? Praise heaven, he was ignorant enough regarding the schemes of nature, but in an old lutrin once he had read of a young woman engendering a missel-thrush through the channel of her nose. It had created a good deal of scandal to be sure at the time: the Holy Inquisition, indeed, had condemned the impudent baggage, in consequence, to the stake.

'That was the style to treat them,' he murmured, appraising the assembly with no kindly eye. The presence of Madame San Seymour surprised him; one habitually so set apart and devout! And Madame La

> Urench, too, gurgling away freely to the fourlegged Father: 'No, my naughty Blessing; no, not now! . . . By and by, a *bone*.'
>
> Words which brought the warm saliva to the expectant parent's mouth.
>
> Tail awag, sex apparent (to the affected slight confusion of the Infanta Eulalia-Irene), he crouched, his eyes fixed wistfully upon the nozzle of his son.
>
> Ah, happy delirium of first parenthood! Adoring pride! Since times primeval by what masonry does it knit together those that have succeeded in establishing here, on earth, the vital bonds of a family's claim? Even the modest sacristan, at attention by the font, felt himself to be superior of parts to a certain unproductive chieftain of a princely House, who had lately undergone a course of asses' milk in the surrounding mountains – all in vain!
>
> But, supported by the Prior of the Cartuja, the Cardinal had arisen for the act of Immersion.
>
> Of unusual elegance, and with the remains, moreover, of perfect looks, he was as wooed and run after by the ladies as any *matador*.
>
> 'And thus being cleansed and purified, I do call thee "Crack"!' he addressed the Duquesa's captive burden.

Here is another quotation, this time from *Prancing Nigger*, the American title, showing Firbank in different but equally masterful mode. The U.K. title was *Sorrow in Sunlight*, Firbank's own and preferred title. The book was published in 1924. This was a new language breaking upon the world.

> Looking gloriously bored, Miss Miami Mouth gaped up into the boughs of a giant silk-cotton-tree. In the lethargic noontide nothing stirred: all was so still, indeed, that the sound of someone snoring was clearly audible among the cane-fields far away.
>
> 'After dose yams an' pods an' de white falernum, I dats way sleepy too,' she murmured, fixing heavy, somnolent eyes upon the prospect that lay before her.
>
> Through the sun-tinged greenery shone the sea, like a floor of silver glass strewn with white sails.
>
> Somewhere out there, fishing, must be her boy, Bamboo!

Firbank used to write his novels on large blue postcards which he also used in correspondence. He travelled widely every year in Europe and North Africa to indulge his homosexual desires safe from prosecution. Osbert Sitwell records receiving a postcard that said simply: "Tomorrow I go to Hayti. They say the President is a *Perfect Dear!*"

* * *

Simon Raven is best known for his series of ten linked novels called *Alms for Oblivion*, a slightly down-market *Dance to the Music of Time*, though some of the books are just as funny as Anthony Powell's. I would especially recommend *Friends in Low Places*, *The Judas Boy*, and *Sound the Retreat*. His two volumes of memoirs are a delight: *The Old School* and *Bird of Ill-Omen*. I find Powell's memoirs, on the other hand, eccentric and rather boring. The novel of Powell's that most holds my attention is not one of the *Dance to the Music of Time* titles but Powell's first book, *Afternoon Men*; it announced along with titles by Evelyn Waugh and Henry Green the arrival of a generation of genius.

Readers who enjoy Simon Raven may well feel an affinity for Julian Maclaren-Ross and for his *Memoirs of the Forties*. Maclaren-Ross was portrayed in Powell's *Books Do Furnish a Room* as the character X. Trapnell.

Julian Maclaren-Ross, along with Dylan Thomas, Augustus John, J. Meary Tambimuttu (editor of *Poetry London*), George Orwell, and painters' model Nina Hamnet all drank at the *Wheatsheaf* in Fitzrovia (Rathbone Place) and at the *Fitzroy Tavern* on Charlotte Street. Hamnet's raucous memoirs are entitled *Laughing Torso*; she boasted that Modigliani said she had "the best tits in Europe." The *Fitzroy* maintains a special basement bar in honour of these roistering bohemians where, surrounded by drawings and photographs, one can raise a pint of Fuller's London Pride to their memory.

Nina Hamnet's best drawings were her portraits – Lytton Strachey, Anthony Powell, Roger Fry, Edith Sitwell – but her promise was destroyed by alcohol. Her work is now probably most easily seen in her illustrations for Seymour Leslie's novel *The Silent Queen*.

A sight of Nina Hamnet by Scottish poet Ruthven Todd one night in 1942. (Quoted from Todd's *Fitzrovia and the Road to York Minster.*)

> In the light of a parachute-flare dropped by a German plane, I saw a most peculiarly flaccid tripod approaching me from the North. The legs

wobbled and wove and crumpled and it was clear that it was only possible for the three persons to move as a tripod linked by arms over one another's shoulders. The tripod seemed unaware of the air-raid and of the nasty sharp splinters of ack-ack shrapnel that were pitter-pattering down in the streets. I remained in the shadow of the Highlander waiting for a lull in the gunfire and stayed there as the tripod wobbled past. The three legs were Augustus John, Nina Hamnet and Norman Douglas, all three, to use an expressive Mallorcan phrase, as drunk as sponges, on their way to the Gargoyle for an unneeded drink.

Evelyn Waugh published *Vile Bodies* in 1930. When the novel was republished in the 1965 uniform edition Waugh wrote in the new Preface: "I think I can claim that this was the first English novel in which dialogue on the telephone plays a large part."

What an astonishing thought!

The following gorgeous performance is from Simon Raven's novel *An Inch of Fortune* – masterful telephone handling – written in 1950 when he was twenty-two years old and still an undergraduate at King's College, Cambridge. It remained unpublished for years because it was considered libelous.

> The phone was answered by a throaty, empire-building sort of voice, presumably but not incontestably feminine.
>
> 'I want to speak to the Honourable Mrs. Sandra Fairweather,' said Esme.
>
> 'Mrs. Fairweather speaking,' said the voice.
>
> 'Oh. Yes. This is Mr. Sa Foy here. I think – '
>
> 'Who?' said the voice.
>
> 'Mr. Sa Foy. I –'
>
> 'Hurry up,' said the voice, 'my dog's just gone on the carpet and if I don't hit it now, it'll forget why.'
>
> 'Mr. McTavish, that is Dr. McTavish, said I was to r –'
>
> 'Oh, it's Mr. Sa Foy, you might have said so. When can you come and be interviewed? Badlock's no way at all from Cambridge and the car can meet you at the station. Whatever I think of you it'll be worth the journey, because I can show you my borders – they're magnificent just now, a great stinking mess, by Heaven, it might have been a horse. Will tomorrow do? McTavish will be here – and a sick friend of mine from

London who may die – you won't mind that? – he's done it all over the place.'

'It sounds very pleasant. What time?'

'Five-thirty at the station. As I say, McTavish will be here. He's made a stench like a sewer. I'll teach you to shit. Good-bye Mr. Sa Foy.'

'Good-bye,' said Esme.

* * *

And here, in contrast to Banville's gorgeousness, is Raymond Carver's anti-rhetoric, emotion achieved by lack of emotion, a scrupulous flatness of emotional effect which is close to heart-breaking.

The Harvill Press in London produced a small memoir of Carver written by Richard Ford. It was called *Good Raymond* and contained a vignette of an early reading.

> On the way out of the building into the watery Texas night, I came up beside Ray and patted him on the back. (We *were* always doing that.) 'Gee,' I said, 'that was a terrific story, Ray. And you read it just perfectly [hesitantly, painfully, reluctantly, almost inaccessibly, as if all the horrors and poignance and comedy were straight from true life, which they probably were].'
>
> 'Oh God, Richard, really?' Ray said, looking nearly astonished and grinning. 'Did you like that? Did you? Oh Christ, I'm glad to hear that, I really am.' He stopped and shook his head. 'I hadn't read a story sober in longer than I can remember. Maybe never. I was shaking in my boots. I was afraid I couldn't finish it. But that you liked it means the world to me. Thanks a lot, my friend. I'm pleased. I really am. Thanks. Thanks.'

Here are the first three paragraphs of "Mr. Coffee and Mr. Fixit" from the 1981 collection *What We Talk About When We Talk About Love.*

> I've seen some things. I was going over to my mother's to stay a few nights. But just as I got to the top of the stairs, I looked and she was on the sofa kissing a man. It was summer. The door was open. The TV was going. That's one of the things I've seen. My mother is sixty-five. She belongs to a singles club. Even so, it was hard. I stood with my hand on

the railing and watched as the man kissed her. She was kissing him back, and the TV was going.

Things are better now. But back in those days, when my mother was putting out, I was out of work. My kids were crazy, and my wife was crazy. She was putting out too. The guy that was getting it was an unemployed aerospace engineer she'd met at AA. He was also crazy.

* * *

Beryl Bainbridge is a darkly comic writer whose plots often shelve off into the surreal. She is very much a theatrical writer, perhaps a result of her early career as an actress in a Liverpool repertory company. She evokes that world in *An Awfully Big Adventure*. I especially relished *The Bottle Factory Outing*, *Sweet William*, and *Injury Time*, a soccer term but here used quite literally. Here's its opening paragraph.

> During the partners' lunch, old Gifford talked indistinctly about the Rawlinson account: something to do with the new man on the board not having a first-class brain – he didn't come up to scratch. From time to time Gifford's shoulder dipped below the level of the tablecloth; he seemed to have dropped something. Halters, from the Overseas department, told a story involving a doctor and a woman patient who heard pop music whenever her husband made love to her. Edward Freeman, who was seated opposite, missed the punch line. The fellow appeared to be muttering, or perhaps his own hearing was at fault. Alarmed by this new defect – lately he had been forced to wear spectacles when attempting the crossword – he stuck his finger in his ear and waggled it vigorously back and forth. Halters, flourishing his fork in the air, was saying quite clearly that the engine of his car needed tuning. Edward allowed Mrs. Chalmers to serve him with a second helping of lamb; he wasn't hungry but he contributed twenty pounds a month toward the cost of the office lunches and was damned if he was letting a penny of it go to waste. Binny said it was killing him, all that meat stewed in wine and all those puddings consumed every day of the week. 'Men of your age,' she constantly warned him, 'are at risk. You'll have a heart attack.'

* * *

I first became aware of Samuel Beckett while I was in my last year of high school. I was listening to the BBC Third Programme and heard the first broadcast of *All That Fall.* That was in 1956. In 1957 I heard Patrick Magee on the BBC in *From an Abandoned Work.* I became a passionate convert. In 1958, hitchhiking home from Pamplona, I bought in Paris Beckett's *Molloy* (Maurice Girodias' Olympia Press *of course*) and Henry Miller's *Tropics.* I was dropped off in London and I remember sitting on the steps of the National Gallery oblivious to pigeons and passers-by, lost in the language of *Molloy.*

Beckett in the plays and the later prose work is inventing a new kind of prose. He is very much *not* writing "prose poetry," as I have seen *Worstward Ho* (1983) described. Nearly everything he wrote becomes more meaningful and pleasurable if read aloud, if the reader so far as possible ignores the "battle horse" and lets the cadences of the sentences work their magic.

Beckett thought of prose as music. In James Knowlson's biography of Beckett *Damned to Fame* he writes of actress Siân Phillips rehearsing the play *Eh Joe.* She said of Beckett: "It was explained to me that every punctuation mark had a precise value and I began metronoming my way through the text, reading appallingly but gradually remembering that a full stop is not a colon is not a hyphen is not an exclamation mark is not a semi colon. We worked like machines, beating time with our fingers and, after some hours, the relentless rhythm and the beautiful, but equally relentless, blue eyes were making me feel ill . . ."

Actress Billie Whitelaw on rehearsing the play *Not I.* "'For instance, there is no time to breathe.' She therefore went into training, practising verbal sprints and time trials (sometimes using the time clock [like those] at athletic meetings on television) until she could build up the required speed, enabling herself to cram so many words into such a brief time span. 'I've been practicing saying words at a tenth of a second . . . No one can possibly follow the text at that speed but Beckett insists that I speak it precisely. It's like music, a piece of Schoenberg in his head.'"

To hear Beckett's music there is no better instruction than to listen to the Irish actor Jack MacGowan. In 1966 MacGowan recorded a selection of extracts from Beckett's works. The record, *MacGowan Speaking Beckett,* was made for Claddagh Records in Dublin.

James Knowlson writes: "Coached in his detailed phrasing and rhythms by Beckett, MacGowan was in splendid form and produced an exceptionally fine recording." Pale praise. The recording is superb, possibly the finest theatrical rendition I have ever heard, the Irish brogue revealing rhymes and comedy not obvious in conventional spoken English.

Whenever Simone Vauthier, the University of Strasbourg-based critic, came to stay we played MacGowan for her; she had a delight for *From an Abandoned Work* and for the "sucking stones" set piece. She said more than once that the recording had changed the way she came at literature, high praise for a critic so intelligent.

When Myrna and I went to Dublin a few years ago I sought out Claddagh Records and bought eight or nine copies of the tape version to give to my younger writer friends I was publishing at the Porcupine's Quill. To this day Steven Heighton does a mean MacGowan imitation.

Here is the opening music of *From an Abandoned Work.*

> Up bright and early that day, I was young then, feeling awful, and out, mother hanging out of the window in her nightdress weeping and waving. Nice fresh morning, bright too early as so often. Feeling really awful, very violent. The sky would soon darken and rain fall and go on falling, all day, till evening. Then blue and sun again a second, then night. Feeling all this, how violent and the kind of day, I stopped and turned. So back with bowed head on the look out for a snail, slug or worm. Great love in my heart too for all things still and rooted, bushes, boulders and the like, too numerous to mention, even the flowers of the field, not for the world when in my right senses would I ever touch one, to pluck it. Whereas a bird now, or a butterfly, fluttering about and getting in my way, all moving things, getting in my path, a slug now, getting under my feet, no, no mercy. Not that I'd go out of my way to get at them, no, at a distance often they seemed still, then a moment later they were upon me. Birds with my piercing sight I have seen flying so high, so far, that they seemed at rest, then the next minute they were all about me, crows have done this. Ducks are perhaps the worst, to be suddenly stamping and stumbling in the midst of ducks, or hens, any class of poultry, few things are worse. Nor will I go out of my way to avoid such things, when avoidable, no, I simply will not go out of my way, though I have never in my life been on my way anywhere, but simply on my way.

Intellect will not deliver this to you.
Music will.

* * *

There are so many felicities in these cited passages, so many instances of verbal glory. To think that Katherine Mansfield in a letter to an old friend, in a *letter*, could toss away "very still silvery sea with gulls moving on the waves like the lights in a pearl." Or those "old hands holding up satiny baskets" – woven osiers polished by ages of handling to a soft sheen.

I have always enjoyed the comedy of Waugh's rendition of Dr. Fagan's oratorical style – "wind instruments of plated silver" – the comic power of "plated" – and the sweeping list of bad Welsh influences on English history – the equation of Lloyd George with the dissolution of the monasteries – what a delightful exhibition of pseudo-scholarly bigotry. Part of the fun is the rationality of tone in which it is delivered.

The social complexities and comedy that hover around the word "unseemly" in Dr. Fagan's remark about King Edward II have always given pleasure – "a perverse life, Pennyfeather, and an unseemly death" – this said of a man who died in the dungeons of Berkley Castle, murdered, by way of comment on his sexual proclivities, by the insertion of a red hot poker up his rectum.

I remember seeing Marlowe's *Edward II* staged when I was a boy. The murder took place off-stage but one could see through a doorway part of the interior of a room. The stage was in gloom. Giant shadows loomed inside the room, red light flickered from the imagined brazier, the screaming, smoke rising. I nearly vomited.

Marlowe would have derived all this grisly detail from Raphael Holinshed's *Chronicles* (1577). He and Shakespeare are thought to have used the 1587 revised edition. Holinshed wrote: ". . . with heavie feather beddes (or a table as some write) being cast upon him, they kept him downe, and withall put into his fundament an horne, and through the same they thrust up into his bodie a hote spitee . . . the which passing up into his intrayles, and being rolled to and fro, burnt the same, but so as no appearance of any wounde or hurt outwardly might bee once perceyved."

Unseemly!

When I was a beginning teacher at a secondary modern school in Bristol I once took the fifth form School Leavers class on a daylong history field trip to Berkley Castle. It was a day that shortened my life. Two girls claimed to have had their knickers pulled down in the dark of the dungeons and a boy with ginger hair got his entire arm stuck down the barrel of a cannon. This eventually involved an ambulance, a police car, a humiliating phone call from the psychotic Mr. Stine, Headmaster of Bluebell Secondary Modern, the saga resolved some two hours later by one of the castle's custodians with a bucket of hot water and a box of Persil soapflakes.

I love the *pacing* of the final line of the Sylvia Townsend Warner's extract and admire the resolute non-explanation of Professor Abernethy's use of an egg cup in the making of tea.

John Banville's Christmas pudding is positively studded with verbal sixpenny pieces. Consider "manhandled," and "zinc-white cerements." "Zinc-white" catches almost magically the colour El Greco uses. And as for "ascending in a transport of erotic agony amid alleluias and lip-farts" and the pure perfection of the rising rhythm of the entire last sentence until it lands triumphantly "into just such a patch of pellucid bleu céleste" . . . the mastery leaves me almost speechless.

Firbank's comedy irritates some readers who find it "baroque;" I think what they tend to mean by this is that they are irritated or made uncomfortable by Firbank's homosexual sensibility. My suggestion is that Firbank, like Beckett, is one of those writers to whose work the reader must simply surrender. Firbank is not immediately easy but treasures await. The puppy licking the "splendid uncertainty" of the Duquesa's chin. Now there's a phrase to think about. Madame La Urench "gurgling" to the puppy's sire: "No, my naughty Blessing; no, not now! . . . By and by, a *bone*."

There are possible ambiguities in what Madame La Urench *means* when talking to Blessing whose sex, two lines later, is "apparent." But whatever might be being implied, the gurgling, doting, maternal, teasing Madame La Urench is marvellously suggested in "By and by, a *bone*." I've often thought that speech is the fastest way to conjure *appearance*.

The opening paragraph of Beryl Bainbridge's *Injury Time* isn't marked by any such verbal exuberance but it is a brilliant example of oblique exposition and foreshadowing, a diving in *in medias res* involving the reader by making him do the work. So *very* much more interesting than being told. The influence of film is obvious.

* * *

What, then, have all these extracts in common? Not really very much. Except that each represents a masterly use of the English language exactly tailored to the writer's ends. Each uses English in a heightened and charged way. (That is true, too, of Raymond Carver.) If there *is* one thing all the extracts have in common it is a focus on language, on words, on words deployed into rhetorical structures. The concern of all these writers is aesthetic.

Aesthetic concerns have dominated our efforts at the Porcupine's Quill for all my years of association with the press. I am well aware, of course, of all the arguments that are marshalled against an aesthetic approach to art of all kinds, all of which boil down to the charge that aesthetic judgements are simply subjective opinion. I would concede immediately that this is so – rather obviously so – but I still have more faith in connoisseurship than I do in theory. Not for me logic-chopping in a littered classroom with orange plastic chairs but, rather, intense concentration in the presence of the thing. If I wished to try and buy a painting of the Italian Quattrocento, I'd be a fool not to turn for advice to the earned authority of a Bernard Berenson, a John Pope-Hennessy, or a Sir Kenneth Clark.

It is always instructive to listen to artists talking about art. Writers judging other writers are connoisseurs; a lifetime in the craft has taught them what to look for, what to value. How foolish we'd be not to listen to what engages them.

Here is Martin Amis in an essay entitled "The American Eagle" writing on Saul Bellow's *The Adventures of Augie March*.

> Attentive readers will, I hope, have noticed that this is an extraordinarily *written* novel. There are mannerisms or tics in the way words squirm up against each other. The compounds – 'worry-wounded,' 'lair-hidden,' 'bloody-minded,' 'pimple-insolence,' 'gum-chew innocence' – which in Bellow's heavily sprung rhythms, sometimes career into train-wreck compression: Trafton's gym with its 'liniment-groggy, flickety-rope-time, tin-locker-clashing, loop-darkened rooms.' There are the verb couplings: trams 'lumbered and clanged,' billiard balls

'kissing and bounding,' traffic 'dived and quivered,' cars 'snoring and trembling,' or 'fluddering and shimmering.' It is a style that loves and embraces awkwardness, spurning elegance as a false lead, words tumbling and rattling together in the order *they* choose: 'glittering his teeth and hungry,' 'try out what of human you can live with,' 'the long impulse from well out in the ocean bobs the rotten oranges,' 'a flatfooted, in gym shoes, pug-nosed old woman,' '[he] sobbed in the brakes of, he thought, most solitude,' 'I hoped there'd something show on the horizon,' 'I could not find myself in love without it should have peculiarity,' 'hypocritic,' 'honestest,' 'ancientest,' 'his brittle neck would be broke,' 'waked-up despair,' 'loud-played music.' Why is 'loud-played music,' in a dimestore so much better than 'loud'? Because it suggests wilfulness, vulgarity and youth, whereas 'loud' is just *loud*. *Augie March* isn't written in English; its job is to make you feel how beautiful *American* is, with its jazzy verbs: 'it sent my blood happy,' 'to close a deal,' 'to run [a nickel] into a fortune,' 'we were making twelve knots,' 'cover the house' (get around it), 'beat a check' (leave without paying it), 'to make time with Mimi' (seduce), 'This is where I shake you, Augie' (reject). Never mind the p's and q's of fine prose. Whatever works . . .

Style, of course, is not something grappled onto regular prose; it is intrinsic to perception. We are fond of separating style and content (for the purposes of analysis, and so on), but they aren't separable: they come from the same place. And style is morality. Style judges.

* * *

I would like to quote again the words of Maurice Denis.

> Remember that a picture, before being a battle horse or a nude, or some anecdote – is essentially a flat surface covered with colours assembled in a certain order.

It is, of course, always dangerous to compare painting and writing because words *do* have meanings whereas paint does not but comparisons can sometimes be suggestive and fruitful. To circle back to John Banville's *The Untouchable*; there is a passage where the Sir Anthony Blunt figure, Victor Maskell, is thinking again about Poussin's *Et in Arcadia Ego* and I'm wildly tempted to say – though I won't quite topple over the edge – that the way the fictional Victor Maskell feels about painting is much the way I feel about prose. Though I am not *so* far down that formalist road that I cannot laugh at the famous anecdote about that endearingly eccentric critic Roger Fry escorting a lecture tour through the National Gallery in London. Stopping in front of a triptych by Andrea Orcagna, Fry started to explicate. The painting portrays God the Father, in all His awesome power, terrible of aspect, pointing to His sacrificed Son. "And now," said Fry, incidentals dealt with, "we must turn our attention to the dominant central mass."

John Banville, then. Or, rather, Victor Maskell.

> How I used to sneer at those critics – the Marxists especially, I am afraid – who spent their energies searching for the meaning of his work, for those occult formulas upon which he was supposed to have built his forms. The fact is, of course, there is no meaning. Significance, yes; affects; authority; mystery – magic; if you wish – but no meaning. The figures in the *Arcadia* are not pointing to some fatuous parable about mortality and the soul and salvation; they simply *are*. Their meaning is that they are there. This is a fundamental fact of artistic creation, the putting in place of something where otherwise there would be nothing.

A WRITER'S WRITER

On the ground floor of Libya's National Museum in Tripoli in an area devoted to Neolithic artifacts – scrapers, arrow heads, some lumpy pots – sits a pastel green Volkswagen.

I enquired of the custodian.

"It belonged," he said, "to our dear brother."

"Oh," I said, "and who's your –"

"The Great Leader and Dear Brother," continued the custodian, "is the way Colonel Gaddafi prefers to be described."

"Ah, right. Yes. Well, thank you."

"Not 'President,'" said the custodian, making his chest pompous.

He then exhaled.

"No, not 'President' but 'Dear Brother.' The car was his, owned by him, his own personal driving car driven by him at the time of the decline of King Idris."

"Decline?"

The custodian wiggled his fingers in an equivocal gesture.

March and April of 2005 and Myrna and I were on another Swan Hellenic cruise, this time in North Africa visiting Roman Empire sites. We began in Jordan visiting the city of Petra, home of the ancient Nabateans who traded in spices, sending their caravans of as many as fifteen hundred camels at a time down into Yemen. The walk through the Siq, the narrow cleft through the rock wall, is about a mile and a half of sheer enchantment and then you debouch into an enlarging landscape to face the tomb carved from the red rock, the tomb known as The Treasury, the first in the long façade of carved tombs which leads down to the Romanized city.

After Jordan, we crossed into Egypt and drove to St. Catherine's Monastery in the Sinai Desert. The monastery supposedly enshrines the Burning Bush from which "the angel of the Lord" spoke to Moses (Exodus 3:2). The desert has an implacable beauty but I can never get enthused about Greek Orthodox churches. With their hanging lamps, chandeliers, brass chains, candles, votive offerings, dubious icons, notices forbidding photography and bare shoulders, fuming thuribles, all beneath murky frescos of martyrdoms and presiding ceilings of Christ Pantocrator, they always put me in mind of jumbled Bargain Barns.

After the Sinai we joined a convoy through the Suez Canal to Port Said and later Cairo and the pyramids at Giza. The buses carried gunmen on board and were guarded in front and behind by trucks of very young soldiers who handled their battered weaponry with alarming nonchalance. The day after we left Cairo a suicide bomber killed three tourists and wounded eighteen.

In Benghazi we went to the British War Cemetery and walked for a couple of hours reading the gravestones of boys nineteen and twenty killed mainly in the Desert War. Reading the names and ages, ranks and regiments – and occasional markers chiselled: Known Unto God – left us in a mood of sombre gratitude.

We visited the Roman sites of Tukra and Tulmaytha. Tulmaytha was dotted everywhere with fresh molehills and I remembered my brother's habit of always spreading the earth because moles sometimes pushed up coins, Roman denarii and Anglo-Saxon Thrymsas and Sceattas. I spread one of the fresh mounds and found two potsherds, one black ribbed ware, probably Greek, and a piece of red Roman pot. They're sitting now on my desk, fragments shored against my ruin.

Leptis Magna in Libya, a whole Roman city preserved, was an overwhelming experience. One enters the city through the vast triumphal arch of the Emperor Septimus Severus. Leptis was his birthplace. A forum with adjacent temples, a porticoed market with two circular market halls, streets and houses, a completely intact theatre which looks out onto the sea. The Hadrianic Baths boasted a marble-clad lavatory, a 20-some holer with running water in channels beneath the holes. It was most ingenious, even handsome, but I was not converted to the idea of communal bowel movements. For some irreverent reason, I imagined Sid James, his toga hoicked up, carrying on lavatorial boorishness with a very prim Kenneth Williams.

We also went to El Djem to see the amphitheatre. It was built in AD 230 and seated 30,000 spectators. I went down underneath the ring to look at the rooms and cages where the gladiators and wild animals were kept; one could imagine the smell and almost hear the roar of the crowd.

In Tunis we went to the national museum, the Bardo Museum, to see the Roman mosaics. The museum is housed in an eighteenth century palace built by the Ottoman Turks to echo the Alhambra. The rooms are high and intricate, dancing with light and ornate colour. The palace was the former home of the ruler, the Bey of Tunis.

This Turkish title "Bey" reminded me of one of John Newlove's favourite anecdotes. John was in the habit of copying onto index cards admired poems, anecdotes, interesting quotations, snippets of detail from the history books that were his constant reading. We had been working together before his stroke on a commonplace book drawing on index cards going back over a quarter of a century. I had intended publishing this book with the Porcupine's Quill. I thought that not only would the entries be interesting in themselves but would illustrate the refined vagaries of John's mind. His stroke ended the project as it was a job so intimate I could not do it for him.

The Bey of Tunis, then, and John Newlove.

The Prince Regent, later George IV, was being pressured in 1794 to marry a German princess and produce an heir to the throne. He agreed to marry Caroline, Princess of Brunswick-Wölfenbutell. Lord Malmesbury was sent to Brunswick to fetch the bride. *The Wordsworth Book of the Kings and Queens of Britain* describes her thus: "She was wildly eccentric. She was coarse, exhibitionist, flamboyant, dirty and highly sexed. She scarcely ever changed her linen and never washed. The Prince was overcome when he met her. To Malmesbury he said: "I am not well, fetch me a glass of brandy." The marriage took place on 8 April 1795. The Prince was drugged with drink; she behaved immodestly; the marriage was consummated that night; a daughter, Charlotte, was born precisely nine months after. It was the only occasion."

The Prince still hankered after Mrs. Fitzherbert and she soon returned to his bed. Princess Caroline portrayed herself as a wronged woman. To get rid of her, attempts were made to convict her of adultery. She left England and travelled widely for years. She visited the Bey of Tunis. And here I can see the gleam of amusement in John's eyes as he works up to the punch line.

Asked how did the Princess Caroline in Tunisia, one of the British politicians, eager to further smear her reputation, replied:

"She is as happy as the Bey is long."

We flew home from Valetta in Malta.

My overwhelming impression of Jordan, Egypt, and Libya was of plastic bags. Garbage is strewn everywhere and the trees and bushes are festooned with wind-blown plastic. Even deep in the Sinai the few acacia trees – source of gum arabic – flutter with plastic tatters. The countryside is despoiled by abandoned cars, stoves, refrigerators, broken tile, building waste. Domestic rubbish litters every field. I assume from this that there is little sense of public, community space. It is perhaps petty to react more to plastic than to pyramids but Samuel Beckett's phrase "the turd world" often came to mind.

We flew home from wild poppies blowing and mimosa everywhere in bloom to Ottawa's brown twigs and to a rush of work with the Porcupine's Quill and the fast burgeoning Biblioasis.

For the Porcupine's Quill I was reading – I would not dare use the word "editing" – W.J. Keith's updated *Canadian Literature in English* and David Helwig's autobiography *The Names of Things*. I was also working on the Clark Blaise special issue of *Canadian Notes & Queries* and arranging another special issue to follow on the poetry of Eric Ormsby; Amanda Jernigan, a very sound, conscientious, and imaginative young critic and poet, accepted the guest editorship.

Some years back I had told Tim Inkster that I intended resigning from the Porcupine's Quill in 2008 as I would then be seventy and I would have been editing for him for twenty years. I felt that the Porcupine's Quill had become fully what I'd intended and I also felt that at seventy I was probably too old to be on top of the game. Perhaps there were young writers out there I was getting too hidebound to hear?

But then Daniel Wells hove into view and I felt energized by him and again romantically attracted to the idea of helping to shape another publishing house. Years seemed to fall away. Seventy seemed suddenly younger.

For Biblioasis I was editing Michèle Adams' first book, a story collection called *Bright Objects of Desire*; I'd read a story of hers in *Event* magazine and written to her. I was also editing a novel by Mike Barnes entitled *Catalogue Raisonné*, a brisk and involving look at lives in the unknown world of Canadian art. David Helwig sent us a lovely new novel entitled *Saltsea*. Negotiations had been continuing between Dan and Tim Inkster about the purchase of *Canadian Notes & Queries* and the sale was now agreed, Dan to take over after Amanda Jernigan's Eric Ormsby issue.

I was busy discussing books for Biblioasis with Clark Blaise, Leon Rooke, Jeet Heer, Terry Rigelhof, Ray Smith, and Patricia Robertson. Dan and I decided that we'd edit an annual anthology of Canadian short fiction to be entitled *Ampersand*. Eric Ormsby, now living in England, agreed to become the Biblioasis poetry editor.

In addition to all this ferment I was reading manuscripts, writing fiction and criticism, and keeping up daily with correspondence. I had been writing regularly to Norman Levine because I knew that he was lonely and, in a literary sense, rather isolated. Letters were important to him though mine were often pedestrian.

His replies to my letters grew briefer and briefer, the handwriting on some of them shaky and childlike. And then a letter arrived saying that he had had a heart attack, that his doctor had him on a regimen of pills to reduce high blood pressure, that he was forbidden to walk uphill from his rooms to the post office.

Some time after this a truly alarming letter arrived. He claimed that a woman had phoned him – he thought from Ottawa – to inform him that his Old Age Security Pension had been cancelled. It was usually paid into his bank account in Toronto but the latest statement did not record the deposit. He wrote, "Someone in Canada's been reading *Canada Made Me*."

I asked him if the woman had identified herself. He said she had not and that he was so shocked he hadn't asked and she had suddenly hung up. I showed this to Myrna who thought this was all of Norman's invention, paranoia, apparently, being one of the first signs of Alzheimer's.

I went to talk to the people at the offices of Human Resources but they said they could not give me any information as it would violate Norman's privacy rights; I would need a dated letter from him in handwriting authorizing me to act on his behalf. I went home and phoned him, dictating a letter for him to copy. I also insisted that he phone his bank manager in Toronto to check on his account. The next day he phoned back to say that the pension *had* been paid into his account. There had been a mistake of some sort. He didn't quite understand what the man had said. It had happened in the back.

Not long after this I received a letter from the secretary of the Canadian Writers' Foundation. Years earlier I had secured from the Foundation a monthly pension for Norman. The Foundation assists writers living in straitened circumstances. Norman certainly qualified; he had been reduced to reading in his flat with an overcoat on because he could not afford to switch on the electric fire, information I'd gleaned from his daughter Rachel in St. Ives. The Foundation's accountant now needed Norman's Social Insurance Number and Norman had sent them a seven-digit number which he insisted was correct. SIN numbers are all nine digits. I phoned and grilled him on the matter. He became quite obstinate saying that the seven-digit number had always sufficed in the past. I had to write him a stern letter warning him that the Foundation had to comply with federal law and that if he didn't co-operate the pension might be withdrawn. I urged him to search for official-looking papers and send me any numbers he found. I felt mildly ashamed of this bullying. Scarcely a month later his sister Irene phoned to tell me he had died.

The *Ottawa Citizen,* in continuing disparagement, headlined an obituary piece*:*

"Death ends short-story writer Norman Levine's struggle for recognition."

Irene sat shiva for him which would have caused him embarrassment.

I organized obituaries in the *Citizen*, the *Globe and Mail* and the *Toronto Star*. Norman's oldest daughter, Cassie Flint, phoned from Barnard Castle asking me to write a piece myself. What follows appeared in *The Independent* (UK) on June 20, 2005.

Norman Levine
Author of *Canada Made Me*

Norman Albert Levine, writer: born Rakow, Poland 22 October 1923; married 1951 Margaret Payne (died 1978; three daughters), 1983 Anne Sarginson (marriage dissolved); died Darlington 14 June 2005.

In the late Forties, after having served as a pilot and bomb-aimer with the Royal Canadian Air Force, flying Lancasters out of Leeming, North Yorkshire, the writer Norman Levine decided to leave Canada's cultural desert and return to an England he had come to admire.

What had attracted him, he wrote, was "seeing paintings, hearing concerts, reading new books and *New Writing*. And especially, seeing how the English lived and behaved in wartime." In those early days he was introduced in a Thames-side pub to the poet George Barker, who said to him: "Sorry, chum, nothing personal. But coming from Canada, you haven't got a chance."

Levine spent many years of his life in St. Ives, Cornwall, proving Barker profoundly wrong. Like all modernists, he spent his life forging and honing a signature style. His was fragmentary and imagistic, prose stripped to the bone, conventional expectations of rhythm denied, forcing the reader into a new, intimate and uneasy relationship with the word on the page. His most important story collections were *Champagne Barn* (1984), *Something Happened Here*(1991), *By a Frozen River* (2000) and *The Ability to Forget* (2003).

Canada never recognized Levine's amazing talent and achievement. The country's cultural nationalists have never forgiven Levine for his 1958 autobiographical travel book *Canada Made Me*. The book closed with the words,

> I wondered why I felt so bitter about Canada. It was foolish to believe that you can take the throw-outs, the rejects, the human kickabouts from Europe and tell them: Here is your second chance. Here you can start a new life. But no one ever mentioned the price you had to pay, and how much of yourself you have to betray.

Written at the beginning of a boosterish period, this rather sour look at Canada's underbelly closed for Levine the possibility of Canadian publication. It was to be 17 years before another Levine title appeared in Canada.

Levine was always by temperament and choice an outsider. As a Jew, as a resident alien, as an immigrant, he was always on the margins, observing with an unsentimental eye. His stories usually have an elegiac quality and typically explore loss, impermanence, and the fragility of human hopes. He wrote in the story "Soap Opera": ". . . whenever I go to a new place and walk around to get to know it, I inevitably end up in a cemetery."

The son of an impoverished fruit-pedlar who plied his trade with a horse and cart, Levine at 18 volunteered for officer training and was sent on a course to take what he used to call "gentleman lessons." These he duly learned, but he belonged to no class or cause. If he believed in anything, it might have been Chekhov.

If Levine was ignored in Canada, his reputation in England and Europe was high. *The Times Literary Supplement* described his work as "masterly." *The Times* talked of his "timeless elegance . . ." and *Encounter* wrote: "Norman Levine is one of the most outstanding short-story writers working in English today." His German translator was the Nobel laureate Heinrich Böll and in recent years Levine's work has been translated in Holland, Switzerland, and France.

Younger writers in Canada are slowly discovering his work and some have been influenced by his stylistic experiments. Michael Winter, a young writer directly influenced by Levine, said of him:

"His style is not one that appeals to a lot of people, but a lot of writers marvel at his talent . . . His economy of so little saying so much – when you try to write like that, you realise how hard it is to capture things accurately and truthfully with very few words. He was a writer's writer."

Norman Levine was married twice, and the companion of his later years was Moira Dale.

CONTINUO

Sailing out of Istanbul and through the Bosphorus cradling in a chunky square glass a hefty measure of Laphroig. Past Scutari and Florence Nightingale's Old Barrack hospital. On the top deck of *Minerva II* in the Orpheus bar as she glided past ruined Byzantine walls, Turkish fortifications, Genoese-built towers and battlements, heading into the Black Sea for Sinop and Trebizond in Turkey. September and October of 2005, Myrna and I on another Swan Hellenic cruise. Small flocks of shearwaters skimming the waves, the spirits of sailors drowned.

I was still rigid with tension, my neck creaking and crackling every time I turned my head. My mind was churning with thoughts, anxieties, memories of sights seen when I wished it empty, calm. I was concerned about the future of the Porcupine's Quill, worried about its writers, depressed by the decline in readership, anxious, too, about Biblioasis though its list for 2006 was shaping nicely. Michèle Adams, Mike Barnes, Patricia Young, David Helwig, Patricia Robertson, Leon Rooke, Eric Ormsby . . . a glittering list but was Dan Wells going to be able to withstand the constant pressure? The rebuffs, the defeats, the indifference? Small fishing boats everywhere, a police launch surging a cream wake around them stopping at each boat with a slop.

Professor W.J. Keith and yurts were in my mind and black and gilt Ottoman land grants, the Arabic calligraphy like wind-bent fields of wheat. Bill had told me he was going birdwatching in China and had to live in a yurt. The day before I'd actually seen one in Istanbul's ethnographic museum, three mannikins inside the yurt, one spinning, one braising gobbets of lamb, one offering to the other two a pitcher of – what would it be? – koumiss. No Laphroig in yurts. Though equally as likely Diet Coke.

Recalled with great concentration the Seljuq metal work in that museum; I wanted to set it in my mind. Shapes new to me. The little signature Seljuq birds sitting atop the handles of jugs and ewers. Twitchers. Why were birdwatchers called "twitchers"? Sitting on the mantelpiece in our living room a Seljuq bronze jug, its handle broken from the body, a body of swelling erotic beauty, described by the dealer caressingly as "zooiform." A welding task for a silversmith the next time I was in Montreal. So many tasks, the weight of manuscripts unread, the weight of judgements not rendered, the weight of help selfishly withheld.

The Laphroig reminded me of Terry Griggs – Laphroig her favourite tipple – remembering a happy lunch with her in Alcalá de Henares, hunks of bread on the paper table cloth, Terry picking out offending meat from her supposedly vegetarian dish, shreds of the sort of meat described in Chinese menus as "assorted," me putting away *lomo de cerdo*, all of us quaffing *Rioja Alta reservas*. Thinking, too, about a menacing story of hers in production with Biblioasis. A story called *Bigmouth*. Wondering as I've always wondered why her fragrantly nutty mind and sparkling prose hasn't brought her a fanatic following. My mind churning on and on ceaselessly without peace, sights seen I was finding hard to digest, The Blue Mosque, the Aghia Sophia, the Spice Market at the end of the Galata Bridge.

I was saddened and made weary by the impasse with the McGill Rare Book Room. I had been asked by Frances Groen, the Trenholme Director of Libraries, on the occasion of delivering the Hugh MacLennan Memorial Lecture "Something Happened Here" to keep on collecting books for future sale to McGill and to maintain the Porcupine's Quill archives but this was an informal, verbal agreement. Frances Groen had then retired. I received from her successor, Janine Schmidt, a legalistic letter disclaiming any responsibility on McGill's part and informing me that McGill had no interest in acquiring the remaining archives of the Porcupine's Quill. And equally no interest in the books I'd carefully acquired.

Janine Schmidt's interests seemed to lie in "information technology" and "e-journals." She had made reference in an internet article to living in the "CyberAge." She seemed to fear the acid in paper. She actually used the words "Cybrary" and "Cybrarian." She had arrived in Canada from Australia.

I was wearied by her stance, saddened, too, by the loss to Canada, and by my squandered time. Her stance meant that the story collection stopped dead. The annual anthologies stopped. The press collections of Oberon and the Porcupine's Quill stopped. The magazine-runs stopped. The conversation of the vast correspondence was cut off in mid-sentence. Her stance meant that a significant part of Canadian literary history, conservation work that had taken me thirty years, sat now in McGill inert and incomplete while rare books and unique archives were piled in my study on the dusty floor.

She was known in the household as "The Australian E-Thing at McGill."

I was driven by her slipperiness, deliberate obtuseness, and intransigence to write her a letter which Myrna considered mildly intemperate. Its concluding sentences read: "I find corresponding with you rather like having conversations at the Mad Hatter's Tea Party. Conversations with a kangaroo would be more fruitful."

At the end of the Hugh MacLennan Memorial Lecture I had lamented the loss to Canada of the manuscript of *Canada Made Me* but had suggested that McGill would be making amends by accepting into the Rare Book Room the next earliest state of the book, the Advance Proof.

The proof of *Canada Made Me*, almost certainly the only copy in existence, a book of national significance, was, almost inevitably, among those scorned by Janine Schmidt.

"O God!" as Samuel Palmer wrote, "O Montreal!"

I was also mildly saddened by the fate of my memoir of the literary life *An Aesthetic Underground*. It had achieved a lifetime (i.e. two year) sale of 579 copies before being remaindered at Book City in Toronto for $6.99. But equally I was thinking of Eric Ormsby's poetry collection *For a Modest God* – so *extravagantly* talented – being remaindered by an outfit called *Liquidation World*. His indignation!

Ah, well . . .

Stiffen the sinews, laddie, summon up the blood.

Thinking of the continuing battle, the drawing to a close of things, the looming possibility of defeat, I found myself thinking too of the Prologue and the Chorus in *Henry V*. The parts were spoken in the Elizabethan period by an actor wearing simply a long black velvet cloak. How exactly right! The self cloaked, effaced, the epic language painting the empty stage.

Now entertain conjecture of a time
When creeping murmur and the poring dark
Fills the wide vessel of the universe.
From camp to camp through the foul womb of night
The hum of either army stilly sounds,

That the fix'd sentinels almost receive
The secret whispers of each other's watch:
Fire answers fire, and through their paly flames
Each battle sees the other's umbered face;
Steed threatens steed, in high and boastful neighs
Piercing the night's dull ear; and from the tents
The armourers, accomplishing the knights,
With busy hammers closing rivets up,
Give dreadful note of preparation . . .

Agincourt again.

I had year after year tried to rally and reassure, inspire, praise, sustain, but I was finding it increasingly draining now trying to work that magic of Harry in the night.

Along with this sadness for an unwanted culture there was an underlying continual rumble of thought about writing. Constantly in my mind of late a remark Constance Rooke made years ago about my writing, that the central concern of all my work was entropy. I could feel all the time the tensions of a strong emotional current driving me towards shapes I could only dimly discern.

Minerva II started to shudder as she hit the Black Sea's opposing currents.

Ahead lay fable and history.

Ahead lay Trebizond.

* * *

Trebizond!

In Turkish, more muddily, Trabzon.

The name seems to have slipped out of history. Many readers will perhaps only know it from the title of Rose Macaulay's 1956 novel *The Towers of Trebizond*, a novel concerning the efforts of Mrs. ffoulkes-Corbett, her niece Laurie, and the Rev. the Hon. Hugh Chantry-Pigg to bring High Anglicanism to the Turkish Muslim population of the Black Sea. The writing is often funny but is perhaps too much marked by the "utterly blushmaking" style of her youth, intelligent froth but froth undeniable. The book's sprightly opening sentence reads:

"'Take my camel, dear,' said my aunt Dot, as she climbed down from this animal on her return from High Mass."

But Trebizond is ancient indeed. Trapezous was founded in the 7th century BC as a colony of the nearby city of Sinope, a colony, in turn, founded by Greeks from Miletus, a city-state in Ionian Greece. The city prospered because of the great caravan route south to Tabriz and the Persian Gulf.

Much fought over and under the sway of an array of differing rulers, Trebizond eventually became the capital of the Kings of Pontus most of whom bore the name Mithridates. The most famous was Mithridates VI (Eupator) 120 to 63 BC, "the Great." He was eventually defeated by Pompey and Trebizon and its lands became a province of Rome.

In 1204 Trebizond was cut off from the Byzantine world of which it had been part and the city became the centre of a Christian Empire founded by Alexius Comnenus. The dynasty of the Grand Comneni lasted until 1461 and throve on the overland trade bringing Chinese silk, Ceylonese pearls, Tibetan rhubarb and East Indian pepper to the leading markets of Italy.

In 1461, eight years after the fall of Constantinople, Mohammed II took Trebizond and the 14th century church of St. Eugenius, patron saint of Trebizond, became the Yeni Cuma Cami (New Friday Mosque).

Greek merchants and residents hung on until the end of the 19th century but in 1922 Ataturk completed Mohammed II's work and deported 164, 000 of the surviving Greeks to Greece, a land which their ancestors had not seen for over 2,500 years.

Trebizond was being written about long before Dame Rose Macaulay's foray in the 1950s. Trebizond is mentioned in Xenophon's *Anabasis Kyrou* (The Expedition of Cyrus) and as *Minerva II* sailed towards port it was this robust, even heroic, story that was filling me with that irreplaceable pleasure of being close to, part of, an ancient past.

Xenophon's book has been variously titled in translation; some call it *The Persian Expedition*, others *The March Up-Country*. The book is less taught now than formerly so I'll give a much curtailed account.

In 401 BC Cyrus the Younger (c. 430-401 BC), the younger son of Cyrus the Elder, founder of the Persian Empire, held office under his brother Artaxerxes, the Great King, as a military governor in Asia Minor. Cyrus decided to depose his brother and secretly gathered an army of 10, 000 Greek mercenaries. Cyrus marched from Ionian Greece in Asia Minor. The two armies met in Persia and joined battle at Cunaxa. Cyrus was killed and chaos set in. The Greeks regrouped and began the long march north towards the Euxine (Black) Sea.

Xenophon's army was made up of heavily armed hoplites in the centre, with more lightly armed peltasts on the flanks and skirmishing forward. A woefully small squadron of cavalry brought up the rear. The march north to the Euxine Sea was some 1,500 kilometres through unknown and hostile territory. They pillaged as they went, living off the land. When under attack, they marched in a hollow square, women, slaves, and baggage animals in the centre.

To understand the psychological hardships of this epic march, we must remember that it was said of the ancient Greeks that no Greek lived more than 40 or 50 miles from the sea. The seas were their roads. Here they were in unknown countries, crossing desert sands, battling through mountain ranges, fighting constantly, week after week not knowing where they were nor if they would ever again see their homeland. It was in the Pontic Alps, breaking through a mountain pass that they glimpsed the water below them at distant Trebizond. Here is Rex Warner's rendering of that lovely passage.

> They came to the mountain on the fifth day, the name of the mountain being Thekes. When the men in front reached the summit and caught sight of the sea there was great shouting. Xenophon and the rear guard heard it and thought that there were some more enemies attacking in the front, since there were natives of the country they had ravaged following them up behind, and the rearguard had killed some of them and made prisoners of others in an ambush, and captured about twenty raw ox-hide shields, with the hair on. However, when the shouting got louder and drew nearer, and those who were constantly going forward started running towards the men in front who kept on shouting, and the more there were of them the more shouting there was, it looked then as though this was something of considerable importance. So Xenophon mounted his horse and, taking Lycus and the cavalry with him, rode forward to give support, and, quite soon, they heard soldiers shouting out 'The sea! The sea!' and passing the word down the column. Then suddenly they all began to run, the rearguard and all, and drove on the baggage animals and the horses at full speed; and when they had all got to the top, the soldiers, with tears in their eyes, embraced each other and their generals and captains.
>
> 'Thalassa!' the men shouting. 'Thalassa!'

Centuries come and gone, vast palaces built and destroyed and dynasties defeated . . . Trebizond today affords little evidence of former glories. The decayed remains of the mainly Byzantine city stand on a hill between two ravines. At the seaward end are the remains of Hadrian's harbour, walled lower and upper cities and finally, at the point where the two ravines meet at the southern end, the ruins of the golden palace of the Comneni. Cardinal Bessarian, Trebizond's most famous native, later the patriarch of Constantinople, first read his Homer in the palace library. Years on, Bessarian's own collection of Greek manuscripts became the nucleus of St. Mark's library in Venice. Now in the ruins of the library of the Grand Comneni, open to the sky, nettles grow.

When Rose Macaulay visited Trebizond in the 1950s she had the character Laurie describe the expectation and reality thus:

> When we saw Trebizond lying there in its splendid bay, the sea in front and the hills behind, the cliffs and the ravines which held the ancient citadel, and the white Turkish town lying along the front and climbing up the hill, it was like seeing an old dream change its shape, as dreams do, becoming something else, for this did not seem the capital of the last Byzantine empire, but a picturesque Turkish port and town with a black beach littered with building materials, and small houses and mosques climbing the hill, and ugly buildings along the quay. The citadel, the ruins of the Comnenus palace, would be somewhere on one of the heights, buried in brambled thickets and trees; a great cliff, grown with tangled shrub, divided the city into two parts. Expecting the majestic, brooding ghost of a fallen empire, we saw, in a magnificent stagey setting, an untidy Turkish port. The ghost would be brooding on the woody cliffs and ravines, haunting the citadel and palace, scornfully taking no notice of the town that Trebizond now was, with the last Greeks expelled by the Father of the Turks twenty years back.

In the building boom of the late fifties, some years after Rose Macaulay's visitations, Trebizond knocked down nearly all its domestic buildings of any age except for the more expensive suburban houses on the heights and replaced them with breeze block and brick slapped together with mortar oozing out of every course. We were taken by bus to see the Ataturk

Villa, a mansion originally owned by a Greek merchant and built in an art deco-ish style, where Ataturk stayed for one night in 1924. It had been fitted out with buttoned, paunchy, horse-hairy-stuffed great-grandmotherly furniture, the walls hung with photographs of Ataturk and family, black and white and sepia in massy bronze frames. In a room off the foyer a billiard table without pockets, the American version of the game where scoring was by caroms only. Bronze chandeliers of floral theme and sconces bronze and floral. I gave the second floor a miss.

Waiting for Myrna I pottered around the garden beds in the drizzle and looked at dahlias.

"Interesting, perhaps," I noted later in my diary, "to Turks."

We were then transported to the Sultan Mehmet Mosque but again I waited outside in the courtyard for Myrna. At the Alaeddin Mosque in Sinop I had felt deeply embarrassed at being guided inside to watch seven old men at prayer, reading and dovening, dovening. Not much different from a synagogue. Our presence had seemed to me insensitive and bad-mannered.

And the courtyard afforded matters of interest though I dissembled as best I could. The washing place where worshippers performed the ritual of *wodaa* was an octagonal stone structure once upon more gracious times, I guessed, a constantly flowing fountain. Eight low stone perches facing niches each with a faucet inside. The men were washing hands, feet, and faces, cleansing ears and even nasal cavities with snortings, snottings, dramatic excavations, gobblings.

A mildly retarded girl of eighteen or so, pertly nubile, greeted each arrival with what was obviously sexual banter and barracking. She was treated not unkindly as a sort of pet. It felt odd understanding all this in a language I'd never heard before though her gesticulations provided unambiguous help.

Or had this been in Sinop? It scarcely mattered. Most of these Turkish towns in terms of their shops and goods for sale were almost identical. The number of furniture shops was surprising, all of them giving pride of place to swollen settees. I had expected the bakeries to be selling sweet and sticky things but most displayed savoury pies and borek. Jewellers' windows displayed bars and poles of gold and silver bangles, a few pairs of earrings, but bangles insistently. They were significant, apparently, in the various stages of courtship and for married women formed an ambulatory bank account, each bangle having a fixed value. In trays, pans, shallow bins, the fish stores displayed the catch of the day; that day in Trebizond the choice was bonito. Painted plaster child-mannikins stood in all the clothes stores windows, suits and bow ties for three-year-old boys and puffy-sleeved froufrou dresses for tiny girls.

But shouting their presence louder than other stores, small store fronts selling film, cameras, phones, CD players, electronic doodads, their windows a blare of posters and logos: SONY, TOSHIBA, SAMSUNG, OLYMPUS, CANON, PANASONIC, FUJI, KODAK, HITACHI, NIKON.

Towards the end of the morning we were again transported by bus west of the imperial ruins to the church of Aghia Sophia which stands by the sea. It was recognized, our guide informed us, as one of the major monuments of late Byzantine art. The church stands inside what I would have thought of as a churchyard but which had been, apparently, a monastic enclosure. The campanile had possibly been a famous medieval observatory. No one seemed to know. In the shell of the building, the salt wind blew through empty window-spaces and the gaps above arched doorways, sagging chicken-wire failing to keep out pigeons. I stared around at the decaying patches of colour.

Outside in the enclosure, a few yards from the main entrance of the Aghia Sophia, the marble-sided plinth of an altar. The remains of a temple to Apollo. Two small marble Doric columns were still standing. The component drums of another lay tumbled in the grass.

* * *

St. Paul in the First Epistle to Timothy urges "... use a little wine for thy stomach's sake and thine often infirmities;" I was using a little Famous Grouse for mine as Myrna and I lay in our cabin, the *Minerva* running before the wind towards Sochi in Russia. We had been bound for Batumi in Georgia but a Force Nine gale had blown up, long running swells, and Batumi harbour had declared itself closed. The lurching corridors were dangerous and supine seemed the only position that eased the queasiness.

I was not entirely discontented to be resting and reading. The day before in Trebizond, after the Ataturk Villa and the Aghia Sophia, we had gone up by bus into the Pontic Alps to visit the cliff top Sumela Monastery. The last three-quarters of a mile can only be done on foot and the path is steep and broken, in places more scramble than walk, and we were moving at a fair pace to get out of the rain.

When we reached the tiny forecourt of the monastery, one last long flight of steep steps climbed into the building itself. I'd stood puffing a bit and propped back against a wall.

"What's the matter?" said Myrna.

I shook my head.

"Just a bit winded."

Perhaps my eyes were closed.

"Stop being so bloody British."

"Well, it's in my arm . . ."

"Christ!" said Myrna.

We made our way slowly down to where the vans waited. In the front van sat the Catholic priest and his flannel-mouthed minder who barely comprehensibly extolled the beauties of County Wexford, the soft silver sheen of the Slaney's sweet waters, the potency of Wexford's potheen, a potheen that was your only creature, your only man, a potheen, now, for only the throngest of men . . .

I had tuned out his blather and had sat watching through the van's open door the quick picking of a sparrow under a picnic table. I was feeling drawn deep inside myself, cautious, tentative in the world.

Back in Canada I had another much stronger angina attack and spent the day on oxygen in Emergency. Shortly after this I was sent for a stress test at the The Ottawa Heart Institute.

Injection of "radioactive material."

The technician said, a tap on my wedding ring, "The wife'll like this."

"Pardon?"

"Make your willie glow in the dark."

Eighteen minutes of photographs. Injection of a drug called Persantine to stress the heart. Five unpleasant minutes later the injection of an antidote. Followed by the injection of more "radioactive material." Followed by a chopped egg sandwich. Followed by eighteen more minutes of photographs.

Results were . . . not exactly well-defined. Nor much discussed. The surgeons at the Ottawa Heart Institute are a taciturn cadre. There was, apparently, no blockage of arteries. But from that day on I was advised to carry a pumpspray of sublingual Nitroglycerin. There was talk of alleviating tension and stress. I was to return to the Institute immediately in the event of an episode of arrhythmia.

As the *Minerva* bucked and plunged towards Sochi I was reading *Wilt in Nowhere* by Tom Sharpe. He was acclaimed in reviews quoted on the back of the book as:

"The funniest novelist writing today." (*The Times*)

"Our funniest living novelist." (*Daily Telegraph*)

". . . his position at the heart of British comedy is as assured as that of the seaside postcard." (*Observer*)

No! No! and No!

The book was laboured, mechanical, forced, the writing humdrum and workaday.

Some even more lumpen reviewers have compared Sharpe's writing with that of Evelyn Waugh and P.G. Wodehouse.

When I read Sharpe's first two novels *Riotous Assembly* and *Indecent Exposure* at the beginning of the seventies I was quite taken with them because grotesque and savage farce seemed a more fitting way of dealing with the savagery of South African apartheid and the Sharpsville Shootings than distressed soul searching or Marxist strictures.

Riotous Assembly opens with the visit of Kommandant van Heerden and Konstabel Els to the anglophone estate of Miss Hazelstone who has just shot and killed with an enormous elephant gun her black cook Fivepence. The almost subhuman Konstabel Els trips and falls onto Miss Hazelstone's Doberman Pinscher which promptly bites the Konstabel's balls. In retaliation and self-defence the Konstabel locks *his* teeth into the Doberman's balls and they lie on the lawn conjoined until separated by Miss Hazelstone with an ammonia-soaked cloth.

All this seemed a promising beginning in a head-butting kind of way. The problem with the books was that they had nothing to sustain them beyond grotesquerie piled on grotesquerie. As the novels kept on appearing and the settings became British rather than South African, it became obvious that Sharpe was simply a genre writer of farces uncomplicated by political intent. What the novels lacked was language.

* * *

An aside. I have nothing against good genre writing. Indeed, I have learned much from it. Kingsley Amis wrote a James Bond continuation after Ian Fleming's death called *Colonel Sun* and in a subsequent essay "A New James Bond" published in *What Became of Jane Austen and Other Questions* offered this defence of genre writing.

> It might well be agreed that the best of serious fiction, so to call it, is better than anything any genre can offer. But this best is horribly rare, and a clumsy dissection of the heart is so much worse than boring as to be painful, and most contemporary novels are like spy novels with no spies or crime novels with no crimes, and John D. MacDonald is by any standards a better writer than Saul Bellow, only MacDonald writes thrillers and Bellow is a human-heart chap, so guess who wears the top-grade laurels?

Amis being Amis. But he makes a couple of interesting points. Curious that Saul Bellow's *The Adventures of Augie March* was the book celebrated in an earlier chapter by Kingsley's son, Martin, as one of the greatest of American novels. It's many years since I read MacDonald's Travis McGee books but many, many more since I read *Dangling Man* or *Henderson the Rain King*. Both, in memory, uphill work. I especially enjoyed the titles of two early MacDonald books when he was still writing paperback originals for, I think, Fawcett Gold Medal Books: *One Monday We Killed Them All* and *The Girl, the Gold Watch, and Everything*.

Amis' *Colonel Sun* was, I'm afraid, a stinker. The three further continuations by John Gardner were sorry flops. Although Amis specifically denied it, the Fleming Bonds were very much about social class and surely James Bond is not unrelated to Dorothy L. Sayer's Lord Peter Wimsey and Margery Allingham's Albert Campion. Fleming's imitators were uncomfortable in evening dress. None of their Bonds sported – exquisite touch, this – a slim *gunmetal* cigarette case.

I caused some consternation many years ago by declaring that Elmore Leonard was a better writer than Margaret Laurence and that he wasn't alone on those convenience store racks. It's not all Clive Cussler in there with the Diet Coke and Cheezies. Were I wanting a sly and moving look at South African racial politics you'd probably find me reading not Tom Sharpe nor Nadine Gordimer – though I greatly admired her novel *The*

Conservationist – but rather the stories of James McClure with his detective team of the Afrikaner Lieutenant Tromp Kramer and the Zulu Sergeant Zondi. There are pleasures to be had in *The Steam Pig*, *The Gooseberry Fool*, *The Artful Egg* and *The Blood of an Englishman*. Zondi, the servant who is less subservient than he seems, is a character who well might derive at a remove from Sir J.M. Barrie's *The Admirable Crichton*. Who in turn might derive from the plays of Titus Maccius Plautus c. 254 – 184 BC. Literature's a lengthy business.

But Amis glosses over genre writing's principal flaw – the tyranny of plot. I read thrillers and detective stories as relaxation from the demands of the human-heart chaps. Sometimes I'm rewarded by superb writing. Usually not. But there's enough to keep me turning pages, a hunt, a chase, funny dialogue, new slang, entertaining spots of mayhem, arcane information about forensics, ballistics, triads, forgery, antique furniture, the Union Corse, but late at night when there's no more of that kind of thing to be gleaned and the plot hammers on and on I often can't be bothered to finish because ultimately I don't *care* who did it or why or how. Because the characters are thin, I don't *care* whether the private eye keeps off the sauce, whether he wins the girl with auburn hair . . . The onward rush of narrative engages, but the plotted destination and conclusion become uninteresting. And because such books pose questions and end with some kind of answer they cannot be re-read.

To circle back to Tom Sharpe's use of language. I remember years ago my anticipation of the BBC productions of P.G. Wodehouse episodes involving Jeeves and Bertie Wooster and, despite fine actors, how dead and boring and silly the shows were. The essence of the matter was that a man in a bathtub washing his foot is not funny whereas the following sentence *is*:

"As I sat in the bathtub, soaping a meditative foot and singing, if I remember correctly, 'Pale Hands I Loved Beside the Shalimar,' it would be deceiving my public to say that I was feeling boomps-a-daisy."

To watch Drones and Crumpets zipping about in sports cars, losing the antique silver cow-creamer, breaking into the wrong bedroom, stealing the necklace is to be watching *actions* and damn silly ones at that.

There is no pleasure in seeing a butler entering a room bearing a silver salver. But to *read* "Jeeves shimmered in . . ."

Shimmered.

Within that word is all the joy.

Lying there in that ship's cabin thinking of Tom Sharpe and Wodehouse and Waugh I had with a grab of grief a sudden memory of Hugh Hood. Shortly after we'd first met we were trying each other out with quotations, measuring who knew and valued what. Hugh said that his favourite Waugh lines concerned Mr. Salter's luggage in the novel *Scoop*. Mr. Salter chooses to walk from the tiny railway station to the country house where he will be staying. His luggage is sent on ahead on a farm truck full of fertilizer. When he arrives at the house, the butler (a markedly Wodehouse butler) says to him:

> 'I regret to say, sir, that your luggage is not yet available. Three of the outside men are delving for it at the moment.'
>
> 'Delving?'
>
> 'Assiduously, sir. It was inundated with slag at the time of the accident.'

Hugh and I were besotted with P.G. Wodehouse. Hugh used to say that one had to regard with reverence the man who had written "the unmistakable sound of an Anglican bishop sitting up in bed." Evelyn Waugh himself was greatly influenced and owned a nearly complete collection of P.G., many of which he'd had rebound in full leather – a hideous practice, anathema to serious modern collectors, but in keeping with his anachronistic life. Frances Donaldson in her *Evelyn Waugh: Portrait of a Country Neighbour* says that he always referred to P.G. as "The Master" and when she demurred Waugh replied, "One has to regard a man as a Master who can produce on average three uniquely brilliant and entirely original similes to every page."

There isn't much writing in English that can equal the delights of Bertie Wooster in full flow. Here's a treasured example from *Jeeves and the Feudal Spirit.*

> I don't know if you happen to be familiar with a poem called 'The Charge of the Light Brigade' by the bird Tennyson whom Jeeves had mentioned when speaking of the fellow whose strength was as the strength of ten. It is, I believe, fairly well known, and I used to have to recite it at the age of seven or thereabouts when summoned to the drawing-room to give visitors a glimpse of the young Wooster.

'Bertie recites so nicely,' my mother used to say – getting her facts twisted, I may mention, because I practically always fluffed my lines – and after trying to duck for safety and being hauled back I would snap into it. And very unpleasant the whole thing was, so people have told me.

Well, what I was about to say, when I rambled off a bit on the subject of the dear old days, was that though in the course of the years most of the poem of which I speak has slid from the memory, I still recall its punch line. The thing goes, as you probably know,

Tum tiddle umpty-pum
Tum tiddle umpty-pum
Tum tiddle umpty-pum

and this brought you to the snapperoo or payoff, which was

Someone had blundered.

I always remember that bit, and the reason I bring it up now is that, as I stood blinking at this pink-boudoir-capped girl, I was feeling just as those Light Brigade fellows must have felt. Obviously someone had blundered here, and that someone was Aunt Dahlia.

Many people can quote Amis, Waugh, and Wodehouse, perfected language burned into their hearts and minds by pleasure; only an idiot savant, I'd wager, could quote Tom Sharpe.

* * *

Over the next couple of days something about Evelyn Waugh and P.G. Wodehouse and Trebizond was lurking in the mental undergrowth but I couldn't catch a glimpse of it. During a sleepy breakfast it stuck its head out and I grabbed its neck and hauled it into the light of day. Nearly fifty years earlier I had read, I realized, an historical novel about the last of the Pontic kings of Trebizond. It was concerned with the three Pontic wars against Rome. It was called *He Died Old: Mithradates Eupator, King of Pontus.* The connection to Waugh was that it had been written by his Oxford contemporary and friend Alfred Duggan.

What follows is from *Evelyn Waugh: No Abiding City 1939-1966*, the second volume of Martin Stannard's commanding biography, with a quotation interpolated from another Oxford contemporary, Peter Quennell.

Waugh and Alfred had been Oxford contemporaries when the young man from Golder's Green had been awestruck by his friend's extravagance.

[Here, interpolated, Quennell's description of Duggan. The quotation within the second sentence is from Waugh himself.]

Alfred Duggan . . . was a dashing Restoration rake, who, having at length been converted to Catholicism, developed into a successful and prolific historical novelist. At Oxford, Alfred 'was very rich . . . He was, moreover, the stepson of the Chancellor of the University, Lord Curzon. This connection irked the authorities, who otherwise would have summarily sent him down. We were often drunk, Alfred almost always.' And not only did he keep a string of hunters, but every night of his life, wearing full evening dress, he would have himself driven off to London, and there spend the next three or four hours at a then-notorious Soho nightclub. Driven back again, he would scale the façade of the college and struggle through his first-floor window. The bribes that he paid his scout, I remember him telling me, ran into several hundred pounds a year. But, drunk or sober, he was always polite and impassive; and his starched shirt-front, with its lustrous pearl studs, seldom showed a crease or dent.

Stannard again:

But the glamour had soon faded as Duggan ran through his inheritance and succumbed to chronic alcoholism. In 1933 he had returned to Catholicism and during the 1930s, through Waugh's influence, had begun writing for the *Tablet* until one day, after another 'blind,' he had failed to send in his copy. After that, he had dropped from the novelist's life, seemingly a burnt-out case, until the summer of 1949.

Duggan had emerged from the war a man purged. Having enlisted as a private and suffered badly during the retreat from Norway in 1940, he had been invalided out, his health permanently impaired, and had worked in an aircraft factory. Reckless arrogance had been replaced by humility bred of religious devotion. In the spring of 1945 he had happily begun an ex-serviceman's apprenticeship to train as a cowman at £4 a week. Then, when he felt his life at long last settled, his mother, Lady Curzon, had insisted that she was too ill to live alone and he had returned without complaint to care for her in Sussex.

[Lady Curzon in the delicious words of a recent biographer of Lord Curzon was "unencumbered by intellectual interests" and after Curzon's death took as her lover a grand cad and bounder called Sir Mathew "Scatters" Wilson who had squandered her fortune and left her destitute. *His* son, Peter Wilson, became the more than dubious chairman of Sotheby's.]

There, at Bodiam Manor, he had spent his spare time in the library and had developed a considerable knowledge of medieval history and theology. For want of anything better to do, he wrote an historical novel, more to amuse himself than with any hope of publication, and Faber offered him a contract. It was at this point that he wrote to Waugh, thanking him for advice about establishing a literary career. A man of extraordinary industry, Duggan simply wanted something to do. 'Actually I am extremely happy,' he wrote. 'It is the financial result of being teetotal that is astounding. Nowadays I always have money in my pocket.' If he survived his mother, he said, he intended to enter the Christian Brothers or some other teaching order.

A long correspondence ensued, concluding only with Duggan's death in 1964, by which time he had written 'fifteen historical novels . . . , three biographies and seven historical studies for young readers.' This proud listing is from Waugh's panegyric, delivered first on the radio and then published prominently in the *Spectator*. It was an astonishing accolade. Reading it quickly, one might think that Waugh was speaking of a close friend whom he considered a great writer. In fact, he ingeniously avoids stating either proposition while implying both. His literary chums were baffled. Why this ceaseless promotion of a widely (and they believed, justly) neglected author? Had Waugh's fine sense of aesthetic discrimination deserted him? Was this not merely a pathetic display of his clinging to the coat-tails of the aristocracy, come what may? The answer, surely, was simpler and more creditable to Waugh. The article, indeed the whole relationship, was another act of *pietas*.

Waugh kept some fifty of Duggan's letters, replied to them all, sent him his own new books and offered generous encouragement in reviews. It was immensely satisfying for Waugh to watch this former wastrel, a man who at Oxford had professed Marxism and atheism, settling into Catholic domesticity and earning his living by the humble trade of letters. Duggan married, adopted a child, and lived for the rest of his life on a few pounds a week. Waugh attended his funeral, cared for his widow and organized a trust fund. But the social circles of the two men rarely intersected. Waugh and Laura went to tea in 1952 to meet the fiancée, but the two men never visited each other's houses. Indeed, during those fifteen years they scarcely met. Cured of drink and extravagance, Duggan perhaps seemed an admirable but dull character to one cured of neither, and Waugh politely sidestepped further invitations.

* * *

An aside. Stannard mentions the low opinion Waugh's contemporaries had of Duggan's work; it is not a judgement I share. Some of the novels are unarguably better than others but I've gained pleasure from them all. Not aesthetic pleasure so much as the pleasure of information and its stimulus to the imagination, simple historical facts which had not previously dawned. Duggan, for example, tells us that knights wore white linen surcoats over their armour to keep off some of the sun's murderous heat. Obvious, I suppose, but it had never occurred to me. That little nudge led me to imagine chafing, washing, laundry, horse lather, the stench of a Frankish army – perhaps all of it for Duggan relating back to "the string of hunters" he kept at Oxford and the rigours of the Norway fiasco in 1940. The accumulation of such little nudges opens up a time and place to our greater understanding. My favourite Duggan titles are *Knight with Armour* about the First Crusade, *Winter Quarters* about the First Triumvirate, *Three's Company* about the Second, *Lord Geoffrey's Fancy* about Frankish Greece in the thirteenth century, and *Leopards and Lilies* set in thirteenth century England.

Historical novels are, of course, genre writing but when they aim beyond being costume dramas they can give – and especially to young readers – gifts beyond the pleasures of narrative. They can foster an interest in and love of the past without which no individual is really civilized. Kipling had an almost mystical grasp of this love which he exhibited in *Puck of Pook's Hill* and *Rewards and Fairies* – along with *The Jungle Book*, *Kim*, and *Just So Stories*, perhaps his best work.

Reading an adventure story such as *Eagle of the Ninth* by Rosemary Sutcliffe may well have given thousands of children their entry into the past urging them up onto, say, the chalk downs, past the White Horse of Uffington cut into the turf in the Iron Age, and along the ancient Ridgeway down which Boadicea led the Iceni against the Roman Legions. Iron Age hill forts and long barrows thrown in for good measure.

In the hollows below the White Horse, Alfred the Great rested his army overnight on his march to the Battle of Ashdown in 871 where he wreaked slaughter upon the invading Danes. Perhaps my imagined young readers will find their way to Alfred Duggan's novel about Alfred the Great, *The King of Athelney*. And perhaps the British heroics of Alfred will lead these golden readers back, in the way that reading does, to what is called by the twelfth-century French writer Jean Bodel "the matter of Britain" – King Arthur and the Knights of the Round Table. And here await Mary Stewart's *The Crystal Cave*, *The Hollow Hills*, *The Last Enchantment*, and the deeply imagined work of T.H. White's *The Once and Future King*, and perhaps at the end of the trail Sir Thomas Malory's *Le Morte D'Arthur*. And, one would hope, as a comic byway, *Monty Python and the Holy Grail*.

Similarly, stirred by the imagining of *Knight with Armour*, an older reader might be drawn towards Sir Steven Runciman's three-volume *A History of the Crusades*.

* * *

For lazy people like me genre writing often delivers, sugar-coated, splendidly useless knowledge I would never otherwise have come across. Thriller writers, especially first-time ones, often endow their private eyes with their own authorial hobbies so as the story zips along the reader is given odd information about Clovis points, say, daguerreotypes, Penny Blacks and Twopenny Blues, netsukes, lost Stan Getz recording sessions, Dinky toys.

In my own case, I've always been grateful to whatever historical novelist it was – and it may very well have been Alfred Duggan – who alerted me to *garum*, a substance which has come to fascinate me.

Garum was inherited by the Romans from the Greeks *(garos)* and was one of the staples of Roman cooking. It was a fish sauce which gave a briny pungency to many dishes. Pliny in his *Natural History* describes *garum* as "consisting of the guts of fish and the other parts that would otherwise be considered refuse; these are soaked in salt, so that garum is really liquor from the putrefaction of these matters . . ."

There seem to have been grades of *garum;* the highest grade, according to Martial, was made from the blood of a still-breathing mackerel. In *De re Coquinaria*, ascribed to Apicius (mid-4th century AD), the highest grade is claimed to be made from mullet. Tuna fish sauce, the second grade of *garum,* was called *muria.* The lowest grade could be made from any small fish left in the net. We might imagine these to be sardines and anchovies.

In later years, the use of the word *garum* seemed to fade out and fish sauce came to be called *liquamen.* A faint idea of what it might have been like can be gained by tasting fish sauce available now in most Asian stores, *ngan-pya-ye* from Burma, *nam pla* from Thailand, and, strongest of all, *nuoc mam* from Vietnam, though people who have cooked Roman recipes seem to think that *garum* would have been more powerful still.

Ancient commerce traded in three liquids, wine, olive oil, and *garum* and each liquid had its own specially shaped amphora much in the same way that we have instantly recognizable shapes for claret, Burgundy, and Riesling bottles. The Royal Ontario Museum years ago had a wall-mounted display of the amphora shapes.

I like to think that there are ghostly connections between their world and ours, echoes, family likenesses too marked to be coincidence. Pliny the Elder tells us that *garum* looked like aged honey wine and was often mixed with wine to drink. Apicius' recipes suggest that fish sauce was sometimes mixed with wine or vinegar. In parts of Italy today people drink tiny glasses of Modena balsamic vinegar as a digestif. Wine is still watered. And the Mediterranean still produces, not sauce, but fish salted in much the same method, anchovies.

I always go out of my way to eat anchovies. Myrna credits me with inventing an anchovy quiche which calls for one-and-a-half cans of flat anchovy fillets. The effect of egg on anchovy . . . but I obviously can't go into that now.

Before we set out on this holiday, David O'Meara lent us Neal Ascherson's *Black Sea.* Ascherson writes about Black Sea anchovies which annually travel clockwise around the sea feeding and spawning. There are, he says, so many of them, that it is hard to find a word to describe their accumulation. None of the conventional words for congregations of fish is sufficient. "School" or "shoal" are inadequate to describe millions upon untold millions of anchovies travelling in a swirling mass like a vast living ball.

To my perfect delight, Ascherson describes this phenomenon as a "biomass."

* * *

First Prize: one week in Sochi. Second Prize: three weeks in Sochi. The utilitarian bus throbbed and shuddered as it waited for stragglers from the Botanical Gardens making their way back from gawking at the Tree of Friendship.

The wood slat seats gave little ease. Someone had pasted a festive frill of scissored gold foil round the inside top two inches of the windows obscuring the view. Glued to every fourth or so strip of fringe a cotton wool bobble. The long gear shift was dressed in a knitted sheath. The punctilious guide kept testing his mike, peering into his briefcase, fingers questioning the knot of his tie. The Baden Powell man with the cravat and cratered boils who'd fought alongside Glubb Pasha began his daily bellowing and pounding on the floor with his brass-bound walking stick.

"You! Bloody driver! You! The tout with the microphone! Music *off!* Music *off!*"

The bus juddered on its way. The guide resumed his litany. There wasn't much to see. One after another, large white buildings, gardens surrounding. High hedges of dark yew. Sanitaria for apparatchiks.

. . . what do you call in your countries not – hospitals? Spa. Just so mmmm. There are many baths 50 metres by 25 metres that is mmmm in the measurements of your countries 164.042 feet by 82.02 feet and these baths are full of water from the hot springs. The water is full of health but the smell is very rude.

The State Winter Theatre. Riviera Park with an opportunity to buy local handicrafts. In the grounds of the Zelyonaya Roscha Sanatorium, Stalin's Dacha.

. . . and a big surprise are the baths full of mud which is heated to mmmm 41 degrees centigrade or in the measurement of your countries 105.8 Fahrenheit which is 4 degrees higher than your blood . . .

I squirmed on the unforgiving seat.

. . . and there are also mud mmmm cabinets with just heads . . .

"The Cabinets of Doctor Caligari," I said to Myrna.

... and the mud sucks out the poison from the body ... not mmmm suck ...

He riffled through some notes.

... leaches mmmm leaches poison ...

"Leeches?" said Myrna making a sucking face.

"Well, Mother," I said to her, "exfoliation they may call it but I've always said you've a long way to go to beat an old-fashioned scourging."

"And what do *you* know, you old stick in the mud!"

And this got us launched into riffs on soviet spas, gleaming white resorts from the outside but inside crumbling Gormenghasts with lavatory-tiled rooms staffed by smelly crones and doctors with steel teeth. The Beria Room full of people wrapped in wet sheets and stacked. Skink-Extract treatment in the Maceration Room. The Gherkin Diet. The Dry Cupping Room. Korean massage administered by Oddjob aided by the sinister Blowjob. In the Malenkov Room, Borscht enemas performed by Enigma Machines. On Thank God It's Fridays, the Siberian Plotz executed turn and turn about by the Smersh Sisters, three ex-KGB houris.

This giddiness possesssed us until we reached Dagomys in the mountains and the bus bumped over the gravel parking area of the most northerly tea plantation in Europe. I had not particularly wanted to visit a tea plantation – rows of small, green bushes – and listen to a lecture in Russian with simultaneous translation into halting English but the only alternative had been more sanitariums. Not even the prospect of free tea and folkloric entertainment had won me over.

"Remember," I had said to Myrna, "the wisdom of Sir Arnold Bax."

"Who's he?"

"A well-known composer I've never heard *but*, but smart enough to say 'you should make a point of trying every experience once, excepting incest and folk-dancing.'"

In front of me down the bus' steep steps, Alan and Martin, the American couple, today wearing gabardine windbreakers with plaid linings. They always introduced themselves with, "We're Alan and Martin from Cincinnati." The day before they'd worn seersucker jackets that made me think of ice creams. Alan was studying the writing on the back of the bus.

"Hey!" he said. "This bus is from Korea. *This is a Korean bus.*"

"Get a picture," said Martin.

Myrna was helping along the aisle of the bus the woman with the walker.

I held out my hand to steady another old lady, much bedizened, down the steps. I'd noticed her before. Her make-up was so elaborate, so excessive, that the word "make-up" seemed inadequate to convey . . . "Maquillage," perhaps . . .

"What a lovely – would one call it a choker?"

She smiled.

"Victorian, isn't it?"

"Clever boy," she said.

"And not jet," I said. "Rather too matte for that."

She was watching my face.

"It wouldn't possibly be . . . coal, would it?"

"*Very* clever boy," she said. "How did you know that?"

"I've seen pieces in museums and at auction."

"I *love* auctions," she said. "*My* name's Bronwyn."

"They still do it, you know," I said. "I've seen modern pieces – not with *that* refinement – for sale from a barrow on the sea front at Whitby. John," I said.

She took my arm.

"Nice sleepy auctions in country towns – *such* a pleasure," she said. "Like boxes of chocolates. Magical boxes, always full and waiting to be opened. I lead a lovely, selfish life going to antique shops and auctions buying little things of beauty for myself. Of course," she continued, "I wasn't brought up here . . ."

"Here?"

"England, I mean. Which rather explains it all. No. I spent my early years in Sarawak. My parents were missionaries, you see."

"Anglican?"

She batted her ancient lashes.

"Do I have a Baptist *look?*"

I smiled.

"And then I was shipped off to boarding school in England. Nine at the time. Plenty of love for the dusky indigenes but precious little for me. Anyway, that was the way I felt as a girl. Poor Bronwyn, less loved than a Dyak. So I've always comforted myself ever since with *objets d'art* and yummy *delectabilia* and . . ."

"Wait for us!" called Myrna.

We paused outside the listing wooden swayback shed which served as a lavatory. Myrna joined the line. Seconds after entering she shot out again.

"Christ!" she said.

"It's easy to see," said Bronwyn, "*you've* never been to China."

The four of us proceeded along the uneven path through the woods towards the wooden shed where the lecture and tea-drinking and folkloric entertainment were to take place.

"No," I said to Myrna at the door, "I'll go for a stroll in the woods. At least they're not wearing clogs."

"Clogs?"

"Mmm."

"Why should they be? They're not Dutch."

"No, but the hulking *bulk* of them, and the jolliness and head scarves, and *accordians*. I don't know. Perhaps I was thinking of Lancashire."

It was warm, cloudless, the shapes of hawks slow-wheeling and slipping down the sky. The rows of tea bushes were planted on hillsides that looked as though the trees had been bulldozed into wreckage. The soil looked dark and acidic. Rank bracken had grown back in between the rows.

A flicker of movement on the fringe of dappling oak leaves caught my eye. Familiar brown wings laced by demarcating black lines and dots. Two fritillaries. I was excited and intensely pleased.

When I had first seen Monarch butterflies on coming to Canada I had been reminded of fritillaries, the colouration, the black lines of demarcation like niello jewellery, but Monarchs had seemed burly and muscle-bound in comparison, NCO's of the butterfly world while fritillaries were officers and aristocrats, the browns and ochres, umbers, burnt siennas of their wings like exquisite marquetry.

I used to wander in the New Forest when I was a child catching butterflies and hunting adders. The boy I wandered with was a little older and I existed in a haze of love and hero-worship. The butterflies had been shaken from the net into a killing jar, glass and wide-mouthed with a large cork bung. Onto a pad of folded cotton at the bottom of the jar, a rag of an old shirt perhaps – not cotton wool as insect legs tangled in its wisps – I'd pour a few drops from a bottle of *Thawpit*, a commercial solvent used in dry cleaning and then freely available in chemists' shops. It was only years later that I learned that *Thawpit* was actually carbon tetrachloride and considered to have near fatal effects on the liver. We used to like the sweetness of its smell.

And into an old pillow case went adders which we tended to handle with dangerous familiarity. We carried an old tobacco tin containing a razor blade and purple crystals of potassium permanganate as first aid. We swore to each other that we'd cut a cross over the two fang marks and suck and spit and let blood flow and then force in the purple crystals, a nightmare that still recurs. The thought of cutting. Doing the cutting.

We sold the adders to the Ferndown Zoo for a shilling a foot, a large sum then for a child. It kept us in cigarettes. We smoked a brand called *Park Drive.*

Even then, nearly sixty years ago, fritillaries were seldom seen, very local in their distribution. I knew only three rides in the New Forest near Ringwood where they might reliably be found.

I remembered reading that in England they were now considered extinct. But here in the sunlight, in all their remembered grace and beauty . . .

I stood transported.

* * *

"Sir Charles," said Bronwyn, "was a nasty old man. Very fierce and rude."

"But to think," I said. "That you . . . I mean, The White Rajah of Sarawak! It seems somehow . . ."

"He didn't die until quite recently, you know – the sixties, I think it was. In Cheltenham. Or Cirencester." She waved a dismissive hand. "Had a horrible glass eye he'd got from a taxidermist. But yes, he was there – in Sarawak, I mean – well, until the Japanese soldiers came."

"And when you were a child, you remember . . ."

"Oh, but it was the Ranee all the stories were about! Sylvia, her name was. Oh, she *was* a baggage! Of course, I never saw any of the goings-on but all the children heard the stories from the servants and the agency men and *their* servants . . . Not that she was in Sarawak all that often. She much preferred London and Paris. 'Frivolous' was the word my father used – such a *weight* of disapproval. She was Lord Esher's daughter, you know. Sylvia Brett, she used to be. And a merry dance she led him, by all accounts. Do people *use* the word 'trollop' nowadays?"

Through the trees the buses in the parking lot came into sight.

"It was the drink," said Bronwyn. "Gin for breakfast rarely ends well. She was a living scandal. She even made the Dyaks nervous, and some of *those* johnnies weren't exactly straitlaced."

"Shrunken heads and such?"

She waved her free hand dismissively, again.

"Nasty, smelly things," she said.

She paused to pat my arm.

"She refused, just *refused* to leave the table and stayed on after dinner for the port. Smoked the cigars and drank the port. Utterly foxed. And by then she'd be quite *raucous*. Not, apparently, that the esteemed Sir Charles Vyner Brooke appeared to care! He'd be as fuddled as she was and fumbling in some creature's placket."

I tutted.

"Too sordid, my dear," said Bronwyn.

She shook her head.

"It is *said*," said Bronwyn, "it is *said*, that after dinner the men repaired to the billiard room and she used to hoist up her skirt and clamber up onto the table . . . I'm not embarrassing you, am I dear?"

"No, no. Fascinating."

"And work herself against a corner pocket and open her legs wide . . . and shout . . . you're sure I'm not . . ."

"Please."

"By this time, of course, she'd be hectic with drink."

"And shout what?" I said.

"And she used to shout . . ."

Bronwyn paused and drew herself up.

"Come on, boys!" she cried. "Pot the red!"

* * *

The Alupka Palace was designed, read Myrna, *by the Scottish architects Edward Blore and Henry Hunt and was built for Prince Michael Vorontsov between 1828 and 1846* . . . "Are you listening?"

"No," I said. "I'm watching this snail."

Myrna's dedication to reading plaques and notices had irritated me all our married life. She seemed to prefer reading maps to looking at the landscape they represented. Similarly with attributions in art galleries. It was a level of abstraction I did not want interposed. I always wanted urgent, unmediated contact with things. If I liked them, I'd told her, I'd find out more. And I'd already decided I didn't like the Alupka Palace.

Vorontsov's father had been the Russian ambassador to Great Britain and Prince Michael had grown up and been educated there. A passionate anglophile, he had, apparently, wished to create on the shore of the Black Sea an English country house.

The rear of the house where tourists entered was got up as a courtyarded mock castle, turreted, spired, crenellated, a wispy echo, perhaps, of Walpole's Strawberry Hill but with "oriental" effects added to "Tudor" chimney stacks. The front of the house in contradiction was confected in three styles in a row, Cotswold Manor House joined onto a glass and iron conservatory in the Palm-House-at-Kew-Gardens style joined onto which was a bloated bandshell-like entrance surmounted by verandas and balconies with balusters and balustrades all furbished with "oriental" finials and furbelows, the whole pot-pourri a feeble echo of Brighton's Royal Pavilion. It was less house than folly.

It was overwhelmingly . . . *silly*.

Leaving Myrna reading informative notices about "Chinese" style and bamboo wallpaper in the bedroom where Sir Winston Churchill slept during the 1945 Yalta Conference, I wandered out into the gardens.

The gardens funnelled out to the drive which led down to what was now a parking lot at the entrance to the estate. The Palace had been set into a ledge cut in the mountain side. The long drive was walled on both sides. On the mountain side of the drive was a retaining wall well above head height. The other side was lower providing a barrier against the mountain's fall to wards the sea where the sun sparked on water and Raoul Dufy sails stood white on blue.

The mountain side was wooded and I noticed an ochre scar carving down through the trees, a shallow gully of erosion. I probably wouldn't have seen them if not for the movement. They seemed to blend into the tumbled stone. A file of dogs.

The leading dog was tall and wiry-haired, greyish with something about it of an Irish wolfhound. The following dogs were mongrels, brown mostly, here and there a flash of white. Where the gully widened into grass and weeds, the dogs stopped and looked about. Then they sank almost out of sight as they worked forward to the coping on the top of the wall. Then nothing.

They gave a strong impression of tenseness, wariness, almost as though they were a commando behind enemy lines. I waited until no one was near and gave a sharp whistle. A greyish ear flicked above the grass.

"What are you doing?" said Myrna. "Watching snails?"

I felt rather than saw covert movement along the top of the wall and out of the corner of my eye caught the grey dog appearing at the foot of a flight of steps some twenty yards away. He sat. He waited until the drive was clear then led the pack across the drive into deep shadow on the sea wall side. They trotted down towards the car park seeming almost to flow.

As we entered the parking lot, we saw the last two dogs, back legs splayed, squirming and scrunching themselves under the edge of our bus.

"Why are they getting under there?"

I shrugged.

"What if they get run over?"

"I expect they've done it before."

Myrna bent and banged the side of the bus with her umbrella.

A ferocious snarl ripped back.

"Perhaps," I said, "he's taken up a *querencia*."

"A what?"

"It's when a bull decides . . ."

"I'm not having Hemingway," she said, "before lunch."

She reversed her umbrella again.

"If something of that size has taken a fancy to the underneath of the bus I, personally, would be jolly circumspect about challenging it."

"I'm *not* challenging him. I just don't want . . ."

"It's not important whether you're challenging him or not, it's what he *thinks* you're doing."

"This is a ridiculous conversation," said Myrna.

"And especially," I added, "if you are armed only with a collapsible umbrella."

"WHY," said the man with the antique hearing aids with the batteries and volume control knobs in a leather case hanging from a strap around his neck, "IS THAT WOMAN HITTING THE BUS?"

"Snails!" said Myrna.

* * *

After the Alupka Palace, the day's itinerary had promised a wine tasting of "unique Crimean wines" followed by lunch on the nabereshna Lenina featuring "wholesome Ukrainian cuisine," and then visits to Chekhov's White Dacha on vulitsya Kirova, the house he built in 1898 and where he spent his last five years, the day ending with a visit to a summer residence of Tsar Nicholas, the Livadia Palace.

In the yard surrounding the winery building stood rusting industrial-looking container tanks. The building itself was surrounded by straggling lilac bushes under one of which lay two unconscious drunks.

Each visitor was given a tray holding twelve numbered glasses of wine, glasses slightly larger than a shot glass, the glass itself thick. A man in a suit expatiated on the qualities peculiar to each wine. They were all utterly undrinkable, each vilely sweeter than the last. A saucerful would have killed a cat.

As counterpoint to the suit man's amplified drone, the priest's minder was weaving repeated words and phrases into a soothing babble of sound, a song almost, an Irish croon from which I could distinguish now and then the words "a nice little thrink." This flow of words did not seem to be directed at the priest personally but struck me rather as oil on generally troubled waters, placatory, a hush-now, hush-now.

Tilting his head back, the priest swilled each glass. Then his head came down again, his tongue searching into the glass, filling it, magnified, raw.

With a small movement of my head and a glance I guided Myrna's attention to the sight of the fat tongue pushing in.

My distaste for him was hardening into something harsher.

On the way to Chekhov's dacha, the priest sat next to the youngest woman on the bus, a woman travelling with her mother, a woman in her thirties. He was talking to her, talking and looking her over, talking and making a meal of her. His eyes were as cold as the eyes of the gulls that had stalked the lunchtime pavements of the open air cafés on the nabereshna Lenina.

A strange and alarming thing happened to me, something that had never happened before. I saw upon the air words as if printed on a page. I did not see the back of the seat in front of me, the window, or, looking down, my thighs and knees. I saw a white blank like a page. I wondered if this was a sign of a new affliction, the herald of some new erosion.

The words were laid out as though they were some sort of verse. The spacing was precise. Some words were in italic. What I saw said this:

under the flat cloth cap
jumbled mental jelly
chanting

juicy *juicy*
juicy *juicy*

* * *

Filing along the stone-paved path in Chekhov's garden towards the White Dacha I was thinking about an essay I'd written in 1982 in *Kicking Against the Pricks* entitled "Punctuation as Score." It had stirred as much interest in Canada as peasepudding in the pot nine days old. How delighted I was, then, many years subsequently to discover a letter Chekhov wrote to a young author in 1897 urging her "to learn the correct and literate use of punctuation marks because in a work of art they often play the part of notes in a musical score, and you cannot learn them from a textbook, but only from instinct and experience."

Chekhov had lived in the White Dacha with his mother, Eugenia, and his sister, Maria Chekhov (Masha), and his wife, the actress Olga Knipper. "This mangy Yalta" he had called the place and likened his exile from Moscow there as akin to Dreyfus' imprisonment on Devil's Island.

"I'd like to talk to somebody about literature . . ." he wrote, ". . . but here there is only irritating swinishness."

I was excited to somehow get closer to the man Raymond Carver in *No Heroics Please* called ". . . the greatest short story writer who has ever lived."

I'd lived with his work for many years. I'd lived with, among others, "The Steppe," "The Student," "The Bishop," "The Bride," "In the Cart," "The Lady with the Little Dog," and "The House with the Mezzanine."

But I'd been drawn to him for other reasons too.

The theatre.

His love of fishing.

Crayfish catching.

Picking wild berries and mushrooms.

His pet mongoose called Sod.

That painter's eye. In a piece of casual writing he described being out in the country waiting in a siding for eight hours for a train to come through: "I went out for a pee and pure miracles outside: the moon, the boundless steppe with its barrows and wilderness; the quiet of the grave, the carriages and rails stand out in the twilight – you'd think the world had died."

The small house was packed with people from the bus and I hung back in an outer room, a summer kitchen, I think, until the crowd thinned out. I was hoping to get some sense, some feeling of the life coughed out in that house, where Chekhov, lesions on both lungs, had summoned the heroic energy to write *Three Sisters* and *The Cherry Orchard*.

For years he had suffered from colitis, diarrhoea, and haemorrhoids. For the haemorrhaging from his lungs he took creosote which further destroyed his gut. To stave off pleurisy he endured compresses of cantharides. To sleep he drank chloral hydrate. As the pain and weakness bit in he was given injections of camphor, arsenic, morphine, opium, and heroin. As his heart deteriorated, he was treated with digitalis. And through all this horror, he wrote.

But the house gave nothing of this; it remained resolutely ordinary. The feel was Victorian, respectable, regulated. Chairs covered in loose slip covers, every table covered with fringed tablecloths, along the top of the piano with its brass swing-out candle brackets a long runner patterned like a doily. Pelmets and flouncy valances. The furniture was massy and unattractive. Iron bedsteads. Heavily framed photographs hung in nearly every room. There were few paintings in the house and only one of any merit, a landscape of the Istra River in Chekhov's study by his friend Isaak Levitan.

This temple to Anton Chekhov was the work of Maria Chekhova. She did not die until 1957 when she was 94. What emanations I was feeling I did not doubt came from the rather sadly oppressed Masha. The house was, I decided, a doily house.

Each room was closed off to visitors by a furry velvet rope across the doorway. Hanging behind the crowd, I looked into the rooms, the dining room, the sitting room, Chekhov's bedroom, Olga Knipper's room, Evgenia's stark room with an icon on a table beside the bed. Taking pictures was difficult because of the ropes and because of the reflections off the glass framing the photographs on the walls.

I stood looking into the sitting room at the upright piano and thinking of Chekhov's friendships with Rachmaninov and Tchaikovsky and how promptly they had grasped his innovative structures and heard his music. Interesting that Tolstoy turned out to be a dead end and that Chekhov was the trailblazer.

When Chekhov published his second story collection *In the Twilight* in 1887 a hack reviewer moved in to attack:

"Questions without answers, answers without questions, stories with no beginning or end, plots with no dénouement . . . Mr. Chekhov should turn on his work lamp in his study to light up these half-lit characters and dispel the gloom that conceals their silhouettes and contours."

Chekhov died just seventeen years later in 1904 and four thousand mourners walked in this great artist's funeral procession to Moscow's Novodevichie cemetery.

That genius of the short story, Eudora Welty, wrote in *The Eye of the Story*: "The revolution brought about by the gentle Chekhov to the short story was in every sense not destructive but constructive. By removing the formal plot he did not leave the story structureless, he endowed it with another kind of structure – one which embodied the principle of growth. And it was one that had no cause to repeat itself; in each and every story, short or long, it was a structure open to human meaning and answerable to that meaning. It took form from within."

It was with such stuff as this that my head was filled as I leaned into the sitting room trying to take a photograph of a portrait of Chekhov which stood on top of the piano. The glare off the glass was defeating me. I leaned in further over the rope. There was some sort of bustle and to-do in the hall behind me, shuffling, a sudden uprush of conversation, someone calling out. I glanced round and saw the guide rounding up stragglers and ushering people towards the front door.

"We must go now," he called, "and the door be locked."

"John!" called Myrna.

"Coming!" I called back, my eye still at the camera.

I turned to see her alone in the hall. She was laughing.

The guide took my arm.

"Sorry," I said.

"You must be quick!"

Unhooked the furry rope which blocked entrance to Chekhov's study. Gestured me in.

"Get in front of the couch," said Myrna unzipping her camera.

I stood just to one side of the Levitan painting.

"Hurry!" said the guide. "Hurry, hurry."

"Couple more to make sure," said Myrna.

The guide was shifting his agitated weight from foot to foot.

Took my arm again, snapped the furry rope into place, hurried us to the front door and out into the small forecourt where the people from the bus were milling about.

He scurried off to find the driver.

"Well!" I said to Myrna. "What in hell was *that* all about!"

"I told him that you were a writer and how much it would mean to you."

"Good God!" I said.

"Not the kind of thing *you* would do, I know, being so British and all, but . . ."

"Oh, that was so kind of you, Myrna, really . . . *And* of him. I mean, just to up and chuck everyone out."

"And after I told him how much it would mean to you," said Myrna, "I gave him a bribe."

* * *

When Myrna read through these last few pages she complained.

"You're doing it again," she said. "Just as you did in *An Aesthetic Underground.*"

"Doing what?"

"You're making me into a Wanda."

"Well," I said, "just a bit. But *lovingly.*"

We were talking in that verbal shorthand, as it were, common to marriages. Myrna was complaining that I was using her as Eric Newby used his wife Wanda in that glowing travel book *Slowly Down the Ganges.*

Newby writes lovely English, precise, easy flowing, no striving for effect, charming. Nearly every page affords visual and verbal pleasures. That Evelyn Waugh furnished a Preface to *A Short Walk in the Hindu Kush* might suggest the writing's quality.

This is typical Newby.

> . . . a number of turtles which stuck their heads out of the water and remained motionless with their mouths open like a lot of floating beer bottles.

Or this of a procession of pilgrims on a holy day.

> There was even an elephant with a painted head, chained, all alone at the side of the road. It was chewing grass and swishing its decorated trunk up and down, curling it delicately so that it looked like the initial letter on a page of illuminated manuscript but one that was constantly changing its shape.

We first met Wanda in *Love and War in the Apennines.* She was Slovenian but international boundary changes had placed her in northwest Italy. Newby was a prisoner of war held by the Italians. After the Italian surrender, Wanda helped to hide Newby from the Germans. His portrait of Italian peasant life is unlike anything else I've read.

Wanda does not appear in Newby's *A Short Walk in the Hindu Kush,* his account of a journey to Afghanistan, but he uses her as wonderful comic punctuation in *Slowly Down the Ganges.* Soon we were eagerly awaiting her every appearance.

> Each night I seemed to be doomed to be woken by somebody, and always in the small hours. This time it was Wanda. It was three o'clock in the morning. Everything was swaddled in thick fog. 'I have heard voices and seen figures,' she announced in a sepulchral Middle-European accent which only comes to the surface in moments of stress.

And,

> I had a row with Wanda. It was about something so ludicrous that after it had been going on for some minutes neither of us could remember the reason; but it was no less bitter for that.
>
> 'I shall leave you here,' she said. 'Boo-hoo!'
>
> It was not a convenient place to leave from. Besides what the devil would I do without her?

'Where will you go?' I said, really alarmed.

'I shall go back to my country and my people,' she answered majestically.

Wanda raises interesting questions. Is the Wanda of the book really Wanda or has she, in Myrna's words, been "made into" a character called "Wanda"? Is "Myrna" in this travel piece really Myrna? Is the writer using the techniques of fiction to "improve" a scene, enhance its pacing, insert light relief, impose a slant or direction? And underneath these persistent questions are other related questions all of which boil down to: is this recorded experience true?

My own response to the "Is it true?" problem is simply to deny that a problem exists. Let me illustrate my approach with an anecdote. Last year I was walking across the park in Russell Square near the British Museum. Myrna and I were staying at the Russell Hotel which boasts a room called The Virginia Woolf Bar and Grill. It was, to my sorrow, closed for refurbishment. I would definitely have had a Virginia Club or a Woolf Burger. Just imagine, ghastly snob that she was, how *appalled* she would have been!

Coming towards me on the path were two men deep in conversation. I was talking to Myrna and paid no attention to them other than to register that one was tall and the other of average height. As they passed, the smaller man was saying earnestly: "I do like something of a creamy consistency on my porridge."

I know these were his exact words as I had stopped in my tracks and written them in my notebook knowing them to be beyond price.

Later, I started playing with this unconsciously comic utterance and soon arrived at a different word arrangement.

What I wrote was this: "Not necessarily milk or cream," he said, "but I do like something of a creamy consistency on my porridge."

I felt the sentence had needed a "build-up" towards "porridge." The slightly odd placement of "Not necessarily milk or cream" suggests the speaker is finicky. The "he said" acts largely as punctuation of delay and delay in reaching "porridge' makes arrival funnier.

Later still, I played with a second version. What would happen if I moved "porridge" to an earlier position in the sentence giving the *weight* of the sentence to "something of a creamy consistency"?

Like this:

"Not necessarily milk or cream," he said, "but I do like on my porridge something of a creamy consistency."

Finally, I arrived at what I thought was the funniest version of all, a sentence exquisitely performed.

"Not necessarily milk or cream," he said, "but I do like on my porridge something *of a creamy consistency.*"

The average reader would probably say that all the versions say the same thing, the only element of invention being the words "Not necessarily milk or cream." But the average reader would be wildly wrong. The three versions which follow the first entirely accurate quotation are moving words into different positions for a rhetorical purpose. The three versions are moving step by step towards the suggestion of character. Through one line of speech a character begins to emerge; if I listened more I'd soon see what he *looked* like. A story might arrive.

Moving "porridge" to an earlier position in the sentence begins the creation; the speaker becomes more old-fashioned, more pedantic, precise, a fusspot. Italicizing "of a creamy consistency" hints to me that the speaker might well be gay.

Italicizing "of a creamy consistency" rather than "something of a creamy consistency" has interesting effects. "Something" in this particular sentence is what I think of as a "weakener;" it muffles the sentence slightly. By *not* italicizing it, a space in the speaking of the sentence is created; the reader is forced to pause for a beat before pronouncing the forceful "*of a creamy consistency*" and that pause makes the words even more portentous. Imagine yourself on a stage. Try it out loud.

The point of the anecdote?

Simply that the act of writing, of putting words on paper, is an act of creation rather than an act of transcription. Perhaps those who want to know if Wanda and her utterances are "true" or "real" are asking the wrong question. It could well be that many writers are not even faintly interested in transcribed truth. Perhaps they are more interested in word-order, in pauses, in emphases, in what I might call stage-effects. I have insisted all the way through this book on the artificiality of art. *Slowly Down the Ganges* is as much about language as it is about India's sacred river.

The two poles of travel writing seem to me to be books where the traveller effaces himself and attempts to portray encounters and adventures as objectively as possible and books where the personality of the traveller is at least as much the subject as the place being visited.

The traveller effaced is probably more typical of older, conservative writers who would consider personal revelation to be "not done," writers such as Wilfred Thesiger in *Arabian Sands* and *The Marsh Arabs* or Sir Laurens van der Post in *Venture to the Interior* and *The Lost World of the Kalahari*. V.S. Naipaul could also represent this pole. In *An Area of Darkness* his infrequently alluded-to "companion" was in fact his wife.

Naipaul's stance in this is not merely a matter of what he would doubtless consider well-bred reticence but also a matter of sound artistry. In 1981 Naipaul visited four Islamic countries, Indonesia, Iran, Malaysia, and Pakistan, and wrote an account entitled *Among the Believers: An Islamic Journey*. In 1998 he wrote a follow-up book called *Beyond Belief* and in the Prologue wrote:

> *Beyond Belief* adds to the earlier book, takes the story on. It also moves in a different way. It is less of a travel book; the writer is less present, less of an enquirer. He is in the background, trusting to his instinct, a discoverer of people, a finder-out of stories. These stories opening out one from the other, make their own pattern and define each country and its promptings; and the four sections of the book make a whole.
>
> I began my writing career as a fiction writer, a manager of narrative; at that time I thought it the highest thing to be. When I was asked – nearly forty years ago – to travel about certain colonial territories in South America and the Caribbean and to write a book, I was delighted to do the travelling – taking small aeroplanes to strange places, going up South American rivers – but then I wasn't sure how to write the book, how to make a pattern of what I was doing. That first time I got away with autobiography and landscape. It was years before I saw that the most important thing about travel, for the writer, was the people he found himself among.
>
> So in those travel books or cultural explorations of mine the writer as traveller steadily retreats; the people of the country come to the front; and I become again what I was at the beginning: a manager of narrative.

The opposite pole to Naipaul's self-effacement might well be the mordant ebullience of his erstwhile American friend Paul Theroux. (The bitter collapse of their friendship is detailed in Theroux's *Sir Vidia's Shadow*.) Theroux's priority is not Naipaul's "cultural exploration" and he is hilariously present in such books as *Kingdom by the Sea* (1983) and *The Great Railway Bazaar* (1975).

In *Kingdom by the Sea* Theroux wrote:

> The British had invented their own solution to travel writing. They went to places like Gabon and Paraguay and joked about the discomforts, the natives, the weather, the food, the entertainments. It was necessary to be an outsider, which was why they had never written about Britain in this way. But it was a mystery to me why no one had ever come to Britain and written about its discomforts and natives and entertainments and unintelligible dialects. The British, who had devised a kind of envious mockery of other cultures, and who had virtually invented the concept of funny foreigners, had never regarded themselves as fair game for the travel writer. They did not encourage aliens to observe them closely. They were like a tribe that plundered abroad and were secretive and inhospitable at home. The British did not make me think of Shakespeare but rather of head-hunters – their travel writing a literary version of head-shrinking that had never been used on them. I was eager to try.

Before setting out on his journey around the British coast, he gives us a foretaste of the drubbing the British are about to receive.

> Once, from behind a closed door, I heard an Englishwoman exclaim with real pleasure, 'They are *funny*, the Yanks!' And I crept away and laughed to think that an English person was saying such a thing. And I thought: They wallpaper their ceilings! They put little knitted bobble-hats on their soft-boiled eggs to keep them warm! They don't give you bags in supermarkets! They say sorry when you step on their toes! Their government makes them get a hundred-dollar licence every year for watching television! They issue drivers' licences that are valid for thirty or forty years – mine expires in 2011! They charge you for matches when you buy cigarettes! They smoke on buses! They drive on the left! They spy for the Russians! They say 'nigger' and 'Jewboy' without flinching! They call their houses Holmleigh and Sparrow

> View! They sunbathe in their underwear! They don't say 'You're welcome'! They still have milk-bottles and milkmen and junk-dealers with horse-drawn wagons! They love candy and Lucozade and leftovers called bubble-and-squeak! They live in Barking and Dorking and Shellow Bowells! They have amazing names, like Mr. Eatwell and Lady Inkpen and Major Twaddle and Miss Tosh! And they think *we're* funny!

I'm sure that Naipaul's view of travel writing is the more responsible but I have a weakness for comedy and find certain writers irresistible. I've read many modern travel writers – Bruce Chatwin, Jan Morris, Colin Thubron, Gavin Young, Paul Theroux, Dervla Murphy, Bill Bryson – but no travel writer as dementedly funny as Redmond O'Hanlon, author of *Into the Heart of Borneo*, *Congo Journey*, and *In Trouble Again*.

In Trouble Again recounts a journey undertaken by O'Hanlon through the Venezuelan Amazonas in company with his friend Simon Stockton, croupier at a Kensington casino and photography enthusiast. Martin Amis called the book "hallucinogenic, scrotum-tightening." Bill Bryson wrote of it, "*In Trouble Again* is, in my view, the best travel book of the twentieth century. If you have not read it before, you are about to become a very lucky person."

I'll leave the topic of travel-writing with Simon Stockton's speech to O'Hanlon outlining his reasons for quitting the expedition.

> 'Why should I be stung by ants and wasps and hornets and bees all day? I've been thinking about it. It's nothing but rain and mosquitoes and the same bloody awful trees and endless rivers and disgusting food and being wet all the time. There's no comradeship. There's no wine and no women and no song and nowhere sensible to shit.'
>
> 'I'm sorry,' I said, 'you'll think differently in the morning.'
>
> 'No I bloody won't,' said Simon, his eyes white in the murk, 'oh no I bloody well won't! I've been thinking about it *for four weeks*. And when I had that supper with the doctors in San Carlos I realized exactly what I was going to do. I only came back to tell you properly. It's not that I'm frightened. It's not really your fault. *It's just that I can't bear to go back in there'* (he waved the bottle in the direction of the landing-stage and the uncut jungle) 'and why the hell should I?'

'Do you think you are so unstable already,' said Juan, in his most precise way, his beard outlined in the light of the kerosene lamp, pressed forward in interrogation, 'because of the sudden withdrawal of drugs and alcohol on this journey?'

'You stupid dago,' said Simon, exasperated, 'how the hell would I know?'

'Don't do it,' I said. 'You'll feel bad about it later. About deserting me.'

'Redmond,' said Simon, relaxing, 'I'll handle all that with the first pint of cognac.'

'Don't be silly. You'll never forgive yourself.'

'Oh yes I damn well will. I have already. Redmond – I've cried four times in my adult life. Once when my father died; once when my wife left me; once when Pinky my cat was run over in front of me; and every night when we were lost up that stinking pitsville of a swamp.'

'What about the Yanomami? What about your pictures?'

'I don't want to see the Yanomami. *I can't stand all the poverty.* These people are bad enough. *They don't own anything.* And anyway, my cameras are totally, but totally full of mould and gunge and parasites, and the odd fish too, I shouldn't wonder. It's the pits. I can hear the films turn to soup as I wind them on. But I've worked it out – I'll leave you the manual Minolta I haven't used, in the sealed bag; the small zoom; the flashgun; and all the remaining black-and-white rolls. Then with your Nikonos as well you'll be ready for anything. It's different for you, all this. You've got no taste-buds at all. You think everything's wonderful. You wouldn't know a good meal if I shoved one down your throat. You're a fat brute. You're about as sensitive as a rhinoceros. And there again, you're manic on top of it. You get excited every time you see a new bird. Whereas me, in all honesty, Redmond, to be totally frank with you, I just think, well, *there goes another fucking bird.*'

'What will you do,' I said, suddenly envious, 'when you get home?'

'I will drink *top-class* wine,' said Simon, '*in huge quantities.* I'll take Liz and the kids to Portugal for a holiday. And when we come back we'll have pork and beef, on alternate Sundays, for family lunch. But I'll always do the potatoes because Liz never gets them quite crispy enough, just round the edges, know what I mean? In fact, now I come to think of it, I'll damn well marry her. We'll buy a decent house together, *well away from you.* And I'll go back to the casino and graft like a shitcake and never ever complain about anything ever again.'

* * *

We filed dutifully into the Great White Hall of the Livadia Palace. Here in 1945, Churchill, Roosevelt, and Stalin decided the fate of post-war Europe. I looked at the long tables down the length of the hall where the functionaries and politicians had exchanged paper. In a small anteroom was a circular table where the big three had sat. I felt nothing much, curiosity perhaps about how much Churchill had known of Stalin's monstrousness, a distaste perhaps for Churchill's ingratiatory manner towards him.

Churchill must have known of Stalin's suspicion of any Russians who had witnessed the immeasurably higher standard of living enjoyed by Western workers, must have known of Stalin's fear of the taint of that information spreading. Churchill, in exchange for his desired occupation zones in Germany, acquiesced in Stalin's demand for the forced repatriation of all Russian prisoners. Stalin in earlier obstinacy over the Geneva Convention and the activities of the Red Cross had said: "There are no Russian prisoners of war. The Russian soldier fights on till death. If he chooses to become a prisoner, he is automatically excluded from the Russian community."

The British sent to Odessa in convoys 32,295 Russian soldiers, men of the *Ostlegionen* and Todt Labour Battalions captured in Normandy. A British naval officer in a contemporaneous account described his ship's docking in Odessa. NKVD men boarded with lists and led away named men. Two bombers appeared over the harbour and circled low for twenty minutes filling the air with their uproar. At the same time a mobile sawing-mill on the dock was put into howling operation – all to mask the sounds of the slaughter in the dockfront warehouses. Those left alive were boxed into trains for Siberia.

How could Churchill not have known that "repatriation" meant death or the Gulag?

* * *

The upstairs Romanov Apartments yielded a different kind of sadness. The Tsar's study was furnished in green leather with a large writing table, large wood-and-leather chairs where he had received. The study and the Tsarina's living room were hung everywhere with photographs, picture-taking having been a family obsession. Some were formal portraits of the Tsar in varying military and naval uniforms but most were family pictures, snapshots.

Here is a record of the summer life of the family. Nicholas II, Tsar of All the Russias, the Tsarina Alexandra Feodorovna, (born Princess Alix of Hesse-Darmstadt, granddaughter of Queen Victoria, and cousin to George V and Kaiser Wilhelm II) the Grand Duchesses Olga, Tatiana, Maria, and Anastasia and the Tsarevich Alexei.

The girls in summer white with wide, flowered hats.

On country walks.

Picking wild flowers.

Sitting at elaborate picnics in the woods, white linen tablecloths.

Paddling in the sea.

Playing tennis.

Lessons on the terrace with their Swiss tutor, Pierre Gilliard.

Sitting side-saddle on their ponies in practice for reviewing regiments.

Alexei on his tricycle built to safeguard him from falls and subsequent haemophilia.

Anastasia, feet swinging under the piano bench, doggedly working on her baggy knitting.

Within the family, the Tsar apparently called Alexandra by her childhood nickname "Sunny" or "Sunshine;" she spoke Russian and German badly having been brought up almost entirely in England. The Tsarevich was known as "Baby;" the youngest of the Grand Duchesses, Anastasia, was always known as "Schwibzik" – Little One.

Anna Vyrubova, the Tsarina's confidante, wrote in 1923 in *Memories of the Russian Court* about the coming out ball of the Grand Duchess Olga at Livadia Palace in 1911. Olga was sixteen. Only seven years later she was murdered with all the others at Ekaterinburg.

> It was a very charming ball that marked the introduction to society of the oldest daughter of the Tsar. Flushed and fair in her first long gown, something pink and filmy and of course very smart, Olga was

> as excited over her debut as any other young girl. Her hair, blonde and abundant, was worn for the first time coiled up young lady fashion, and she bore herself as the central figure of the festivities with a modesty and a dignity which greatly pleased her parents. We danced in the great state dining room on the first floor, the glass doors to the courtyard thrown open, the music of the unseen orchestra floating in from the rose garden like a breath of its own wondrous fragrance. It was a perfect night, clear and warm, and the gowns and jewels of the women and the brilliant uniforms of the men made a striking spectacle under the blaze of the electric lights. The ball ended in a cotillion and a sumptuous supper served on small tables in the ballroom.
>
> This was a beginning of a series of festivities which the Grand Duchess Olga and a little later on her sister Tatiana enjoyed to the utmost, for they were not in the least like the conventional idea of princesses, but simple, happy, normal young girls, loving dancing and parties and all the frivolities which make youth bright and memorable.

After the abdication and the exile of the family to Tobolsk in Siberia it became increasingly apparent to them that they might be murdered. Or anyway, apparent to the Tsarina. Nicholas seems to have been vague and fatalistic by nature, rudderless. In letters smuggled out to Anna Vyrubova, the Tsarina dwelt on the last things and the hope of the life everlasting.

That she painted and hand-lettered and decorated while in Tobolsk the following *troparion* from the Orthodox Requiem Service suggests the direction of her thoughts.

> O Thou who, with wisdom profound, mercifully orderest all things, and who givest that which is expedient unto all men, Thou Only Creator; Give rest, O Lord, to the souls of Thy servants who have fallen asleep; for they have set their hope on Thee, our Maker, the Author of our being, and our God.

When the family was moved from Tobolsk to Ekaterinburg they were imprisoned in the Ipatiev House, the former home of a merchant. The Ekaterinburg Soviet renamed the house "The House of Special Purpose" – the corruption of language the herald of atrocity.

(Though even George Orwell would turn in his grave at the recent foul invention by the Americans of the word "rendition" to mean "shipped to compliant countries to be tortured.")

The simple, mainstream, generally accepted account of events in July 1918 is as follows. The White Army led by two crack Czech divisions was eight days away from Ekaterinburg and obviously bound to take it. The Ekaterinburg Soviet decided it was a matter of political urgency to kill – and obliterate – the Romanovs. Like the Allies after World War II, the Bolsheviks wanted no rallying point, no hallowed tombs of fallen leaders to focus resistance. Preparations were made; 200 gallons of gasoline were ordered, 50 gallons of sulphuric acid.

On the night of July 16, a murder squad of Chekists shot in a downstairs room of the Ipatiev House, Tsar Nicholas II, the Tsarina Alexandra Feodorovna, the Grand Duchesses Olga, Tatiana, Maria, and Anastasia and the Tsarevich Alexei. Also murdered with them were the family physician Dr. Evgenii Botkin, the footman Alexsei Trupp, the cook Ivan Kharitonov, and the housemaid Anna Demidova.

The bodies were taken in a truck to the mine shaft of the Four Brothers Mine some thirteen miles away. There the clothing was stripped off and the bodies hacked into pieces. They were then burned and what remained doused in sulphuric acid and thrown down the mineshaft.

The White Army broke the line at Ekaterinburg days later and officers raced to the Ipatiev House but the only living creature there was Alexei's half-starved spaniel, Joy.

That is the generally accepted account of events.

There were three official investigations into the murders conducted by Whites and, as the fortunes of war changed, the Reds. There were also various investigations by amateurs and journalists and George V sent an experienced diplomat to assess the situation. The forensic evidence was totally contaminated and physical evidence stolen or destroyed. Almost simultaneously with the announcement of the "execution" there were rumours and assertions that what was to be seen in the Ipatiev House was the *simulation* of a mass murder scene; blood there was, but not enough, and bullet holes there were but not in the numbers that might have been expected according to confessions and depositions made by Yakov Yurovsky and others of the killers. *Between* official investigations the number of bullet holes in the wall seemed to increase from seventeen to twenty-seven.

King George V's envoy reported to the Foreign Office and to the King that on July 17 a train with all the blinds lowered left Ekaterinburg for an unknown destination and that it was believed it carried the surviving members of the imperial family.

Who, then, was murdered in the House of Special Purpose? Those who contest the generally accepted account claim that Nicholas and Alexandra were killed immediately and the four servants were then murdered to supply a convincing amount of flesh. The Grand Duchesses were secretly saved on Lenin's orders for use as leverage with the Germans.

But this theory is contradicted in a recent book (1992) by the Russian historian and dramatist Edvard Radzinsky entitled *The Last Tsar*. Radzinsky quotes Yakov Yurovsky and others of the killers, all Chekists, concerning the hellish night of July 16. They describe bullets as *bouncing off* the girls' bodies, bayonets as unable to penetrate. They allege that the girls and Alexandra were wearing double bodices and corsets filled with diamonds. At the Four Brothers mine when the clothes were stripped off and burned the men recovered from the clothes half a pood of diamonds (eighteen pounds). According to their depositions the fusillade in the Ipatiev House by the twelve Chekists was so concentrated that the smoke from the guns began to fog out the electric light. Eventually all were dead except Anastasia and, despairing of bayonets, they finished her off with rifle butts.

Some rumours claimed Nicholas' last words, echoing Christ's, were, "You know not what you do," but this is obvious hagiolatry. Yurovsky said that he said to Nicholas, "In view of the fact that your relatives are continuing their attack on Soviet Russia, the Ural Executive Committee has decided to execute you."

Nicholas' reply and last words according to Yurovsky before Yurovsky shot him in the head were, "What? What?"

Lord Emsworth-like and more believable.

But how believable is *any* of this material?

There are detailed problems with every aspect of the evidence presented. I became so wrapped up in the minutiae of accounts that I found myself phoning my son-in-law Ethan, a gun enthusiast who hand-loads his rounds for competition shooting, to ask him if in his opinion the smoke from those guns in the Ipatiev House – seventeen shots fired, or possibly twenty-seven – could have been so dense as to have fogged out the electric light. He tolerantly informed me that smokeless powder had been in use since the 1880s.

The murder squad according to one eyewitness account was armed only with twelve Nagant revolvers. Another said two men had Mauser machine pistols. Yet another specified two men as being armed with a Browning and a Colt .45.

The infernal scene at the mine shaft creates more problems. Not enough bones were found to suggest eleven bodies. No teeth, the most indestructible part of the body, were ever found. Women's corset-stays were found but were unmarked by bullets.

Two BBC investigative reporters, Anthony Summers and Tom Mangold in their book *The File on the Tsar* (1976) come to the conclusion that the four Grand Duchesses were aboard that sealed train which left Ekaterinburg on July 17. They were taken to Perm where they were imprisoned but seen by several witnesses who later gave testimony. The testimony is not overwhelming. The explanation the authors offer is that Lenin wanted the girls as pawns to counter German intervention but with the Treaty of Brest-Litovsk safely signed and with the Germans facing stalemate if not defeat on the Western Front, Lenin thought intervention increasingly unlikely and that he could afford to have the girls dispatched.

This explanation, however, does not take into account the murder of the Tsarina, Kaiser Wilhelm's cousin.

And then there's the Grand Duchess Anastasia who may have escaped and who may have been living as late as 1976 as Anna Anderson (Mrs. John Manahan) in Charlottesville, Virginia.

But documents are missing from archives, various royal families are uncooperative, evidence of this or that has disappeared, is thought to have been suppressed . . .

As I read further in this morass of conjecture and coincidence it occurred to me suddenly that I'd been through all this before with the murder of John F. Kennedy. Was there one man or two on the sixth floor of the Texas School Book Depository? Were shots fired from The Grassy Knoll? Who was Lee Harvey Oswald? Why did Oswald kill Police Officer J.D. Tippit? Why did Jack Ruby kill Oswald? Was the information gathered by the Warren Commission and published as the Warren Report inclusive and unbiased?

Who was behind the Kennedy assassination? Texas oil interests? Anti-Castro groups in Miami angry that Kennedy denied them air support at the Bay of Pigs? Was it renegade CIA agents? The dapper New Orleans District

Attorney Jim Garrison brought a notorious case against Clay Shaw, a CIA contract man, and suggested assassination evidence was being suppressed by Lyndon Baines Johnson. Was it the mafia sending a message to Bobby Kennedy to let up the pressure? What was Kennedy's relationship to the mob? Jack Ruby was mob-connected. JFK enjoyed the ministrations of the same call girl, Judith Exner, as Sam Giancana, boss of the Chicago mob. Was it the John Birch Society in New Orleans which regarded Kennedy as communist? Other theorists thought that the New Orleans tentacles stretched down into South America and connected with United Fruit and Standard Fruit and Steamship – two of the biggest banana companies in the world – which . . .

And bananas is exactly what one would go after prolonged exposure to the "evidence" of either the assassination of John F. Kennedy or the murder of the Romanovs in the House of Special Purpose.

And to what end was all the killing?

Revolutionary zeal led not to the establishment of a visionary society but to the roar of two planes circling over Odessa harbour and the howl of a mobile sawing mill.

Despite the millions who died, my thoughts – perhaps, sentimentally, perhaps not – lingered with one person, "Schwibzik" – Little One.

* * *

Few people now remember the Canadian novelist Juan Butler. I knew him slightly, an unpleasant man unpleasantly unhinged. He committed suicide in a psychiatric hospital in 1981. He wrote three novels which are forgotten by everyone but are embalmed with too much else in the *Oxford Companion to Canadian Literature* (First, Second, and Concise Editions). The novels were *Cabbagetown Diary* (1970), *The Garbage Man* (1972) and *Canadian Healing Oil* (1974).

(The *Companion* entry on Butler was written by that savant of Canadian literature Professor All-Purpose Staines who refers to *Canadian Healing Oil* in all three editions as *Canadian Heating Oil.* But as Bill Hoffer used to say, this is Canada and approximations are good enough.)

The novels are deservedly forgotten but whenever my mind turns to problems political I always remember the material Butler used as an epigraph in *The Garbage Man.*

QUESTION

Tell me, in the anarchist society that you envisage, where all men will be free, where no one will ever be in a position to impose his will upon his fellow man, where 'doing your own thing' will be the norm rather than the exception, where creative leisure – as opposed to material success – will be the aspired-for work goal, where all political authority will disappear and economic controls will exist on a purely voluntary basis, who will pick up the garbage?

ANSWER

The garbage man.

* * *

Myrna had bumped into Alan in the *Minerva's* passenger laundry. He'd been washing two white cable-knit sweaters that he and Martin from Cincinnati were to wear the following day in Odessa. They put her in mind, Myrna said, of lawn bowling or yachting. Alan had confided that they were 60 per cent cotton and forty per cent the P-word but strictly, *but strictly,* for travel.

We walked up the noble Odessa Steps where Tsar Nicholas' troops had savaged the mutineers from the *Potemkin* in the 1905 revolution, impossible not to be seeing in the mind's eye the baby-carriage montage from Eisenstein's 1925 *Battleship Potemkin,* impossible for *me*, at any rate, not to be thinking of the profundity of the visual language of silent films and its overwhelming impact on fiction writing.

Odessa was lucky to have been built at exactly the right time – very late 18th century to mid-19th. The influences were classical – a touch of Baroque here and there getting out of control – and the design generally refined. The town is largely the creation of Armand Emmanuel du Plessis, Duc de Richelieu (great-great nephew of the cardinal), who was Governor General of the city in 1803-14. The result is something like a miniature Paris or Madrid. The buildings are mostly three-story and based on the idea of the interior courtyard. The boulevards are tree-lined and spacious and people actually do promenade in the graciousness of the Prymorsky Bulvar at one end of which stands Prince Vorontsov's Palace built in impressive classical style but rundown now, partly boarded up and sadly still called Palace of the Pioneers.

The Pioneers was a Party organization with compulsory membership to indoctrinate elementary school children in communist thought. Upon completing the curriculum of the Pioneers, the children moved into the organization for teenagers, the Komsomol, before graduating into the full-blown embrace of Soviet life.

Fortunate Prince Vorontsov that he died in 1854.

Beside the Cathedral of the Assumption or was it the Ilinsky Cathedral – a bewilderment of places to see, the Archeological Museum with at least two dozen Greek pottery shapes new to me, Pushkin's house, the lodgings favoured by Gogol, Isaac Babel's house . . .

Babel! I still treasured the Cossack slang in Babel's stylish stories in *Red Cavalry* which I'd read for the first time in Montreal in the sixties when I was educating myself in the genre. Isaac Babel. Arrested 1938, died in the Gulag.

In the precinct of whichever cathedral it *was*, Alan and Martin pounced on two stalls, rough tables draped with old bits of carpet, the one displaying icons, the other naval memorabilia of the Russian Black Sea Fleet, badges, medals, oddments of uniform.

They bought an icon each, the wood distressed and pitted with precision worm-holes, but were even more overjoyed by the Russian high-peaked officers' caps, the badges worked in gold wire against an oval ground of white felt. They urged tour members to take their photos on the cathedral steps.

Alan saluted.

Click

They mugged.

Click

Linked arms.

Soyuz Sovetskikh, intoned Martin, *Sotsialistichesskikh Respublik.*

He turned his head to one side and with a rigid forefinger at the cap's rear edge tipped it forward over one eye.

Click

I feared that they might in tandem clack into slick dance steps.

"Make way!" called a quavery old man from the tour. "Make way for a naval officer."

* * *

The three boys in the front row carried assault rifles held across their chests, the three girls behind them held their arms rigidly at their sides. They were all in ceremonial sailor uniform, white belts with gold buckles, gold lanyards, white gloves. The girls in blue serge skirts. They marched down the ceremonial approach past the flanking red polished granite graves of resistance fighters killed in World War II and took up positions of respect at the cardinal points surrounding the Monument to the Unknown Sailor, a granite obelisk on the cliff edge overlooking Odessa's harbour and wharves.

The ceremony was apparently repeated every hour throughout the day, the cadets, if that was what they were, drawn in rotation from Odessa's high schools. The goose step marching was obviously inherited from the Russians. It always chilled me rather. I've seen the same march performed by the Nazis, the Soviets, Il Duce's Fascists, by the dementedly vigorous North Koreans, lately by Hezbollah parading through Beirut. Such a marching style proclaims the suppression of the individual and implies, in W.B. Yeats' line, the loosening of the "blood-dimmed tide." There's viciousness in it yet that part of me that isn't intimidated finds something in it grotesquely funny, the martial equivalent, say, of synchronised swimming.

We made halting conversation with the cadets, the girls in white knee socks and wildy unlikely strapped high heels. Was this sanctioned formal attire in the Ukraine? Or did they change into these shoes after leaving the house? The girls were so pretty in the morning sun but probably doomed, I thought in sudden gloom, to grow to great bulk and play the accordion. As I sauntered back towards the bus, one of the boys called out, "Goodbye, American friend."

I sat on the bus and watched a pack of dogs lying in the park under the shade of a tree. There were eleven of them. None of them had collars on and I presumed they were feral. I thought of the ones we'd seen at the Alupka Palace. These were in worse shape. They were rib-thin. One showed patches of raw skin the size of saucers and the colour of ham. A female dog was lying on her side with what could have been the right hind leg broken. There was blood on it and its angle odd.

If anyone approached on the nearby path, the dogs tensed, watchful and still. I wondered what they thought about people. If any had once been pets? Danger past – if people *were* a danger – they returned their attention to their flea-bitten flanks and haunches chawing, chawing through the dulled fur. The dog with the injured leg had two half-grown pups. Whenever she tried to get up, they pounced in biting the dragging leg and toppling her. If she snarled at them, one in particular chop-chopped her mask, his lips drawn back in a manner that seemed not at all like play.

Then the driver switched on the engine, the Baden Powell man was shouting about having the radio turned off, the Honour Guard was marching *stomp, stomp, stomp* back up the avenue and an old man stood suddenly to photograph them through the window and dropped with a cry, felled into his seat by the overhead storage rack.

"And now," cried the amplified lady guide, "away we go to the Lenin Monument!"

* * *

Constanza, Romania's principal seaport, was originally called Tomis and was the city to which Ovid was exiled in 9 AD, poor sod.

Tomis was founded in the 7th century by Greek settlers from Miletus in Anatolia. The Romans annexed the region – known to them as Scythia Minor – in the first century BC, and in the 4th century AD Tomis was reconstructed by Constantine the Great and renamed Constantiana.

Constantza depressed us. Stained concrete. Poverty mixed with stores selling international brand names. Decaying buildings. Abandoned lots strewn with rubble and refuse. Doorways reeking of piss. A used-up place, an old rind, all the juice squeezed out of it. And a miasma over all of a scarcely-ousted bureaucracy.

"Well, I don't in any way want to hurt your feelings, Myrna . . ."

"No," she said, "that's all right. I'm just glad my grandparents had the energy to leave."

In the afternoon we drove to Histria, Romania's oldest city. The countryside was as sad and bleak as the city. Single ploughed fields stretched seemingly for miles with no trees or hedges in sight. Tractors stood in these limitless fields five and six abreast. I assumed the fields had years before been collectivized, the smallholdings and family histories with them, obliterated. It was a desolation that made me angry.

The two villages we passed through were in vibrant contrast to this Passchendaele landscape. They were squalid, ramshackle, two-or-three room houses patched with corrugated tin, beaten-earth yards with hens, ducks, and geese pecking over the garbage, fly-twitched donkeys and ponies tethered to fruit trees. The gardens were growing cabbages and beans and grapes and in some stood teepees of cut rushes stooked to dry for bedding. The villages looked as I imagined a *shtetl* might have done. What inhabitants we saw were swarthy with grime.

Histria was set at the edge of a vast reed-fringed swamp. The bus pulled onto a rough parking lot of broken brick mixed with asphalt in front of a glass box of a museum set down beside this waste of reeds and stagnant water. Mosquitoes whined. On a tussock rising above the water some two hundred yards away stood a large bird startlingly white, a crane perhaps, or an ibis. The dampness in the air turned to drizzle.

The museum was intensely boring. The contents, mainly red Roman ware, had nearly all been broken and the missing shards had been reconstituted in white plaster. The two big rooms at a glance were a leprosy of red and white. No effort at aesthetics or even selection had been attempted; if it had been uncovered at the site, in it went. Shapeless, rusted lumps of iron were identified as "anchors;" the profusion of broken pots was labelled as "storage vessels," "wine vessels," "conical vessels;" a row of corroded pieces of bronze was labelled "mirrors;" scraps and unidentifiable fragments were identified as "decorative elements." Here and there the accumulation was adorned by a stele with an inscription so weathered and eroded as to leave visible only such words as *hic* and *est*.

The three main periods of the site, Greek, Roman, and Byzantine were recorded in three massive and profusely illustrated hardcover tomes which gave off a strong whiff of State Publishing. They had been compiled in the 1920s. The authors all wore pince-nez and wing collars with loosely-knotted ties. The books cost 25 new *leys* each.

Outside the museum a muddy path led to the site itself through an arch in a tumbled brick wall. Feral dogs scoured the parking lot for crumbs. The path ended. The baulk of turf I was negotiating crumbled and my right foot slipped deep into the cold mire. A mosquito *zizzizzed* in my ear.

"I hate this place."

"Oh, stop being childish."

"My foot's wet."

"Oh, look, these must have been houses."

I looked at the jumble of low walls, footprints of buildings. Nothing was recognizably anything. Some of the walls were stone; some brick. Some bits of wall contained pantile so were probably Byzantine.

I slapped at mosquitoes.

Stared down what might have been a street.

Inside the stone squares grew sedge and wind-stunted bushes.

The drizzle turned to a steadier rain.

"And what was this big place over here?" called Myrna.

"Fuck!" I said.

"What?"

"Blood!"

"Oh!" she called. "Here's a plaque!"

"I'm going back to the bus!"

"But we haven't seen everything."

"I don't wish to discommode you," I said, "but I am swelling rapidly."

"So *this*," she said, pointing to an expanse of debris, "was the apse but the dome fell in. *So*," she said, glancing down at the diagram, "over *here*, this must be . . ."

"I don't care," I said, "if it's the collapsed apse of a fucking Byzantine *whorehouse*! It is raining. My foot is wet. I am getting bitten to death. My body is covered in infected Romanian lumps."

I glared at her back as she bent again over the plaque and diagram.

"Goodbye!"

The dogs were lying now in the ditch at the edge of the parking lot watching the buses and the tourists straggling back out of the murk and mire.

On the steps of the museum the custodian was stooping above a deformed puppy which kept trying to lurch through the open glass door. Its belly was swollen huge and one eye was much larger than the other and bulged out from its face reminding me of those grotesquely overbred goldfish, goggle-eyed and trailing white fungus-like growths round the sockets.

The custodian kept making scooping-water gestures with his cupped hands and shouting what sounded like "Marsh! Marsh!" and every time he shouted the puppy whiddled on the step.

Some of the stragglers appearing through the gloom had umbrellas, others wore plastic hoods. Mosquitos whined on the coach windows. The crinkle of Cellophane, somebody opening a packet. Rain drumming on the roof. The smell of damp clothes.

"How are your bites?" said Myrna.

I gave her a cold glance.

"You smell," I said, "like a cloakroom."

"Air-conditioning ON," shouted the Baden Powell man.

". . . thirteen fourteen, fifteen . . ."counted the guide.

"Not *another* museum," said the man behind.

"It's mosaics," said his wife.

"I'd rather an early dinner."

"They're *Roman*," said his wife.

"Oh!" he said. "Why didn't you say? Roman! Well, If I'd known they were *Roman* . . ."

"Now, Harold!" she said.

". . . nine, ten, eleven . . ." re-counted the guide.

The custodian had retreated into the museum and closed the door. The pack had materialized behind the puppy and sat watching the lighted windows.

". . . the lady," Baden Powell was saying to the guide, "will have got on one of the other buses – silly old trout."

The driver turned the key in the ignition.

"Jaldi!" roared Baden Powell. "Jaldi jao!"

The bus bumped across the parking lot and ground up onto the approach road. As it began to pick up speed and the museum receded, the custodian shrank smaller and smaller, a black speck within the lighted cube.

A LETTER TO MICHAEL

Michael Carbert
P.O. Box 2023
Marathon, Ontario
POT 2EO

Dear Michael,

I must again thank you for typing up the "Continuo" chapter for me. Hands stretched out to rescue the drowning. And congratulations again on the move to Montreal. I rather suspected that Marathon, Ontario, was not going to be your Shangri-La when a while back you mentioned the squashed bear on the town's main street getting flatter by the day.

During the time you've been typing this stuff for me you've mentioned that it seemed to be heading somewhere but that you couldn't really figure out what I was up to. And I promised a letter Revealing All. So this is it.

In his Author's Foreword to *Finding the Centre: Two Narratives*, V.S. Naipaul writes: "The two personal narrative pieces that make up *Finding the Centre* were written one after the other and occupied the best part of two years. They are offered as a book principally for that reason; and also because, over and above their story content, both pieces are about the process of writing. Both pieces seek in different ways to admit the reader to that process."

That, in essence, was what I was setting out to do in "Continuo" – admitting the reader to the process of writing. The chapter is, in a way, meditating on my own work. It is most definitely *not* "What I Did on My Summer Holidays." But to make sense of these declarations I shall have to meander at some length in a preparatory way – so please bear with me in patience.

Do you remember an early story of mine called "Dandelions"? It was in *The Lady Who Sold Furniture* and is now effectively out of print. I'll include it here for your convenience as I need to talk about the making of it before I can really get at the "Continuo" material.

Dandelions

George Kenway straightened his shoulders and sat upright to ease the pang of heartburn. He breathed deeply until the pain began to fade, its sharpness settling into a dull ache in his teeth on the left side. He took the bottle of aspirins from the centre drawer of the desk and shook a couple out onto his palm. When the pains had first started he had thought he was suffering heart attacks.

It was probably lack of exercise. That, and sitting hunched over the desk. When the spring came again he would really try to get himself into shape. He pulled his stomach in and looked down, but the grey cardigan Mary had knitted him still bulged. Tennis might do the trick. He stared down at the mother-of-pearl buttons. Or walking. Walking was quite pleasant. He pushed his spectacles higher on the bridge of his nose.

On both sides of the central aisle, the shelves stretched down the length of the narrow shop. There were no customers. In the silence, he could hear the sounds of the old beams and floor boards. On the desk lay *Imprint* and *Book News*; he had not yet read them. The paperback order-forms, too, were waiting to be completed. The pencil in his hand doodled over the yellow pad drawing tiny, interlocking circles in endless repetitions.

The bell above the door jangled. A woman with a child came in. He looked at her over his glasses and inclined his head in welcome. He never approached customers now. He did not want to say *Can I help you?* and hear the ritual *I'm just looking, thank you.*

"A book for a boy, madam? This boy? Over in the far corner."

Over in the far corner with all the trains and planes, the fire engines and the spaceships, the brown bunnies and the cuddly bears; with all the fat, pink pigs in trousers, the winsome pups and patient horses. He glanced at his pocket watch. The glass was scratched and yellowed. It had belonged to his father. Mary had made a shammy-leather pocket for it in the waistband of his trousers.

Business was slow, even for a Monday. Twenty-odd paperbacks, a book about the care of budgies, two copies of *Middlemarch* because they were doing it on TV and an enquiry:

I can order it for you.

And the traditional lie:

I especially wanted it for today.

He wrapped the book in brown paper, sticking down the flaps with tape. So much more sensible than string. *Farm Friends.* And change from the tin cash box in his drawer. He walked toward the door with the woman but stopped to straighten the Penguins and Pelicans. He would have to re-order, too, on the new gardening books. A very popular line.

He moved back past Gardening and Cookery, Religion (Common Prayers in white leatherette and Presentation Bibles), Modern Literature (low again on the Cronin's and Shute's), Hobbies, Travel, and Adventure, towards his desk.

He had put his sandwiches in the desk drawer. He wondered what they were today. Cheese and tomato, perhaps? He hoped they weren't fish-paste or luncheon-meat. Those always left him so thirsty. She'd promised shepherd's pie tonight. He'd always liked that. It was an attractive name, too. Shepherd's pie. As he put his hand down to open the drawer, he noticed the sticking plaster across the back of his thumb. He thought, as he always did, what an unpleasant colour it was; that unnatural flesh colour, almost salmon, that children produced in their paintings. A nasty scrape on one of the wing nuts of Roy's bicycle. And the wheel still wasn't straight. That would be another job for tonight. He'd probably have to take off the brake blocks. And the front hedge couldn't go much longer. It was silly, though, how upset she got about things like that. He would have to buy a bottle of machine oil for the clippers on the way home.

The sandwiches were wrapped in grease-proof paper and secured with an elastic band. He looked at his watch again and decided to wait until one o'clock. Another ten minutes. Perhaps he could lose weight if, every day, he left one sandwich. But then, he knew that he would eat it with his afternoon cup of tea.

Sometimes, in the long afternoons, after the day had been divided by the sandwiches, he saw the shelves as he had always imagined them, the rows of calf-bound volumes, gilt titles, gilt decoration on the spines, the light hinting on the mahogany richness of the old leather. Standing along the bottom shelves, the massive folios – heraldry, county visitations, voyages, theological disputations and chronicles. The air would be heavy with the must of old paper. Lying open on his desk, or perhaps propped against his works of reference, would be a sixteenth-century German blackletter with quaint woodcuts, and in the glass-fronted cases behind him a few incunabula and the Aldines and Elzevirs and the volumes with the fore-edge paintings. In the heavy portfolio beside the desk there would be the Speed and Bartholomew maps, single leaves from Caxton, a few autographs, and pages of medieval manuscript brilliant with gold, blue, and scarlet illumination. And to his few customers – for most of his trade would be through his scholarly catalogues – he would say:

"Well, the title's foxed and there's some worming in the last signature, but it's a rare volume. Not recorded in Wing, I believe."

Or he'd say:

"It's a pleasing book. A very representative binding."

He still bought catalogues of the sales and read the report from Sotheby's every week in the *Literary Supplement.* It was Friday's chief pleasure.

He unwrapped the sandwiches, leaving them out of sight in the open drawer in case a customer came in. They were egg and lettuce. The coffee in his thermos flask was the kind without caffeine. She was always worrying about his health. On winter mornings, when he stooped to kiss her goodbye, she always tucked his muffler more firmly inside the old mac.

The afternoon sun was quite strong for September and the narrow room was becoming uncomfortably warm. He got up from his desk and walked down to the window where he lowered the Venetian blind. He checked to see that the sign on the door said Open and then went back to his desk.

He took out his fountain pen, a gift from Mary eleven years ago, and unscrewed the cap. He took the bottle of Permanent Black from its place in the left-hand drawer and filled the pen, wiping it clean on a piece of rag he kept with the ink bottle. He placed the pen beside his memo pad on the blotter and then started to work his way through *Book News* but it was difficult to concentrate; his eyes jumped lines of print and he had to keep on going back to grasp what he was reading. He did not like to admit it, but he often felt quite sleepy after lunch. It would have been most refreshing to stretch out, just for a few minutes.

With the blind down, the room was rather dim, except for a single patch of sunlight where a slat in the blind was buckled He took off his glasses and rubbed his eyes. The bridge of his nose, too, was sore from the pressure.

He raised his head and stared down the warm gloom towards the window. His eyes were caught and dazzled in the burst of light. As he stared, the light seemed to grow brighter like a climbing candleflame, and larger, until he saw nothing else. Then, slowly, in the white centre of the light, a picture grew.

He saw a small boy standing in a familiar room looking towards the window. The boy was himself. He was standing alone in the big stone-flagged kitchen. He could feel the coolness of the stone through his stocking-feet. Behind him, on the mantel piece, the black clock was ticking.

On the red-tiled window sill stood a jam jar full of dandelions. The window burned. Between the lace curtains, sunlight, sunshine glittering off the silver tap, gleaming in the white sink, glowing on the crowded yellow heads.

He had picked them in the orchard.

The details of the picture faded, faded until he saw only the burning flowers in the jam jar, and then, blinking, he found that he was staring at the sunpatch, the Venetian blind with its buckled slat, the shelves of books, and his desk in front of him with his glasses lying on the green blotter. For a few moments, he stared at the glasses as though he did not know what they were for. Then he reached out and picked them up, settling them cautiously on his nose. He sat motionless in his chair and the afternoon ebbed quietly away.

The bell above the door jangled. A young man, an untidy young man in jeans and a sweater, a student, walked up the shop towards him and stood in front of the desk.

"*Economic Theory* by Woodall? I don't believe I have . . . no, I'm sure . . . I beg your pardon? Order it for you? Oh, yes. *Order* it. Certainly, sir. Certainly."

When the young man had gone, he took out his watch and, looking at it, shook his head. He felt rather fuzzy; a cold coming on perhaps, or possibly the aspirins. He put the thermos flask into his briefcase and snapped shut the clasp. His raincoat was in the cupboard behind the desk and he took it out and shrugged his shoulders into it. He pulled the belt tighter and stood looking round the shop.

He was surprised to see his fountain pen still lying on the blotter. He put it in the right-hand drawer in its proper place in the *Castañeda* cigar box.

He put the lock down on the door and turned the *Open* sign around. He pulled the door shut after him and shook the handle to make sure, as he always did. And as he always did, he looked up at the sign above the door: Geo. Kenway: Bookseller.

Because he was earlier than usual, there was not such a long queue at the bus stop and when the bus came he managed the luxury of a seat to himself. The familiar landmarks passed in their usual order and he got automatically to his feet just before his stop.

The fresh air seemed to clear his head as he walked down Cherril Avenue and turned into The Grove. Down at the far end, by the bowling green, a group of boys were straddling their bikes and talking. He recognized Roy, and Peter from next door.

He had forgotten to empty the tin cash box.

The painters were at work at number fifty-three. He hoped the green they were using was an undercoat. Mr. Glover waved to him.

"How are you keeping, Mr. Glover?"

"Sprightly for an old one. Keeping busy, you know. And yourself?"

"Oh, very well, thank you," he called.

"Yes, it's been a beautiful afternoon."

He turned in at number forty-seven. The front door was ajar. As he hung up his rain coat and pushed his briefcase under the hall table, he called, "Hello? Mary?"

She came out from the kitchen and as he bent to kiss her she said, "Is anything wrong, George?"

"Wrong?"

"You're so early."

"Oh, no. I had a bit of a headache and things were quiet. I just thought I'd come home."

"Would you like a cup of tea?"

"Yes," he said. "Yes, that'd be nice."

"It was so lovely this afternoon," she said, "just like summer, so I made a salad for you. With salmon. And Roy's off somewhere playing speedbike."

"Speedway," he said.

He had forgotten the oil for the clippers.

"Whatever he calls it," she said.

"I think I'll do the hedge before supper," he said, as he followed her into the kitchen.

It was still warm, although, as the sun set, a breeze was springing up.

He moved gradually into the rhythm of the work. It became enjoyable and he frequently stepped back to see if the line was straight. The higher sprigs would have to be tackled from the other side. But he had managed a smooth curve towards the crown of the hedge. Very smooth, in fact. He stepped back to look again and then moved in to trim a straggling spray.

His hands were hot and sweaty and a heavy pulse beat in his neck. Leaning on the front gate, he rested for a few minutes before starting on the other side.

The light was thickening and the houses opposite were becoming shapes against the flushed sky. Shepherd's delight. Shepherd's pie. Another fine day tomorrow. He could hear the distant whirr and clack of a lawnmower, and across the road the Romilly girl was practising scales on the piano, the notes falling softly into the evening.

There was a light, sharp scent in the air, a faintly acid smell. The smell of sap and bruised privet leaves. It seemed to move a memory in him . . . a recollection . . . but he could not remember what it was.

* * *

That story started for me with the memory of the jam jar of dandelions. It was one of those acute visual memories that for unknown reasons stay with us as if they are visions or revelations. I was ten or eleven at the time and this memory is of the kitchen at my uncle's farm, Low Bracken Hall, in Westmoreland. The dandelions began revisiting me in dream or reverie. The sunlight, the sink, the gleaming tap, the flowers, have no meaning – until they are given meaning by being placed in a context.

The next part of the story to arrive was insistent memories of an actual bookstore I frequented in Bristol when I was a student. I can even remember particular books I bought there: *Herself Surprised*, *The Horse's Mouth*, and *To Be A Pilgrim*, the wonderful Joyce Cary trilogy in the Carfax uniform edition. I brought these to Canada and years ago gave them to Amanda Jernigan fairly confident that *The Horse's Mouth* would lure her into a life of art and penury.

I also remember buying there an omnibus edition published by Grey Walls Press of the four main works of Nathaniel West: *Miss Lonelyhearts*, *A Cool Million*, *The Dream Life of Balso Snell*, and *The Day of the Locust*, all writing which exploded upon me.

But in these memories, it was the store itself, the long, narrow central aisle and its gloom which seemed important to me. Gradually the store became in my mind a different *kind* of store, not the solid used book store it actually was but one that sold books bound in white leatherette. Slowly the store's owner began to appear. And then I began to hear the owner's voice. I suspect, looking back at the story now, that its lack of dialogue was the influence of Katherine Mansfield's "Miss Brill" where although the writing is in the third person, an "I," a speaking voice, is implied and invoked in the rhythms of the prose.

I know I've quoted that wonderful paragraph before in this book but what's wrong with celebrating that exquisite opening music again?

"Although it was so brilliantly fine – the blue sky powdered with gold and great spots of light like white wine splashed over the Jardins Publiques – Miss Brill was glad that she had decided on her fur. The air was motionless but when you opened your mouth there was just a faint chill, like a chill from a glass of iced water before you sip, and now and again a leaf came drifting – from nowhere, from the sky."

Magic.

That paragraph has been one of the building blocks of my writing life.

But it is the end of the story that particularly interests me. I wrote it in Montreal during the school summer holidays. I was staying with a friend while we worked together compiling an anthology. I was working on the two final paragraphs of the story and they were not going well. A summer evening in a middle-class neighbourhood, through the open window hearing the sounds of a hand-pushed lawnmower and a child practising scales. The two sounds were drawn to my story and led perfectly up to the final paragraph.

"The light was thickening and the houses opposite were becoming shapes against the flushed sky. Shepherd's delight. Shepherd's pie. Another fine day tomorrow. He could hear the distant whirr and clack of a lawnmower, and across the road the Romilly girl was practising scales on the piano, the notes falling softly into the evening."

This paragraph of soft summation leads into the final paragraph.

"There was a light, sharp scent in the air, a faintly acid smell. The smell of sap and bruised privet leaves. It seemed to move a memory in him . . . a recollection . . . but he could not remember what it was."

The memory, of course, is the dandelions. And we are to understand that the vision of the afternoon will not disturb the shape of his life; rather than the Aldines and Elzevirs of his dreams, he will continue selling books bound in leatherette.

What are we to understand the dandelions to mean? Principally *themselves*. It's up to you. But one could say "beauty." Or "intensity." Or "promise." They're certainly associated with sap and all that is implied in that word of youth, growth, power, sexuality. But it is not this reductive junk I want to talk about. I want to talk about my earlier sentence: "The two sounds were drawn to my story and led perfectly up to the final paragraph."

In an effort to elaborate on that sentence I'm going to try something risky, an analogy with a scientific process. Risky because I don't understand the science and I don't really understand what happens. I'm just groping for a way of suggesting to you how a mysterious process works. I'm going to suggest that a lot of story-writing – not all, of course – is something like electro-plating. I did go down to the Children's Library in search of a modern equivalent of *The Boys' Wonder Book of Science* to get a grip on this plating business but the lady librarian obviously had me pegged for a mackintosh-man so I quickly fled.

So let's try anyway to compare writing with the electro-plating of silver onto copper – the end result being lovely (and now vastly expensive) Sheffield Plate. The process is something like this: into a bath of sulphuric acid are placed a copper shape, a wine coaster, say, and a small ingot of silver. These are wired positive and negative and the current is switched on. Here's where we get into oxidizing and increasing or decreasing the positive or negative valence of an element or ion – *haven't a bloody clue, dear boy, just take all this cobblers as read*. All we need to know for our purposes is that silver from the ingot is *somehow* transferred, *drawn* to the copper wine coaster and plates it.

There are a couple of things here to notice. The silver of the ingot and the silver on the wine coaster are identical – though I'm led to believe that some scientific jiggery-pokery of difference went on during the transfer. So the nature of the silver hasn't changed but its form and shape have.

The second thing to notice is that two existing things have been connected by the electrical current and the effect of the current has been to produce a third thing – the Sheffield plate coaster – which did not exist in the world before.

Both these points have bearing if you are considering the questions "Did this really happen?" or "Is this true?"

I believe that all writers – indeed, all people – have a characteristic current. It flows all the time and in the large sense we'd call that current temperament, outlook, disposition, personality. It is formed by all of a person's history, family, class, race, education, intelligence – an immensely complicated mixture. But in writers working on a story the current is much more intense, naked, dominating.

So the copper wine coaster, then, is the initial shape or notion of the story, the silver ingot provides details which plate the copper shape and make from it something new in the world. The copper object need not be a rigid, defined thing like an idea or a thought-out structure with meaning – usually isn't – but can simply be, as in "Dandelions," two pictures placed in conjunction – the dandelions and the long narrow central aisle of the bookshop. Or the copper could be the overheard words: "I do like something of a creamy consistency on my porridge." In the Foreword to his selected stories *Hitting the Charts*, Leon Rooke records the copper of the story "Winter is Lovely, Isn't Summer Hell" as his finding in a library book in New Orleans a scrap of paper on which was written in a childish hand "she have to check up on her hygiene."

All the way through this book I've been downplaying plot or story. Remember the quotation in an earlier chapter from Alice Munro: "What happens as event doesn't really much matter. When the event becomes the thing that matters, the story isn't working too well. There has to be a feeling in the story."

Remember Maurice Denis writing that ". . . a picture, before being a battle horse or a nude, or some anecdote – is essentially a flat surface covered with colours assembled in a certain order."

The intense current of feeling draws to itself the details, the silver, and the details combine to create feelings in the reader. The silver can be real (that is, transcribed), imagined, drawn from books, drawn from a variety of sources which might range over continents and a lifetime. The story's current summons whatever particles are needed.

The writer, because of the power of the current, actually sees and hears things that non-writers don't. In "Dandelions" I heard the lawnmower and the child practising scales because I *needed* to hear them, because the current demanded them.

As "Dandelions" began to accumulate, as details were drawn in, I began to understand more clearly that I was writing about the power of routine in a particular life, a routine that had deadened more joyous possibilities. I don't convey these ideas by statements but by rhythms.

> The bell above the door jangled. A woman with a child came in. He looked at her over his glasses and inclined his head in welcome. He never approached customers now. He did not want to say *Can I help you?* and hear the ritual *I'm just looking, thank you.*
>
> 'A book for a boy, madam? This boy? Over in the far corner.'
>
> Over in the far corner with all the trains and planes, the fire engines and the spaceships, the brown bunnies and the cuddly bears; with all the fat, pink pigs in trousers, the winsome pups and patient horses.

Repetition and alliteration make the statements, set the mood. The routine of his life is palpable in the words and their placement.

Similarly, the slightly infantilized quality of his life is suggested by the comfort of his food, by his sandwiches, by his promised Shepherd's Pie. Everything proceeds not by statement but by things, by nouns. The Permanent Black ink. The fountain pen in the *Castañeda* cigar box with its special rag to wipe off excess ink.

His fading visions are of real things, *nouns*, German blackletter, Aldines, Elzevirs, the maps of Speed and Bartholomew.

Much of this is craft, but it is a craft that burnishes *after* the current has drawn in the silver. I wrote this story about thirty-five years ago; the opening sentence speaks of "a pang of heartburn" and heartburn of a kind, a pang of bewildering pain, is the story's subject matter. In those days I used to work with an intricate brush; I'm more interested now in theatre, in gestures more extravagant.

Remember that story by Norman Levine – "A Small Piece of Blue"? I edited an anthology about twenty-five years ago called *Making It New* and included that story and asked Norman, as I asked all the writers, to comment on the selected story. Here's what he wrote and it is strikingly related to what I've been writing about "Dandelions."

> I wrote 'A Small Piece of Blue' towards the end of 1955 in St. Ives, Cornwall. I was waiting to go to Canada in order to do a trip across the

country (the trip was to form the backbone of the book *Canada Made Me*) and I had made a list of the places I would visit. One of the places was Helen Mine, an iron mine in northern Ontario, where I had worked during the summer of 1948 after graduating from McGill. In the autumn I would return to McGill for my M.A. then go off to England. Meanwhile I had to earn some money. A summer job, in the past, usually meant working in Ottawa, for the government, in an office. But there had been a war. I had been in the RCAF. And I didn't want to go back to what I was used to. So going to work in the mine was also an act of bravado.

I didn't have a clear notion of the story when I started. Only a definite intention – of wanting to show something of what living and working in this iron mine was like. Yet, some of the ingredients in this story came not from the mine but from people and incidents I had met elsewhere.

The woman with no nose – she came from Barnstaple, in North Devon. She was a music teacher and let out a room. I took it for a few months in 1954.

The shooting with a gun, indoors, at a lit candle was told to me about what went on aboard the French Crabbers, anchored in the bay off St. Ives, at night.

The poem that begins:

> *All your experiences:*
> *Those bits.*
> *Those pieces you carried away with you.*
> *How long will they last?*

I wrote that separately, as a poem, in 1952. I had not long been married and we were staying, very briefly, with my wife's parents in London. I remember I was in a pub reading a newspaper. An American professor had come over to England to exhume a tomb to try and prove that Bacon had written Shakespeare's plays. There was another customer in the pub as well. We got talking. He said he worked at an undertakers. And he told me some technical things about his job: what was the best wood to have and how even that didn't last very long . . .

I did not think of these separate pieces as parts of a jigsaw that I had to get to fit in order to make the story. As I remember it, all I wanted was

> to write a story about the experience of living and working in the mine. And it was the pressure of writing the story that made me remember these disconnected memories. The pressure of writing the story was like a magnet that pulled these pieces from my past. And by the time I came to the part of the doctor I found I had to invent him in order to make the story work.
>
> A few months after finishing 'A Small Piece of Blue' I was in Northern Ontario again, at Helen Mine. And one of the first things I did was to go to the lake to see if it was shaped like a heart. It wasn't. And I don't know why I expected it to be.

See what I mean, Michael?

The pressure of writing the story was like a magnet that pulled these pieces from my past.

And here's something else interesting. If Levine is to be believed, he wrote "A Small Piece of Blue" in 1955. The noseless lady, he says, was actually drawn from a woman in Barnstaple, Devon, and transported into a Canadian setting because the current of "A Small Piece of Blue" demanded her presence. Yet in *Canada Made Me*, purportedly a factual account of his journey across the country, the noseless woman from Barnstaple reappears in Sault Ste Marie in 1956 or 57.

Clearly, Levine is driven more by the "pressure of writing the story" than he is by the obligation to transcribe "reality." What drives him is the need to create mood, feeling. Are we detecting Levine in a falsehood or is he simply dealing in a different kind of truth? Remember that the silver on the coaster and the silver of the ingot remain exactly the same: only the form has changed.

Again in *Making It New*, Alice Munro wrote an essay for me called "What Is Real?" This, too, is germane to what I've been talking about.

> What I would like to do here is what I can't do in two or three sentences at the end of a reading. I won't try to explain what fiction is, and what short stories are (assuming, which we can't, that there is any fixed thing that it is and they are), but what short stories are to me, and how I write them, and how I use things that are 'real.' I will start by explaining how I read stories written by other people. For one thing, I can start reading them anywhere; from beginning to end, from end to beginning, from

> any point in between in either direction. So obviously I don't take up a story and follow it as if it were a road, taking me somewhere, with views and neat diversions along the way. I go into it, and move back and forth and settle here and there, and stay in it for a while. It's more like a house. Everybody knows what a house does, how it encloses space and makes connections between one enclosed space and another and presents what is outside in a new way. This is the nearest I can come to explaining what a story does for me, and what I want my stories to do for other people.
>
> So when I write a story I want to make a certain kind of structure, and I know the feeling I want to get from being inside that structure. This is the hard part of the explanation, where I have to use a word like 'feeling,' which is not very precise, because if I attempt to be more intellectually respectable I will have to be dishonest. 'Feeling' will have to do.
>
> There is no blueprint for the structure. It's not a question of 'I'll make this kind of house because if I do it right it will have this effect.' I've got to make, I've got to build up, a house, a story, to fit around the indescribable 'feeling' that is like the soul of the story, and which I must insist upon in a dogged, embarrassed way, as being no more definable than that. And I don't know where it comes from. It seems to be already there, and some unlikely clue, such as a shop window or a bit of conversation, makes me aware of it. Then I start accumulating the material and putting it together. Some of the material I may have lying around already, in memories and observations, and some I invent, and some I have to go diligently looking for (factual details), while some is dumped in my lap (anecdotes, bits of speech). I see how this material might go together to make the shape I need, and I try it. I keep trying and seeing where I went wrong and trying again.

"Pressure," "soul," "current" – Alice Munro's "feeling" that "seems to be already there" – you can see that Norman Levine, Alice Munro, and I are all talking about much the same experience.

So now that we've suggested some terms and a vocabulary, let us, *at last*, I can hear you say, approach the material of "Continuo."

Near the beginning of "Continuo" you'll recall my quoting Constance Rooke as saying that the central concern of all my work was entropy, that is, decline, fallings away, defeat, degeneration. I also say "I could feel all the time the tensions of a strong emotional current driving me towards shapes I could only dimly discern."

Apart from those places where I loosen the grip of narrative to talk about genre writing, comedy, and travel writing, nearly everything in "Continuo" in some way or another sets a mundane present against a grander and heroic past.

In Trebizond, for example, I evoke the *Anabasis Kyrou* and the epic march to the sea after the battle at Cunaxa, the triumphant shout of the warriors, "Thalassa! Thalassa!" I record the ruins of the golden palace of the Comneni. Set against this feat of arms, this defeated Byzantine splendour, is Ataturk Villa with its "horse-hairy-stuffed great-grandmotherly furniture" and the modern buildings of Trebizond built with "breeze block and brick slapped together with mortar oozing out of every course." At the mosque, the "octagonal stone structure once upon more gracious times, I guessed, a constantly flowing fountain" and the retarded girl. And the shops of Trebizond featuring "swollen settees," bonito, and electronics. Later I visit the Aghia Sophia with its "decaying patches of colour" where there might have been a famous medieval observatory but its possible location now forgotten, lost, all as meaningless as the tumbled column-drums of the temple of Apollo in the church precincts.

This section pretty much sets the pattern for the rest of the set pieces. What I am trying to show the reader is the silver-plating process arrested. The current is allowed to flow but is then deliberately stopped before a story starts defining itself – in this case by a section about genre writing.

If I wanted to write a short story set in Trebizond – a plot? – an incident? – my piece of copper? – nothing could be simpler. How about this? One of the local youths offers one of the tourists Roman coins or a small bronze bull, a votive offering from the Turkish bronze age. It happens all the time. And is strictly illegal. Can you see how the current would pull in detail? What some of that detail might be? And let us imagine that the story ends with the tourist, increasingly fearful of apprehension, throwing the bronze bull into the sea from the deck of the tour ship.

Or this: Alan and Martin from Cincinnati caught by a custodian in lascivious embrace in the Ataturk Villa. An international incident in the making.

There's a story in "Continuo" about dogs. And they are somehow linked to politics. The murder of repatriated Russians in Odessa. The marching style of the high school kids in Odessa. The murder of the Romanovs. I don't see how the dogs relate to these events. Perhaps I'm thinking of politics more generally. Perhaps I'm simply feeling that these diseased dogs sit in silent judgement on the societies that allow them to starve and shiver, that they make a mockery of Odessa's classical architecture, of Odessa's pride in Pushkin.

The material bulges everywhere with the possibilities of stories. I found it difficult to restrain myself, to stick to showing arrested current. Only in the section about Sochi did I let it run and that was because I couldn't resist Bronwyn.

Was Bronwyn "real"? To me, very much so. I'll tell you how she came about. The spark of her was the words of the Ranee of Sarawak, "Come on, boys. Pot the red!" This anecdote was another of John Newlove's gems gleaned from some period autobiography. I've seen it quoted subsequently in a critical book by Anthony Burgess so it is probably entirely authentic. Sylvia Brett was notorious. Her sister, the Hon. Dorothy Brett, was the confidante of Katherine Mansfield and the recipient of the Mansfield letter quoted in an earlier chapter. Dorothy Brett was a disciple of D.H. Lawrence and went with him towards the end to Mexico. In his *Flame into Being: The Life and Work of D.H. Lawrence* Burgess writes of her:

"She is the only woman in the history of the married Lawrence with whom the master considered going to bed (the anecdote goes that he actually got there and desisted saying 'Your pubes are wrong')."

What an *ungentlemanly* remark!

I stick these salacious details in only to keep you awake, Michael.

So, Sylvia Brett.

When she married Charles Vyner Brooke, George Bernard Shaw sent this doggerel as a wedding gift.

Ride a cock horse
To Sarawak Cross
To see a young Ranee consumed with remorse.
She'll have bells on her fingers
And rings in her nose
And won't be permitted to wear any clo'es.

Actually, the family crops up everywhere. John Glassco worked for a member of the family in Paris and writes about the experience in the final pages of *Memoirs of Montparnasse*. One of the mixed-race offspring, Esca Brooke, actually came to Canada and worked as what the slang of the day called a "sky-pilot" ministering to the spiritual needs of lumberjacks in the Ottawa area.

Uphill work, one would have thought.

And that business about Sir Charles wearing a glass eye he'd got from a taxidermist is absolutely true. He'd lost an eye to a twig when he fell off his horse hunting and for some time went about with an open socket. He was prevailed upon to do something about it and so went to a taxidermist's and wore stuck in his socket according to the whim of the day the eyes of rabbits, deer, foxes, and tigers.

Bronwyn's coal necklace or choker was drawn to my current in the first place from a novel by Jonathan Gash called *Firefly Gadroon*, one of a series of cheerfully awful books about an antiques dealer called Lovejoy which I read for what I can glean about fakes and forgery. Gash has, wisely, started calling these books not novels but "Lovejoy narratives." Subsequently, I did see worked coal for sale in Whitby in Yorkshire.

The detail was drawn to me, I suppose, because my recognition of the coal establishes an immediate connection between us, a shared and rather recherché knowledge and interest.

Bronwyn had to have had a reason for having known about the Ranee and English people would have been in Borneo only to run businesses and banks or as missionaries. Making her the child of missionaries allowed me to bring in Dyaks and amuse myself by having Bronwyn refer to them as "some of *those* johnnies." The exact word, I think, she would have used.

Given the class set-up, such missionaries could only have been Anglican. Children would have been sent back to England for health reasons and for schooling. Feelings of having been abandoned must have been common. Poor Rudyard Kipling comes to mind and his bitter short story "Baa, Baa, Black Sheep." And so Bronwyn stepped out of her history into her ancient, bedizened present.

Because she would have been of the lesser gentry, I gave her some eighteenth and mid-nineteenth century usages which would likely have survived in the rural aristocracy of her time. "Baggage" and "trollop" are definitely old-fashioned. "Placket" hovers on the archaic. "Foxed" meaning "drunk" is pure eighteenth-century.

When I wrote "By this time, of course, she'd be hectic with drink," I was hoping that my ideal reader would – even if subliminally – register "He rages like the hectic in my blood . . ." Claudius' words concerning Hamlet spoken as if to the King of England, the noun "hectic" meaning "a persistent fever."

I decided I had to interrupt Bronwyn by the fritillaries scene for three quite different reasons. The first was that I was getting far too interested in her – I was, in other words, not stopping the current to show the process. The second reason was a technical one; the whole scene builds towards the final line and the scene simply works better, becomes funnier, if delay is built into it. The third reason was that the Bronwyn scene was beginning to feel as if it belonged to a larger structure.

So I needed a new building block to be lowered into place. But notice that the emotional flow of it continues the same concerns – the trees bulldozed into wreckage, rank bracken growing back in, the beautiful and elegant fritillaries now extinct in England, the pillow case of adders, the razor blade and the horror of cutting one's friend. Implicit in all this, the aging of the narrator. His childhood; Bronwyn's childhood.

All this material is entirely factual down to the "shilling a foot" we were paid for the adders. Bronwyn, however, is a figment of my imagination.

Notice I used the words "building block" for this section. That is actually how I think of making fiction. The emotion is there right enough, the current is powerfully switched on, but formalist concerns are never far from my mind. I don't know if the comparison is really helpful but I *feel* it should be, Le Corbusier defining architecture as "the masterly, correct and magnificent play of masses brought together in light." I absolutely want to say *yes* to that.

Now let's glance at that priest and his minder. How does *he* fit in? He is sadly alcoholic and sexually dangerous. I suppose I'd have to say that he, too, exemplifies degeneracy, a betrayal of faith and tradition. Under that very plebian cloth cap sits a damaged brain. He probably needs more aggression built into him, more violence, more aggressive ignorance, but it is all too easy to imagine what he could get up to in the dark recesses of the ruined Aghia Sophia, in the ruins of Histria, or in the passenger laundry of the *Minerva*. I found rather frightening his raw tongue magnified by the thick glass.

Alan and Martin from Cincinnati would need to appear more often to reveal their true awfulness. I'm not concerned with their Americanness or with their homosexuality. It is their shallowness that interests me. I see them as being forty-five to fifty. They are concerned with things being comfy for them, with getting their own way. They tend to look upon the world as a bazaar through which they're entitled to rootle. I was trying them on as a kind of Chorus which points up the decline from past to present.

When they buy their Russian naval caps and an old chap from the cruise calls out "Make way for a naval officer!" the words are from a favourite book of my childhood and appear under an illustration of a man making his way through a market crowd, a stack of empty wicker baskets on his head. The book was by Elizabeth Goudge and is called *Green Dolphin Country*. There's the current, the magnet at work. The fake icons and the real caps add to the suggestion of the scene. As do the cathedral steps.

I realize, too, looking back over these sections that I am very interested in my fellow passengers. They are all middle-aged to old, middle-class in the main, reasonably well-educated, most of them with a more than passing interest in history. Nearly all of them attend lectures which are sometimes as abstruse as a reading, register by register, of Trajan's Column recording his victory over the Dacians.

Think of the awful Baden Powell man who had fought under the command of Glubb Pasha. He *was* transcribed reality, I'm ashamed to admit, but it is also true that the flower of his generation lie in Benghazi and Tripoli, and in cemeteries in France, Holland, and Germany. These aging tourists are also the end of something, the end of Empire, the very last gasp of a vanishing England, the remnants of a kind of people we will not see in numbers again.

I said earlier that nowadays I'm more interested in large theatrical effects than in delicate brushwork. I should have had the artistic intelligence to absorb *The Day of the Locust* much earlier than I did. But anyway, damned if all this talk with you isn't tempting me to reassemble much of this stuff as a Robert Forde story to be included in *Travelling Northward.* After all, there's already some deliberate blurring of the line with Bronwyn. In the writing of the scene I am becoming the attracting copper. I notice that in talking about the scene I refer to myself as "he" and "the narrator." Is "I" me? Is "Myrna" Myrna? The Wanda question popping up again.

If "I" became Forde, I would immediately re-arrange my building blocks. I might well start with Forde's angina at the Sumela Monastery and his sitting in the van with the priest and his minder. For I already have a suspicion the story ends with the priest at Histria and in between these two blocks "Death" as the line from a Basil Bunting poem goes "is written over all."

I can see immediately I need two sets. One set will be the historical sites, the other will be the ship. I need to sketch up more small character actors as a supporting cast. Might bring up some characters described in the Greek holiday section – the lady in the man's suit who struck the waiter with her stick saying "Tardy," the woman "greedy, greedy for the sun." I'd shift my Odessa dogs to Histria. Increase the gloom and drizzle to black skies rent by lightning. Wuthering Heights. Dammit, I'll let Alan and Martin in their naval caps dance a shuffle-off-to-Buffalo routine on the steps of the Histria Museum and leave you with the strong suspicion that the priest has murdered Bronwyn with a brick in the Roman rubble of the Histria site.

How do you like *them* apples?

The Decline and Fall of *Everything.*

Götterdämmerung.

More thanks than I can express,
John

P.S. If you're flush from your labours in Marathon, go and have dinner at Le Paris on St. Catherine. About three blocks west of Rue Guy.

THE CENTURY LIST

It seems fairly obvious that the efflorescence in the short story in Canada in the period 1958-2000 will receive much future scholarly examination – well, hold on a minute – probably not "scholarly" examination but certainly academic examination, a rather different creature. Before these bald scavengers flop down, furl their wings, and sidle towards the corpus – and by God! they're taking their craven, carrion time – I thought how much fun it would be to pre-empt them by making a List.

The sort of List that occurred to me was Cyril Connolly's *The Modern Movement: One Hundred Key Books from England, France and America 1880-1950*. Or Anthony Burgess' *99 Novels: The Best in English Since 1939*. Or Elizabeth Diefendorf's *The New York Public Library's Books of the Century*. Or H.R.F Keating's *Crime and Mystery: The Hundred Best Books*.

The figure of One Hundred is attractive and apposite and I thought of calling my List *The One Hundred Best Canadian Story Collections in the Twentieth Century* but even a glance over my shelves suggested that the title was preposterous. I was eventually forced to settle for *The Best Forty Canadian Story Collections in the Twentieth Century*. In short, the *Century List*.

(It also occurred to me that I'd feel pushed to find even ten novels worthy of inclusion in a companion list. There's something wickedly accurate about Randall Jarrell's line that a novel is "a prose work of a certain length with something wrong with it.")

We have produced so few books of tolerable literary essays that a List would be impossible. We have little to compare with Randall Jarrell's *A Sad Heart at the Supermarket* or W.H. Auden's *The Dyer's Hand*, or Kingsley Amis' *What Became of Jane Austen*? or Orwells' *Inside the Whale and Other Essays* or V.S. Naipaul's *The Overcrowded Barracoon*. I continue to be dismayed, however, at the refusal of Canadian readers to acknowledge – acknowledge, hell! *Delight* in! – John Mills' essay collection *Thank Your Mother for the Rabbits*. The Irving Layton-Steam Laundry-John Richmond-Aviva Layton rigmarole is alone worth the price of admission.

Making a List is, of course, an act of literary criticism. Lists always seem to provoke discussion and argument and this is obviously important for the literature. Lists can champion unexpected or forgotten works as was the case with Anthony Powell's support of Jocelyn Brooke, author of "The Orchid" trilogy, or Philip Larkin's and Lord David Cecil's resurrection of the delightful novels of Barbara Pym. They can also suggest a reordering within the hierarchy of a writer's work; when I choose Margaret Laurence's *The Tomorrow-Tamer* over *A Bird in the House* my List is jousting with conventional wisdom; I am choosing craft over nation. Perhaps most importantly, Lists can pull a period into a clearer focus; instead of readers being faced with many hundreds of volumes which range from the superb to the execrable, the List enables readers to see an informed estimate of the size and shape of the period's accomplishment.

Anthologies are a form of List and it is at anthologies that we must first look. The first nationally important anthology of Canadian short stories was published in 1928. *Canadian Short Stories* was edited by Raymond Knister. This volume contained stories by Duncan Campbell Scott, Frederick William Wallace, Edward William Thompson, Sir Gilbert Parker, Charles G.D. Roberts, Marjorie Pickthall, Merril Denison, Morley Callaghan, Stephen Leacock, Norman Duncan, Allan Sullivan, McLaren Imrie, Will E. Ingersoll, Mazo de la Roche, Harvey O'Higgins, Thomas Murtha, and Lesley McFarlane.

Knister had compiled *Canadian Short Stories* while living on his parents' farm in Northwood, Ontario; this circumstance explains the last line of Morley Callaghan's letter to him.

> Dear Raymond,
>
> Today I got a copy of the Canadian stories. I read the Introduction and then I read D.C. Scott's story in the book. What is the matter with you?
>
> Though it will come as a relief to many schoolmarms throughout the country to learn that the venerable Duncan is a great writer, since they have always suspected it, you know better. Then why do you do it? Are you thinking of retiring definitely? You had a chance to point the way in that introduction, and you merely arrived at the old values that have been accepted here the last fifty years: *id est*, Duncan C. Scott, G.D. Roberts and Gilbert Parker are great prose writers. In any other country

> in the world they are not taken seriously. Why do you do it? Since you know better and are willing to put your name to the book. Or is it the mellowing effects of the soil?

Only five of these seventeen reputations survived the thirty years which separated Knister's anthology from the first international anthology in 1958, Robert Weaver's *Canadian Short Stories* published by Oxford University Press. Only five of Knister's deadbeats appear in Weaver. Not a single one will survive on my List, not Knister, not Leacock, not Callaghan himself.

The barrenness and bankruptcy of Canadian writing in the early years of the twentieth century might be suggested by the jacket copy on Paul A.W. Wallace's *The Twist and Other Stories* published by Ryerson in 1923. I assure the incredulous reader that I am quoting verbatim.

"A purely Canadian book of Short Stories is considerable of a novelty. Those included in this volume are characteristic, striking tales of romance, adventure and whimsical nonsense written in a most vigorous style and set in such familiar locations as Banff . . . ."

Between the anthologies of Knister and Weaver, Desmond Pacey published *A Book of Canadian Stories* (1947). The "modern" was represented by P.K. Page, Raymond Knister, William McConnell, Sinclair Ross, Leo Kennedy, Morley Callaghan, and Mary Quayle Innis. Again, not a single one will appear on the Century List.

Why is that? The simplest answer is to say that these writers were not fully in touch with the genre.

Knister in his 1928 Introduction remarks that: "People like to listen to an interesting tale . . ." and later writes of Sir Gilbert Parker's "warm-blooded, courageous tales . . ." The word "tale" implies, I think, a story whose main emphasis is on the contrivances of plot. Similarly with the word "yarn." Both imply entertainment. Adventure. Exotic climes. We might talk of "a pirate tale" but if we were talking about Katherine Mansfield's "The Daughters of the Late Colonel" we'd be unlikely to describe it as "a tale about two sisters" or "Miss Brill" as a tale about "a spinster sitting in a park."

"Tales" seem typical of the nineteenth century. Kipling and Robert Louis Stevenson spring to mind, Rider Haggard's tales of Gagool and the Zulu impis, A.E.W. Mason's *The Four Feathers*, R.D. Blackmore's *Lorna*

Doon, Stevenson's *Kidnapped* and *Treasure Island.* All, it should be noted, wonderful books for children. Stevenson refused to take his writing seriously: "Fiction," he stated, "is to grown men what play is to the child." His historical fiction he described as "tushery."

Such swashbuckling, though, had vigour. The tales in Knister's anthology couldn't rise even to that. They are from the tired end of a tradition of commercial magazine writing.

"Tale" suggests a kind of story which preceded modernism and it is modernism and its developments which have dominated writing in the twentieth century. It wasn't until the sixties that modernism impinged on Canada. In the rest of the western world modernism had been roaring on since the early years of the century but Canada languished in its time warp with the Ryerson Press and The Book Steward. Canada remained loyal to "the venerable Duncan" and academic dullards later kept him on life-support by declaring his cut-price idyll *In the Village of Viger* our "gateway ancestor," the book from which we all derive, nationalist tomfoolerie still officially promulgated.

History, literary history, must give a place to, say, the stories of Sinclair Ross but *The Lamp at Noon and Other Stories* really cannot stand alone outside its historic context. We can say the same, and in spades, for Raymond Knister's stories. The passage of time and subsequent achievement reveal the work stranded and diminished. This chapter is not concerned with literary history; it is, *pace* Margaret Atwood and other nationalist drearies, concerned only with "good writing."

Knister was described by Desmond Pacey in 1962 as "one of the most promising young writers whom Canada has yet produced." This estimation was unfortunately probably correct.

Knister was struggling to free himself from plot. Like other aspiring modernists he was more interested in character and emotions and psychological states. He was, in brief, trying to lead Canada away from "tale" and towards "story." The problem was that he was a very bad writer.

In "The Strawstack," published in *The Canadian Forum* in 1923, a man is returning, pursued by a "posse" after having committed a murder, to the abandoned farm of his childhood. He is consumed by guilt and anguished by the sordid horror his life has become. The story ends with his braiding binder-twine with which to hang himself.

Here he is at the beginning of the story approaching the homestead.

> The sun had set when he came forth from the woods, and the incomparable quiet was there which comes before the moon rises or the greater dark begins. He found himself asking, 'I wonder if there will be a moon tonight,' before his memory told him of last night's dark as he tramped the endless bald road.
>
> Dark splotches in one little field were peacefully still, and the cool munching of cows had something obscene about it, like the ravening of wolves at the finding of a dead hunter: the field, dead, was not the less silently complaining, he saw.
>
> He came nearer, and they woofed and scampered leadenly away, turning about to face him at a distance. He went on without seeing them.
>
> The wind lifted again, and he stopped with a jerk which drew his head back, stiffened as before a brink. His face was compressed in a colour of terror which made his unshaven features frightful. Then he stepped on again after an instant, with limp strides as before . . .

". . . scampered leadenly . . ."?

". . . limp strides . . ."?

Cows (?) that "woof"?

And Gold Medal with Bar to any reader able to make any sense *whatever* of paragraphs two and three.

Professor Michael Gnarowski in his Introduction to the *Selected Stories of Raymond Knister* describes this story as "avant garde" and as one of "those published stories of Knister's which have proved to be most fascinating and rewarding."

Such obscurantism and mouldy antiquarianism are, in a way, something of an insult to the forty writers discussed in this chapter.

It behooves us to keep our comparative feet on the ground and to remember that James Joyce had completed *Dubliners* in 1907, the book actually appearing in 1914, and that Katherine Mansfield had published *Bliss* in 1920.

Knister is now eclipsed entirely, his awkward efforts deservedly forgotten. Canadian achievement in the story form is now so sophisticated that the present has pulled the past into a different shape.

Academic response to short fiction in Canada has normally been inadequate because uncomprehending of, or immune to, aesthetic pleasure. Many academics – and some writers – consider the form inherently minor. Professor Solecki of St. Michael's College of the University of Toronto refers to short stories as a "sub-genre." Professor Solecki wrote: "The short story writer resembles the miniaturist in painting or the composer specializing in preludes or the featherweight boxer: the interesting action is elsewhere."

I debated this estimation of the short story with Professor Solecki and W.J. Keith in the book *Volleys*.

I passionately reject such views and consider Professor Solecki's remarks as wilful or indicative of a deeply flawed understanding.

I would stand absolutely with Malcolm Bradbury. In his Introduction to *The Penguin Book of Modern British Short Stories* Bradbury wrote:

> The short story has become one of the major forms of modern literary expression – in some ways the most modern of them all. For what we usually mean by the genre is that concentrated form of writing that, breaking away from the classic short tale, became, as it were, the lyric poem of modern fictional prose. The great precursors were Chekhov, Henry James, Katherine Mansfield, James Joyce, and Sherwood Anderson. It took on a strong modernist evolution in the work of Hemingway, Faulkner, Babel, and Kafka which, in the period after 1940, was followed by a new wave of experiment led by Beckett and Borges, and provided the short story with a repertory of late twentieth-century forms. The modern short story has therefore been distinguished by its break away from anecdote, tale-telling and simple narrative, and for its linguistic and stylistic concentration, its imagistic methods, its symbolic potential. In it some of our greatest modern writers, from Hemingway to Mann to Beckett, have found their finest exactitude and most finished stylistic practice. In fact, for many prose-writers it has come closest to representing the most 'poetic' aspect of their craft.

The centrality of short story writing was movingly asserted by Jonathan Franzen in his *New York Times* review of Alice Munro's *Runaway*. He wrote in part:

> I want to circle around Munro's latest marvel of a book, *Runaway*, by taking some guesses at why her excellence so dismayingly exceeds her fame . . .

. . . with short stories the challenge to reviewers is even more extreme. Is there a story in all of world literature whose appeal can survive the typical synopsis? (A chance meeting on a boardwalk in Yalta brings together a bored husband and a lady with a little dog . . . A small town's annual lottery is revealed to serve a rather surprising purpose . . . A middle-aged Dubliner leaves a party and reflects on life and love . . .) Oprah Winfrey will not touch story collections. Discussing them is so challenging, indeed, that one can almost forgive the *New York Times Books Review's* former editor, Charles McGrath, for his recent comparison of young short-story writers to 'people who learn golf by never venturing onto a golf course but instead practicing at a driving range.' The real game being, by this analogy, the novel.

McGrath's prejudice is shared by nearly all commercial publishers, for whom a story collection is, most frequently, the distasteful front-end write-off in a two-book deal whose back end is contractually forbidden to be another story collection. And yet, despite the short story's Cinderella status, or maybe because of it, a high percentage of the most exciting fiction written in the last 25 years – the stuff I immediately mention if somebody asks me what's terrific – has been short fiction. There's the Great One herself, naturally. There's also Lydia Davis, David Means, George Saunders, Lorrie Moore, Amy Hempel and the late Raymond Carver – all of them pure or nearly pure short-story writers – and then a larger group of writers who have achievements in multiple genres (John Updike, Joy Williams, David Foster Wallace, Joyce Carol Oates, Denis Johnson, Ann Beattie, William T. Vollman, Tobias Wolff, Annie Proulx, Tom Drury, the late André Dubus) but who seem to me most at home, most undilutedly themselves, in their shorter work. There are also, to be sure, some very fine pure novelists. But when I close my eyes and think about literature in recent decades, I see a twilight landscape in which many of the most inviting lights, the sites that beckon me to return for a visit, are shed by particular short stories I've read . . .

Here's the story that Munro keeps telling: A bright, sexually avid girl grows up in rural Ontario without much money, her mother is sickly or dead, her father is a schoolteacher whose second wife is problematic, and the girl, as soon as she can, escapes from the hinterland by way of a scholarship or some decisive self-interested act. She marries young, moves to British Columbia, raises kids, and is far from blameless in the break-up of her marriage. She may have success as an actress or a writer or a TV personality; she has romantic adventures. When, inevitably, she returns to Ontario, she finds the landscape of her youth unsettlingly altered. Although she was the one who abandoned the place, it's a great blow to her narcissism that she isn't warmly welcomed back – that the world of her youth, with its older-fashioned manners and mores, now sits in judgement on the modern choices she has made. Simply by trying to survive as a whole and independent person, she has incurred painful losses and dislocations; she has caused harm.

And that's pretty much it. That's the little stream that's been feeding Munro's work for better than 50 years. The same elements recur and recur like Clare Quilty. What makes Munro's growth as an artist so crisply and breathtakingly visible – throughout the *Selected Stories* and even more so in her three latest books – is precisely the familiarity of her materials. Look what she can do with nothing but her own small story; the more she returns to it, the more she finds.

This is not a golfer on a practice tee. This is a gymnast in a plain black leotard, alone on a bare floor, outperforming all the novelists with their flashy costumes and whips and elephants and tigers.

'The complexity of things – the things within things – just seems to be endless,' Munro told her interviewer. 'I mean nothing is easy, nothing is simple.'

She was stating the fundamental axiom of literature, the core of its appeal. And, for whatever reason – the fragmentation of my reading time, the distractions and atomizations of contemporary life or, perhaps, a genuine paucity of compelling novels – I find that when I'm in need of a hit of real writing, a good stiff drink of paradox and complexity, I'm likeliest to encounter it in short fiction.

I have quoted Bradbury and Franzen at such length because the points they are making would not be widely conceded in Canada's literary world – or in many cases even understood.

In a recent issue of *Quill and Quire: Canada's Magazine of Book News and Reviews* three story collections were reviewed under the general heading: "Short Tales for Grownups." The reviews were introduced as follows:

> With the recent success of books such as David Bezmozgis' *Natasha and Other Stories*, as well as the relative prominence of short fiction on the shortlists for this year's big literary prizes, the perception of short stories as the publishing industry equivalent to the NDP [New Democratic Party] – admirable and virtuous, if a little foolhardy and, well, *not quite grown up* – may be changing.

* * *

The Century List runs, inclusive, from 1900-2000 and the order is simply alphabetical. When writers have published a selected stories I have always accepted their estimation of their own work rather than choosing an earlier title. In three cases – Clark Blaise, Norman Levine, and Leon Rooke – I have cited more than one title per author because the titles, are, in effect, a Selected or Collected. A few titles were published in the 21st century but the work they present was written well within the period under consideration. The necessarily brief quotations are intended as a *menu dégustation.*

The Century List

Caroline Adderson	*Bad Imaginings*
Margaret Atwood	*Good Bones*
Mike Barnes	*Aquarium*
Clark Blaise	*Collected Stories*
Mary Borsky	*Influence of the Moon*
Ann Copeland	*The Golden Thread*
Libby Creelman	*Walking in Paradise*
Shirley Faessler	*A Basket of Apples*
Cynthia Flood	*My Father Took a Cake to France*
Keath Fraser	*Thirteen Ways of Listening to a Stranger*
Mavis Gallant	*Selected Stories*
Paul Glennon	*How Did You Sleep?*
Douglas Glover	*Bad News of the Heart*

Shut Up He Explained

Terry Griggs	*Quickening*
Steven Heighton	*Flight Paths of the Emperor*
Jack Hodgins	*The Barclay Family Theatre*
Hugh Hood	*Light Shining Out of Darkness*
Isabel Huggan	*The Elizabeth Stories*
Mark Anthony Jarman	*Dancing Nightly in the Tavern*
Susan Kerslake	*The Book of Fears*
Margaret Laurence	*The Tomorrow-Tamer*
Elise Levine	*Driving Men Mad*
Norman Levine	*By a Frozen River* and *The Ability to Forget*
Annabel Lyon	*Oxygen*
Alistair MacLeod	*Island*
K.D. Miller	*A Litany in Time of Plague*
Lisa Moore	*Degrees of Nakedness*
Alice Munro	*Selected Stories*
Gayla Reid	*To Be There with You*
Patricia Robertson	*City of Orphans*
Leon Rooke	*Painting the Dog* and *Hitting the Charts*
Robyn Sarah	*Promise of Shelter*
Diane Schoemperlen	*Red Plaid Shirt: Stories New and Selected*
Carol Shields	*Collected Stories*
Ray Smith	*Cape Breton Is the Thought-Control Centre of Canada*
Russell Smith	*Young Men*
Linda Svendsen	*Marine Life*
Audrey Thomas	*The Path of Totality: New and Selected Stories*
Guy Vanderhaeghe	*Man Descending*
Michael Winter	*One Last Good Look*

Tim Inkster in full flow . . . 2003 . . .

at Harbourfront . . .

. . . to a possibly sceptical audience of Kim Jernigan, editor of *The New Quarterly*, her daughter Amanda, and Russell Smith. (AUTHOR)

Above: Jack Illingworth at Eden Mills in 2003. PQL's second intern. (AUTHOR)

Right: Tim Inkster with Leon Rooke at Eden Mills. In the background Sandra Sabatini talking to Annabel Lyon. (AUTHOR)

Below: Elizabeth Hay at Eden Mills in 1998 signing copies of (and earning) *Small Change*. (AUTHOR)

Above: Tim Inkster at Eden Mills, 2003.

Right: With Annabel Lyon in Ottawa in 2004. (MYRNA METCALF)

Below: Tim and Elke Inkster with their second intern Jack Illingworth at the Book Shelf Café in Guelph, 2003. (AUTHOR)

Above: Norman Levine in the St. Ives years. (SAM TATA)

Right: With Norman Levine in 2003 at Richmond Castle in North Yorkshire. (MYRNA METCALF)

Below: Norman Levine in 1993 in St. John's. (MICHAEL WINTER)

Above: With Elke, Tim, and Amanda Jernigan, PQL's first intern, 2003 in Ottawa. (MYRNA METCALF)

Right: Eric Ormsby at the launch at Concordia University in 2002 of *Facsimiles of Time*. (AUTHOR)

Below: Mary Swan, author of the haunting novella *The Deep*.

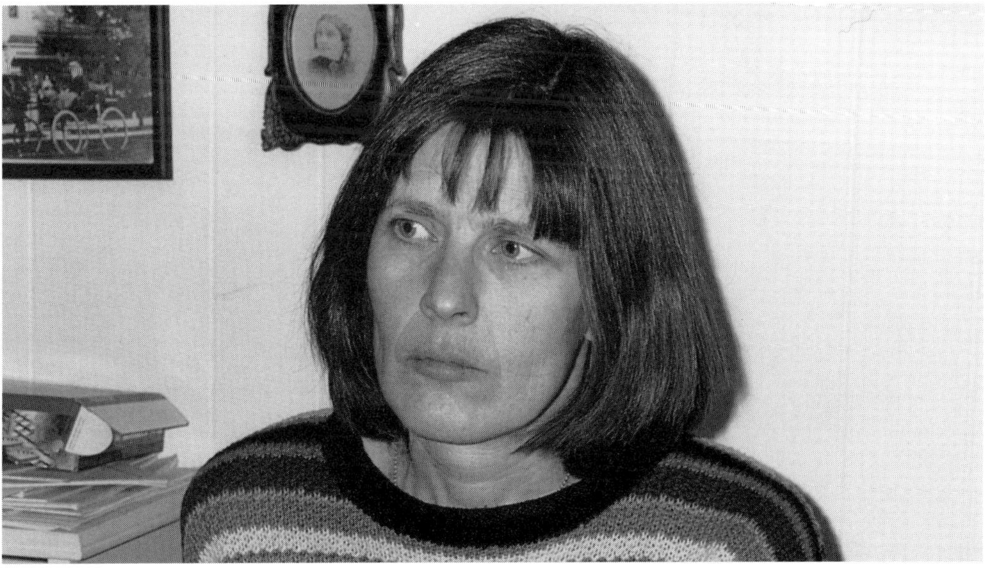

Above: Caroline Adderson. Hailed by Philip Marchand, book critic of the *Toronto Star*, as "one of the four most notable emerging writers in Canada." (JOHN HANEY)

Right: Steven Heighton visiting and coveting our David Bolduc painting, what David calls "an icon for your eye to rest on." (AUTHOR)

Below: Ray Smith staying in Ottawa with us while we worked on the conclusion of *The Man Who Hated Emily Brontë*, 2003. (AUTHOR)

With Dan Wells at Eden Mills, 2005. For sale in front of us, the first of the signed limited edition chapbooks of short stories by Clark Blaise and Judith McCormack. (JACK ILLINGWORTH)

Tim Inkster and Dan Wells at Eden Mills, 2005.

Above: Francesca Piredda, author of *Bambina*, my last title with the Porcupine's Quill, with Patricia Young, author of *Airstream* and the first winner of the Metcalf-Rooke Award sponsored by Biblioasis.

Right: Kathleen Winter, author of *boYs* and second winner of the Metcalf-Rooke Award. (DAVID WITTEN)

Below: Biblioasis Poetry Chapbook launch at Goran Simic's restaurant Fellini's Shoe, May 2006. Dan Wells, A.F. Moritz, Chris Banks, Adam Getty.

Above: Zach Wells, *CNQ* Book Review Editor, with Ottawa poet Bill Hawkins. (AUTHOR)

Right: Ryszard Kapuscinski. Biblioasis is set to publish the Polish great's *I Wrote Stone: Selected Poems* in the fall of 2007.

Below: With Myrna in the Elgin Street Diner. Another photo by David O'Rourke after a working lunch discussing his forthcoming book with Biblioasis on the Montreal forties poets – *Once There Were Giants.*

Above: Dan Wells and fellow publisher and mentor Kitty Lewis (from Brick Books). The elusive bookseller and publisher Nicky Drumbolis in the rear. (DON MCLEOD)

Right: David Hickey reading from Gerald Lampert Award nominated collection *In the Lights of a Midnight Plow*. Biblioasis will be publishing his first children's book in 2009.

Below: Joint Biblioasis/Porcupine's Quill Launch for David Helwig (*Saltsea*) and Sharon English (*Zero Gravity*) at Fellini's Shoe, October 2006. Wayne Clifford, Tim Inkster, Goran Simic, Sharon English, Dan Wells, Mike Barnes, Jack Illingworth, David Helwig. (DON MCLEOD)

Above: Chekhov's house in Yalta, the White Dacha. (AUTHOR)

Right: The living room in the White Dacha, Chekhov's photograph on top of the piano. (AUTHOR)

Below: Chekhov's study. The wallpaper made me think of the room where Oscar Wilde lay dying. His last words were directed at the wallpaper and were alleged to have been: "One of us must go." (MYRNA METCALF)

Above: With daughter Liz, and son-in-law Ethan in Salisbury, Connecticut. (MYRNA METCALF)

Right: Oct/Nov 2003. Sitting in the stadium at Delphi above the Temple of Apollo. Halfway up Parnassus. (MYRNA METCALF)

Below: With Tony Calzetta and Myrna in L'Isle-sur-la-Sorgue, Provence. Tony being unnecessarily Gallic in sporting a baguette. (AUTHOR)

The British War Cemetery in Benghazi. Reading the marker of Flying Officer T.H. Dibb. Navigator. Royal Canadian Air Force. 2nd June 1944. Age 29. HE DIED THAT WE MIGHT LIVE (MYRNA METCALF)

Left: At the Prado on my 66th birthday, a morning of Hieronymous Bosch followed by lunch at Restaurante Botin where Goya had been a dishwasher. (MYRNA METCALF)
Right: Part of the student Honour Guard at the Tomb of the Unknown Sailor in Odessa. (AUTHOR)

With my mother and brother at the celebration of her 100th birthday in Yorkshire. (MYRNA METCALF)

The Humber School for Writers (2005)

Bottom row (left to right): Paul Quarrington, Erika de Vasconcelos, Olive Senior, and Joe Kertes.
Second row: Kim Moritsugu, John Metcalf, Alistair MacLeod, D.M. Thomas, and Bruce Jay Friedman.
Third row: Richard B. Wright, David Bezmozgis, Wayson Choy, and Barry Unsworth.
Fourth row: Antanas Sileika, Charlotte Empey, Guy Vanderhaeghe, Ha Jin, Nino Ricci, and Isabel Huggan.

Above: Drs. Denys Arcand and Clark Blaise trying to work out how many more hundreds of students are yet to cross the stage. (MYRNA METCALF)

Right: Receiving the Order of Canada from Governor General Adrienne Clarkson, 2004.

Below: Clark Blaise receiving an Honorary Doctorate at McGill in 2004. Dick Pound, Chancellor of McGill, Clark Blaise, and, identified by one wing of the bow tie, Eric Ormsby adjusting Clark's hood. (MYRNA METCALF)

Walking on the Ridgeway along which Boadicea led the Iceni against the legions. My brother and I are heading towards Wayland's Smithy, one of the most romantic of the neolithic tombs. (ELIZABETH METCALF)

Caroline Adderson is the author of two short story collections, *Bad Imaginings* and *Pleased to Meet You*, and two novels, *A History of Forgetting* and *Sitting Practice*. Philip Marchand, book critic for the *Toronto Star*, has hailed her as one of the four most notable emerging writers in Canada.

The stories in *Bad Imaginings* have an astonishing range both in subject matter and emotion. She moves, always with great authority, from stories about troubled children – "Bread and Stone," "And the Children Shall Rise," and "Shiners" – to the complex comedy of "The Planet Earth," to fanciful pastiche of nineteenth century memoir-writing in "Gold Mountain: A Tale of Fortune-Seeking in British North America." She is somewhat drawn, perhaps, to the macabre but any Gothic tendency is countered in the crispness of her language and the directness of her gaze. Nothing she writes is touched by sentimentality.

Her stories tend to make the reader uncomfortable; there is nothing emotionally easy in any of them and the poetry of her language increases our unease as it makes us work closer and closer in to the depth of the experience she is creating and making us share.

At the *Wild Writers We Have Known* conference in Stratford in 2000, recorded in *The New Quarterly* Volume XXI, Nos. 2 and 3, Terry Griggs began her comments on Caroline Adderson's writing by talking about the story "Shiners":

> 'Laurence is wading stiff-legged into the lake, plastic bucket in one hand, the other reassuring the top of his head. Their grandmother has got him to put on a little sailor cap. Blue trunks, Thad's of two years before, sag at the crotch. On his chest are raw pink marks, a tender mottling where scabs were peeled off too soon.'
>
> The writing is deft and swift and telling: Laurence's tentative 'stiff-legged' wade into the lake, his own hand 'reassuring the top of his head,' the 'little sailor cap' (a wrenching detail), the 'sag at the crotch' (another one), the 'raw pink marks,' the 'scabs . . . peeled off too soon.' The effect this has is an immediate plunge into uneasiness, if not dread – you know this story is going to hurt, that something unpleasant is going to happen to this vulnerable child, that scabs are going to be ripped off too soon and that very likely they will be yours. Instinctively, protectively, one wants to turn away and not read further, but that is really not possible because of the appeal of the writing

> itself, the sheer loveliness of it. It is as alluring as the minnows, the 'shiners,' that attract Laurence's attention: 'Sun-warmed shallows show minnows. Like the blades of small new knives, they are painfully silver, alluring. A cluster hovers over grey-green pebbles.' By loveliness of the writing it's clear that I'm not referring to a lushly romantic style, but to a style of exactitude and particularity, in which words have been chosen very carefully and are placed just-so on the page with an economy – and an economy of metaphor – that nonetheless resonates, that has poetic impact.

This is the essence of Caroline Adderson's writing but there is another aspect of her work that Terry Griggs only touches on but which I consider central – Caroline Adderson is very, very funny. Her humour flashes and glints throughout the book in a controlled way, but when deliberately let rip as in the story "The Planet Earth" a comedienne stands revealed. The story records the friendship of two school friends, Denise and Barbara.

> Denise was sick of her parents. Sick, sick, sick. It wasn't that they hounded or cramped her. Rather, they left her too much alone, starring in their own little melodrama with Denise as their audience. She booed and cat-called. 'Get a divorce!' were her parting words. As for Barbara, her three older sisters were all pregnant at the same time. When the extended family united for Sunday dinner the vomiting terrified her. She wanted to live a little before that happened to her.
>
> They rented a furnished bachelor suite in Kitsilano, its proximity to the beach compensating for the mildew. 'Furnished' meant a kitchen table, two unmatching chairs and a Murphy bed that pulled out of the wall like a drawer. Opening the bed that first night, they shrieked in disgust; the mattress was a record in splotches of all the previous tenants. Or, as Denise imagined, it was an astigmatic cartographer's projection of the earth – the stains the continents misshapen and askew. South America was obviously blood. Barbara thought menstrual blood; Denise said, 'Somebody picked a cherry.' Neither wanted to lie down on it so they bought a cot and made this rule: the last one home sleeps with Murphy.
>
> Denise didn't show her skinny legs. She wore long tie-dyed skirts

and got a job in a café on Fourth Avenue, the Planet Earth, that specialized in vegan cuisine.

'I don't get it,' said Barbara. 'It's called Planet Earth but you sell food from Venus.' Tofu made her fart so they instituted another rule: Denise couldn't bring any home. Instead she brought her contempt for the clientele of the Planet Earth. 'I am a flower' she sang, swaying on the Murphy bed, arms swirling around her. 'Feel my good vibrations.' She claimed to despise everyone in Kitsilano except Barbara, Max – bus boy from the Planet Earth – and her boss, Peter, who owned the café but was at the same time a supposedly penniless Hare Krishna distributing the *Bhagavad Gita* downtown in front of the Bay.

Denise also brought home men she met in the café.

'This is Frank. Frank, tell Barb your favourite colour.'

'Psychedelic.'

Such fast, deft characterization. Such verbal pleasures . . .

A profile of Caroline Adderson appears in *CNQ* No. 71, 2007.

Margaret Atwood is the author of six collections of short fiction, *Dancing Girls, Murder in the Dark, Bluebeard's Egg, Wilderness Tips, Good Bones,* and *The Test.* She has been internationally lauded for these volumes but I remain unconvinced. While her wit and intelligence are obvious the stories in general fill me with disquiet. My unease revolves around what she wrote in "An End to Audience?" which I quoted from in my talk at Alcalà de Henares: "I believe that fiction writing is the guardian of the moral and ethical sense of community. Especially now that organized religion is scattered and in disarray, and politicians have, Lord knows, lost their credibility, fiction is one of the few forms left through which we may examine our society not in its particular but in its typical aspects; through which we can see ourselves and the ways in which we behave towards each other, through which we can see others and judge them and ourselves."

She goes on: "Writing is a craft, true, and discussions of the position of colons and the rhyming of *plastic* and *spastic* have some place in it . . ."

Her statement in the first quoted passage that fiction enables us to examine our society "not in its particular but in its typical aspects," and the implication in the second that the craft of writing is separable from and subsidiary to the "message" of the writing, fundamentally differentiates

Margaret Atwood from most of the other writers on the Century List. Characteristically, she is committed to presenting ideas and political positions. The central problem with fiction which advances ideas is that we can take issue with the ideas advanced *as ideas*; we can disagree intellectually with particular moral and ethical positions or with the political ideas of left, right, and centre. But it is impossible to "disagree" with our experience of the particularities of a Mavis Gallant story.

All too often her messages seem to me to urge a raucous and almost hysterical feminism. Bill Hoffer used to grump that Atwood's work was most appreciated "by girls of the most unpromising kind." Doubtless less perceptive criticism than irritated misogyny. Yet the work *does* have designs on us. She does indeed want to send us messages. And like telemarketing, they're messages I'm not interested in listening to. It comes down to a question of artistry. I would stand, rather, with William Faulkner who is supposed to have said to a lady who asked him what message he had wished his book to send that had he wanted to send messages he would have used Western Union.

Clark Blaise reviewed *Wilderness Tips* (1991) in the *Chicago Tribune* and wrote:

> . . . she works a secure but narrow band of settings and characters. Men still murder, women still create. The stories are not profound and certainly not charming. What they are is stylish, very, very Atwoodian.

He went on:

> In the duality of the sexes, men and women can never be intimate. They can never fully trust or be worthy of trust. Like great scarred hunting cats, they gather in temporary prides for gorging and breeding and seem curiously susceptible to urges unworthy of their cunning and experience. Atwoodian men are especially ineffectual, over-matched little boys, worthy of giggles even in the height of their passions.

Despite such savage and ghastly stories as "Hairball" in *Wilderness Tips*, Atwood can be generously funny. What follows is an excerpt from "Hurricane Hazel" from *Bluebeard's Egg* (1983). The story is an almost perfect comic performance. The feminist position which is inherent in the story is not advanced as an argument; the uncouth young male, Buddy, is seen through the grave eyes of the narrator as something as alien as a being from

Mars, and the rituals of teen courtship are described almost as by an anthropologist observing the rites of savages.

"Hurricane Hazel" has for me only one flaw and it is that place in the story where Margaret Atwood intrudes into the comic texture to hammer home unnecessarily a point that was being made delicately by the whole shape of the scene. I draw attention to this because it illustrates my reservations about her editorializing, her deforming didacticism.

The narrator and Buddy, along with Trish and Charlie, are swimming in Pike Lake and, typical Atwoodian detail this, "Part of a hot-dog wiener floated near where we waded in, pallid, greyish-pink, lost-looking."

Under a shady tree Buddy plights his troth.

> Then he said, 'I want you to have something.' His voice was offhand, affable, the way it usually was; his eyes weren't. On the whole he looked frightened. He undid the silver bracelet from his wrist. It had always been there, and I knew what was written on it: *Buddy,* engraved in flowing script. It was an imitation army I.D. tag; a lot of the boys wore them.
>
> 'My identity bracelet,' he said.
>
> . . .
>
> It was years later too that I realized Buddy had used the wrong word: it wasn't an identity bracelet, it was an identification bracelet. The difference escaped me at the time. But maybe it was the right word after all, and what Buddy was handing over to me was his identity, some key part of himself that I was expected to keep for him and watch over.
>
> Another interpretation has since become possible: that Buddy was putting his name on me, like a *Reserved* sign or an ownership label, or a tattoo on a cow's ear, or a brand. But at the time nobody thought that way. Everyone knew that getting a boy's I.D. bracelet was a privilege, not a degradation, and this is how Trish greeted it when she came back from her walk with Charlie.

Messages. Messages.

It may be that Margaret Atwood's best work in short fiction will turn out not to reflect the bleak world of "great scarred hunting cats gathering in temporary prides for gorging and breeding" as Clark Blaise put it. She is not so much "stylish," as Blaise said, but, rather, fashionable. Her talent is, as he said, "not profound" and her best work in short fiction just might be in the idiosyncratic bits and pieces in *Murder in the Dark: Short Fictions and Prose Poems, Good Bones,* and *The Tent.*

Mike Barnes is the author of two collections of poetry, *Calm Jazz Sea* (1996) and *A Thaw Foretold* (2006), two novels, *The Syllabus* (2002) and *Catalogue Raisonné* (2005) and two collections of short stories, *Aquarium* (1999) and *Contrary Angel* (2004). *Aquarium* was the winner of the first Danuta Gleed Award for the best first story collection of the year.

Calm Jazz Sea was the first Barnes book I read and poetry is probably at the centre of everything he writes. His observation is keen, observations, which, to use Robyn Sarah's phrase, "resonate in more than one frequency," observations which the story elevates to the status of image.

The story "Dr. Lekky's Rose" in *Aquarium*, for example, concerns the efforts of an alcoholic couple to make a new start and achieve sobriety. By the end of the story we realize that life for them is going to be simply more of the same. Here is the story's opening.

> Paul was on his way into the liquor store when he heard a small, bright sound. *Chip. Chip.* He looked up. A little above him, large white letters spelling Liquor Control Board projected from the brick wall. Inside the O in Liquor, a sparrow was sitting on an untidy nest, chirping. It looked down at at him, switching its head from side to side. When it opened its beak the bright sound sprang out. Other letters – the C, the B and D – had bits of sticks and dried grass stuck in them, the beginnings or remains of other nests.

This seems, as we read, simply observed detail, but as we read on it becomes clearer that the paragraph is, in fact, an image informing the story's emotional direction. The image is not defined; there is no "equals" sign. But the bird presides over the Liquor Board amid "the beginning or remains" of nests and utters "the bright sound." Two emotional states or currents are being suggested here. And observations become images repeatedly as incident follows incident.

In my 1972 anthology *The Narrative Voice* Clark Blaise wrote in "To Begin, to Begin"

". . . the story seeks its beginning, the story many times *is* its beginning, amplified . . . The first paragraph is a microcosm of the whole, but in a way that only the whole can reveal."

In the light of this, consider the following paragraph near the opening of the story "Bitter Lake." Don Tremaine, a teacher on a remote northern Ojibway reserve, estranged from his wife, Becky, receives from her a box of supplies.

> He was glad that Becky had got his letter in time to send the foodstuffs he had requested: Red River cereal, oatmeal, dried fruit; but disappointed that she had sent them in such small quantities. Her little twist-tied bags bespoke a proximity to malls and supermarkets. Around them she had packed useless, sentimental things. Another mug, his desk lamp, two brass duck heads (he leaned back and shook his head at those), two framed pictures. The glass over the Monet print had cracked. Glass! Broken parts rattled in the clock radio.

Broken, broken.

So much going on here.

At the Stratford Conference, David Bergen said, "As a writer, Mike Barnes circles a problem or a character, dropping hints and pulling back, drawing closer, lifting the lid slightly and then closing it, as if we are voyeurs with the author and are being invited to look."

Jim Bartley, the *Globe and Mail's* brilliant reviewer of first literary fiction, captured the *shape* of a Barnes story when he wrote of *Aquarium*: "Barnes chooses his narrative turns with delicacy, avoiding high drama and epiphanies in favour of keen, incremental observation of characters. His climaxes approach like dawning understanding."

"Dr. Lekky's Rose" ends with Paul and Jean sitting on the balcony of their new apartment watching the sunrise. They had been awakened in the night by the scrabblings of an animal above their heads – another detail turning into image. Paul later awakes again to hear sounds from the kitchen and suspects Jean might have been drinking more gin.

The story ends bleakly with these three paragraphs.

> She flicked her cigarette over the railing.
>
> 'Hey,' he said. 'We live here.'
>
> Jean said something back to him, but he didn't catch it because he was watching the butt go spinning end over end down to the grass. It had already landed but he could still see it falling, like a scene on video

> loop. There was a good inch left beyond the filter. He would have to go down in a minute and pick it up, before Mr. Rice found it and decided that he'd rented to a couple of bums.

And that butt, falling, falling, falling, is our "dawning of understanding" of the sparrow's "bright sound" in the first paragraph.

Chip. Chip.

Not all, however, is brooding poetry. Mike Barnes is disgracefully funny in writing sex scenes –see *The Syllabus* – and capable of lively humour modulating to sudden warm depth as in this polished paragraph from *Catalogue Raisonné*:

> Angela rolled her eyes my way at Robert's 'jitterbugging,' but she was having fun. Her cheeks flushed, laughing when he cranked her around in a spastic spin. But next up she got Jason, who shuffled awkwardly to 'Start Me Up,' the usual masculine jerks and jolts, like a man forced to be sprightly in body armour. Our registrar was an earnest, thoroughly decent guy, a fitness buff capable of telling you far more than you wanted to know about lactic acid and proteins. Executing a neat turn away from him, Angela shot me a pained look of appeal. I spoke to Ramon, and rescued her when the next song started. 'Avalon' by Roxy Music, one of her current favourites. We danced in a slow tight circle, her body humid and warm. It felt like high school. Almost that magical again.

With his second collection, *Contrary Angel*, Mike Barnes dramatically extended his range and ambition.

Kim Jernigan conducts an interesting interview with Barnes in *The New Quarterly* Volume XX, No. 4 (Winter/Spring 2001).

David Bergen writes on the stories in *Aquarium* in "The Blue Bic Pen" in *The New Quarterly XXI,* Nos. 2 and 3.

Clark Blaise's *Selected Stories* appeared from The Porcupine's Quill in four volumes: *Southern Stories* (with an Introduction by Fenton Johnson) 2000; *Pittsburgh Stories* (with an Introduction by Robert Boyers) 2001; *Montreal Stories* (with an Introduction by Peter Behrens) 2003; and *World Body* (with an Introduction by Michael Augustin) 2006.

Along with the Selected Stories of Mavis Gallant, Norman Levine, and Alice Munro, these four books constitute one of the most important bodies of work in Canadian fiction.

In his Afterword in the final volume Blaise wrote:

> Fate, family and marriage have conspired to make me into a hydroponic writer: rootless, unhoused, fed by swirling waters and harsh, artificial light. In Canadian terms, a classic un-Munro. A Manitoba mother and a Quebec father, an American and Canadian life split more or less equally, can do that to an inquisitive and absorptive child. I never lived longer than six months anywhere, until my four-year Pittsburgh adolescence and fourteen years of Montreal teaching. As a consequence, when I was a young writer, I thought that making sense of my American and Canadian experience would absorb my interest for the rest of my life.
>
> But a five-minute wedding ceremony in a lawyer's office in Iowa City forty-two years ago delivered that inquisitive child an even larger world than the North American continent. I married India, a beautiful and complicated world, and that Canadian/American, French/English, Northern/Southern boy slowly disappeared. (I wonder what he would have been like, had the larger world never intervened.) The stories in *World Body* reflect a few of those non-North-American experiences. I now live in California, but my California, strangely, presents itself through Indian eyes.

When I first knew Clark forty years ago as a member of the Montreal Story Tellers I was a young English immigrant from a still insular England. We gathered from his stories that he had spent his childhood among redneck crackers having chigger-like worms removed from his feet with the aid of carbolic acid and pouring fresh quicklime down the seething, hissing squatty-hole. In Cincinnati he attended school with Israelites and "the coloured," elementary school students either balding or with moustaches. He spoke French; even more impressive, he understood *joual.* His mother had studied art in Germany during Hitler's rise to power; his father, a thuggish, illiterate womanizer, was, in Clark's words, "a salesman, a violent, aggressive, manipulative man specializing in the arts of spontaneous misrepresentation." Bernard Malamud was his friend. He had been at Iowa in much the same years as Raymond Carver, Andre Dubus, and Joy Williams. And to top off all this outré richness, he was married to Bharati Mukherjee, a novelist and story writer of great beauty who dazzled us with saris. I found him (and her) exotic.

A few years ago my son Daniel married Chantal Filion and Clark said to me, "At last your people have joined my people." But by then I was less clear who my people were. I was no longer, as I had been, simply a part of the Metcalf diaspora from Wensleydale in North Yorkshire. I had acquired another country, another citizenship. My first wife was of Lebanese origins, her people from a village not far from Mount Hermon, so my daughter is half British, half Lebanese-Canadian. Though American in upbringing. My wife is Jewish as, therefore, is my stepson. My wife connects me to Quebec where she was born and to Rumania, Poland, and Israel. My younger son and daughter are from Kerala or Tamil Nadu State –no one knows. My wife and I were the guardians of boat children, a brother and sister from Cholon in Saigon. Over the forty years I've known Clark, my life, I realized slowly, had become a Clark Blaise life, a Clark Blaise story.

Alexander MacLeod wrote an interesting essay on Blaise in *CNQ* No. 67 entitled "I once was lost but now am found: Re-reading Clark Blaise in 2005."

> After so many years of emigration and immigration, and after decades of cultural and linguistic inter-marriage, and after generations of ever-increasing personal mobility and travel, I think the world outside Blaise's fiction has caught up to lives led inside the books. When we re-read these stories in 2005, we see that Blaise's characters are not nearly as unusual as we may once have thought. Rather than imagining that they are lost and alone, it seems now that Blaise's characters are actually leading the way, carving out a path that millions have followed in recent decades. It may be true that seventy years ago most of the North American population lived and died within fifty miles of the places where they were born, but that simply is no longer the case. 'The past' as L.P. Hartley famously put it 'is another country' and we do not live there any more. When scholars study Blaise's work they are not reading anthropological reports on some strange group of lonely overeducated misfits who just can't fit in no matter where they go. If it were only possible to shake off the nostalgic fog that so often clouds our reading on the issue of place, we might finally see the mirror Blaise is holding up.

> We might finally understand that when we look at his people, we see ourselves – an entire population haunted by visions and stories of a stable home place that never actually belonged to us.

In "A North American Education" Clark wrote a story which is one of the glories of Canadian literature though it touches on Canada only briefly, It begins:

"Eleven years after the death of Napoleon, in the presidency of Andrew Jackson, my grandfather, Boniface Thibidault, was born." In the opening paragraphs, Blaise refers to Flaubert's *A Sentimental Education* and Flaubert's novel is to be understood as a ghostly presence, a running commentary on and contrast to the events of Blaise's story. Though Blaise's story is less about sexual love than it is about the love the boy longs for from his father.

A *Sentimental Education* takes place largely in Paris in the years leading up to the overthrow of Louis-Philippe in 1848 and the establishment of the Second Republic. Paris serves as a vibrant backdrop to the obsessional love affair between Frederic Moreau and Mme Marie Arnoux.

> The Seine, mud-coloured, had risen almost to the keystones of the bridges. A chilly breath came off the river. Frederic sniffed it with all his strength, savouring that delicious Paris air, which seems to be fraught with the redolence of love and the exhalations of the intellect.

The book climbs towards the events of 1848 and the early rapture of those who took to the streets is suggested by Dussardier's speech to Frederic during the fighting.

> The Republic has been proclaimed! We shall be happy now. I heard some journalists talking just now; they said we were going to liberate Poland and Italy. No more kings! Do you understand? The whole world free! The whole world free!

This fervour is wonderfully undercut by the subsequent scenes of rioting, wanton destruction, and drunken looting.

Frederic's unconsummated and consuming love for Marie Arnoux, which is the book's central strand, is summed up in his final speech to her:

> Your figure, your smallest movement seemed to me of more than human significance on earth. When you passed by, my heart lifted like dust after your footsteps. The effect you had on me was like a moonlit night in summer, when the world is all perfume, soft shadows, milky paleness, and dim horizons; when I repeated your name, I tried to kiss it with my lips; for me it contained all the joys of the flesh and the soul.

This is the presence behind "A North American Education." The idealized, madly romantic passion between Frederic and Mme Arnoux stands in contrast to the narrator's North American education in matters sexual.

> I had known from books and articles my mother was leaving in the bathroom, that I was supposed to be learning about sex. I'd read the books and figured out the anatomy for myself; I wondered only how to ask a girl for it and what to do once I got there. Sex was something like dancing, I supposed, too intricate and spontaneous for a boy like me. And so we toured the Fair Grounds that morning, saying nothing, reviewing the prize sows and heifers, watching a stock-car race and a miniature rodeo. I could tell from my father's breathing, his coughing, his attempt to put his arm around my shoulder, that this was the day he was going to talk to me about sex, the facts of life, and the thought embarrassed him as much as it did me. I wanted to tell him to never mind; I didn't need it, it was something that selfish people did to one another.
>
> He led me to a remote tent far off the fairway. There was a long male line outside, men with a few boys my age, joking loudly and smelling bad. My father looked away, silent. So this is the place, I thought, where I'm going to see it, going to learn something good and dirty, something they couldn't put on these Britannica Films and show in school. The sign over the entrance said only: *Princess Hi-Yalla. Shows Continuously.*

So much for a *moonlit night in summer, when the world is all perfume.*

The shadow of *A Sentimental Education* which stands behind "A North American Education" and intensifies its power and depth also suggests other sadnesses, diminishments, varieties of loss.

An avuncular adult once asked one of Clark Blaise's sons what he wished to be when he grew up.

The child replied, "A European."

Mary Borsky is the author of two story collections, *Influence of the Moon* and *Cobalt Blue.* The limitations of the List allow me to consider only *Influence of the Moon.* This gem of a book of linked stories chronicles the growing up in the fifties of Irene Lychenko in the small northern Alberta town of Salt Prairie.

"Salt Prairie" is Mary Borsky's reinvention of the actual town of High Prairie. In her childhood, she said, a sign on the outskirts read:

Welcome to High Prairie
Population 2,500
"Where Culture and Agriculture Meet"

That small Ukranian world is captured with an astonishing vividness. The intensity of these stories will remind readers of Alice Munro's "Walker Brothers Cowboy" or Dylan Thomas' "The Peaches" – evocations of an enchanted time and place. The lyricism of the stories is tempered, however, by a dry, wry humour and, as Irene grows older, by a sly and insidiously engaging feminism.

Writers' first books often recreate the intensity with which children experience and apprehend the world. Those remembered worlds, worlds outside time, live in luminous and holy detail. That impulse to enshrine is movingly expressed by Del Jordan in the Epilogue to Alice Munro's *Lives of Girls and Women.* Del is thinking about the little town of Jubilee:

> I would try to make lists. A list of all the stores and businesses going up and down the main street and who owned them, a list of family names, names on the tombstones in the cemetery and any inscriptions underneath. A list of the titles of the movies that played at the Lyceum Theatre from 1938 to 1950, roughly speaking. Names on the cenotaph (more for the First World War than for the Second). Names of the streets and the pattern they lay in.
>
> The hope of accuracy we bring to such tasks is crazy, heartbreaking.
>
> And no list could hold what I wanted, for what I wanted was every last thing, every layer of speech and thought, stroke of light on bark or walls, every smell, pothole, pain, crack, delusion, held still and held together – radiant, everlasting.

We can, I like to think, recognize enshrined detail. It seems to signal itself. Here's a passage from near the opening of Dylan Thomas' "The Peaches."

> He [Uncle Jim] backed the mare into Union Street, lurching against her side, cursing her patience and patting her nose, and we both climbed into the cart. 'There are too many drunken gypsies,' he said as we rolled and rattled through the flickering lamp-lit town.
>
> He sang hymns all the way to Gorsehill in an affectionate bass voice, and conducted the wind with his whip. He did not need to touch the reins. Once on the rough road, between hedges twisting out to twig the mare by the bridle and poke our caps, we stopped at a whispered 'Whoa,' for uncle to light his pipe and set the darkness on fire and show his long, red, drunken fox's face to me, with its bristling side-bushes and wet, sensitive nose. A white house with a light in one bedroom window shone in a field on a short hill beyond the road.
>
> Uncle whispered, 'Easy, easy, girl,' to the mare, though she was standing calmly, and said to me over his shoulder in a suddenly loud voice; 'A hangman lived there.'

The writing in which the experience is delivered bears the hallmarks of Dylan Thomas' razzmatazz; it is carefully, even elaborately worked.

"cursing her patience and patting her nose"

"conducting the wind with his whip"

"hedges twisting out to twig the mare by the bridle"

The sentence that signals to me, a sentence unadorned and very visible, a detail I feel sure that the child-Dylan in his best suit in the frightening dark actually saw and enshrined:

"A white house with a light in one bedroom window shone in a field on a short hill beyond the road."

And Thomas starts here to really rev up the rhetoric, splashy effects which I adored when I was sixteen. But when I was sixteen I also had a liking for Harvey's Bristol Cream. It took years to rid myself of Thomas' baneful influence. The centre of the problem in the following two paragraphs is that there is something ingratiating in the performance, a betrayal of the experience itself by manipulative charm. By charm itself.

Thomas goes on:

> I pushed the door open and walked into the passage out of the wind. I might have been walking into the hollow night and the wind, passing through a tall vertical shell on an inland sea-shore. Then a door at the

> end of the passage opened; I saw the plates on the shelves, the lighted lamp on the long oil-clothed table. 'Prepare to Meet Thy God' knitted over the fire-place, the smiling china dogs, the brown-stained settle, the grandmother clock, and I ran into the kitchen and into Annie's arms.
>
> There was a welcome, then. The clock struck twelve as she kissed me, and I stood among the shining and striking like a prince taking off his disguise. One minute I was small and cold, skulking dead-scared down a black passage in my stiff, best suit, with my hollow belly thumping and my heart like a time bomb, clutching my grammar school cap, unfamiliar to myself, a snub-nosed story-teller lost in his own adventures and longing to be home; the next I was a royal nephew in smart town clothes, embraced and welcomed, standing in the snug centre of my stories and listening to the clock announcing me. She hurried me to a seat in the side of the cavernous fireplace and took off my shoes. The bright lamps and the ceremonial gongs blazed and rang for me.

These days when I read with a colder eye, it is a relief to turn to a different kitchen, one enshrined more austerely, the kitchen of Irene Lychenko's mother in the story "Blessing."

> It was cooler inside the house and the kitchen had its same sour, salty smell. The cupboards were still red and blue, each door bordered with pictures of flowers cut from seed catalogues, glued on, then covered with clear nail varnish. The window was crowded with African violets, geraniums, and various cuttings rooting in jars. Under the window sill and along the counter were stacks of margarine containers, jars of keys, tacks, ballpoints.

And here from one of Canada's stellar short story writers with *all* the elements in play – plot, characters, dialogue – is the high octane opening of the first story in *Influence of the Moon*, "Ice."

> When the Russians shot a dog up into space, my father celebrated for three days. Later, when he got sober, he took us fishing, me and my brother Amel.
>
> 'B.B. Hunt and the other guys, when it's Russian, they think it's something bad,' my dad said. He almost had to shout to be heard above

the pounding of the tire chains on the winter road. Amel and I sat next to him on the front seat of the dark blue Dodge. I was wearing boys' clothes, the same as Amel, a parka, extra pants, tuque, winter boots.

'But you and me, we like that dog in space, don't we Daddy?' I shouted back. 'We think it's fine, right Daddy?' Amel and I were drinking root beers. It pleased me to sit with a bottle in my hand and talk of grown-up matters to my dad.

'The Russians,' my father said, shifting down to go up a hill, 'when they want to send a dog in space, do they ask The-Important-B.B.-Hunt, or do they just go ahead and do it?'

I took a moment to drain the last of my root beer. Sometimes I didn't understand anything my father said – Power of the Proletariat, Science and Progress, the Emancipation of the Working Man. Still, I believed every word he said.

'They just go ahead, Daddy,' I said. 'They don't ask anybody.' Then I checked my father's face, although I was pretty sure I'd answered right.

As we neared the crest of the hill, I could at last see the lake through the grey tops of trees. The ice, mostly blown clear of snow, was grey and flat as a cookie pan, so bright in a strip where the sun reflected, it was impossible to look at. The sky was as blue as the spark from an electric plug.

Influence of the Moon ought to be on its way to becoming a Canadian classic but remains, I'm afraid, largely unknown.

There is a useful interview with Mary Borsky in *Writers Talking* (Eds. J. Metcalf and Claire Wilkshire) Erin: Porcupine's Quill, 2003.

Ann Copeland is the pseudonym of Virginia Ann Furtwangler (née Walsh). Born in Connecticut, Copeland was educated in Catholic schools before entering the Ursuline Order as Sister John Bernard. She left the convent shortly after the reign of Pope John XXIII and the upheavals of Vatican II. After thirteen years of convent life, she married and moved in 1971 to New Brunswick. In her fiction she calls the Ursulines the Agnetine Order, the sisters of St. Agnes. Her short story collections are *At Peace* (1978), *The Back Room* (1979), *Earthen Vessels* (1984), *The Golden Thread* (1989), *Strange Bodies on a Stranger Shore* (1994) and *Season of Apples* (1996). I had the pleasure of editing her first book for Oberon Press in 1978, not that much editing was called for.

In the collection *The Golden Thread*, Copeland reworks the material in *At Peace* to focus on Claire Delaney. We follow Claire from schoolgirl to novice to Sister and in the final story to the now-married Claire revisiting her past. What Copeland sculpts here is something close to a novel. The story Copeland tells falls into fairly conventional forms. The first story where Claire as schoolgirl deliberately misses taking her part in a religious pageant to go dancing with a "Yale man" foreshadows Claire's sexual attraction to a priest, her general rebelliousness against the chafing constraints of convent life, her growing longing for freedom. Some might say that we have here little more than the elements of a Harlequin romance – strong-willed heroine struggling against oppression towards eventual escape and fulfillment in the arms of a husband, a spiritual bodice-ripper, as it were.

Nor can it be denied that the material itself exerts a strong voyeuristic appeal which is extra-literary. What do they *do* in those convents? What is it *for*? What is it *like*? And Copeland amply satisfies our curiosity.

From "The Golden Thread":

> As she tucked hospital corners, she thought of one morning conference in the novitiate – nine years ago now but unforgettable. Right after spiritual reading that golden October morning the novices gathered for their usual conference with Mother Theodore, the novice mistress. As they filed in and took their places on the straight chairs lined up in the library, they found that in place of Reverend Mother's desk an unmade cot had been set up. In those days one didn't comment by even a surreptitious whisper about such things. Their observance of silence was scrupulous and, equally fastidious about modesty of the eyes, they studiedly avoided the exchange of quizzical glances such a break in routine would normally evoke.
>
> Then Mother Theodore came in – a stern woman in her early sixties, straight, silent, awesomely detached from the things of this world. Secretly afraid of her uncompromising otherworldliness, in moments of deepest spiritual aspiration they longed to achieve just such detached clarity of vision and practice.
>
> 'Sisters,' she said after the opening prayer, 'I want to impress on you this morning a lesson for your entire religious life.' She paused and

> looked around at their attentive faces. 'There is no task too small to do well for the sake of Our Lord.' They knew what was coming. 'You will read in Rodriguez many examples of the saints taking care in the minutiae of their daily lives to imitate the patience and humility of Our Lord. It is not given to many of us to carry a great cross. But it is in the humble, day-to-day tasks of our religious lives that we must strive to be conformed to Jesus.' She paused again, gravely. 'Starting with the senior in rank, Sister Jonas, I want each of you to come forward and make and unmake this cot for us this morning.'

Nor do we find in the technique, the rendering, of these stories, anything unconventional or experimental. There is no pushing at the constraints of language and form as there is in the work of, say, Mark Jarman, Michael Winter, Leon Rooke, Annabel Lyon, or Elise Levine. What, then, singles out the work of Ann Copeland?

There is in everything she writes clarity and lucidity. I have over thirty-five years of reading typescripts come to realize that these qualities are rare indeed. Her very clarity is a form of passion. Add to this her command of telling detail – Sister Barney's cluttered cell in "At Peace," for example – and the stories sweep the reader unresistingly on. I have never read anything quite like them.

Here from "Cloister," as a further taste, is Claire Delaney's recollection of her acceptance of vocation.

> 'Reverend Mother, I have failed in several ways this month in observing the rule and constitutions. I feel I've given in to my curiosity and disedified my sisters by carelessness in religious modesty. Especially during Office I have looked around a good bit.'
>
> 'Yes, Sister. A few of your sisters have mentioned this to me.' Reverend Mother leaned forward slightly, raising one hand to touch the wooden crucifix in her cincture. 'It is very easy to become careless about mortification of the senses. Yet our Lord rewards those who curb their curiosity about the outer world by speaking to them within. Unless we quiet worldly curiosity and mortify the tendency to look about, we shall never hear Him when He speaks.'
>
> Sister Claire held her expression steady. The inner voice. She thought of Saint Bernard looking the other way as he passed the beauties of Lake Desanzano, Saint Somebody spitting out his tongue at the temptress.

> She remembered Keats' nightingale and Steven's Ursula. God was about, that she believed. Where should she look to find him? Yet, Reverend Mother was right. God spoke to the soul in silence, not noise. There had come that final crucial moment when, kneeling in the college chapel during her senior year, praying that she would know, she felt in the depths of her soul a stirring . . . a sense. That stirring – call it a voice – touched the subtle thread of her own most deeply felt freedom. 'I want you,' He said. And on her free response in that moment hung her future, her life. Perhaps her eternity. She was prepared. She had responded '*in toto corde*.' That had been the moment of her true profession.

In addition to the six story collections, she has written a book about writing *The ABCs of Fiction Writing.* (Story Press, 1996). There is unfortunately little or no commentary.

Libby Creelman is the author of *Walking in Paradise* (2000). She is currently working on a novel. The stories in *Walking in Paradise* are about, in Stan Dragland's words, "brittle adults and sharp, bewildered children." When I first read the title story "A Walk in Paradise" which describes a cavalcade of mothers and children and bikes and strollers on its way to the grocery store it was like listening to a scintillating run of notes in a jazz piano solo; it was like an eruption of Oscar Peterson.

> The children have reached Main Street and are waiting at the stop sign, all shouting at once for the go-ahead to cross over.
>
> 'I hope no one's trying to take a nap,' Mary Catherine says.
>
> 'A nap? Who takes naps?' Aunt Darby says musically. 'On a beautiful day like today?'
>
> 'CAN WE GO? CAN WE GO?'
>
> 'Yes, yes.'
>
> 'Walk your bikes on Main Street It's the law.'
>
> They cross over in a tight cluster and coast up onto the sidewalk. Georgiana's son Peter crashes into the outside of the electric company office.
>
> 'Oh, my. God,' Georgiana says and Mary Catherine recognizes in her cousin's voice that whine of exasperation that only a mother can

produce: that certainty that she will not survive one more fall-down, bloody knee, stubbed toe, broken bone or set of stitches.

The stories repay close reading and that suggests to me that an interesting way to present Libby Creelman's writing is to look at one story, "Three Weeks," in some detail. It is a story about a brother and sister, Mike and Rosanna, who go to stay for three weeks with their cousin Peter and his girlfriend Debbie on a family hobby farm in Maine. Later they are joined by Louie, a college friend of Mike's. Rosanna is sixteen. Peter, Mike, and Louie are growing on a hillside a field of marijuana.

Libby talked about the origins of the story at the Stratford Festival Conference in a panel discussion moderated by John Vardon.

> I don't keep a notebook, but I do know that, for me, there's an intellectual component and a non-intellectual component. The non-intellectual component is really important . . . Like everybody else, I always have my eyes open and my ears open, and I'm always collecting things, not so much in a notebook, but more as in remembering anecdotes and storing things away. Before I can start a story, I need to be emotionally charged in a certain way. It's really hard to put this into words, but I think it happens to everybody – it's a feeling. Say you look at a photograph, or the way the light hits something – or maybe it's a movie you've seen – and you get a feeling. For the story 'Three Weeks,' the feeling that charges that story, and charged the writing of it, was based on a visit I made to a countryside in inland Maine about twenty-five years ago, just for a weekend. It was the feeling of the landscape that weekend that stayed with me. Nothing in the story, in terms of action and characters, is related to that weekend. It was the feeling of the landscape – it was late summer, really lush and abundant and very, very sexual – that's how it struck me. I knew that it was rich, that there was something there that I could work with . . .
>
> The anecdote that forms the backbone for the story, is not even a full anecdote. Someone described to me this scenario of these young kids – well, young adults – trying to grow dope in the country, having this business. What was described to me was the atmosphere, the paranoia, the tension, the youth, and some of the details of growing dope and stripping the buds, and all this business. Eventually – I don't remember

how this happened – I sat down and those two components – one (the anecdote) was more intellectual, the other (the feeling of that landscape) more intuitive – were married, so to speak, and I began to write the story.

Mike and Rosanna squabble and fight from long custom. They are not only growing dope but smoking it in, literally, stunning quantities.

'You blacked out?' Mike was saying.

It was dark now in the house.

'Go away.'

'Don't get stupid Rosanna.'

'Shut up. Go away.'

He punched her shoulder. The sofa springs creaked beneath her and someone in the room inhaled sharply. 'Rosanna, go to bed. We're gonna go look for a bar, all right, so just go to bed and don't smoke any more or else.'

'Maybe your sister wants to come,' Louie suggested. Rosanna figured he was standing just inside the doorway; she couldn't see him where she lay.

'Or else what?' she asked.

'She's fucking sixteen, Louie. Look at her.'

Along with the sweaty heat, tensions and paranoid fears rise in the house. Violence might erupt. Rosanna sleeps for long stretches and smokes dope in her room avoiding the others. Louie seems interested in her. The world outside the farmhouse is green-swollen, luxurious, the liquid sky hazy, heat waves cast up from the earth, engulfing the house, the woodshed and barn, Rosanna and Mike.

'I thought I heard a helicopter today,' Mike said one evening. He flicked a piece of oatmeal cookie across the room. It landed neatly in Rosanna's hair.

'Fuck you, Mike,' she said.

Peter was looking wearily at Mike. 'They don't go over with helicopters any more. I think I mentioned that to you about eighty-one times already.'

At this, Debbie giggled, the sound of it a rutty laziness that Peter appeared unable to resist . . .

They harvest the crop. An obliquely sensual scene in the barn.

At best, from a distance – outdoors or in the house – the smell was sweet, like cloves, like Christmas cookies, honeyed and luscious. She lay in her bed at night and it lingered in the air above her as a reminder of her day, standing across from Louie, his class ring flashing in the gloomy light as he stripped buds as thick as his thumb.

The ripening of the marijuana parallels other ripenings, hints at other possible readiness.

After swimming at Sharpe's Lake, an ambiguously erotic scene.

She had her shirt on and was balancing on one foot, poised to step into her underpants, when she heard footsteps and realized suddenly several things: she was half dressed and wet, her clothes were dirty, she would be starting grade eleven in only a week.

Louis was passing, on his way to the road.

She stepped quickly into her underpants and began yanking them up. Pine needles on the soles of her feet dropped into the crotch. She knew that Louie had stopped, that he could not resist noticing this. She swiped at the needles, gave up and pulled at her underpants but they rolled under and tangled on her wet thighs.

'Wait. Don't,' he said, coming over. He leaned down and lifted the crotch at the sides and shook it until it was cleared of debris. Then he moved his fingers around one of her thighs, then the other, thoughtfully and with his face averted, like a person picking a raffle ticket from a hat, and untangled her underwear. Despite some distant, dreary mortification, she waited to see if he would pull them up.

As the squirrel rounded a trunk only a few feet away, its voice gone, its tail swishing, its need to see getting the better of it, she stared at Louie's head bent over her, at the tight curls of black hair flashing with oil and water. Here was a proximity to something she had not planned on. He was a man. And he was very near. I'm only sixteen, she wanted to remind him.

She thought he would say, 'What are you afraid of?' because that's what boys had said before, but he said nothing.

It was only when she realized her underpants were stained an ugly yellow that she blushed. Louie straightened with an expression she could not read. As he walked off across the needle floor she considered how remarkable it was that his breath should have felt so hot.

Brooding, hot, pungent, violent, and sexually gamey, the complete story unfolding at Libby Creelman's pace is a memorable performance.

Shirley Faessler was the author of a novel *Everything in the Window* (1979) and *A Basket of Apples and Other Stories* (1988). She died on March 24th, 1997. Most of the stories were written in the late sixties and early seventies. I anthologized "A Basket of Apples" in a high school text I edited in 1970 called *Sixteen by Twelve* and through that circumstance came to know Shirley quite well. She was then retired from running her house on Sherbourne Street in Toronto as a boarding house catering to the actors and actresses of the New York Yiddish theatre companies.

Shirley spent most of the day secluded in her bedroom. She descended at about 4 o'clock in the afternoon and settled herself in the kitchen with the first drink of the day. Her brother Louis would also drift in at about the same time just awake and gradually assembling himself into evening dress, cufflinks, tea, shirt studs, toast, black leather shoes burnished with an orange Ilford Anstaticum camera cloth. He dealt cards every night at high-stakes poker games. Drivers would arrive later to take him to the houses where the games were played.

The stories flowed with the whiskey. "Stories," as she wrote in *Sixteen by Twelve* "of my stepmother, my stepmother's relatives (whom my father called the Russian Hordes), stories of my sister, my brother, myself. I established a reputation as a raconteur and it was flattering to be sought after, to be coaxed to tell again the story of Mrs. Baskin's love affair with Katz the fishmonger; the story of the two prostitutes who rented a room with the Oxenbergs next door to us, claiming they were office workers; the story of Mrs. Spinner who, while her husband (an amputee) was still in hospital, had gambled away at rake-off five card stud poker the money he had put aside for an artificial limb."

One afternoon I was treated to a story of Louis' younger days. Louis had spent some years in Kingston segregated from society because he had a weakness for banks. On this particular afternoon, said Shirley, her mother was baking in the kitchen when Louis ran in, through, out down the outside stairs, having handed off to her a revolver which she buried in the flour bin. Seconds later, madly in pursuit, two policemen burst in.

"Oy, gevald!" screamed Shirley's mother. "It's a pogrom!"

The stories in *A Basket of Apples* are all about Jewish immigrants from Russia and Rumania who settled in the Kensington Market area of Toronto in the years before the Second World War. Mordecai Richler said of his novels that he wanted to be a witness to his time and place and that he wanted to "get it right." The same kind of impulse lies behind Shirley's work which chronicles the activities of what her father, known as "The Romanian Beast" or "The Mamaliga Eater," called, in turn, "The Russian Hordes."

Reading *A Basket of Apples* it is impossible not to think of Mordecai Richler's stories like "The Summer my Grandmother Was Supposed to Die" collected in *The Street*, a book which would have been on the List were it not that some of the pieces are more essays blurring into sketches. Shirley's stories are certainly not essays but might, perhaps, share something with the sketch.

The Richler comedy of St. Urbain Street is often supplied by smart-ass adolescent boy narrators with slicked-back hair.

> 'Knock, knock.'
> 'Who's there?'
> 'Freda.'
> 'Freda who?'
> 'Fre-da you. Five dollars for any one else.'
>
> *Question:* What happened to Helena Rubinstein?
> *Answer:* Max Factor

Shirley Faessler's comedy is more layered, often tinged with sadness, emotionally deeper. From the story "Henye" here are the brothers Yankev and Yudah.

> When I knew the brothers, their fish-peddling days were behind them. It was during Prohibition and they were making an easier dollar peddling illicit booze. The fish cart, however, was still in use. For deliveries. The topmost tray, concealing the bootleg booze in the interior of the

> cart, contained for the sake of camouflage a few scattered pickerel, a bit of pike, a piece of whitefish packed in ice. Yankev, to accommodate expanding trade, had a phone installed in the hall of his house and it rang at all hours, a customer at the other end asking for Jack. Their customers, for the most part Gentile, could not get their tongues around Yankev so they called him Jack. Yudah was called Joe.
>
> The brothers had acquired a bit of English, enough to see them through their business. Their inventory and records were kept in a lined exercise book, in Yiddish. Customers were designated by descriptive terms, nicknames: The Gimpy One on Bathurst, Long Nose on Lippincott. Using their fish carts mocked up with a scattering of moribund fish in the topmost tray, they made their deliveries to Big Belly, Short Ass, The Murderer, Big Tits, The Pale One, The Goneff, The Twister, The Tank.

At the end of the story, Yankev, his first wife dead and he re-married, is talking to Chayle:

> ' . . .You're not happy?'
>
> 'Happy,' he echoed. 'It's like you said – what kind of life is it to be alone?'
>
> All at once he was his old self again. He smiled at my stepmother, a look of mischief coming to his face. 'She bought me a pair pyjamas,' he said. 'Yankev sleeps now in pyjamas, and his missus like a man sleeps also in pyjamas. First thing in the morning she opens up a window and makes exercises. First of all she stretches,' he said, demonstrating with his arms aloft. 'Then she bends down and puts her ass in the air. And that's some ass to put in the air, believe me. And all day, busy. Busy, busy, busy. With what? To make supper takes five minutes. Soup from a can, compote from a can – it has my *boba's* flavour. A piece of herring? This you never see on the table, she doesn't like the smell. A woman comes in to clean – with what is she busy, you'll ask? With gin rummy. True, gin rummy. They come in three or four times a week, her friends, to play gin rummy. They cackle like geese, they smoke like men. 'Dear,' my wife says to me, 'bring some ginger ale from the frig, the girls are thirsty' – she hasn't got time to leave the cards. Girls, she calls them. Widows! Not one without a husband buried in the ground,' he said with sudden

> indignation. 'Dear, she calls me, nu? Before me there was another Dear and she buried *him*. Once in a while without thinking, I call her Henye. She gets so mad, oh, ho, ho. So I make a mistake sometimes, it's natural. How does a man live with a woman all his life and blot out from his memory her name –'
>
> He rose suddenly from his chair, took a handkerchief from his pocket and blowing his nose in it went to the mirror over the sink and peered in it, dabbing at his eyes. 'Cholera take it,' he said, 'there's something in my eye.' My stepmother looked away; next minute we heard the sound of a horn. Yankev went to the window. 'There she is, my prima donna.' He embraced his niece. 'Drives a car like a man,' he muttered and took his leave.

Yankev's and Yudah's lined exercise book reminds me of a detail from another of Shirley's stories "The Night Watchman." Blum is talking to Pa.

> 'Did I ever tell you about my old man's bookkeeping system when he ran a grocery store? He bought from wholesalers on credit, and some of his customers bought from him on credit. To keep track of what he owed the wholesalers and what the customers owed him, my old man bought himself a nickel notepad and on one side he wrote "I owe Pipples," and on the other side, "Pipples owes me."'

Both *The Street* and *A Basket of Apples* delight in and celebrate the magnificent mangling of English by Yiddish speakers. Both were witnesses to their time and place and both got it comically and movingly right.

Cynthia Flood is the author of two story collections *The Animals in Their Elements* (1987) and *My Father Took a Cake to France* (1992).

The stories are surprising in the wide range of their styles. They are stories about parents and children, about wider family relationships, about aging, about dying. They range from elegiac to angry to the oddly-focussed comic. There is a trademark quality about Cynthia Flood's writing; it has always a particularity – nouns, nouns, nouns – and rigorous verbs – but at the same time there plays over it an abstracting, directing intellectual quality. The total effect is rather difficult to describe. To say it lumpishly, the writing is a mixture of "hot" and "cool," the heat of detail, the coolness of an interpreting fierce intellect.

The following paragraph from "The Man, the Woman, and the Witch of New Orleans" will, I hope, illustrate the effect.

> The city of New Orleans, built on clamshells and river sand along a crescent moon of the Mississippi and well below the level of that river, exists in pulsating tension between decay and new growth. A child's wooden wagon left out for a fortnight grows a green skin, while a vine sprouts and begins to twine about the toy. In their elevated graves, in vast glare-white cities of the dead, black and white New Orleanians rot so briskly that one modest tomb may readily hold all that's left of a hundred and seventeen nuns and yet stand ready to take on dozens more. Once, the local foods were highly spiced to delay or mask corruption. Still spiced, they are now refrigerated, frozen, microwaved, convected . . . but still the spoon sinks into the fragrant, maybe, gumbo, like a foot into the marshes by the Gulf. What lies beneath that surface? What condition is it in? Delicious . . . . Rot, mould, rust, peel, blister, burst, sag, mildew – against these ferocious verbs the citizenry send forth one noun: paint. Coat upon coat upon coat of paint, white and cream and pearl and bone and ivory and palest rose. Paint to fill, seal, protect, prevent, maintain. Barely, until next year. Throughout the city, fish and mud smell hairily in the nostrils. Sun and green contend. The full-leaved summer sky is green heat.

Such a paragraph amply repays repeated slow readings.

Cynthia Flood can move from this complex gumbo to such a comic performance as "Design and Spontaneity," a rendering of a dotty dinner party that reads like a mixture of Beryl Bainbridge and Ivy Compton-Burnett.

> Mrs. Mortimer emerged from the kitchen, carrying a cut-glass dish of hot toasted almonds rolled in salt.
>
> 'Timothy, what are you thinking of? Introductions. Julian help Webby. Dr. Beardsley, Bessie, a nut. Mrs. T, my dear, it seems more than a month, I do like that dress, wonderful peacock blue. Bessie Beardsley, Mrs. T, my aunt by marriage. A nut? Bessie Beardsley, Webster Willoughby, my uncle by marriage. The living-room, a glass of sherry, a nut, do . . . .'

> At the eastern head of his table, Mr. Mortimer aimed his carving knife straight through the animal. 'Shall we all hear now from Bessie, on her impressions? The flight? Her recapitulation, so much swifter than our forebears could have dreamed, of their journeys? The sword of the ice-blue river aimed at the heart of the country?'
>
> 'You know my stomach, Timothy,' said Uncle Webby, confidingly. 'I trust there will be no surprises.'
>
> 'Your digestive tract is surely familiar by now with roast beef and two veg,' said Mrs. T, between uncle and niece.

Such sophisticated writing is far more difficult than it appears; it's dancing, yes, but it's Fred Astaire and Ginger Rogers you're watching.

The title stories of the two volumes, "The Animals in Their Elements" and "My Father Took a Cake to France" are both among the most powerful in Canadian writing. In "The Animals in Their Elements" the aging Harry suffers a stroke. He has been living alone save for his cat Princess. The story is structured around imagery relating to birds – Harry's love of watching them in the maple and walnut trees in his tangled old garden. A mere excerpt violates the texture of the whole but it does allow us to see the delicacy of the writing, the way that style absolutely matches subject matter.

> These unknowns were nurses and doctors, that was all. There was nothing to be said to them. He must just work hard, very hard, to get better. One young doctor, Jewish he must be from the nose, had dark bright eyes, and Harry liked it when he visited. There was a sandbox in which he must feel for letters, to match them with letter-shaped holes in a container. The sand felt silky but it got under his nails. He worked hard, got pretty good at the matching. Now an exercise book. C dash T, put a letter in the middle to make a word. Impossible. No such. Then, as when a bird lands on a rainy branch and the drops frill off the leaves on to those below, there was an infinitely small touch in his head and the letter A presented itself. He smiled. The young doctor smiled too. Then Harry wept, and pointed to the word and wept. Some time later a nurse came saying, 'He says to tell you Princess is all right.' Belief and incredulity nested together in his mind. No speech. Birds flew distantly over the parking lot behind his plate-glass window.

> Some of the food was surprisingly familiar. Shirley had made jelly like this, with bits of fruit suspended in it. Harry wished he knew how, and how to make his left leg work. He thought he was doing his best, but nothing happened. At first young girls helped him to the bathroom but of course he could not go, and finally they brought a man. People got him to move his limbs in a way he saw, but did not yet feel, was rhythmic. In time, in time the leg felt more, though it was ponderous, dragging, with dry skin shaling off like fish scales under an invisible knife. Once, perhaps a dream? Mrs. Chang was there, grinning at the end of his bed with a paper bag. Later, fat pale buns on his bedtray.

Harry's mental struggles and lapses are suggested by the simplified or broken syntax ("Now an exercise book. C dash T, put a letter in the middle to make a word. Impossible. No such.") His dislocated grasp of his world is suggested in the mysterious "fat pale buns" which appear on his bedtray. ("Once, perhaps a dream?") Birds are used throughout the story because they mean for Harry – beauty? intensity of life? excitement? freedom? – perhaps all these. His sudden apprehension of the letter A is likened to a bird's alighting, a kind of blessing. The possibility that all is well with Princess ("Belief and incredulity nested together in his mind.") is capped by the concluding sentence of the paragraph "Birds flew distantly over the parking lot beyond his plate-glass window." He sees birds, the embodiment for him of good emotions, in this case of hope, but they are "distant" still and he remains a prisoner of his body behind plate-glass.

Cynthia Flood uses repetition in the writing to great effect. Indicating the slowness of the *meaning* of CAT coming to Harry, she writes, "Then Harry wept, and pointed to the word and wept." Writing of his physiotherapy she says, "In time, in time the leg felt more," the repetition suggesting the repeated exercise movements. Notice, too, that she writes not "his leg" but "the leg," "the" suggesting dead flesh, something that is not him.

It is the accumulation of such small, deft touches which creates a believable world and which delivers delight.

This is writing of a very high order.

KEATH FRASER is the author of four story collections: *Taking Cover* (1982); *Foreign Affairs* (1986); *Telling My Love Lies* (1997); and *Thirteen Ways of Listening to a Stranger: The Best Stories of Keath Fraser* (2005).

Keath Fraser is not a writer for lazy readers. *The Oxford Companion to Canadian Literature* says of him: "He is one of the most gifted of the new generation of fiction writers . . ." Constance Rooke in *The Malahat Review* said: "Keath Fraser is one of the most intelligent writers working in Canada." I wrote in *An Aesthetic Underground* about first reading him: "I was later to learn that Keath's work bulges with puns, play, complexities; it is best approached with humility and an array of dictionaries."

In the Kingston Conference issue of *Canadian Fiction Magazine* (No. 65, 1989) Geoffrey Hancock wrote:

> Also unique is his play with language and voices. 'Both,' said Fraser, 'are inextricably linked. Language is at the root of literature, and any work of literature with any sort of integrity has to pay homage to language and it has to keep its attention focussed on the language. Literature that lasts surely has an important foundation in the language on the page.'
>
> *Taking Cover*, his first collection, is about the uses and abuses of language, words, communication. One story is appropriately titled 'Roget's Thesaurus' . . . His fiction has been described as a river of language, sophisticated, colloquial, metaphorical, even surreal at times . . .

During a panel discussion at the Stratford Festival Conference, Keath said: "The thing that inspires us to write is often, I think, a reaction against the kind of language that we're assaulted with daily, the kind of words – the kind of buzzwords – that drive us up the wall as we watch television and read newspapers. And our desks are the last refuge for us as writers, where we can see how physical and concrete language can be. As writers, we're trying to inspire other people – readers – with examples, with illustrations, of how else language can act, in a way that doesn't have anything to do with the received language or the issues of the day."

There is no one Fraser voice or style – just endless variety and sentences strangely, and sometimes inexplicably, memorable. Here is the old Roget talking in "Roget's Thesaurus": "My young wife died of tumours the size of apples. That I was a practitioner of healing seemed absurd. It smothered me like fog, her dying, her breath in the end so moist."

How intensely moving! How almost magical.

Or the voice of the Hindu waiter in "Waiting":

> This is a calling like any other, except I was not called. I was not chosen. I was born to it, as some bird to flight. People ask me, what is the secret of waiting? People ask me, do you like waiting? Okay, no one asks me, but I have a mind to tell them . . .

The voice of Maurice Ringspear, psychotic monster, in the opening of "Healing":

> That summer my countrymen were in the news abroad. A violinist was found nude, gagged, dead at the bottom of an airshaft at the Metropolitan Opera House in New York City. In August, the Playmate of the Year died in a West Los Angeles house when a shotgun blew away her face; she was from the West Coast too. We all were. Even the one-legged cancer victim, the most famous of us, hopping across Canada on an aluminum hinge. Only I survived.

The narrating voice in "Le Mal de l'Air":

> Miles, on the other hand, started smoking Dutch cigars, drinking Domestica wine, and at night dropping his front tooth and plate in a glass of water made rabid by an extra Polydent tablet.

In the story "Foreign Affairs," Silas, suffering from MS, long confined indoors, taken out in a wheelchair, hungry to see the world:

> That evening she takes him strolling along English Bay to the bathhouse, where they park to watch the sea festival. His aroused vision of the world dilates. Like Krish [his dog] he drools. His gaze is determined to cover everything. The filmy blouses of thin-strapped, heavy-breasted girls in white jeans and black heels. Helium balloons shaped like silver salmon tied to the wrists of Oriental infants. Bowling pins in the air around a juggler's head.

These snippets – every one – mesh with the world's particularities and catches them in "physical and concrete language."

At the 1986 Kingston Conference, Keath also said this about his fiction: "For me pleasure is the ability to bury a reader in the story even if we don't understand it at all. Have respect for the mystery. A fiction is more than understanding; it's perception and delight."

Louis K. MacKendrick of the University of Windsor, a critic noted for his generous and unusual engagement with the work of younger writers, has written well on Keath Fraser in an essay in *Canadian Fiction Magazine* (No. 65) and in *Writers in Aspic* (Ed. J. Metcalf), Montreal: Véhicule, 1988.

Mavis Gallant is the author of two novels *Green Water, Green Sky* (1959) and *A Fairly Good Time* (1970), and eleven collections of short fiction, *The Other Paris* (1956); *My Heart Is Broken* (1964); *The Pegnitz Junction* (1973); *The End of the World and Other Stories* (1973); *From the Fifteenth District* (1979); *Home Truths* (1981); *Overhead in a Balloon* (1985); *In Transit* (1988); *Across the Bridge* (1993); *The Moslem Wife and Other Stories* (1994); *The Selected Stories of Mavis Gallant* (1996).

It is not really possible to treat the work of Mavis Gallant and Alice Munro in the same way I have treated the work of most of the writers on the Century List. Mavis Gallant has written so many stories and comes at them in such a variety of ways that brief quotation cannot suggest typical voice or style. Alice Munro's stories have been getting longer and longer – verging almost on the novella – and are complex with time shifts and subtle digression so that limited quotation again cannot suggest overall flavour. There is little doubt that they are the commanding writers in Canadian short fiction – and therefore in Canadian literature; the debate amongst writers concerns which is better than the other. Alice Munro's career has been more visible but many readers and writers think that Mavis Gallant's rather cold eye and stringent intellect will age better.

Mavis Gallant has had to endure childish and disgraceful hostility in Canada. Mordecai Richler in his Afterword to the New Canadian Library collection *The Moslem Wife and Other Stories* writes:

> Once, during the '70s, Mavis, who had come to Canada on a university reading tour, phoned me in Montreal. She had been astonished by the hostility of Canadian cultural nationalists who demanded to know why she wrote stories about damn foreigners and why she continued to live abroad, as if that were an act of treachery.
>
> There is a story I cherish about Mavis. Once, I'm told, a naive young Canadian reporter asked her, 'Why do you live in Paris?'
>
> To which Mavis replied, 'Have you ever been to Paris?'

In 2006 Mavis Gallant was honoured in New York City at the reading series Selected Shorts. To an audience of more than seven hundred Russell Banks delivered this tribute:

> From her early twenties, when she left Montreal for Paris, she became a writer whose life and work resisted the narrow confines of national identity. In some ways this has been a small liability – not to her work, certainly, quite the opposite – but perhaps to the shape of her public career. Her fame, if you will. She has not been a writer who represents and is thus claimed for the exclusive appreciation of a single national literary readership. She's not the exclusive property of Canadian cultural consciousness, its witness and celebrant. She's not a French writer, certainly, not even a French writer who writes in English. She's not North American or European. She's a world writer who happens to tell her stories in the English language. She would probably hate me for saying this, but in an important way, like my colleagues here tonight, Michael Ondaatje and Jhumpa Lahiri, she's a post-postmodern writer, a post-postcolonial writer, a post-multicultural writer, one of those artists who refuse the hyphen and reject the claims of national fealty. She belongs to no one but herself and therefore her work belongs to all of us.

It is probably fair to say that general approval of Mavis Gallant and her work was withheld until some time after 1978 when Geoff Hancock brought out a Mavis Gallant Special Issue of *Canadian Fiction Magazine*.

Apart from living abroad and writing about "damn foreigners" another possible reason for her tardy acceptance is that her stories make big demands on the reader. They are complex, highly intelligent, wry, and ironic. In remarks quoted in the introduction to my anthology *Making It New: Contemporary Canadian Stories*, Clark Blaise said of her work ". . . what, pray tell, is the difference between a Mavis Gallant story when she's working at her richest and fullest and most polyphonic and someone else's novel? It's just that the novel becomes smaller and thinner than her story."

By "thinner" Blaise means thinner in texture, less rich in detail, less particular, less rooted in the real world. Her rootedness in the real – often a reality that seems "foreign" to the Canadian consciousness – is another possible reason for the slowness of her acceptance in Canada. She is a writer passionately interested in politics and we have to be able to recognize a wide range of reference and allusion to European history and culture if we are to respond adequately to the experience of her stories. In an interview by Debra Martens, Mavis Gallant says of "The Pegnitz Junction": "I wrote it in high spirits, and it was such fun to write because a great deal of it has some references to German writing – parodies and take-offs and skits and all sorts of things that people didn't get . . ."

In the *Canadian Fiction Magazine* interview by Geoff Hancock, she gives some background for her deep interest in politics. She talks of "being twenty-two, being the intensely left-wing political romantic I was, passionately anti-fascist," and seeing the first pictures out of the concentration camps. She was bewildered that Germany could have allowed this to happen. And she thought: "If we wanted to find out how and why this happened it was the Germans we had to question. There was hardly a culture or a civilization I would have placed as high as the German."

Thinking back, she comments: "I never lost interest in what had happened, the *why* of it, I mean. Nothing I ever read satisfied me . . . I had the feeling that in every day living I would find the origin of the worm – the worm that had destroyed the structure. The stories in *Pegnitz Junction* are, to me, intensely political for that reason. It is not a book about Fascism, but a book about where Fascism comes from. That is why I like it better than anything else. Because I finally answered my own question. Not the historical causes of Fascism – just its small possibilities in people."

Her interest in politics is not in party politics, in advancing a theory or a cause. She is concerned with the emotional lives of individuals and families within social and political structures. In the Debra Martens interview (*So To Speak: Interviews with Contemporary Canadian Writers*. Montreal: Véhicule Press, 1987) Mavis Gallant says: "I would think that everything is political, in a certain sense, in people's lives. They don't always realize it; they're either the victims of it or not aware of it . . . I don't think I could consider people, even in a small domestic entanglement – even if I didn't mention it or write about it – without saying what the structure was that they lived in, and what created it, and what at that particular moment was acting on it . . ."

But her concern is always the individual within the structure rather than the structure itself, the particular rather than the abstract.

If all this sounds off-puttingly rigorous, start *The Selected Stories* backwards and read first the four richly comic stories about Henri

Grippe. And if I have somehow made her sound rarified think of the simple and earthy power of what she wrote for me in *Making It New*.

"Like every other form of art, literature is not more and nothing less than a matter of life and death. The only question worth asking about a story – or a poem, or a piece of sculpture, or a new concert hall – is, 'Is it dead or alive?'"

Essential reading is *Canadian Fiction Magazine* No. 28 (1978). Pages XVI and XVII in the Preface to *The Selected Stories of Mavis Gallant* offer a fascinating description of the typical genesis of her stories. Constance Rooke offers a sensitive reading of the story "Irina" in *Writers in Aspic*. J. Metcalf (Ed.) Montreal: Véhicule Press, 1988.

An important profile of Mavis Gallant by Janice Kulyk Keefer appeared in *The Macmillan Anthology (1)* edited by John Metcalf and Leon Rooke. (1988).

Paul Glennon is the author of two story collections *How Did You Sleep?* (2000) and *The Dodecahedron or a Frame for Frames* (2005)

One of the more acerbic of my female writers at the Porcupine's Quill said that Paul Glennon's work stands in the same relationship to Literature as M.C. Escher's does to Art. She clarified this by saying that the sort of people who liked Escher wore plastic shields and multiple ballpoints in their shirt pocket. This tart comment probably reflects an instinctive defence of the norms of social realism. Paul Glennon's is a territory into which Ray Smith, Leon Rooke, Diane Schoemperlen, Patricia Robertson, and Douglas Glover also stray. It is a territory which encompasses farce, whimsy, metaphysics, surrealism, pastiche and play. The spirit and practice of Jorge Luis Borges stand close.

Glennon has written of his interest in Oulipian principles, "that is on the principles of the Ouvroir de la Littérature Potentielle (OuLiPo). OuLiPo is a group of mostly French authors who create literature based on highly arbitrary constraints of their own making. Amongst the most famous of these are Georges Perec's *La Disparition*, a novel written entirely without the letter E and Raymond Queneau's *Exercices de Style* in which the same object is described over and over in different rhetorical styles."

On the home front, Diane Schoemperlen's novel *In the Language of Love* was "structurally based on the 100 words of the Standard Word Association Test, originally devised by Carl Jung. It's an intriguing list, the first five words being: Table, Dark, Music, Sickness, Man. The last five words are: Street, King, Cheese, Blossom, Afraid. I conceived of this structure early in 1988 but did not begin writing it until August 1990. The form was compelling and clear but it took me that long to figure out what the book was going to be *about.*"

My acerbic author at the Porcupine's Quill would probably consider Paul's and Diane's writing as "like farting Annie Laurie through a keyhole. It may be clever but is it worth the trouble" – Gulley Jimson's immortal words in Joyce Cary's *The Horse's Mouth* to Sir William and Lady Beeder concerning her watercolours. As should be obvious through my insistence throughout this book on the centrality of artifice, hers is not a position I share.

We might do well to remember that Gulley Jimson was attacking in Lady Beeder's work the trite, the worn-out conventions.

> Sir William got out an easel and a big portfolio, in red morocco with a monogram in gold. And he took out a big double mount, of the best Bristol board, cut by a real expert, with a dear little picture in the middle. Sky with clouds, grass with trees, water with reflection, cows with horns, cottage with smoke and passing labourer with fork, blue shirt, old hat.

Paul Glennon's stories are very much not "old hat." In "Chrome," for example, a man awakes to see the world as if everything had been coated in chrome:

> I lifted the pillow off my head and put my hand in front of my face, slowly examining the gleaming metallic curves of my palm and fingers. My hand was featureless except for little splinters of wire that used to be body hairs . . . Nothing looked dirty. Balls of dust and lint in floor corners looked like brooches of finely wound silver wire. The breakfast cereal on my spoon seemed more like highly specialized parts for a European car or appliance . . .

The danger of such writing, it seems to me, is that it is easy to descend into mere cleverness and to lose touch with emotion; the challenge is to domesticate the fantastical and invest it with feeling.

"The Museum of the Decay of Our Love," the first story in *How Did You Sleep?*, seems to me to do just that triumphantly. The husband visits the Museum and tours the various exhibition halls – The Colonial Period, The

Revolution, The Republic, The Civil Wars, The Reconquista, The Junta.

In the Civil Wars Hall:

> All the small space would accommodate were paintings, a few small icons with peculiar compressed perspective and a dozen wide, mostly brown and gloomily realistic battle paintings.
>
> The director gestured quickly to the icons as we passed. 'Aloofness, Intellectual Pride, Disdain, Domestic Drudgery, Ennui, Justified Resentment, Estrangement, Sorrow Inconsolable' . . .
>
> His voice was a drum roll of vibrato as he read off the battle names: 'the Stand-off in the Kitchen, the Long March, the Night of the Rebuff, the Marsh Wars, the Campaign of the Chaco, the Mountain Stronghold, the Final Meeting.'

A bravura performance. And *strangely* moving.

Douglas Glover is the author of five story collections and three novels. The last, *Elle*, won the Governor General's Award for Fiction in English in 2005. The story collections are : *The Mad River, Dog Attempts to Drown Man in Saskatoon, A Guide to Animal Behaviour, 16 Categories of Desire,* and a selected stories *Bad News of the Heart.* Normally I would represent him by the selected stories but *Bad News of the Heart* is published by Dalkey Archive in Normal, Illinois and may prove awkward for Canadian readers to obtain. *16 Categories of Desire* would be a good substitute.

Glover's stories are comedies of unhinged sadness. Professor Lawrence Mathews has written of them, "His art aims to reveal not 'the meaning of life' but 'only the mystery of it, its insolubility, its resistance to meaningful explication.'"

The narrating "I" in "State of the Nation" might be speaking for many of Glover's protagonists when he says:

"I am out of there, a crushing weight on my chest – heartburn or love, I can't tell which."

Glover's protagonists, some in mental hospitals, others wandering lost, are trying to escape "emotional confusion and darkness."

> . . . In session with Dr. Gutfreund, I had once let slip (possibly under the influence of sodium pentathol injections administered surrepti-

> tiously) details of my youthful fascination with 'lifelike' mechanical toys. What did I mean by lifelike? Gutfreund had demanded. He was always trying to get me to explain myself to myself, which I understand is standard therapeutic technique.
>
> What did I mean by lifelike? I meant moving about, performing complex and repetitive actions up to and including making simple speeches. I loved my little tin drummer boy, a barking dog that turned somersaults when wound up and a frog that hopped. I also loved automated bank tellers, self-serve gas stations and vending machines (there was one in the hospital cafeteria which I took to calling Mother.)
>
> Somehow, I told Gutfreund, these machines managed to essentialize all that was good in life while subtracting the emotional confusion and darkness. You never saw a vending machine beat an old woman to death for her handbag, I said. With a machine you know where you stand.

Over these wildly funny stories of despair broods the fathering spirit of Samuel Beckett; it is possible to hear something of the familial cadences in "My Romance":

> I call it love, for want of a better word – I don't know what it is really. Beyond us there is a void, and inside us there is a void. At the centre, the self is inscrutable. We ride the dark, lunar surfaces of unknown objects our whole lives long; we are receivers of messages the provenance of which is as obscure as death itself. It seems to test us, to drown us, grow us, betray us, destroy us. Before it, we are alone. And yet between this void and the shallow dogmas of psychotherapeutics there remains some residue, some faint sediment of – what? The thing you can't see for looking at it, the thing disappearing at the corner of your eye, the thing not conceived in any of your philosophies, the thing that is not the void and not the half-crazy, shambling beast of desire that dogs our lives (what the Buddhists call 'the little self'). This is the place where loves resides, if love resides.

Glover is profoundly interested in rhetoric and reveals his many tricks-of-the-trade in an interview with Melissa Hardy entitled "Essential Furniture of the World" in *Paragraph* Volume 13, No. 1 (1991) and in the transcription of a panel discussion "The Theatre of the Page" in *The New Quarterly: Wild Writers We Have Known.* Volume XXI, Nos. 2 and 3.

The dedication of *16 Categories of Desire* reads, perhaps unsurprisingly, *This book is for my dog Nellie.*

Terry Griggs is the author of the story collection *Quickening* and two novels, *The Lusty Man* and *Rogue's Wedding*. She has also written *The Cat's Eye Corner* trilogy for younger readers.

The stories are usually set in Manitoulin Island where Terry Griggs grew up and where her parents owned a fishing camp. "This land included miles of shoreline, forests, fields, a river, a bay in front of our house, etc., and it was the work of my childhood to get to know every inch of it." She was not, she says, much of a reader when a child. "Which is not to say that there weren't other sources of story. You need look no further than the Catholic Church for a packed and bizarre fund of that. As well, anecdote came with the summer breezes, for our camp was always full of people many of them American (never tight-lipped), and many of whom returned year after year – so you got the ongoing saga. In town there was a whole community of interwoven narratives of which I was aware (to a degree) and a part. Hence my immediate attraction to *Under Milk Wood* when I later encountered it – I had lived the form."

Her tomboyish spiritual attachment to the natural world, her later imaginative recreation of that world – "The ice was still in the bay. The ones who live below, the green-haired women with blue bodies and flowing black dresses . . ." – her participation in anecdote and gossip and the stories she was told of saints, martyrs, and miracles and her sharing in what in one story she called "the communal daydream," all this is mixed together, pure recollected detail and imagined magic, no dividing line between them, to form her own myth of Manitoulin and its characters, a Canadian counterpart to Dylan Thomas' lovely village of the very Welsh-sounding Llareggub, Bugger All spelled backwards.

Here is the *feel* of that mythic landscape, the opening two paragraphs of the story "A Laughing Woman."

> A laughing woman with flame-coloured hair and a dress green as leaves wanders down the road and it's summer, luminous summer, the sun dropping haloes and scarves of light. Clothes are cast off, shades are

> raised. Putty-soft babies, born and coddled in the long winter, are put out on lush new grass and later, in photos, are seen to be playing with sunspots and flashing bolts. Summer spreads over the island like a thousand voices carried over water, like a thousand tongues of fire, engulfing, inciting.
>
> Even the ghosts, packed like larvae in the earth, grow restless and refuse to stay put. Mari knows this. Within sight of her place, down the hill on the other side of the road, lies a graveyard. Evenings sitting on the front step with Whip beside her, chasing birds in his sleep, she watches them rise like brume. Some drift toward town, others stay close, anchored to the last of their possessions – mossy bones, names carved on stone, a spelling of themselves they no longer understand. It fascinates her, how they weave like swifts through the falling dark caught in patterns of unrest that never vary. . . .

In her interview in *Writers Talking* she said: "But stories, yes . . . Possibly it's the form I'm best suited to, as I love language – charged, heightened – and style and narrative. (You know, I do find it annoying when critics say I pay no attention to the story in stories, simply because it is not done the usual way, or they can't be bothered to read with a degree of attention.) As Elizabeth Bowen has said, 'The short story avoids routine, it is the most fluid and experimental of forms.' At a time when even literary novels are becoming more formulaic, the story may be the best and most artistically open place to play."

Play is present in every Griggs story, play couched in an eruption of baroque language – perhaps she'll forgive me if I went so far as to say *rococo.* Lovely endless verbal invention. Lava thrown into the night sky and then running in glowing rivers of gold. The creation of myth demands excess.

In my *Freedom from Culture: Selected Essays 1982-1992* I quoted Terry as writing:

> If anything, a story is a complexity, a puzzle, an involved telling, and it is form that makes available to us a story's intricacies and depths as well as its surface. Form carries out intention, that of plot and character naturally, and that of the writer who may be after a certain texture or density in the prose, or who may have something else up her sleeve. Something private but there nonetheless for discovery. Like the generative impulse

> behind 'Suddenly,' which was simply to define in narrative terms the word suddenly. The result being a head-on collision of the dictionary and the short story that gives 'Suddenly' its episodic and immediate character, as if it is saying, 'I am this, and this, and *this!*'
>
> Form in my stories often takes its cue from the dominant metaphor. In proper metaphor fashion the story becomes in structure, in its very bones, what it is about. (Everything, imagery, symbolism, just piles into the metaphor like kids into a station wagon and the story takes off.)

I was for some reason much moved years ago when Terry told me that before she settles to the day's prose she reads poetry to spiritually prepare herself for what faces her.

Two brief quotations from "Man with the Axe."

First, the almost symphonic:

> All that week her ear itches with a telltale trickle of melt like a tap dripping somewhere, and soon water speaking in a hundred, then a thousand voices through rocks and trees and shifting earth . . .

Second, the domestic:

> Erie had been listening all that week to thaw, a trickle of melt tickling her inner ear, the sound of water dripping off the eaves, *drip* into that handful of bare stones by the corner of the barn, *drop* off the branches of the forsythia out front. Like tears, she thought, cold tears.

Like poetry, I thought.

Terry Griggs is interviewed in *Writers Talking* (Eds. J. Metcalf and Claire Willkshire) Erin: Porcupine's Quill, 2003. There is another important interview conducted by Michael Carbert in *Carousel Magazine*, No. 11, 1996.

Steven Heighton writes poetry, essays, short stories, and novels. His two story collections are *Flight Paths of the Emperor* and *On Earth As It Is*. Another collection is in progress.

A travel-writer said that for thousands of young men and women from the States, Canada, and England, teaching English in Japan has become almost a rite of passage, the 20th century equivalent of the Grand Tour.

In the *Writers Talking* interview Heighton says: "We easily found jobs teaching English – like thousands of other *gaijin,* foreigners – and an eight-tatami flat in Osaka. During our ten busy, happy months there I strove to learn the language, mainly from a second-hand book published a few years before by two elderly, venerable Tokyo philologists. Page by page, chapter by chapter, the sentences the student was asked to render into English grew more disturbing and macabre. *Shitai* – corpse or cadaver – was one of the first words I was required to learn."

Heighton is unashamedly romantic in his attitude to literature. He offers interesting comments on romanticism in an interview in *The Notebooks* and in *Writers Talking* he said: "At the turn of the millennium being a true rebel means being, by postmodern standards, unabashedly uncool – an aesthete, devoted to the old pursuit of truth and beauty in artistic form."

The most powerful of his stories in *Flight Paths of the Emperor* – "The Beautiful Tennessee Waltz" and "Five Paintings of the New Japan" – deal with his narrator's romantic veneration of the "old Japan" only to find that for the Japanese the situation is more equivocal. Of his young Japanese friends at The American Dream café in "The Beautiful Tennessee Waltz" he writes: "At first we had seen each other as spiritual guides to remote Promised Lands, then discovered our maps were obsolete, our purposes at odds. We were falling out of love, but at first we would not give up. I pestered them with queries about Mishima and the Emperor. I patronized them and they patronized me. . . . They stopped mentioning my 'quaint obsession' with the old culture, and when I ordered saké (only old people and foreigners drink saké) they smiled beatifically and said nothing."

Not all, however, is sensitive exploration of West meeting East. Heighton is too much a poet not to revel in the rich comedy of Japanese English. Here from an unpublished story, "Dialogues of Departure," the narrator is riding home after the day's teaching.

> My favourite moment on the ride 'home' to my tatami closet: as the train crossed under the river and climbed out of the tunnel and shot into the open night, a long line of huge neon billboards reared across the river like false-front structures in a midway, luminous and festooned – a commercial phantasmagoria of imagery and Japanese script and twisted English, all mirrored in the sluggish Ara. On a towering billboard, a wry *gaijin* – seemingly James Coburn – sipped whiskey above a

> slogan rendered in gothic script, as if it were a plug for a prog rock band: OF YOU DREAM, BE HANDSOME CAD, FOR YOU PARTY LIFE AND NIGHTIES OF BACHELOR FUN.

In the splendid comic story "A Man with No Master" the narrator is kidnapped from the Amanogawa American English School

English Language
Made Not Exactly Easy But
Helpful For Your Better Life.

by Katana-san and a man the narrator calls Ray-Ban because of his glasses. They are *yakuza* hired by a rival school. They take him to a bar where the TV is playing Kurasawa's *The Seven Samurai*. Ray-Ban gets progressively drunker talking at the film.

"'*In the belly!*' urged Ray-Ban. '*Like a dog!*'"

Heighton talks about what kind of writer he is in the *Writers Talking* interview.

> Writing of what she knows, the chronicler of home renews or reorients our view of the familiar, showing us how strange and foreign the domestic really is. ('She' because I think first of Alice Munro.) Writing of what he doesn't know, so as to discover it in the telling, the explorer of 'away' makes the foreign and exotic feel as familiar as home. ('He' because I think first of Malcolm Lowry and Paul Bowles.) Clearly I was that second kind.

And here is Heighton making the foreign and exotic restaurant *Yume No Ato* as familiar as home in that truly masterful story "Five Paintings of the New Japan."

> I was the first foreigner to wait tables in the *Yume No Ato*. Summer enrolment was down at the English school where I taught so I needed to earn extra money, and since I'd been eating at the restaurant on and off for months it was the first place I thought of applying. It was a small establishment built just after the war in a bombed-out section of the city, but when I saw it the area was studded with bank towers, slick boutiques, coffee shops and flourishing bars and the *Yume No Ato* was one

of the oldest and most venerable places around. I was there most of the summer and I wish I could go back. I heard the other day from Nori, the dishwasher, who works part-time now in a camera store, that our ex-boss Mr. Onishi has just fought and lost a battle with cancer.

'We have problems here every summer,' Mr. Onishi sighed during my interview, 'with a foreign tourist people.' He peered up at me from behind his desk, two shadowy half-moons drooping under his eyes. 'Especially the Americans. If I hire you, you can deal to them.'

'With them,' I said automatically.

'You have experienced waitering?'

'A little,' I lied.

'You understand Japanese?'

'I took a course.'

'Say something to me in Japanese.'

I froze for a moment, then was ambushed by a phrase from my primer.

'*Niwa ni wa furu-ike ga arimasu.*'

'In the garden,' translated Mr. Onishi, 'there is an old pond.'

I stared abjectly at his bald patch.

When Heighton's first novel, *The Shadow Boxer*, appeared the *Independent on Sunday* (UK) wrote of it: "Steven Heighton's first novel comes out of its corner with both fists swinging . . . Essentially the story of one man's troubled love affair with literature, *The Shadow Boxer* fizzes with life and energy, its prose a heated mix of lyricism and muscularity. A bravura performance . . . a post-beat bildungsroman of the sort that isn't written anymore . . . its adhesion to the old vanities of authenticity and the primacy of experience [make it] nothing less than a full-blooded argument with postmodern trickery. Intense and poetic . . . has a swaggering, larger-than-life quality."

Exactly the same could be said of *Flight Paths of the Emperor* and *On Earth As It Is*.

See Heighton's interview in *The Notebooks* edited by Michelle Berry and Natalee Caple. Toronto: Random House, 2002.

Jack Hodgins is the author of three story collections *Spit Delaney's Island* (1976), *The Barclay Family Theatre* (1981) and *Damage Done by the Storm* (2004).

When I was re-reading these books and thinking about the shape and composition of The Century List I was in two minds about the work. I had never been a great fan of *Spit Delaney's Island*; its "parable" quality had never persuaded me. *The Barclay Family Theatre* had to be the decider. But that, too, posed a problem because I liked three of the eight stories but found that the remaining five made me, for a variety of reasons, cringe. Compounding this mixed response was the knowledge that it involved one of my prejudices and that therefore my judgement might well be skewed or unfair. And the considerable weight of Hodgins' reputation in Encyclopedias, Guides, and Companions militated against my instincts. I decided to attempt to explain my judgement and let readers make up their own minds.

The stories in *The Barclay Family Theatre* I liked were "More than Conquerors," "The Lepers' Squint," and, with reservations, "The Plague Children." The other stories I thought cute, overwritten, and "folksy." If you liked these other stories you'd call their humour "broad;" if you didn't, you'd call the humour "crude" or "plonking." If you liked them, you'd say they were "expansive" or "full of zest for life;" if you didn't you might say they were "formless" or "sprawling." But for me "folksy" remains the central reason for my baulking.

I have an uncontrollable distaste for populist work. There is the prejudice naked and unapologetic. I find this folksy quality in the work not only of Jack Hodgins but in W.O. Mitchell, Bill Gaston, Alden Nowlan, Hugh Garner, W.D. Valgardson, W.P. Kinsella, and Ken Mitchell among others. It is a minor but persistent strain in Canadian writing.

Is this simply class prejudice on my part? Or is it more complicated? Folksy, it seems to me, wants to turn back the clock. Folksy wants to praise the "simple," wants to renounce "literature" and revert to "good old-fashioned story-telling." Folksy wants to undo modernism; folksy wants to banish "story" and restore "tale." And in the process it makes language cruder, simpler, less demanding, and in its pandering to "approachability" betrays a hundred years of very sophisticated thought, feeling, and effort. So, yes, I do think that rather more than class is involved.

In Hodgins' story "Invasions '79," Bella Robson's academic son James becomes enamoured of a Russian girl in distant Ottawa. Bella, at the insistence of her daughter Iris, flies from Vancouver to investigate. James' ". . . speciality (when anyone asked) was some old poem she'd never had the pleasure of reading. Its title went something like *Toil Less and Crusade*, though she couldn't guarantee that she'd remembered it right."

> *Troilus and Criseyde.*
> Groan.
> Dear Sweet Old Mum.
> The flavour of this laboured comedy can be tasted in what follows.

> There was little ambiguity, however, when Iris called one evening in late October. 'You'd better come see this for yourself,' she said. 'Your brilliant son has got himself involved with the Russians!'
>
> Bella Robson nearly dropped the receiver. Was it possible? This might be the end of a decade that had seen the whole world trying to act like friends, but to her a word like 'Russians' still conjured up images of barbed-wire fences and spies and firing squads. Iris assured her it was even worse that that. 'A woman.'

> Iris meets her mother at the airport.

> 'Well, he's not in the salt mines *yet*,' she said, stepping forward to take her mother's tote bag from her hand. Her tone of voice made it clear that she didn't expect this state of affairs to last long. 'But I can tell that his phone's been tapped.'
>
> Bella Robson felt her heart skip a beat but she kissed her daughter's cheek and told herself to stay calm. 'If you can tell,' she said, 'it must be amateurs who are doing it.'
>
> Iris lifted her eyes to the ceiling. 'If it's amateurs who throw him in jail, will that be all right with you too?'

Despite the Encyclopedias, Guides, and Companions, this reads to me like Amateur Hour.

Bill Gaston's stories, too, are rambling, episodic, anecdotal, some not much more than expanded jokes. He is capable of much more powerful work. Indeed, I've recently selected a story of his, "Honouring Honey," for *Best Canadian Stories 07* which I'm now again editing for Oberon Press. But his conversational, colloquial style contains the built-in weaknesses of verbal simplicity and restricted vocabulary.

Consider this paragraph about the landlady Mrs. Barastall in "The Walk," one of the better stories in *North of Jesus' Beans* (1993).

> Maybe the worst part about the boarding house was having to sit beside old Mrs. Barastall, in front of the TV, with nothing to say. He thought

> he could smell her: under the waft of floral cheapness an ominous undertone of something a little sour. Andy joked to himself that Mrs. Barastall was the only reason he did well in school, forced as he was away from *Cheers* and *Twin Peaks* to be alone in his room with his books.
>
> In truth, because of the old woman he watched more TV than he ordinarily would have. For one, she seemed to like the same programs he did. But it was more that he found it hard to walk by – harder than her own family did, in any case – without sitting down and watching a show with her. She was, in his opinion, too often left alone, especially after her cancer was diagnosed.
>
> And now he was starting his fourth year here!
>
> Friends would still ask how he could stand living 'with, you know, other people around.' They seemed to love being away from their families, and would speak with dread, only half joking, about a coming Christmas. Andy knew now that boarding houses were weird. He didn't know himself why he stayed. He didn't really like it, but he didn't really hate it.

The only interesting sentence in the four paragraphs is the only untypical one: ". . . under the waft of floral cheapness an ominous undertone of something a little sour." And I'm not totally at ease with "undertone" when we're talking about a smell. The last three sentences, on the other hand, are about as plonkingly flat as it is possible to get. (For the concept of "plonking" see Stephen Potter's *The Theory and Practice of Gamesmanship* (1947) and *One-Upmanship* (1952).)

A quarter of a century ago now I was in correspondence with W.D. Valgardson who told me that he deliberately wrote in a simple manner because he was writing for "the people." I was astonished at such naïveté in one who had studied at the Iowa Writers' Workshop.

Valgardson wrote four story collections: *Bloodflowers* (1993), *God Is Not a Fish Inspector* (1975), *Red Dust* (1978), and *What Can't Be Changed Shouldn't Be Mourned* (1990). In the late seventies and early eighties he was widely considered one of Canada's most important story writers. Even the usually level-headed George Woodcock rated him a leading practitioner. It was never an estimate I shared. I would imagine that today Valgardson is scarcely read at all, his career a warning shot across the bows of those who would structure anthologies and make Lists.

In *Kicking Against the Pricks* (1982) I wrote: "I recently re-read all his work when I was compiling an anthology for school children; I was appalled to discover that there was not a single story that was not suitable."

Hugh Hood was the author of ten story collections, the last, *After All!* appearing posthumously in 2003. Hood's work is so stylistically various that no one volume of the ten conveys his range so I have chosen to represent his work by *Light Shining Out of Darkness and Other Stories*, the volume I selected for the New Canadian Library published in 2001 and titled after a story in *Around the Mountain*, a title presumably referring to the opening verses of the Gospel According to Saint John.

If we come to Hood's work expecting it to be like the mainstream we are likely to be disappointed and baffled. A Hugh Hood story is an experience unto itself and it is a demanding one. In the introduction to *The Isolation Booth*, Hood wrote: "Almost all my work is designed to be read silently by very intelligent and attentive readers, a large majority of them women, three or four times."

It is not only, however, the range and vigour of Hugh's mind and its occasional eccentricities which challenge the reader but also the depth of his religious beliefs. Religious belief permeated his every thought. As it was with Wordsworth that "the meanest flower that blows can give / Thoughts that do often lie too deep for tears" so it was with Hugh and Canadian Tire and Mac's Milk stores, with advertising fliers, with the packaging of Air Canada meals; the presence of God was everywhere apparent to him. When he published a story entitled "The Fruit Man, the Meat Man, and the Manager," a story about three employees of a grocery store, I can still remember his *astonishment* that I had not immediately grasped that they had correspondences with the three persons of the Holy Trinity.

If we do not share his beliefs, must these stories then be alien to us? Do they exclude us?

Hugh was aware of the problem but remained serene. In the Introduction to *Around the Mountain* he wrote: "My religion makes its predictable appearance in the composition of the book. I have always been a religious believer, a Catholic by birth, upbringing, and mature conviction. While I always draw a distinction between religious conviction and ideology I realize that most secular discourse does not. Catholic belief is far from incidental to the production of *Around the Mountain*. Whether faith and dogma have here degenerated into disingenuous propaganda is a question for readers of other ideological persuasions to propose to themselves."

Hugh is far too sophisticated a writer, far too subtle and refined, to topple into didactic mode. His religion is the emotional ground of his being, not a series of debating points he wished to score. His tendency is always to celebrate and question rather than instruct. One does not have to be Catholic to see-saw with the narrator at the end of "Going Out as a Ghost;" one does not have to be a Catholic to understand and share in the joy and celebration that is "Getting to Williamstown."

Hugh's religious convictions had an almost inevitable influence on the forms of his stories. In the introduction to *Flying a Red Kite* he recalls the writing of one of the stories: "'Fallings from Us, Vanishings' has always seemed to me to be the first story in which I am writing wholly as myself, not as a version of Faulkner or Styron or Thurber or Joyce. It has the strongly allegorical cast, the echoes of medieval romance, the Wordsworthian aesthetics and psychology, and the perhaps somewhat abstract quality of my later work."

Hugh had limited interest in plot or character and a decreasing interest as time went by in evocative writing. He often mentioned as conscious influences on his work Dante, Wordsworth, and Spenser; his mind dwelled on the *Purgatorio, The Prelude, Tintern Abbey, The Faerie Queene, The Shepheardes Calender.* Because he was working deliberately outside the conventions of his time, because he was reinvigorating allegory, he was more or less forced to invent new shapes for his stories.

Or does the slight bafflement some of his stories occasion stem from the possibility that we are bringing to his work conventions that do not apply? Is it possible that Hugh should not be considered as in the modernist traditions and conventions at all? Perhaps he was writing inside a Catholic tradition much in the way that Morley Callaghan was, the tradition of homilies and *exempla,* a form W.J. Keith calls "moral fables," a form that would have been familiar to him from childhood?

However we approach his large body of work, I remain utterly convinced that *Around the Mountain,* an evocation of Montreal life, should be central in a Canadian canon. Endearingly innocent, Hugh Hood wrote *Around the Mountain: Scenes from Montreal Life* in 1967 believing that it would sell to tourists wanting a souvenir of Expo '67.

> In those days I was spending a lot of time out at the Montrose Record Centre on Bélanger, west of Montée Saint-Michel. As you come over from the centre of town, east on Jean-Talon or Bélanger, you'll be struck by the flatness and lack of charm of this neighbourhood. I've forgotten the boundary streets, if in fact I ever knew them. It's *calme plat, terne,* though you might be interested by the Italian neighbourhood between Papineau and D'Iberville, lots of *gelata* parlours and *sartorie.*

With this book he perfected a trademark style, a mastery of the seemingly casual, what I described once as "that informal formality, that heightened vernacular," a creation more complicated than it seems.

W.J. Keith has written an invaluable, jargon-free book on Hood's stories called *God's Plenty: A Study of Hugh Hood's Short Fiction.* Enthusiastically recommended.

Isabel Huggan is the author of two story collections *The Elizabeth Stories* (1984) and *You Never Know* (1993). In 2003 she published a memoir *Belonging* which also contained three new stories.

I'll concentrate my attention on *The Elizabeth Stories* because I have a personal attachment to the book. In the seventies and early eighties when I was editing *Best Canadian Stories* for Oberon Press I read one day an issue of the Saskatchewan magazine *Grain.* The issue contained a story – I'm almost certain a *first* story – by Isabel Huggan called "Celia Behind Me" which was so precisely written, so rich in detail, so moving that I felt compelled to find the author and, like Oliver, ask for more. After coaxing and cajoling on my part and prevarication and bewailing on hers, *The Elizabeth Stories* evolved and were launched into the world to delight thousands in the book's various editions.

The eight stories chronicle the childhood and adolescence of Elizabeth Kessler growing up in the imaginary town of Garten, a small town with a Mennonite hinterland based, presumably, on Elmira, Ontario. *The Elizabeth Stories* is the same kind of book as Alice Munro's *Lives of Girls and Women* and Mary Borsky's *Influence of the Moon.* That is, it is an evocation of an enchanted time and place. Though Elizabeth did not find Garten enchanting.

The older Elizabeth looking back writes: "By all odds, I should have been dragged down by the life I led as a child in Garten. I should still be there, or somewhere like it, forced under by my upbringing and all the expectations around me. But luck was with me, and small pockets of defiance multiplied beneath my surface, keeping me afloat, preparing me for that final escape."

Of her ballet classes described in "Jack of Hearts" Elizabeth writes, "Along with most of my friends, I had been enrolled in Saturday morning classes at the age of seven. We were beginning that long process of instillation, the steady drip, drip, drip of Values onto our skulls and into our brains. If our parents could only control our lives long enough, we would eventually achieve grace, tidiness and frugality."

Elizabeth's home life is economically sketched in as are her parents Frank and Mavis. Here is Elizabeth with a schoolfriend, Rudy, in his father's butcher shop eating salami. ". . . he divided the pile so we each had a handful of the spicy meat. It was foreign and exciting, the kind of food I never had at home. For although my father's background was German, as it was for many of the people in the town, my mother's was English, and she deplored garlic and anything the least bit European as being not quite clean."

Elizabeth's early transgressions (usually sexual) cause her mother to cry "I'll never be able to lift my head on this street again!" and "How will I be able to hold my head up in this town again?"

Frank, stuffy, stodgy, rigid, is sketched with sprightly strokes by his comments on Mavis' friend, honorary "Aunt" Eadie.

"As much as my mother admired her friend, my father disparaged her. He was critical not only of the way she dressed ('flashy') and looked ('hair is never that colour in nature') but even of the way she laughed ('she has a loose laugh, Mavis, loose!'). She was in a word flamboyant – the epitome of all that Frank Kessler loathed and feared."

(That second "loose" with its exclamation mark strikes me as exquisitely funny.)

Elizabeth meanwhile nurtures "small pockets of defiance" and continues preparing for "that final escape." Even church camp offers an escape from Garten:

> . . . I learned more about God's glory at Camp Zion than I had ever known, and during Bible study I memorized the Beatitudes and several long scripture passages by heart. I learned to make a fruit basket of popsicle sticks, and a wooden plaque on which I glued alphabet

macaroni to read GOD IS LOVE . . . By the third summer, even though Sharon and Amy chose a co-ed camp closer to home, I would have let nothing come between me and Camp Zion. I didn't need friends from home; I was just as happy to leave them behind, to concentrate on these brief, intense friendships with girls from Brantford, Hamilton, London, St. Catherines. These were girls who could teach me about life outside Garten, who knew about things I had never encountered – Chinese egg rolls, pizza, perverts in movie theatres, how to steal stuff from stores, how to wad your brassière with Kleenex (I didn't need to and for that had some status), how to slick your hair back into a ducktail and wear your blouse collar turned up at the neck. Endless, the things there were to discover at Camp Zion.

"They Desire a Better Country" – the motto of The Order of Canada. *Desiderantes meliorem patriam.* I, personally, desire a MUCH better country. Sometimes in moments of mental and emotional weakness I daydream of a national curriculum. I daydream of teacher-training institutions razed, of pedants ejected, of Mrs. Gundy silenced, of pedagogues from OISE harried to exhaustion along Bloor Street. I daydream of a national curriculum in history. Of a national curriculum in literature for secondary school students. I daydream of teaching the beautiful deployment of language, the sheer *pleasure* of *Lives of Girls and Woman, A Basket of Apples, Influence of the Moon, The Elizabeth Stories* . . .

Mark Anthony Jarman published *Dancing Nightly in the Tavern* in 1984. Twenty-two years ago, now. He published it at a time when such short story writers as W.P. Kinsella and W.D. Valgardson were much in vogue. It is not surprising, then, that not much attention was paid. Jarman was not particularly interested in nationalism or regionalism or racial minorities. It would be rather difficult to extract from his stories any moral certainties or comforts. He was not interested in what nationalist political claptrap habitually describes as "telling our own stories."

Jarman's not your man for pablum.

His characters want something but don't know what.

Ray hasn't eaten, has a vision of himself being rolled somewhere, caught with others in the Depression, a post office mural, a Hopper painting,

> in the U.S.A. Think positively, Ray counsels himself. As what we came for eludes us, so we will replace it. At the food bank there is cheese. Hot coffee and three-bean salad in those cheery church basements . . .
>
> This is not the fucking Depression, I will not line up for their handouts, gnaw the bureaucrats' cheddar. There is a bone stuck in my throat. I want, I don't know, something.

Right from the start Jarman went for the jugular of language. A contemporaneous review of *Dancing Nightly* suggested that he might have been influenced by Jack Kerouac but this observation is more true of the characters' wallowing in alcohol and drugs than it is of stylistic influence. Kerouac's a rather flabby writer; Jarman is madly fierce. He reminds me less of Kerouac than of the Cormac McCarthy of *Blood Meridian*.

His landscapes are mythic landscapes of the mind, a mind drunk or drugged with hopelessness. His cities are visions of violence and madness and remind me of Nathaniel West's *Day of the Locust*. His prose is not the delicate register of sociological markers or the accumulation of realist detail for its own sake. His is a prose of apocalyptic incantation.

Here in "Cowboys Inc." are Jankovitch and Ironchild on the road.

> . . . swinging hard across the blue plains and raggedy-ass cottonwood, the endless flight through pale aspens and truckstop botulism, Kmart snakeskin cowboy boots, cheating songs, box elders. This is just after the grain elevator blew over to Missouri: burnt for days and they couldn't get at the bodies. In the blind pigs and roadhouses lizards cringe under the crashing rain of Wurlitzers and chicken bones.

That is the Jarman voice.

For which we should give thanks.

And while Mark Jarman was blowing and honking and screaming these fervent solos, academe ignored him and placidly munched on Marion Engel.

Some reviewers have described Jarman's characters as "blue-collar" but the colour of their collar is wildly beside the point. Jarman's men and women live outside society on the edge of imminent horror. Most, as in "Men Ought Always to Pray and Not to Faint" are dying for the day's first fix or drink.

> Outside it hurts to open my eyes. The pink flamingoes still have price tags on them. Heat steams in the road, the moss-backed elms dry, ready to crumble or burst into flame. I am running with sweat and toxins.
>
> My father moved to the north side to labour in the huge diesel shop, trains humping all night inside the grass berms, flowering my childhood dreams, metal, swearing and coupling. I am parched. My mouth forms phrases. I have the beer.

Not all the stories are equally successful but Jarman had the talent and the literary wisdom to understand from the beginnings of his career that *words* and their deployment were his answer and salvation. He had the insight and courage to sacrifice grammar and punctuation and tradition to grab immediacy.

Douglas Glover offers a fascinating tribute in his essay "How to Read a Mark Jarman Story" published in *The New Quarterly: Wild Writers I Have Known*. Volume XXI, Nos. 2 and 3.

Mark Anthony Jarman's career unfolded – exploded – into *New Orleans Is Sinking* and *19 Knives. Dancing Nightly in the Tavern* is a glittering book, the first expression of a literary samurai.

Susan Kerslake is the author of *Middlewatch* (1976); *The Book of Fears* (1984); *Penumbra* (1984); *Blind Date* (1989) and *Seasoning Fever* (2002). *The Book of Fears* was shortlisted for the Governor General's Award. She is not afforded an entry in the *Oxford Companion to Canadian Literature*.

Susan Kerslake's stories are unconventional. She dispenses largely with plot and character and centres on a voice and a consciousness often in extreme situations. A woman trapped in a car crash slowly regaining consciousness and becoming aware of her injuries. A woman gripped by fear in a heart specialist's examining room awaiting the results of tests.

> The room is dusty. Peculiarly furnished with a large conference table – probably one left over – a sink, several rolls of cheap paper towels, no holder . . . There is nothing to read except the plug in the sink: Crane.

The observations of a woman abducted at gunpoint from a shopping mall and taken to a rooming house.

> Sitting at the bottom of the bed, on the heap of sheets and blankets that seemed to be trying to get away, he would hunch forward, restraining his shaking hands under his armpits and peer at her, the curve of her breast through the pale orange gauze of her blouse, the dip between her thighs where the print cotton skirt hung like a hammock. He wasn't interested, just curious; her kids looked at centipedes the same way. Under his breath he would mumble, 'I have such difficulty . . .'

The thoughts and fears of old Emily in a single room in a slummy neighbourhood.

> Cupping her palm over her mouth and nose, she sniffed the familiar circus of peanut butter, soap, stale cleaning cloths, bleach. Through it all she could identify the unique musk of her old body. Her skin had always been soft and smooth. Now wrinkles slid down in it. Now she could pluck folds and they would peak like beaten egg whites.

The writing is intense, electric, the reader thrown in at the deep end of *medias res*. The writing is usually held in an extremely tight focus. Kerslake's interest is not in resolutions to what she starts but in the movements of minds. The experience of reading her is rather like listening to Pablo Casals playing the Bach suites for unaccompanied cello; the music burrows and winds ever deeper into itself. It is tinged with obsession.

The writing is so unusual that only quotation can suggest its qualities. Here are a series of brief excerpts from "Push-Me Pull-You" about a woman who admits herself to hospital because of unbearable pains in her head. She is given drugs:

> A drug rushes into action; I can feel it taking over, spreading like water over the sand castles of brain.

> In a lucid interval:

> The world is small; it has gathered right around me; a little light, warm air, the slight touch of cotton, the scent of ironing and antiseptic, silence.

Attempts between the administering of drugs to get out of bed:

There is a lady on the other side of the hall. She is holding onto the railing with both hands, humps of fat show through the back of her robe. On the floor is a puddle. She rolls her face from side to side. I never help anyone here. One nurse will coax her on down the hall. An aide will mop the floor and wipe the smear of drool off the wall. I watch from my side of the wall. No one watches me; from time to time I actually believe no one is watching me.

Awake at night:

Looking in the mirror above the sink, I thought I saw my soul fluttering on the surface of my eye. I was afraid it would escape, and death, a small maggoty thing, would invade the black hole to lick up the shine.

. . .

It is dark in the rooms. Light from the nursing station whispers to the walls in the corridor. Sneaking in the rooms, it lights like metallic dream birds on the shiny surfaces of steel and glass. In the bed next to me there is the ghostly shape of a woman. She moans, the sheets are too heavy, too rough for her. I have never seen her face. I don't know if she even has a face, perhaps there is nothing but the moan; grey pulsing lips as large as her head. They always keep the curtain drawn. For a long time I didn't know if anyone was there. I didn't want to see her – it. There was a smell. Antiseptics could not camouflage the green edges. I imagined her seeping into the sheets, dripping off the rubber mattress cover. In the night I would step on her. She wasn't real. It would take more than shadow and smell. This was some sort of test: reality. Or reality – your reality. Do you think this woman is real? Slippery question. If only my head were clear. Be careful.

The building is breathing through its vents. I get up. The floor is cold. It feels so good . . .

Susan Kerslake offers a strange music, original and deeply imagined, and once heard it is difficult to forget. It is heartening that *The Book of Fears* went through three printings.

Margaret Laurence is the author of two short story collections, *The Tomorrow-Tamer and Other Stories* (1964) and *A Bird in the House* (1970). The stories collected in *The Tomorrow-Tamer* were published, largely in Canadian literary magazines, between 1956 and 1963.

The Tomorrow-Tamer is far better written than *A Bird in the House*, the language tighter and brighter, the stories, though with an ideological edge, less sentimental. I find in general that Margaret Laurence's early work is better than her later efforts; I can re-read *A Jest of God* but cannot again plough through *The Stone Angel* or, *much* worse, *The Diviners*.

The Tomorrow-Tamer was less well received than *A Bird in the House* because the stories were set in Africa. *The Bird in the House* stories were set in Canada and were therefore more acceptable. The same thing happened with what is probably Mavis Gallant's best single title, *From the Fifteenth District* (1979); the stories were set in Paris so that the book was not even nominated for the Governor General's Award. For *Home Truths*, stories with Canadian settings, she won the Governor General's Award in 1981. Canadian nationalism in all its malignantly stupid pride.

It has become very much clearer in the twenty years since her death in 1987 that Margaret Laurence's writing was less the beginning of something new and much more the culmination and probably best expression of a tradition of writing that was poised to disappear. Her work makes advances on the work of such writers as Morley Callaghan, Sinclair Ross, Ernest Buckler, W.O. Mitchell, and Hugh MacLennan. Margaret Laurence never fully embraced modernism; she teetered on the brink of doing so but nearly always fell back into the tradition from which she emerged.

"The Drummer of All the World" published in 1956 is the story of Mathew, the son of a missionary returning to Ghana on the eve of its independence from England. The red umbrella was part of the paraphernalia of Ashanti rank and nobility. Mathew concludes:

> We were conquerors in Africa, we Europeans. Some despised her, that bedraggled queen we had unthroned, and some loved her for her still-raging magnificence, her old wisdom. But all of us sought to force our will upon her.
>
> My father thought he was bringing Salvation to Africa. I do not any longer know what salvation is. I only know that one man cannot find it for another man, and one land cannot bring it to another.

> Africa, old withered bones, mouldy splendour under a red umbrella,
> you will dance again, this time to a new song.

This is strong writing and it deserves to last but the essential point to be made is that it is recognizable now as *historical* writing. It recognizably belongs to a particular period. Its self-conscious rhetoric and cadences are no longer of our time.

When I wrote earlier that Margaret Laurence never fully embraced modernism here is what I meant. Consider this passage from "The Drummer of All the World." Mathew, has returned from England to work with the government in Ghana and bumps into his boyhood best friend Kwabena.

> 'Oh, I am a medical orderly.' His voice was bitter. 'An elevated post.'
>
> 'Surely you could do better than that?'
>
> 'I have not your opportunities. It is the closest I can get now to real medical work. I'm trying to get a scholarship to England. We will see.'
>
> 'You want to be a doctor?'
>
> 'Yes –' He laughed in an oddly self-conscious way. 'Not a ju-ju man, you understand.'
>
> Suddenly I thought I did understand. With me, he could never outgrow his past, the time when he had wanted to be another kind of doctor – a doctor who dealt in charms and amulets, in dried roots and yellow bones and bits of python skin. He knew I would remember. How he must have regretted betraying himself to me when we were both young.
>
> I wanted to tell him that I knew how far he had travelled from the palm hut. But I did not dare. He would have thought it condescension.

The construction of this passage – dialogue followed by commentary and summation – is entirely typical of Laurence's work. It accounts for her great popularity at the time she was writing. She did the work for the reader; she showed a little and explained a lot. She was, in a word, easy. And it is that loose easiness which will explain why in the future her reputation will decline drastically.

The seed of destruction is sowed even in the first line of the quoted passage.

"'Oh, I am a medical orderly.' His voice was bitter. 'An elevated post.'" "An elevated post" is – quite obviously – a bitter remark. The sentence, "His voice was bitter" merely clogs the works. It also reveals a very un-modernist mistrust of the readers' ability to read.

Elise Levine is the author of the story collection *Driving Men Mad* (1995) and a novel *Requests and Dedications* (2003).

You can take a paragraph almost at random from any of the stories in *Driving Men Mad* and you will realize immediately that Elise Levine plays her prose as a musical instrument. In this she shares interests with Mark Jarman, Norman Levine, Terry Griggs, and Michael Winter. She cuts and compresses, stretches, squeezes to produce writing which ranges from aria to incantation.

Here's a paragraph from "Boy":

> In Perry I play burnball every day after supper, making do with Mike Hires, a retard from Special Ed. class. Slap-slap down the road, smoking ball against glove faster-fast through the long twilight, everything flattened to two boys one creature purely boy, and a sound like spitting.
>
> There are days and days of this.

The paragraph immediately raises questions of grammar and meaning and we have to accept two narrating voices but the difficulties are easy to overcome; they tend to melt away if you read the passage aloud and surrender to the sounds of incantation.

She is something of a magician; she makes language perform. Silk scarves appear, doves flutter, the Ace of Spades rises through the deck at her command. Here from the story "Angel" is the voice in monologue of the young lesbian abandoned by Angel; she is rehearsing the history of their love. The wild cityscapes of the story are not backdrops but rather embodiments of the narrator's passion; they fulfill the same function as the cityscapes in the short stories of Mark Jarman.

> It was midnight, Angel, and I'll never forget. We did it in doorways up and down Church Street, my back against rotting wood or my hamstrings hurting, crouched down on grey concrete, the club where I'd cruised you receding as we twisted down alleyways and across half-

> empty parking lots. You wooed me that night and I could hear my breath whistling in and out of me and when you pulled my shirt up and over my head and tossed it – just like that, in the middle of the street – it was like a ghost floated up inside me and fluttered out of my mouth, my white shirt sailing up over Parliament Street, and the next morning I saw it lying on the streetcar tracks at Queen and Sherbourne.

Or this, rather astonishing, recreation of desire rising:

> You racked up those balls like a pro and beat those old dykes in their black leather vests who lovingly took their hand-crafted, mother-of-pearl-inlaid cues from monogrammed cases and everyone stood around, and I counted each sudden click as you knocked the balls down, always where you said you wanted them and it was like each click that night brought me closer to something, each click a notch cut closer through the tension thick as the blue smoky bar or the heavenly sweet smell of amyl in the bathroom, and looking up I could see the smooth moves shaking it out there on the dance floor but all I could hear was you, calling, Six ball in the corner pocket, and click, Nine ball in the side pocket, and all night long I felt I was moving, Angel, really moving.

Incantation again, the play of alliteration.

In the interview in *Writers Talking* Elise Levine says of the way she works:

> . . . writing is a process of excavating what is embedded, an extended drive to fill in the centres of the truth of a character. I think of a mouth spotlit, opening and closing in a blacked-out theatre. I flirt with notions of some strange, operatic experience, part Monteverdi, Messiaen, Ligeti, PJ Harvey – equal parts aria and recitative, with performers well versed in the uses of extended techniques. Ahistorical, forever playing away on a lost stage, in a pocket out of time. My job is to press my forehead against the stage door and peek through a peephole, and try to describe, as faithfully as I can, what I see and hear.

What is particularly interesting about this is that the peephole view doesn't even let her see *all* of the stage; she is looking at a scene with everything inessential and surrounding cut off from view. Because of the peephole she is looking at the distillation of a distillation. She is looking at something viewed in a way which makes the scene or action seem strange. Things are presented to us in such a light or with such a magnification or in bewildering close-up that the everyday becomes exotic. When I read Elise's account, I thought of Shkovski's *ostranerie* – "making strange." (Shkovski, Victor Borisovich. Russian Formalist. *The Technique of the Writer's Craft*. 1928.)

In the same interview, she wrote:

> As the piece begins to emerge as a whole, I try to shape (the material feels plastic, three-dimensional). I try to listen as hard as I can for the way the piece should sound (the material is musical, involving timbre and pitch, pulse and rhythm and hypermetre, it unfolds over time, is, like music, abstract). I try to look as hard as I can (fast flat lines or textured and painterly), to imagine. Content dictates form, form equals content: I keep going, and if I'm lucky, I at times find myself awed in the presence of this beautiful, mysterious tautology.

And for a digestif – emotionscape again – here is the night security guard at the Boulevard Club in "Testing, Testing":

> Once on a moonless night when I'd been up two days straight, maybe more, my scalp tingly and tart with Black Beauties, I took the dog outside the club to do her business. As I waited for her to finish, I could dimly make out the marina sailboats rocking, the trees in the nearby park swaying. I could hear the occasional baying of what seemed to be every solitudinous beast of night, from the lost cygnet I saw jerking disconsolately into and out of the water to the stray Canada goose bruising the night sky over Lakeshore Drive. The lights of the city shone to the north, blurring with those from passing cars. Everything, in every place I looked, was speeding ahead, so fast I could barely catch the drift.

Such originality has cost Elise Levine dearly. Again in the *Writers Talking* interview:

This "finding an expressive language" means, she says, "risking being labelled 'unconventional,' 'poetic,' 'experimental' – these underhandedly pejorative terms that smack of a conservative, underimagining, reactive view of literary fiction very much in contrast to commonly held views of other contemporary arts."

Keath Fraser has written on the stories of Elise Levine "How As Writers Do We End?" in *The New Quarterly* volume XXI. Nos. 2 and 3.

Norman Levine is best represented by two volumes which are, in essence, his Collected Stories. These are: *By a Frozen River* (with a Foreword by John Metcalf) and *The Ability to Forget* (with a Foreword by André Alexis) both Toronto: Key Porter Books 2002 and 2003.

As I have written about Norman at some length in this book already I'll confine myself to recommending some secondary material. *CNQ* (*Canadian Notes & Queries*) No. 60 (2001) was a special issue on Levine's work and contains a brilliant essay by Cynthia Flood some of which is quoted in Chapter Two: "Goodbye to All That."

CNQ 70 contains Alison Oldham's essay on early Levine "The Gentleman in the Attic."

Interesting commentary by Levine on his own work appears in *Making It New: Contemporary Canadian Stories* (Ed. John Metcalf) Toronto: Methuen, 1982 and in *Canadian Classics* (Ed. John Metcalf and J.R. Struthers) Toronto: McGraw-Hill Ryerson, 1993.

A truly strange discussion of the story "A Small Piece of Blue" can be found in *Writers in Aspic* (Ed. John Metcalf) Montreal: Véhicule Press, 1988.

In preparation now is *All the Heart Is in the Things: Studies in Norman Levine's Short Fiction* to be published by Biblioasis. It will contain an expanded essay by Cynthia Flood and contributions by Terry Rigelhof, Michael Winter, Simone Vauthier, T.D. MacLulich, Lawrence Mathews and others.

Norman Levine has often talked of the St. Ives painters who so much influenced his work:

> Another thing I got from the painters was the need for immediacy. When they finished a painting they wanted me to see it in their studio. And there it was. At a glance. Through the eyes. Onto the nervous system. I remember thinking: how could I get this immediacy in writing? And I remember Peter Lanyon telling me, in his studio, that all that mattered was the work. 'You take something from life. Make something from it. Then you give it back into life.'

(From an essay "Sometimes It Works" published in *How Stories Mean* (Ed. J. Metcalf and J.R. Struthers) Erin: Porcupine's Quill, 1993.)

A good introduction to the St. Ives literary and artistic scene is the booklet by Alison Oldham *Everyone Was Working: Writers and Artists in Postwar St. Ives*. Falmouth: Tate St. Ives/Falmouth College of Art, 2002.

Also of great interest is the series of books on St. Ives Artists issued by Tate Publishing under General Editor Michael Tooby. Of particular interest to Levine readers are: *Alfred Wallis* by Mathew Gale, *Bryan Winter* by Chris Stephens, *Peter Lanyon* by Margaret Garlake, *Patrick Heron* by Michael McNay, and *Terry Frost* by Chris Stephens.

Annabel Lyon is the author of one story collection *Oxygen* (2000) and a collection of three novellas *The Best Thing for You* (2004).

At the Stratford Conference Diane Schoemperlen illuminated Annabel Lyon's stories by quoting from Raymond Carver's 1981 essay "On Writing."

> I like it when there is some feeling of threat or sense of menace in short stories. I think a little menace is fine to have in a story. For one thing, it's good for the circulation. There has to be tension, a sense that something is imminent, that certain things are in relentless motion, or else, most often, there simply won't be a story. What creates tension in a piece of fiction is partly the way the concrete words are linked together to make up the visible action of the story. But it's also the things that are left out, that are implied, the landscape just under the smooth (but sometimes broken and unsettled) surface of things.

". . . the things that are left out. . . ." Hemingway said almost exactly the same thing. Omission, we might say, is one of the main keys to reading Annabel Lyon. She came early and honestly to the idea. In the interview with me in *Writers Talking* she wrote: "My dad taught me to write when I was small. He had been a journalist and newspaper editor for many years and taught me some particularly ruthless lessons about style that I've had trouble giving up. The main one, which I've accepted as dogma, was to cut out all extraneous words. If you've said something in six words and you can say it in four, you're obliged – by logic, by aesthetics, by Occam's razor, by principles of elegance and an acquired radar for pretentious bullshit – to say it in four."

". . . the landscape just under the smooth (but sometimes broken and unsettled) surface of things."

Her story "Tea Drinks" opens with this menacing sentence:

"Finally she takes me aside to tell me you just can't treat people that way. This is in the garage, behind the house. I try to look preoccupied. I finger the blade of my jigsaw, frowning."

The omission in the opening of the story "Black" reels us helplessly in:

> The old woman upstairs is taking a long time to die. Downstairs, Jones is making some phone calls. Jones calls Barry and Edith, and Tom and Anna, and Jack and Ruby and Glen. He calls Larry and Kate and Bridget and Amy. He calls Foster. He calls Susy and Morris.
>
> 'God, Jones,' Morris says. 'I'm so sorry.'
>
> 'But will you come?' Jones asks.
>
> Morris pulls on the phone cord, stretching Jones' voice out and letting it seize back to coils, a kid with bubble gum, finger to tongue. 'Do you really think,' Morris says. 'At this point, I mean.'
>
> 'Yes,' Jones says.
>
> 'I mean, considering.'
>
> 'Yes.'
>
> 'Will Lorelei be there?'
>
> 'Lorelei, Lorelei,' Jones says. 'Are you coming or not?'

And so on.

The rest of Susy's life – in this opening excerpt she is five – is conveyed in a series of brief imagistic takes until she dies at the age of eighty-five.

The story "Things" is reduced to lists:

"In the grocery store I buy tortillas, juice, milk, condoms, soap. I worry the cashier will write to my mother and tell her I buy tortillas, juice, milk, condoms, soap."

In the narrator's building is a tenant called Calla. The story moves forward in stripped, intense image blocks. Omission intensifies the focus.

> Calla has a social worker named Pippa. Pippa has a braid. She gives Calla sample budgets and meal plans, and encourages her to go on outings with the Group.
>
> Calla brings her sample sheets to my door. She says, Macaroni and

carrot sticks? Whole-grain banana bread?

Also, Calla dislikes the people of the Group. She says they make too much noise at bus stops.

The effect of omission is to involve us more actively in the story; we have to create it for ourselves, to write it for ourselves using Annabel Lyon's suggestive notation. We might recall Norman Levine's remark "the more cryptic you are the more resonance there is."

At the end of our interview in *Writers Talking* Annabel wrote:

> Amazingly (for a [1] first book of [2] short stories from a [3] small press) it was widely reviewed, and well-reviewed, and the criticisms – lack of structure, brevity, opaque character motivations, cuteness in the prose – were criticisms I had already levelled at myself, and was trying to address in my new stories. So I was happy.

This proclamation of a veering more towards the mainstream is already being fulfilled though the writing remains what Caroline Adderson describes as "sparky." In Annabel's latest novella "Palaces" in *The New Quarterly* No. 102 (Spring 2007) – Bonny, Mary, and Jack in mildly inebriated conversation:

> 'You guys are always talking about computers,' Bonny said. 'Computers or motorcycles. Amscray, ackjay. We're having girl talk.'
>
> 'Speaking of motorcycles,' Mary said.
>
> 'Yeah, speaking of motorcycles,' Jack called from the next room.
>
> 'Oh, he's fine,' Bonny said. 'I was exaggerating before.'
>
> Bonny's boyfriend rode a motorcycle. She had shown up an hour earlier saying it was all over.
>
> 'He has all these little habits that just get on my nerves,' Bonny said. 'Food habits, toilet habits, you know what I'm talking about.'

The change is clear. The earlier Annabel would not have accommodated us with: "Bonny's boyfriend rode a motorcycle. She had shown up an hour earlier saying it was all over." And although I understand why she made the change, part of me hankers still for the glittering obscurities of such stories as "Stars," "Tea Drinks" and "Awake."

Alistair MacLeod is the author of three story collections *The Lost Salt Gift of Blood* (1976); *As Birds Bring Forth the Sun* (1986); and *Island: The Collected Stories* (2000).

I emigrated to Canada in 1962 sailing on the *Carinthia* from Liverpool. Just before this I went on a farewell holiday with two university friends to the Outer Hebrides. We crossed from the Kyle of Localsh to the Isle of Lewis landing at Stornaway. Fishing boats were coming in, the sea silver and utterly still and in the silver, black rounded shapes like floats or buoys which soon turned out be the heads of harbour seals following the boats. They heaved themselves up the stone steps onto the dock and whuffed and honked for fish. Their breath was memorable.

We were put in the postman's van who took us on his route until he found a cottage willing to accept us. The landscape was harshly beautiful and haunted by a great weight of history. The people we met were friendly but formal. The crofter had a few acres of land, a cow, a fishing boat, and a shed where he wove tweed. He had been a steward on a P. and O. liner and had travelled the world; his three sons all had degrees from Edinburgh University. We went out along the cliffs together and shot rabbits for a stew.

The family invited us to attend a party they were having on Saturday night, friends and neighbours dropping by to record messages in Gaelic and to sing "mouth music" for relatives in Cape Breton, a place, so they said, in Canada. The singing went on all evening fuelled by liquor which had bypassed officers of Customs and Excise. At minutes to midnight everyone got up to leave. The Sabbath was upon us.

I have visual and emotional memories of Lewis and of the way of life so I can easily empathize with Alistair MacLeod's love of Cape Breton and with the grip it must have on his heart. But my task is to talk not about love of place and past but about writing. The stories in *Island* are presented chronologically; the first story "The Boat" was published in 1968, the last, "Clearances" in 1999. The first six stories are indeed stories; that is, they have elements of plot, character, and dialogue. The last ten stories are not really stories in any conventional sense at all and to approach them with conventional expectation is to be disappointed. There is little dialogue and any forward movement tends to get arrested by descriptive detail; scenery is extensively "painted," a way of life is depicted by a cataloguing of *things*. The effect is rather folkloric, rather like looking at a primitive painting.

> The kitchen is small. It has an iron cookstove, a table against one wall and three or four handmade chairs of wood. There is also a wooden rocking-chair covered by a cushion. The rockers are so thin from years of use that it is hard to believe they still function. Close by the table there is a washstand with two pails of water upon it. A washbasin hangs from a driven nail in its side and above it is an old-fashioned mirrored medicine cabinet. There is also a large cupboard, a low-lying couch and a window facing upon the sea. On the walls a barometer hangs as well as two pictures, one of a rather jaunty young couple taken many years ago. It is yellowed and rather indistinct; the woman in a long dress with her hair done up in ringlets, the man in a serge suit that is slightly too large for him and with a tweed cap pulled rakishly over his right eye. He has an accordion strapped over his shoulders and his hands are fanned out on the buttons and keys. The other picture is of the Christ-child. Beneath it is written 'Sweet Heart of Jesus Pray for Us.'
>
> The woman at the stove is tall and fine featured. Her grey hair is combed briskly back from her forehead and neatly coiled with a large pin at the base of her neck. Her eyes are as grey as the storm scud of the sea. Her age, like her husband's, is difficult to guess. She wears a blue print dress, a plain blue apron and low-heeled brown shoes. She is turning fish within a frying pan when we enter.

This passage is entirely typical.

MacLeod cuts dialogue to a minimum. The stories avoid drama, avoid action. They are static. The foregoing quotation from "The Lost Salt Gift of Blood" where detail smothers is typical of the later work. A story like "The Road to Rankin's Point" collapses completely under what comes to feel like verbiage.

> The sun is rising above the mountains and touching the freshly washed earth. The raindrops glisten and sparkle, and the fog and mists that hang above the dirt roads of high places rise and vanish toward the sky. The bobolinks and red-winged blackbirds bounce and sing from the tips of their springing willows. Orange butterflies glide and float on the drafts of air and the chattering squirrels and chipmunks sprint along the fallen logs like busy proprietors doing morning inspection. The earth is alive, refreshed and new.

When MacLeod wants to stress the beauty and virtuous simplicity of Cape Breton and enhance the nobility of his elemental characters he does so in rather crude contrasts. The son leaving Cape Breton in search of a larger life in the story "The Vastness of the Dark" gets a lift from a travelling salesman from Toronto – a rather obvious representative of the world beyond the Island – whose main expressed interest is in casual sexual intercourse with the small town women left widowed by mine disasters.

Or this from "The Last Salt Gift of Blood":

> And perhaps now I should go and say, oh son of my *summa cum laude* loins, come away from the lonely gulls and the silver trout and I will take you to the land of the Tastee Freeze where you may sleep till ten of nine. And I will show you the elevator to the apartment on the sixteenth floor and introduce you to the buzzer system and the yards of the wrought-iron fences where the Doberman pinscher runs silently at night.

This is not exactly subtle.

And again, there is the question of sentimentality. I can imagine Alistair countering such a charge by claiming *unabashed* sentimentality.

It may be that the most fruitful way of looking at Alistair MacLeod's work is to think of the stories not as stories in the modernist tradition but as hybrid mixtures of memoir, folk tale and sketch. "To Everything There Is a Season" is certainly a memoir and "The Closing Down of Summer" is much nearer meditation than story. These are pieces of writing that are hymns to the past, celebrations, meditations. As one of the stories puts it, "songs of loss." We should listen for the skirl of lament. We should, perhaps, read these pieces with the ballads in mind, such ballads as "The Bonny Earl of Murray," "Sir Patrick Spens," "The Twa Corbies." Joyce Carol Oates in her Afterword to *The Lost Salt Gift of Blood* says: "If I were to name a single underlying motive for MacLeod's fiction, I would say that it is the urge to memorialize, the urge to sanctify." Which is the perfect explanation for the loving, but fictionally inappropriate, description of the kitchen quoted earlier. These stories do not take the same aim as, say, Katherine Mansfield or James Joyce or Ernest Hemingway. Their aim, I would say, is bardic.

> After a while they begin to sing in Gaelic, singing almost unconsciously the old words that are so worn and so familiar. They seem to

handle them almost as they would familiar tools. I know that in the other cars they are doing the same even as I begin silently to mouth the words myself. There is no word in Gaelic for good-bye, only for farewell.

This narrator remembers then a lyric from the fifteenth century.

I wend to death, knight stith in stour;
Through fight in field I won the flower;
No fights me taught the death to quell –
I wend to death, sooth I you tell.

I wend to death, a king iwis;
What helpes honour or worlde's bliss?
Death is to man the final way –
I wende to be clad in clay.

K.D. Miller is the author of two story collections, *A Litany in Time of Plague* and *Give Me Your Answer.* A trio of novellas is in progress. "A Litany in Time of Plague" is, of course, the title of the Elizabethan poem by Thomas Nashe whose refrain at the end of each verse is:

> "I am sick, I must die.
> Lord, have mercy on us!"

The stories in *Litany* about novelist Raymond Mayhugh and his younger lover Robbie are not stories about the plague of AIDS; they are – vital difference – stories about Raymond and Robbie. Kathleen has cast them in the form of monologues or soliloquies spoken and thought by Raymond. They are astonishing *performances.*

K.D. came to writing via acting and directing at Guelph and UBC. She writes:

> . . . one thing I've concluded as a result of rehashing my past is that I am in fact an actor who writes. The exercises I did in acting classes to train my powers of concentration, observation, and emotive memory still serve me well as a writer . . . What I learned as a director comes in handy too. I was taught to 'parse' a script, then go over and over a single

line or bit of business until it worked. The recommended formula was one hour of rehearsal per minute of performance. As a writer, I still think in terms of segments of action – acts, scenes, and 'beats,' like heartbeats. Sometimes when a story appears to be dying, I turn back into a director and try to revive it as I would a play. 'Why isn't anything *happening?* I bark at the hapless page. 'What are you supposed to be *doing?'*

. . . I'm told that musicians are encouraged to hum or sing a difficult passage of music they are trying to master. The act of taking the notes in, of becoming their instrument, can break down technical and psychological barriers between player and score.

For four years when I was in Vancouver, I was employed by the BC Library Services Branch to tape-record books for the blind. I narrated works by Alice Munro, Margaret Laurence, Margaret Atwood, Marian Engel, Audrey Thomas, Mavis Gallant and many other authors who were coming into their own in the mid-seventies. Though I didn't realize it then, that job was in large part my training as a writer. Not only was I being exposed to significant new works, but I was acting as their 'instrument.' I'm still convinced that the best way to appreciate a piece of writing is to read it aloud.

The best way to taste K.D. Miller's work is to listen to her as Raymond Mayhugh. Definitely not Miller Lite. Of Mayhugh she wrote:

A motive. A sense of the character's rhythm. A growing feeling of empathy with that character. These are the things an actor takes along on what is essentially a journey of discovery. To write Raymond was to play him, which in turn was to learn to love him.

What follows is from "A Litany in Time of Plague."

Anyway. I bitched on cheerfully to Robbie about that, and about editors and advances, blah-blahing away. Oh, I love myself when I'm with book. I'm a blur. I never slow down. Everything but the book just melts into distance behind me.

Everything, that is, except too, too solid Robbie. He stayed right in front of me, and the minute I paused for breath stopped me dead by talking about his soul. His *soul.* He actually used the word.

'You know, Raymond,' he began in that self-deprecating way that used to get to me, 'I've been looking at my life a bit too, lately. I've begun thinking again about the state of my soul.'

Now, Robbie does this kind of thing. I was at a barbeque with him once, where everybody was riding along happily on a bubble of beer. All of a sudden Robbie looked up and said, 'When the Indians were here, the sky was black with birds.' Pop.

Well, I refused to be popped. The calamari had arrived, thank God, so I speared one and held it up. 'Does anyone else know about this?' I asked conspiratorially. It's what I used to say to him in bed.

'About what? My soul?'

'No. Calamari in lemon-garlic butter. Does anyone else – Oh, never mind.' God, I hate it when someone won't carry the ball.

. . .

Well, over lunch, I felt the old familiar boredom setting in again. So I decided to head it off. 'Robbie,' I said, 'about your alleged soul. Two things. First, nobody's come back to tell us what's on the other side of the big D. We're not even sure there's anything to worry about, one way or the other. Second, supposing somebody does come back and says, here's the scoop. If you're good, you spend eternity sitting on a stream of jacuzzi bubbles, sipping Chablis. But if you're bad, you stand forever in a cashier's lineup listening to 'Attention, K-Mart shoppers' over and over again. So what? What do you do? Change the past? Change what you are? Start taking the homeless out for dim sum?' I speared another tiny perfect squid and gestured at him with it. 'There's no piece of paper inside the box this board game came in, telling you the rules in seven languages.' I twiddled the squid in the lemon-garlic butter and put it in my mouth. 'Where's all this soul crap coming from just now, anyway?' I asked when I had swallowed. 'You're not dying are you?'

'Well,' he said, 'yes. I suppose I am.' Then he reached out, put his hand on my wrist and said, 'I'm sorry, Raymond.'

There is further discussion of "A Litany in Time of Plague" in *Writers Talking* (Eds. J. Metcalf and Claire Wilkshire) Erin: Porcupine's Quill, 2003.

Lisa Moore is the author of two story collections, *Degrees of Nakedness* (1995) and *Open* (2002).

In *Writers Talking* Lisa Moore wrote:

> A fully-formed story is a rare occurrence for me. I keep a daily journal, switching from the computer to a hard-cover black notebook throughout the day. The journal is full of dialogue, dreams, images, gestures and scenes. It's a journal of impressions rather than facts. My fiction almost always develops from these notes. I write the journal without looking for any cohesion or theme, though over a two-month period I usually find the material has an internal order that can become a short story. I have a kind of illogical belief that certain images are magic, super-saturated with meaning. I write fast in my journal because I want to sneak up on those moments and snag them before I know what I'm doing. Too much scrutiny at this stage can make things fusty.

In further discussion of images – absolutely central to her work – she went on to say:

> Recently I have been learning to edit video on my computer at home. A shot of my daughter and me in a vaulted alleyway in France. We're holding hands and spinning in a circle, our hair flying out behind us. I try cutting the speed halfway through the spin so when our feet hit the pavement the sound is distorted, drawn out, a reverberating *thwack*. It takes more than an hour to edit less than half a minute. Around one o'clock in the morning when vibrant, frenetic pixels have implanted themselves onto my retina for good, it occurs to me that the written word is dead. That a hundred years from now the image will have taken over. The language of images will proliferate and evolve at a tremendous speed. The video blur on the screen in front of me – a splash of orange shirt, the blue shutters – all a swarming mass of tiny pixels seems to be far more *living*, more full of possibility than anything I could write. One frame of video contains so much detail. It would require several pages of writing to capture what the eye devours in a second. At one in the morning, writing seems destined to lose its privileged position as a form of communication.

But she then reverses her position:

> Norman Levine, in an interview with Michael Winter, once said the less a writer gives the reader the better. Levine is referring to what McLuhan calls a cool medium: a medium in which the audience does most of the work. The reader is a fully engaged participant in the act of creation. It's that ambiguity, or coolness, that draws me primarily to writing rather than the visual arts in the end.

In *An Aesthetic Underground* I described the writing of my first book *The Lady Who Sold Furniture* (1970):

> I'd wanted to get away from plot and towards a story that moved forward in a different way. What I was after, though I couldn't quite articulate it, was a story that was powered through images that generated strong emotion. I wanted a story propelled by a series of emotional jolts. This, in turn, implied a close observation of surface and detail . . .
>
> My short stories had been tending in the right direction – 'Keys and Watercress' and 'Dandelions' move forward in intense images – but I could not then have expressed as a theory what I was grappling with. I was listening to CBC *Anthology* one evening when an actor started reading a story called 'Images' by a writer called Alice Munro. I think this was in 1968 but it might have been 1967. It certainly preceded publication of *Dance of the Happy Shades*. I was galvanized by this story. I recognized immediately what she was doing. She had succeeded brilliantly at the very thing that I was still messing with and by using the title 'Images' she'd pointed out the method of her fiction. She allowed my own thinking about these technical problems to expand. I wrote to her in great excitement and we entered into a correspondence which lasted for years.

Lisa Moore creates stories by the accretion and juxtaposition of images; the difference between us is that she is far more radical. Sometimes it is not immediately clear to what the images add up; my experience of her work suggests that meanings will emerge if the reader stops trying to intellectualize the work, if the reader absorbs the full impact of each building block rather than trying immediately to articulate a meaning for the whole structure. Lisa

Moore does not travel in straight lines. She has, after all, admitted that "certain images are magic, super-saturated with meaning."

Here's the sort of thing she means. From "Haloes":

> There's a photograph of the house my parents built together when it was just a skeleton. Blond two-by-fours like a rib-cage around a lungful of sky. They worked back to back shifts in the restaurant they sold before I was born. The house was built on the weekends. I never once heard my parents make love, or saw them naked together. But the photograph of the two-by-fours is like walking in on them, unexpected. The house without its skin. Their life together raw, still to come.

Or this from "Ingrid Catching Snowflakes on Her Tongue":

> I like sitting on the staircase listening to our house. The gravelly voice of the coffee maker in the kitchen, something metal turning over in the dryer, the ebbing of canned laughter from behind a bedroom door on the third floor. Mike's daughter Mary rubbing against the tub, flaccid splashes. The house is a skeleton and our moods surge along the wiring, spilling through the pipes, circulating like currents of heat. Living under the same roof with someone else shapes you both, the way liquid takes the shape of its container.

Sometimes her images are almost surreal:

> When Mike and I make love, a blush comes into his cheeks and the tips of his ears. That's my private colour for him, almost plum. The first time we were together we were behind the row housing under criss-crossing clotheslines, white shirts laughing with their bellies. We were drunk and his tongue in my ear sounded like a pot of mussels boiling, the shells opening, the salty shells clicking off one another, a riot of tiny noises. I got the flu. He made a pot of tea: cinnamon, cloves, apple and orange chunks. The next day we made love in his new house, empty of furniture except for a couch, covered with satiny parakeets, belonging to the former owners. Streetlight poured in. A plastic bag of chicken breasts glowed on the floor where I'd dropped it.

It's of considerable interest to me that Lisa Moore has been reading Norman Levine and has been influenced by him towards experimentation in the story form. She is already in her first book beginning to abandon conventional punctuation in the search for intensity, immediacy. The influence of Norman Levine must date to 1993 when the Porcupine's Quill republished *From a Seaside Town* and *Canada Made Me* and sent Norman on a reading tour of the Maritimes. While in St. John's Norman was interviewed by Michael Winter, editor of the literary magazine *Tickle Ace*, a meeting which seems, over the years, to have had significant ramifications.

The interview with Lisa Moore in *Writers Talking* was conducted by Claire Wilkshire, writer and fellow-member of the fiction collective *The Burning Rock*.

Alice Munro is the author of *Dance of the Happy Shades* (1968); *Lives of Girls and Women* (1971); *Something I've Been Meaning to Tell You* (1974); *Who Do You Think You Are?* (1978); *The Moons of Jupiter* (1982); *The Progress of Love* (1986); *Friend of My Youth* (1990); *Open Secrets* (1994); *Selected Stories* (1996); *The Love of a Good Woman* (1998); *Hateship, Friendship, Courtship, Loveship, Marriage* (2001); *Runaway* (2004); *The View from Castle Rock* (2006).

I would urge on readers all these individual titles.

As I have written on Alice Munro extensively in this book I won't comment further.

"The finest writer of short stories working in the English language today." *The Times.*

"That Munro is a great writer of short stories should go without saying. She is also one of the two or three best writers of fiction (of any length) now alive." *Sunday Times.*

". . . quite possibly the greatest short story writer at work today." *Daily Telegraph.*

"She is one of those few living writers who, in the way of the greats, must simply be read." *The Globe and Mail.*

Gayla Reid is the author of two story collections, *To Be There with You* and *Closer Apart: The Ardora Variations.* The latter is a series of linked stories about Australia from 1901 to 2001. *All the Seas of the World* was her first novel.

If there is one fault to be found with Gayla Reid's stories it is that some them have unsatisfactory endings. This could be said of more than one of the writers among these forty. It is the endings of stories which present the biggest challenge for story writers. Think of a gymnastic performance. The athlete can demonstrate fluid mastery on the bars or rings, each series of movements rhythmically flowing into the next, but the clinching moment for the performer is the dismount, the moment that stops and caps the sequence. If the performer buckles, takes a half-step back on landing, is forced into an unnatural stance to maintain balance, then the performance is marred and the audience feels an inevitable disappointment. If, on the other hand, the dismount is perfect – bang! – the entire performance seems logical and inevitable and our pleasure in it is an aesthetic one. Commentators say of a perfect conclusion that the performer has "nailed" the landing.

Clark Blaise has written two brilliant essays on beginning and ending stories which can be found in *How Stories Mean* (Eds. Metcalf and Struthers, 1993).

"On Ending Stories" begins:

> Stories begin mysteriously, but end deliberately. A writer can't really *will* a story to open, but in the act of writing, the appropriate ending (event, tone, revelation, effect) will probably suggest itself. Most endings arise in the act of writing (a few stories 'arrive' so fully formed that the ending is as mysterious as the opening; the writer is rarely so fortunate) and they all share a single purpose: to give a final emphasis to a particular aspect of the story. Literally, it's the writer's last word on the subject: he'd better choose those words carefully. The opening anticipates the conflict. The ending immortalizes the resolution.

I loved the lyric detail and the texture in such stories from *To Be There with You* as "Sister Doyle's Men" and "Uncle Reg and the Wide Brown Land" but thought that neither was "nailed." However, "To Be There with You" is a perfect performance and its ending resonates. And resonates.

It is narrated by a young woman working as a reporter in the Vietnam war. Here is one of the story's movements. Its quiet horror burns backwards into itself when we reach the domesticity of the image of Ron "coaxing his kids to eat up their peas."

We'd start off drinking at the Grand, then go on to those makeshift places that had sprung up along the beach front – little round huts, they were. I'd try to get Ron and the others to talk about the war. What about Dak To? (Dak To was where the main U.S. fighting was going on.)

What about it? They spoke of the cricket scores back home.

Sometimes in one of these bars you saw a soldier crying his eyes out. 'Ratshit,' his mates would say. Then look away. We are in a bar. It's not long since Ron's best mate, Johno.

A chap called Ian comes up. He's young and he's really handsome. Ian starts slapping Ron on the back, in a familiar way that is part friendly, part hostile. 'Zip 'em right down the middle, mate,' Ian says. 'Whaddya say, mate? Zip 'em right down the middle.'

He's very drunk.

'Beauty, mate,' Ian goes on. 'One for you and one for me.'

Ron, who's quite a bit older, says, 'Take it easy, mate. Just take it easy, eh.'

But Ian keeps on keeping on.

'One for you and one for me. What do you say? Ripper, mate.'

Ron gets up and punches him in the stomach, hard.

That shuts him up.

I didn't see it as any big deal – Ron's punching him. They were all pretty physical men.

What interested me was what Ian had said.

I'd heard it before.

After the drinking and fucking had been pushed to the limit, and Ron was almost asleep, out of it, he'd mumble, under his breath but loud enough for me to hear: 'One for you and one for me.'

He could have been back home coaxing his kids to eat up their peas.

But I didn't think so.

Patricia Robertson is the author of two story collections *City of Orphans* (1994) and *The Goldfish Dancer* (2007).

I usually lie in bed for an hour after waking and turn over what a night's sleep has cast up. On the morning after re-reading *City of Orphans* I found that in my mind was a book by John Livingston Lowes called *The Road to Xanadu* read when I was sixteen or seventeen, a book about Coleridge's reading. I was also thinking about that murky tome, Coleridge's *Biographica*

Literaria. Specifically, I was thinking about Coleridge's distinction between Imagination and Fancy. Fancy, Coleridge claimed was governed by Imagination. Fancy, he said, is a mode of memory; its associative power collects from the artist's past, words, images, rhythms etc. which it delivers to Imagination which fashions these raw materials into Art.

Why was this fusty stuff in my mind? I hadn't the faintest interest in Coleridge's obscure musings and considered wide swathes of the *Biographia Literaria* incomprehensible.

The other thing in my mind was the first two lines of the song sung in *The Merchant of Venice* while Bassanio is contemplating the caskets:

Tell me, where is fancy bred,
Or in the heart, or in the head?

For Shakespeare, the word "fancy" usually meant "love" or "infatuation" though he sometimes used the word to mean "creativity" or "imagination." What Coleridge meant by "Fancy" is still open to much Germanic debate.

I slowly realized that Shakespeare and Coleridge were nothing to do with Patricia Robertson. I was simply thinking about the word itself, not those specific contexts. I was thinking about *City of Orphans* and the word "fancy;" the word "fancy" meaning something like "fanciful," "whimsical," "something based on imagination rather than fact." And I realized that in this entirely convoluted manner I was preparing to confront another of my prejudices.

Patricia Robertson writes two kinds of stories; most of her stories are rooted in the real world while others are what I think of as "fanciful." In *City of Orphans* there are two "fanciful" stories, "Finn Slough" and "Arabian Snow." I've usually felt that fanciful stories have lesser power and authority than stories rooted in the real world. The "real world" I consider a more imagined world. Even things straightforwardly *remembered*, are, in a way, imagined. Though I don't feel that way about Paul Glennon's fanciful stories. The difference, perhaps, is that Glennon's stories are charged with feeling.

For example, in "Arabian Snow" Gabriela gives birth to Minna and starts dreaming of a past life when she was a princess in Norway and betrothed to an Arabian prince.

> They'd begun in the hospital. On the second night, the baby asleep in the crib beside her, Garbriela woke with the sheets in her fists, the

> pillow damp with sweat. She'd been somewhere among sand dunes, palm trees, minarets, her face covered in a white veil . . . In the afternoon, drifting in and out of sleep, she walked through a courtyard of turquoise tiles where a fountain sparkled in sunlight and a nightingale sang in a cage . . .

The "dream-story" is told in italicized paragraphs woven into the non-dream story of Gabriela and Minna.

"My father promised three pairs of gyrfalcons to the traders when they came to Bergen in their djellabas, asking for the master falconer to the king . . ."

Much more typical of Patricia Robertson's work – and much more imaginative – are these paragraphs from "Counting":

> On Saturdays we visit Auntie Edna. My mother puts Billy in his push-chair and we walk up the avenue and under the railway bridge to the high street. Past Bentley & Son Greengrocers, past Boots' Chemists and the sweetshop, rows of jars with silver lids, to Old Lyme road where we turn right. Past Hall's Toffee Works with its warm sweet smell, cauldrons pouring a thick gleaming brown stream into moulds. Under the chestnut trees at the edge of the park with the black metal hobby horses and the Peter Pan statue. After the last houses there are fields with daisies in them. We go through a stile and follow a cowpath which comes out in Wheaton Crescent, where my aunt lives.
>
> Today my aunt is standing in the kitchen with flour streaks in her hair making buns and custard. My mother takes a pile of newspapers off a chair and sits down to talk. She holds Billy on her lap but he struggles down and my aunt gives him a saucepan and wooden spoon to play with.

I find the language of "Arabian Snow" meretricious. I cannot escape the feeling that such stories are manufactured.

On the other hand, *hurrah!* for that saucepan and wooden spoon.

Patricia Robertson has command of a range of styles and rhetorics and with them she embodies one fairly constant theme – her characters seek to make sense of their lives and grope towards larger and more expansive visions through acts of imagination. The expatriate narrator in "City of Orphans" loves hopelessly a beautiful boy prostitute; in counterpart he tells, lying on the grave, a continuing and comforting story of hope to the spirit of a child who died in 1893; Simon in "Pretty Bangs" turns away from the delusions of the conventions and vows to create in the world – astonishment; Stefan Czerwinski, detainee in a Canadian labour camp in the First World War in the story "Ice Palace," sustains himself against the brutalities with a vision of female beauty.

When theme and feeling and language fuse Patricia Robertson creates paragraphs that are positively burnished; here is the narrator in "City of Orphans," a story set in a North African city:

> That night I lay in the airless heat of my room listening to the cries of the old quarter, comforting and abrasive as a cat's tongue. What would entice that sulky boy to stand behind shutters at my balcony window while I ran my fingers down his spine? I wanted to see that pink mouth open, the neck arch, hear him cry out as I bit into downy skin. I pressed my face into the pillow but still he stood there, smiling at me from beneath those long lashes. My little life of carefully counted coins, chalky fingers, bottles of wine – the same life I had, in mid-life, left behind me – lay about me like a husk. Peter stood at a doorway visible only in outline, poised to enter, his face turned away from me.

Leon Rooke has published more than three hundred short stories, most of them written before the year 2000. Representing him by one collection is impractical so I have chosen to represent him by two selections which attempt to do justice to his range. The selections are *Painting the Dog* and *Hitting the Charts*. These volumes together present thirty-six stories which give a fair sampling of his achievement.

Rooke has been one of the driving and shaping forces in Canadian literature over the last thirty years or so. His influence on the short story is incalculable. He is an exuberant performer of his own work and performance is the fundamental key to understanding him. His stories are nearly all voices talking, monologues, soliloquies, the reader buttonholed. In addition to his novels and stories, he has written numerous plays and has had a lifetime involvement in the theatre. To grasp Leon, one simply has to listen. This seems, today, blindingly obvious and simple yet for years many readers were unable to hear him. The dutiful search for "meaning" rendered it the more elusive. All we have to do is listen to the voices and take pleasure in the spate of language washing over us, the torrent of lovely words. Meaning arrives through our acquiescence, through our delight in the performance.

The other key to reading Leon Rooke is to realise that his stories are improvisations. Leon doesn't brood for months over the shape and detail of what he hopes will be a masterwork; he picks up his horn and chases a few runs, a few phrases to see if something is going to happen. Think of him as a tenor sax player and the story as a jazz improvisation. Relax into what he's playing.

Leon's body of work, his teaching, and his many performances over the years have helped to give the short story in Canada a new and different emphasis. In 1982 in *Kicking Against the Pricks* I wrote about the short story in Canada:

> Where twenty years ago Canadian stories stressed content – what a story was *about* – the main emphasis now is on the story as verbal and rhetorical *performance*. Our best writers are concerned with the story as *thing to be experienced* rather than as *thing to be understood.*
>
> *Thing to be understood* implies that the reader is outside the story and regarding it intellectually. *Thing to be experienced* implies that the reader is inside the story and reacting to it emotionally. Leon Rooke has been one of those who effected the verbal and rhetorical revolution.

Here are a few snippets of the multiplicity of voices that call to us, invite us to come in.

> Here's a story.
>
> Although it has been going on for years, the crucial facts are fresh in my mind so I will have no trouble confining myself strictly to what's essential. Nothing made up, have no worry about that. I live in this world too: when my wife, lovely woman, tells me that people are tired of hearing *stories,* they want facts, gossip, trivia, how-to about real life, I'm first to take the hint. So this is plain fact: yesterday my foot was hurting. The pain was unbearable. I was in mortal anguish and convinced I'd been maimed for life.
>
> (The opening of 'The Deacon's Tale.')

> We got fifty-two (52) kids in the nursery, the Henny Penny Nursery, only one teacher, and she's retarded. They come to me, the parents of these kids do, and they say, 'Sir, Mr. Beacon, excuse us, sir, for butting in

> like this, but some of us parents, mostly those of us you see right here, what we've noticed is that Mrs. Shorts, running your place, well, sir, to make no bones about it, she's retarded.'
>
> (The opening of 'Some People Will Tell you the Situation at Henny Penny Nursery Is Getting Intolerable.')

Voice, characterization, the psychology of the scene and its comedy – all are delivered by commas.

Oh, crafty Rooke!

> You have heard about Mama Tuddi. If you got eyes and ears or a brain in your head then you know that Mama Tuddi is a big celebrity, that she have her own show The Mama Tuddi Show on TV and radio where she sell soft drinks by the bottle and the crate, especially on TV where everyone know what she look like and how much she enjoy her work.
>
> (The opening of 'Mama Tuddi Done Over.')

There are almost as many voices as there are stories.

Branko Gorjup has edited a useful and interesting collection of essays by various hands entitled *White Gloves of the Doorman: The Works of Leon Rooke*. Toronto: Exile Editions, 2004.

Robyn Sarah has published two collections of short stories *A Nice Gazebo* and *Promise of Shelter*. Her selected poems were published in 2003 as *A Day's Grace*.

To have one's nose bloodied from time to time can be salutary. I remember when we were readying *Promise of Shelter* for the Porcupine's Quill I was charmed by the detail within the stories, by the acuity of observation, but somewhat troubled by the *shapes* of the stories. They seemed to me, like Gayla Reid's stories, not quite "nailed." I wrote to Robyn suggesting that the closings of the stories needed more – well, I didn't know what, but, well, *oomph*.

Robyn replied at great length, a letter of kindly intent but undeniably stern. She explained that I simply didn't know how to read her, that I was bringing to her work a set of modernist conventions and expectations that did not really fit with her intentions or practice. She showed me how to read her and I have remained appreciative and grateful.

When Kim Jernigan and I were planning the *Wild Writers We Have Known* conference at Stratford we decided to invite two story writers who are also poets to talk about the ways that being a poet influenced being a story writer. Steven Heighton and Robyn Sarah delivered lectures on the topic under the title "Ringing Changes: The Poet's Hand in the Short Story."

Steven Heighton said:

> Robyn Sarah and I have been asked to speak not just in general but in specific, personal terms. Discussing the seminar in advance, we discovered that we'd coined remarkably similar phrases to suggest what we, as poets who often write fiction, attempt to do. In Robyn's case 'serial resonance' is a good description of what she does in fiction almost all the time; in my own case 'serial illumination' describes a form I sometimes use (while at other times I write more traditional fiction). What both terms suggest is a poetics of echo and increment, calling to mind the rhetorical force through artful echoing of key words or phrases, or even images. Both Robyn's and my terms seek to describe texts that accrue meaning and momentum via a slow accumulation of juxtaposed words and images, rather than by following the old 'line of rising action' to a conventional climax and dénouement.

Robyn Sarah then traversed the same ground.

> Insofar as short stories have become more compressed – and the new techniques of storytelling do demand great compression – the ear is more important in the writing. As stories become discontinuous, told in imagistic segments with white space around them like separate 'beads' of prose loosely strung together, each bead in its compression becomes a sort of poem, and wants a poem's or a joke's perfection of timing – the ear attentive at the level of the syllable. Hence, the 'poet's ear' in the short story . . .
>
> Both of us have hit on a structural principle based not on a line of dramatic action or sustained single narrative, but on serial variations spun around an idea, an image, or a phrase . . . I tell one story that is digressive and free-associative – like a person who begins to tell a story, then says 'that reminds me . . .' and continues in this vein, weaving in and out of the primary story. I use this structural principle to set up a

> series of thematic echoes that cumulatively build a mood or explore an idea. In 'Looking for My Keys' [in *Promise of Shelter*], the story begins as being, literally, about a set of lost house keys. As the narrator explains how she happened to lose them – in the process, confiding details of her daily life and routines – the story subtly shifts into being about her personal sense of security, first as an individual and then, as one who is loved. Subsequently, as Hasidic neighbours appear in her narrative, it shifts again, introducing the idea of security based on faith and cultural connectedness. These levels enter the text successively, like lines in a musical fugue, until they are all intertwined – by which point the word 'keys,' and the idea of losing them, should be resonating in more than one frequency wherever it occurs.

And what does this method of accrual and echo look like? In "Looking for My Keys" the narrator leaves her keys on the hood of a parked car while changing hands with awkward shopping bags.

> It seemed too much to expect that the car would still be there, but I walked back over to where I remembered stopping. The car was gone, but even from half a block away I could see something lying on the curb, gleaming in the sun, right where the car had been. I came closer and there were my keys, waiting for me, winking. It's funny how vividly I remember this moment, the immense satisfaction of picking up my keys from the pavement. The squareness and rightness of my keys being *right there*, exactly where I'd figured I must have parted with them. A little feat of memory, a successful exercise of self-knowledge, proof that I could always recover what was important, even if I temporarily lost sight of it.
>
> The children were happy with the newly painted table, and even happier when – having painted it – I was inspired to go out and buy four old Windsor-style chairs in a used furniture store, and to paint them the same colour. Our old chairs, a scruffy and mismatched assortment of leftovers, went out on the back porch. 'It's so nice in here now, Mummy,' said my son, 'like a *real* person's kitchen, like my friends' houses.' And I was a little shocked at this glimpse of how I'd been living, not noticing the shabbiness, unaware that my children noticed, calculated, compared.

> Much has changed since then. My keys are not even the same keys, since I and my children now live in my friend's house, a few blocks away. My peach-coloured coffee mug broke, long before I moved. Since my friend had a perfectly good kitchen table set, a solid oak one that had belonged to his grandparents, there was no need for me to keep my pink table when we decided to live together; but I didn't want to part with it altogether, so it is now at my friend's chalet in the country. Sometimes when we go there I look at it and think about how painting it was the beginning of my being good to myself, after a long time of living numbly from day to day, in the wreckage of my failed marriage. The colour of it warms me, it is the colour I remember waking myself up with.

That "resonating in more than one frequency" isn't difficult to grasp. Once it's been pointed out to you. Robyn Sarah reprints "Ringing Changes: The Poet's Hand in the Short Story" along with Steven Heighton's essay in her sparkling collection *Little Eurekas: A Decade's Thoughts on Poetry*. Windsor: Biblioasis, 2007. Both essays also appear in *The New Quarterly* Volume XXI, Nos. 2 and 3. *Wild Writers We Have Known*.

Diane Schoemperlen has published seven collections of short fiction: *Double Exposures* (1984); *Frogs and Other Stories* (1986); *Hockey Night in Canada* (1987); *The Man of My Dreams* (1990); *Hockey Night in Canada and Other Stories* (1991); *Forms of Devotion* (1998); and *Red Plaid Shirt: Stories New and Selected* (2002).

What follows, "Forging New Shapes" is the Introduction I wrote in 1991 for Diane's *Hockey Night in Canada and Other Stories*. Since then, her technically inventive stories deploying digression and discontinuous narrative, brave new shapes, have won the Governor General's Award for Fiction.

Forging New Shapes

When I was editing *Best Canadian Stories* in the 1970s I can remember receiving stories submitted by Diane Schoemperlen who was then living in Canmore, Alberta. I didn't accept any of these stories but the name lodged in my mind; it joined my list of the names on which to keep a more than casual eye.

Years later – in 1987 – I accepted from Diane two stories for the first *Macmillan Anthology*, stories entitled "A Simple Story" and "The Man of My Dreams," the latter being the title story of the collection she went on to publish with Macmillan in 1990. Diane reminded me when I was talking to her recently that when I accepted these two stories, I had written her a letter saying that she had finally won through to a recognizable "Diane Schoemperlen story." (I also seem to remember going on to say that she now had to avoid the danger of repeating herself, of becoming the captive of the strategies she had developed.)

When I started writing in the early 1960s I faced exactly the same problems she faced, exactly the same problems that each new generation or grouping faces. The writers I was particularly associated with – Hugh Hood, Ray Smith, Clark Blaise, Alice Munro – were all struggling to create new shapes and forms for their stories. The shapes we had inherited from Hemingway and the other great American writers had hardened into an orthodoxy, a classicism, had become what Kent Thompson called "academy stuff." Those shapes were *their* shapes. What young poet today would dedicate himself to writing, say, the villanelle? We could not write *our* stories in *their* voices.

Each of us tackled the same problem in different ways but we were all well aware of what we were attempting. I would say, looking back now, that we succeeded so well that we created considerable difficulties for the younger writers who would follow us. It would have been difficult to avoid the challenge of stories like "Silver Bugles, Cymbals, Golden Silks," "Walker Brother Cowboy," "Gentle As Flowers Make the Stones," "A North American Education," "A Small Piece of Blue," and dozens of other immensely powerful and original works.

(I rush to point out, however, that I am not trying to assert the beginnings of a Canadian tradition in the short story. The idea that an hermetic Canadian literary tradition exists or can evolve is one of the nuttier nationalist fantasies. On the other hand, I know from conversations that some of the younger story writers were influenced by Canadian writers of my generation. Just as they were influenced, though, by American and British writers and, in translation, by writers from Italy and Chile. So rather than positing the birth of a Canadian native tradition I'd be more comfortable suggesting that some Canadian writing has moved out into the mainstream of writing in English).

For the first time since the mid-1970s, I can see now a new formal upheaval taking placed in Canada. Younger writers are everywhere forging new shapes which are *their* shapes. This formal upheaval is not, of course, merely some matter of "technique," some sort of nuts-and-bolts messing about which might well provide fascinating shop-talk for writers but which is of no interest to readers. What readers must understand is that the shape of a story *is* the story. There is no such thing as "form" and "content." They are indivisible; they *are* each other. New shapes are new sensibilities.

Diane is one among a growing number of serious young fiction writers who are allowing us to see and feel in a new way. Other names that spring to mind are Keath Fraser, Linda Svendsen, Dayv James-French, Terry Griggs, Douglas Glover and Steven Heighton. All are concerned in very different ways with the same task.

The stories in *Hockey Night in Canada and Other Stories* can be read as a record of Diane's struggle towards the kinds of stories in her most recent collection, *The Man of My Dreams*. This is not to be patronizing. The remarkable thing about *Hockey Night in Canada and Other Stories* is that all the stories hold up well. All contain surprises, felicities, pleasures.

In 1976, Diane attended a six-week summer writing workshop in Banff. For one of those weeks she was taught by Alice Munro. Some of the stories in this collection – I'm thinking of "The Long Way Home," "Hockey Night in Canada," "Clues," and "Crimes of Passion" – suggest to me the influence of the Alice Munro of such stories as "Walker Brothers Cowboy" and Images."

Then there are the transitional stories which are attempting to break away from the influences, such stories as "First Things First," "Frogs," and "Notes for a Travelogue."

And then there are achieved new forms in such stories as "Life Sentences," "This Town," and "True or False."

But even in her earlier and more conventional stories Diane's work could not be confused with Alice Munro's. And as she develops could not be confused with that of any other young writer in Canada.

Diane's territory is not rural or small town but is rather the gritty urban world of the Safeway, the laundromat, the café whose orange vinyl seats are patched with black electrical tape, a world where men dream of women who are "queens" but settle instead for women they think of as "utility grade," a world where women yearn for true love but end up trading gross recipes for Lazy Day Lasagna and Inside-Out Ravioli.

Life in this world bruises Diane Schoemperlen's heroines in their affairs and relationships and failing marriages and they learn and record small wisdoms with a tough, rueful humour:

> Last August I met this guy Dean at a party. I remember thinking he looked a little tired but I didn't see that as a serious problem at the time. He fell asleep at the party but then we'd all had quite a bit to drink and he wasn't the only one. He looked like a child when he was asleep. It wasn't until later that I discovered this is true of many people and is not an accurate measure of one's character.

Indeed, it is Diane's humour which is, for me, the central pleasure of her work. Nearly all the stories are marked with a sly humour which is wry and dry and sometimes as painful as ingested ground glass:

> She thought of her cousin Denise back in Hastings whom she had always been told had married late in life. For years, the whole family had treated Denise with a hopeful sympathy, as though there were little else she could be expected to do at such an advanced age beside marry a widower or keep working forever at the Bank of Montreal. Ruth had recently figured out that Denise actually got married at twenty-eight. Her husband, Howard Machuk, was a gynecologist who'd never been married and he gave her everything she could possibly want, including a dishwasher for her thirty-first birthday.

Diane creates this work with loving detail and detail itself – trade names, brand names, the banal language of advertising, the plenitude of deliberately flat fact – forms one of her comic devices.

I'm beginning to suspect that she is building, story by story, the Schoemperlen world. I mean by this that as she continues to write we'll begin to pay her the ultimate compliment of recognizing certain things we see as essentially details from a Schoemperlen story. I will never again see an orange vinyl seat patched with black electrical tape without being immediately reminded of her observing eye. And can there *really* be a dish called Inside-Out Ravioli? But one *knows* it's true.

If someone were to ask for an example of the sadly funny world of Diane Schoemperlen, I'd give them to read the following paragraph from

"Notes for a Travelogue." Sharon and Grant are two years into a failing marriage and take a week's holiday camping in an effort to hold matters together. On the first night they pitch their tent in the dark in a campground. The paragraph describes the next morning.

> Morning reveals a white Winnibago squatting just down the way, fat with sleeping strangers. There seems to be ten or twelve of them, with interchangeable heads, emerging one by one in various states of half-dress. The children race down to the lake in a pack while the adults put the coffee on. They holler blindly back and forth at each other through the tree cover – warnings, discoveries, the breakfast menu. While I'm waiting my turn in the fibreglass outhouse, a white poodle licks amiably at my ankles. Grant pumps up the Coleman stove and breaks eggs seriously into a metal bowl.

This paragraph is crammed with pleasures: the Winnebago "fat with sleeping strangers," the choice of the words "amiably" and "seriously." But the real joy of the paragraph in its context in the story is the way it seems to suggest and stand for and comment on the state of Sharon's marriage.

Welcome to the world of Diane Schoemperlen.

Further critical material can be found in "The New Story Writers" in my *Freedom from Culture: Selected Essays 1982-92*.

Carol Shields is the author of three poetry collections. *Others* (1972); *Intersect* (1974) and *Coming to Canada* (1992). She is better known for her novels: *Small Ceremonies* (1976); *The Box Garden* (1977); *Happenstance* (1980 and 1982); *A Fairly Conventional Woman* (1982); *The Republic of Love* (1992); *Swann: A Mystery* (1987); *The Stone Diaries* (1993); *Larry's Party* (1997) and *Unless* (2002). She also wrote three collections of stories: *Various Miracles* (1985); *The Orange Fish* (1989); and *Dressing Up for the Carnival* (2000). These three volumes together with her last unpublished story, "Segue," were published as *The Collected Stories* (2004).

I have never been interested in the novels, considering them rather lukewarm, muted, women's magaziny. There is no technical innovation, no challenge in them. Dialogue tends to be ill-managed. I thought I had Carol Shields pegged. Domestic, a bit sentimental, twee. Imagine my astonishment, then, when I read *Various Miracles* and later *The Orange*

Fish. Observation was acute, language was tight and vibrating, form was dense and packed.

I asked Carol what had happened and she didn't really seem to know, describing the stories in *Various Miracles* as more or less a visitation, a sudden liberation. Stoddart had little clue as to the value of the collection and released it as a paperback original. It did not create much critical stir though writers were acutely aware of it. A copy in fine condition is hard to find. Four years later Stoddart released *The Orange Fish* in hardcover. The two collections remain much more important than *The Stone Diaries* and *Larry's Party* for which she was awarded medals and prizes.

Here is the "social arbiter" Georgia Willows from the story "Good Manners."

> Promptly at three-thirty each Tuesday and Thursday, neatly dressed in a well-pressed navy Evan-Picone slub silk suit, cream blouse and muted scarf, Georgia Willows meets her small class in the reception area of the MacDonald Hotel and ushers them into the long airy tearoom – called, for some reason, Gophers – where a ceremonial spread has been ordered.
>
> Food and drink almost always accompany Mrs. Willows' lectures. It is purely a matter of simulation since, wherever half a dozen people gather, there is sure to be a plate of sandwiches to trip them up. According to Mrs. Willows, food and food implements are responsible for fifty per cent of social unease. The classic olive pit question. The persisting problem of forks, cocktail picks and coffee spoons. The more recent cherry-tomato dilemma. Potato skins, eat them or leave them? Saucers, the lack of. The challenge of the lobster. The table napkin quandary. Removing parsley from between the teeth. On and on.

How this deft, light, sparkling opening leads on to Mr. Manfred's "tube of pink, snouty, dampish flesh" and matters even darker, cannot even be guessed at. This is a dazzling story.

But the machinery clanked into operation and Random House reprinted everything – deleterious in itself – and the media fawned and Carol Shields was elevated to Feminist Icon. Some damn fool referred to her as "our Jane Austen," a comment which other damn fools echoed. This deliberate inflation of reputation did not last long, the weight simply not being there. But when it became known that she was suffering from cancer, sainthood seemed a near possibility.

In the Random House publicity organ *Read* (Volume 3, Issue 2) Marjorie Anderson and Carol Shields contributed a letter about their anthology *Dropped Threads*:

> And, of course, what the stories in the anthology attest to is the profound and the moving in the everyday, how there is no such thing as 'ordinary' in the diverse, rich lives of women.
>
> In her preface to the book, Governor General Adrienne Clarkson writes that these essays are about how we learn to 'become women.' We feel privileged to be part of this intact community of female story telling and understanding.

. . . *this intact community of female story telling and understanding.*

What horsebuns!

All this feminist syrup traduced and obscured the intellect and sensibility which had produced *Various Miracles* and *The Orange Fish* and I wish it hadn't.

Ray Smith is the author of three story collections and four novels; the collections are *Cape Breton Is the Thought-Control Centre of Canada, Lord Nelson Tavern,* and *Century.* His originality and importance lie in the fact that from the very beginning of his career he turned away from the conventions of realism and started to write stories totally unlike those of early twentieth-century masters of the form. His achievement has been undervalued by those who want Canadian literature to "tell our own stories to ourselves," an aim he would consider crude and vulgar. He might shudder just a trifle to consider this but there is about his writing a Firbankian quality, a glittering artifice, a dandyism.

In an invaluable introductory essay in *Cape Breton . . .* entitled "The Age of Innocence" Smith describes his work as belonging to The Alternate Tradition, the tradition that stems from Laurence Sterne's *Tristram Shandy.*

> [The stories are] part of a body of work called 'speculative fiction.' Generally ironic in tone. Aesthetic in approach; which means, I suppose, an indirect approach to many social and political problems of the world

> around us. This is in clear contrast to the other rising [in 1971] body of writing which includes things like revolutionary writings, the new journalism, documentary novels and the like, all of which try to grapple directly with the aforesaid social and political problems. I should emphasize, or repeat, that speculative fiction doesn't ignore the world, but approaches it somewhat indirectly. The telling point is that all these types have pretty much rejected the whole creaking apparatus of the . . . psychological-realism (or whatever it's called) form of writing.
>
> Some big dogs in speculative fiction: Jorge Luis Borges, Vladimir Nabokov. Coming big dog: Kurt Vonnegut, Jr. Prominent younger dogs: Thomas Pynchon, John Barth, Donald Barthelme, Richard Brautigan.

Ray once said to me, "Being a Canadian, of course I have no language." We might well look at all his work as a love affair with other languages, other dialects, other tribes in their heartlands. *A Night at the Opera* immerses us in the German city of Waltherrott and in its opera *Der Hosenkavalier*, written by the city's favourite son, Carl Maria von Stumpf. The stories in *Century* luxuriate in Paris of the *belle époque*, contemporary Venice, the pampered world of Austrian ski slopes, and in the ordered elegance of Edinburgh's New Town. His latest novel, *The Flush of Victory: Jack Bottomly Among the Virgins*, embraces and celebrates the horribly colourful Strine, the Australian vernacular.

What sort of linguistic razzle-dazzle was Ray Smith up to in the late 60s when he was forging a style? A close reading of "The Age of Innocence" and of Ray's commentary on "Colours" in my anthology *Sixteen by Twelve* will help. One of his central concerns was getting rid of what he thought of as the lumber of scene and setting. I'll take just two examples to suggest the kinds of devices he was inventing.

In the story "Colours" the protagonist Gerard wishes to ask questions of an exotic dancer called Patchouli. Ray is mainly concerned with getting Gerard from A to B and doesn't wish to waste narrative time on conventional description of the night club setting. This was his solution:

> So, after Patchouli had read Gerard's note and agreed to the interview, Gerard pushed past the chorus (laughter, sweat, smoke, gaping mouths) into the wings and, led by the man with six fingers, came and sat in her dressing room.

The five words in parentheses are, in effect, a montage. A montage that makes *us* make an instantaneous montage in our minds of all the musicals and show biz/gangster nightclub scenes we've watched in countless movies. Once he's done it, it's not difficult for us to grasp but his having *invented* it suggests we're in masterful hands.

Here's another example of Ray at play from the opening of the second section of "Peril":

> Period watched the carousel from a distance. Between him and the carousel stretched a green lawn with tree shadows like continents on a map. The lawn was so flat that Period had the impression (as had also many before him) that the lawn could be rolled up on a pole and carried away. (The carpet movers stout, slow, their cloth caps . . .)

When he's finished deflating the lawn-as-carpet cliché what does he want me to do with the carpet movers?

stout, slow, their cloth caps . . .

I'm not completely sure, but I think he wants from me something like: British. Black-and-white. Late 50s. Ealing Studios. Possibly involving Alec Guinness . . .

These, and dozens more, are the sorts of games these stories play.

Useful discussion can be found in *The Montreal Story Tellers: Memoirs, Photographs, Critical Essays* (Ed. J.R. Struthers). Montreal: Véhicule Press, 1985. And in an essay of Ray Smith's called "A Refusal to Mourn the Death, by Bullshit, of Literature in the Eighties" in *Carry on Bumping*. (Ed. J. Metcalf) Toronto: ECW Press, 1988.

Russell Smith is the author of three novels, a novella, one collection of short stories, *Young Men*, and a work, written under the pen-name Diane Savage, which old-fashioned booksellers would have catalogued under the heading "Curiosa."

Only in Russell Smith's work would one read dialogue like this:

> 'What a herman. What a fucking howie. You are a dorb, you know that? You are a total dorboid. You rot my bag.'

Only in Russell would we read:

> 'Come on, you know what I've heard. That you're more than friends with that incredible babe with the weird name.'
>
> 'Leyalla. Leyalla Brown. Yes, we've been kind of –'
>
> 'Doing it. Sinkin' the pink.'
>
> 'Danny, really, sometimes you talk like a –'
>
> 'Bonk city. Bonk-o-rama. Good for you. I mean seriously, congratulations. She is incredible.'

Only Russell could write such *good* parody of wine-speak:

> 'It's not special, I know,' he said, pouring, 'but it's the most expensive bottle the shitty little liquor store near here had, and I was lucky to get the last eighty-nine, the rest were ninety-threes or some such. I actually don't mind it. A little thin, but with some earth, country earth, a hint of duck footprint, you know, an echo of a sort of honking, braying –'

Russell's fictional worlds are restaurants, raves, the offices of magazines, catwalks, fashion shoots. His restaurants are run by celebrity chefs "chain-snorting cocaine." They are staffed by anorexic coked-out "Alpha Babe" waitresses. They post Dress Codes that read:

No running shoes
No rugby shirts
No fucking nice sweaters
(Make an *effort*, for fuck's sake)

They are patronized by neurotic girl fashion photographers like Nicola, "Nicola the Ebola babe" whose hair is dyed the colour of "toxic waste."

But always here and there, a lyric touch:

> Behind him, in the open kitchen, Manuel was doing a special of quail and orange glaze; there was the odd *phuff* of a tablespoon of Grand Marnier catching fire, then the warm smell of burned sugar in the air.

A lovely invention, that *phuff*. Persuasive *spelling*.

The homelife of Russell's young men is usually straitened, cash-strapped, grubby.

'GONNA STROKE YOU UP,' boomed the car stereo.

James felt his chair vibrating. Above the bass, the boys outside were shouting at each other.

'She's a cow, man. She's a fucking *pig*.'

'You fucking know shit, Armando. Fuck you, man. Stop pulling the hair out of my ass.'

'Suck my hairy –'

To his momentary relief, someone cranked up the booming even louder, and the voices were lost. He watched his water glass slowly edge across his desk. He wondered what a seismograph would read in his neighbourhood on any midafternoon . . .

Next door, the teenage girls responded to the boys with their romantic tune, the little stereo stretched to breaking, fizzing with white noise. '*And I. Will always. Love you.*' Cigarette smoke in his room. The girls were home all day these days; school out, parents at work. If he put his head out the window he would be able to see them on the sundeck below, in their shorts and T-shirts, smoking, fighting, frequently sobbing. He thought of their long hair, the lipstick and braces, newly Neeted legs glistening in the sun, and tried not to.

It should be obvious by now that I have an extravagant regard for Russell Smith's writing. As I've said before, comparison with early Kingsley Amis is not inappropriate, the exuberant Amis of *Lucky Jim, That Uncertain Feeling, I Like It Here*, and *Take a Girl Like You*. Interesting, too, to note that Russell, as was Amis, is adept at mimicry. His dialogue is impeccable, his eye merciless. Another influence on his work is Evelyn Waugh; I've not confirmed this, but I sense in *How Insensitive* the ghostly presence of *Vile Bodies*.

With such masters of language as his mentors, how could Russell not be gilded?

Linda Svendsen is the author of *Marine Life* (1992), a collection of linked stories related by Adele Nordstrom, often called by her mother, "Coconut" or "Mince Pie," about her father, Humphrey, her stepfather Robert, her sisters Joyce and Irene, her mother June, and her dangerous alcoholic brother, Ray. The matter of the stories, loves and terrors, heartbreaks, marriages and divorces is common enough but what is so astonishing is the economy and elegance of the telling.

Alice Munro wrote of the work: "Linda Svendsen's stories are stunning – so easily embodying such terrific power."

Here is Adele at the age of fourteen in the story "Flight":

> . . . After beating Penny at ping-pong, I biked home. At the bottom of the crescent I could make out my mother and second oldest sister on our front porch. I pedalled hard and pretended I was going to crash into them. 'No brakes,' I shouted. 'Save the children and run for your lives.'
>
> At the last second I swerved, crushing a clump of daffodils. They hadn't budged. Joyce still wore sunglasses, although there was nothing to shield her eyes against. 'Hi, gang,' I said. 'Why're you sitting out here in the dark?' The lamp on my bike beamed across their laps and they seemed hypnotized by a family of moths going tizzy in the light. It was then I realized something wasn't right. I said, 'What happened?'
>
> 'Joyce is leaving Eric,' Mum said carefully, and I was struck by that word *leaving*. Joyce had not actually *left* yet, although her body was beside ours and not his. 'She's going to stay with us until she's on her feet.'
>
> 'Oh,' I said.
>
> 'I'll let her tell you. I'm going to bring the mower in before somebody steals it.' Mum stepped over the zigzag of half-cropped lawn and tugged the machine out from under the dogwood. She called over the rattle, 'Doesn't the grass smell good?' and disappeared into the garage. She was crying.

How poignant and how *very* elegantly put together.

The stories cumulatively become very dense; we become deeply involved in the complexities of the Nordstrom family's emotional life. This impression of density and detail is, in a sense, strange because Linda's influences are American minimalist; she studied at Columbia in New York with Gordon Lish.

All of the stories are lit with a deadpan humour.

> I turned on the air conditioning and we listened to it. Here I was on my wedding night with my father, sitting on a bed, possibly a vibrating one, in a Queens motel.
>
> 'Marriage,' Dad said, 'as I'm sure you've learned during your extensive and, need I add, expensive schooling, is life's most difficult proposition.'

> 'There are no happy marriages,' I said. 'Only unexamined ones.'
> 'Who says that?'
> 'Me,' I said.

And a vignette of June, Adele's scatterbrained mother:

> About 2 A.M. she fetches a small china box and places it before me. She opens it and spreads tiny molars and bicuspids and incisors on the table, beside our saucers, and tells me it's my first set of teeth.
> 'You're kidding,' I say.
> 'No,' she whispers. 'I'll always keep your teeth.'

Adele at the age of ten ice-skating with her father, Humphrey, on one of his Saturday visitation days:

> I hugged the side every few feet. The only way I knew to brake was to slam into the wood. The ice was strewn with teenagers, the normal sort and a mentally retarded bunch. One of them took over the penalty box, pounded his mitts together, and screamed 'Santa' each time Dad whizzed by, until he was given a needle.

Linda wrote the following commentary for me when I was assembling the anthology *Second Impressions* (Ottawa: Oberon, 1981.)

> Frederick Busch, an American novelist and short story writer, says good fiction is 'the song inherent in the fighting through of people who share a room or house or bed or child or journey: they fear to perish of one another, or without each other, and yet, calling each other dead, they won't lie down.' I tend to go along with this stance – looking for the 'song' of a story in its style and language, looking for why it had to be told in just this exact way, a particular voice. Leonard Michaels says, 'Every story has the language of its own occasion.' Storytellers tell the same tales over and over, and what makes these births, deaths and separations new and vivid is the voice (language, tone, the timing). What is told, when and how it's told.
>
> Equally important is Busch's idea of 'fighting through.' And not simply 'fighting.' One can see that on television. 'Fighting through' implies

that things are not black and white, that events have tender repercussions. A story that does not try for its character, or *try* its characters, cannot hold, or move. And that's what I hope my writing will do. As Busch swears, 'Serious writing . . . is dangerous writing. It makes us, with our secrets and lies, hurt. It doesn't keep the darkness out. Nothing so safe; it lets the darkness in.' And Elizabeth Hardwick once said in a seminar, 'It's like that slap when you finally feel the caress in it.'

. . . When I write a story, I'm writing it to a particular person, a mind that I want to parry things with, somebody I'd like to confide in. Happily, so far, this imaginary audience has not been too removed from the rest of humanity, so I could be addressing practically anybody. And then I like to believe I tell an emotional kind of truth. I take scraps from my experience (perhaps envy, an infatuation) or something that excited me in somebody else's, and then make up. Maybe tell it how it should have happened. Sometimes I simply have an ending – a final image or a strong feeling or a phrase – and write what would have had to happen to get there. Robert Bly might say it's 'a growing into a sense of what's inside' or as Stanley Elkin demands, 'What does this story know unconsciously?'

I write slowly. After I figure out what's happening, the basic events, I re-write them so that they interest me. I guess this is the 'song' part. I want to be lured by my own words: I like them to bite. Sometimes I say to myself, 'If you could read only this story in the world, how would you want it to be?' And then I have to make it match a high expectation, as best I can . . .

AUDREY THOMAS is the author of seven story collections, two novellas, and eight novels. The story collections are: *Ten Green Bottles* published in the U.S.A. by Bobbs Merrill in 1967 and reprinted in Canada by Oberon Press in 1977; *Ladies and Escorts* (1977) Oberon Press; *Real Mothers* (1981) Talon Books; *Two in the Bush and Other Stories* (1981) New Canadian Library; *Goodbye Harold, Good Luck* (1986) Viking Penguin; *The Wild Blue Yonder* (1990) Viking Penguin and *The Path of Totality: New and Selected Stories* (2001) Viking Penguin.

According to the rules I've set myself, I must represent Audrey Thomas' achievement by what she herself has selected in *The Path of Totality*; if I were free to do otherwise I'd probably have chosen *Ladies and Escorts.*

The first five books were published by small or literary publishers, the three subsequent collections by Viking Penguin. (*Two in the Bush* is actually not new work; it draws a mixture of stories from *Ten Green Bottles* and *Ladies and Escorts.*) I am recording these dry details because they turn out to be important.

The most striking stories in *The Path of Totality* are "If One Green Bottle . . . ," "The Albatross," "Salon des Refusés," "Two in the Bush," "Joseph and His Brother," and "The More Little Mummy in the World." The stories are tightly written, demanding, experimental, four of them using techniques of collage. All are incisive. And all of them are drawn from collections published by small literary publishers.

When we turn to the stories published by Viking Penguin in *Goodbye Harold, Good Luck* and *The Wild Blue Yonder* the writing has undergone a sea change. The stories have become loose and baggy, sometimes not far removed from anecdote and gossip. What once was taut is now flabby; what once was direct and urgent is now garrulous. The stories seem to drive to no emotional end. The experience of reading them – I am talking of such stories as "The Dance," "In the Groove," "Ascension," and "Survival of the Fittest" – puts me in mind of watching episodes of *Neighbours* or *Coronation Street*, bright and chatty while they're going on but when they've stopped going on unnourishing and oddly unmemorable.

These later stories seem unbalanced in their length and detail. Even an interesting story such as "Local Customs" almost collapses under its embroidery of detail, as does the story "The Dance." Excessive detail furs and clogs the writing, slows and muffles. What follows is an excerpt from "The Survival of the Fittest" which in no way advances plot, delineates character or adds depth to theme. It is uncontrolled wordiness and is unfortunately not untypical.

> Her mother tried to imagine Heather standing in her flat – her 'apartment' – in Boston, talking into a telephone, maybe a fancy one like one of those she saw advertised the week before when she went to pay her telephone bill. There were pictures of all sorts of telephones, for executives and people in a hurry, telephones with memories, telephones without cords, Princess phones in pretty colours, even telephones for the kiddies – shaped like Snoopy or Mickey Mouse. One advertisement had amused her in a grim way, an ad for a 'grannie

phone.' There was a picture of a sweet-looking, white-haired lady, face down on the carpet, and underneath the words – 'Thirty seconds after she fell, help was on the way.' It seemed you just yelled 'help help' and the telephone picked up the sound of your voice. It was the same as dialling 999. When her turn came at the counter she said to the girl, 'Grandpas fall down as well' and pointed to the ad. The girl was busy; she didn't even smile.

'I don't know, I'm sure,' she said, handing back the change and dismissing her. 'Next,' she called, as Mrs. Hutchison moved away.

Dialogue, which in the earlier stories had been crisp, here wilts into archness and art-denying shapes.

Here is the divorced Martha to her daughter Anne in "Breaking the Ice."

. . . Martha said, 'A friend of mine is coming Friday morning.'

'A friend of yours?'

'A new friend. His name is Richard. I think you'll like him.' (Please like him, said the mother's heart to the child's. I like him. I like him a lot.) 'He has a daughter, just about a year older than you.'

'What's her name?'

'Anne, the same as yours. We'll have to call you Anne One and Anne Two.'

Her daughter's voice was cold. 'Nobody's going to want to be Anne Two.'

(*Please*, said the mother's heart to the child's. What do you know about loneliness? Oh please.) 'Well,' she said, 'we can call you Anne T. and her Anne L. No discrimination there.'

The younger Audrey Thomas would not have perpetrated this.

In the Introduction to *The Path of Totality* she writes of the stories "a lot of them have to do with language, with my love of words . . ." In this case, such a love is not a virtue. She self-indulgently permits her narrators to meander into etymology and word play.

The story "Mothering Sunday" begins with this daunting paragraph.

Hail Mary, Wounded art Thou among Women. That's what it means, doesn't it? Still, there in the French: *blesser:* to harm, to hurt, to injure, to wound. '*C'était une blessure grave.*' *Se blesser*, to wound oneself. In English we can trace the word back to *blod*. Hail Mary, Blessed art Thou among Women. All the Marys bleed.

My comment would be: *C'est un blather grave.*

Audrey Thomas' contribution to the short story in Canada was her early and surefooted use of collage techniques, work on which younger writers can still draw.

GUY VANDERHAEGHE is the author of three story collections: *Man Descending* (1982), *The Trouble with Heroes and Other Stories* (1983) and *Things As They Are?* (1992). *The Trouble with Heroes* is not widely known as it was published by a very small literary press in Ottawa called Borealis.

I know absolutely nothing about Guy Vanderhaeghe's upbringing and education. I read his work as it appeared in the literary magazines in the late 70s and 80s. I remember publishing "What I Learned from Caesar" in *Best Canadian Stories 1980*. His work was obviously stronger than most that surrounded it in the magazines. But re-reading him now prompts me to *imagine* his literary self-education. I say "self-education" as his degree work at the University of Saskatchewan was in history rather than literature.

Consider these quotations from "The Watcher," a story published in 1980.

> And in the midst, in the very eye of this familial cyclone of mishap and discontent, stood Grandma Bradley, as firm as a rock. Troubles of all kinds were laid on her doorstep. When my cousin Criselda suddenly turned big-tummied at sixteen and it proved difficult to ascertain with any exactitude the father, or even point a finger of general blame in the direction of a putative sire, she was shipped off to Grandma Bradley until she delivered. Uncle Ernie dried out on Grandma's farm and Uncle Ed hid there from several people he had sold prefab, assemble-yourself crop-duster airplanes to.

And this:

> The yard was little more than a tangle of thigh-high ragweed and sowthistle to which the chickens repaired for shade.

And this:

> In 1958 Grandma Bradley would have been sixty-nine, which made her a child of the gay nineties – although the supposed gaiety of that age didn't seem to have made much impress upon the development of her character.

The prose is well-mannered, formal, slightly old-fashioned. The diction is elevated, the verbal comic effects very slightly ponderous, contrived, *worked.* From where does all this derive? Whose work and influence helped forge this style? The *Oxford Companion to Canadian Literature* in another entry by Professor Staines says that Vanderhaeghe writes "in the prairie tradition to which its author is indebted;" as practitioners of that "tradition" Staines cites Margaret Laurence, Sinclair Ross, and Robert Kroetsch. As though they were snowed in north of Pukatawagan with nothing to read but each other – Margaret Laurence with all her years in Africa and England, Sinclair Ross with his interest in Proust and Claude Mauriac, Robert Kroetsch with his PhD in creative writing from the Writers' Workshop at the University of Iowa and his years of teaching "post-colonial" literature at Binghampton, New York. That "prairie tradition" is – again– nationalist invention, mentally lukewarm Loony Toons.

. . . putative sire . . .

. . . repaired for shade . . .

. . . much impress . . .

The *sort* of writer I seem to hear behind these quotations – possibly an eccentric view – is someone more like Stephen Leacock than Robert Kroetsch. Almost certainly British rather than American. What I *imagine* is simply something like this: in Vanderhaeghe's childhood and adolescence Saskatchewan was doubtless far more British than it is now. The books available to him in schools and libraries would, I imagine, have been fairly British in flavour. Canadian writing was not much of a force. The *kind* of writing exhibited in the quotations need not date back to Leacock; it need not have come from one particular writer or group of writers. It was a kind of educated British *generic* writing. It was, simply, what "writing" was. Vanderhaeghe's distinction was that he turned away from it realising the power and delights of the demotic.

Consider this quotation from the same story:

> My parents didn't own a television and so my curiosity and attention were focussed on my surroundings during my illnesses. I tried to squeeze every bit of juice out of them. Sooner than most children I learned that if you kept quiet and still and didn't insist on drawing attention to yourself as many kids did, adults were inclined to regard you as being one with the furniture, as significant and sentient as a hassock. By keeping mum I was treated to illuminating glances into an adult world of conventional miseries and scandals.
>
> I wasn't sure at the age of six what a miscarriage was, but I knew that Ida Thompson had had one and that now her plumbing was buggered . . .

This splendid descent into the overheard vernacular can stand for what Vanderhaeghe set out to do in his short fiction: wean himself from the style and diction he'd been early influenced by, funny as it often is, and connect into the vernacular and demotic. As his work progresses, he abandons good-mannered formalities and produces instead beautifully heard paragraphs like these farmers at a family gathering in the story "Reunion":

> The conversation ran on, random and disconnected. There was talk of the hard spring, calf scours, politics, Catholics, and curling. Totting up the score after four drinks, Jack concluded hard springs, calf scours, politics, and Catholics weren't worth a cup of cold piss. That seemed to be the consensus. Curling, however, was all right. Provided a fellow didn't run all over the province going to bonspiels and neglect his chores.

That paragraph leaves me envious.

In the splendid story "King Walsh" he writes of some poor and frugal farmers who "squeeze a nickel until the beaver shits."

As he relaxes into the demotic he even writes in the voice of an adolescent. ". . . nobody ever accused Pop of being a religious fanatic by no means. He goes to confession regular like an oil change, every five thousand miles, or Easter, whichever comes first."

When Vanderhaeghe is not aiming at the comic, his increasingly austere style – a style he has won through to – is compelling. Here from "A Taste for Perfection" is Ogle in a hospital ward unknowingly suffering from a brain tumour.

> The sudden glare of the light in the bathroom glancing off rubbed enamel and spanking bright tiles hurt his eyes. The place smelled of antiseptic and somebody else's turds.
>
> Ogle examined his face in the mirror over the sink. It seemed to him that the left side of his face had altered, although he couldn't be sure. There was a sensual droop to the eyelid, and the corner of his mouth felt a little slack and lacking in decision. He flexed the fingers of his left hand and made a weak fist; he felt faint.
>
> He sat down on the toilet seat, lit his cigarette, entwined his long legs about one another and meditatively scratched his shin. All he wanted now was four ounces of Scotch, neat. That would make this an occasion. The cigarette smoke hovered around his head, a blue nimbus.
>
> 'A drink, a drink,' he declaimed to the opposite wall, hoisting an imaginary glass, 'my sterile, christly kingdom for a drink.' Ogle attempted a suitably ironic smile but the stiff, resisting muscles of his face informed him he had failed and produced only a grimace. *There is something radically wrong here*, he thought.
>
> On the other side of the door, Morissey spoke indistinctly to a character in his dreams.
>
> 'Die in your sleep, you old prick,' Ogle answered him.

Guy Vanderhaeghe by Nicholas von Maltzahn in *Profiles in Canadian Literature*, Series 8 is well worth a visit.

Michael Winter is the author of two story collections, a fictional memoir, and a novel. The story collections are *Creaking in Their Skins* (1994) and *One Last Good Look* (1999).

Aiming for immediacy, he has stripped his writing down to a simplicity that makes the world strange in its intensity. In an interview in *The Notebooks* he said "I want to describe sex (and everything else) in a new way, and when you write in a new way, it can seem hard to read or difficult."

This statement should remind us of Hemingway's statement, quoted earlier, from *A Moveable Feast:* "Since I had started to break down all my writing and get rid of all facility and try to make instead of describe, writing had been wonderful to do. But it was very difficult, and I did not know how I would ever write anything as long as a novel. It often took me a full morning of work to write a paragraph."

In dialogue, Winter banishes much conventional punctuation. He dismisses entirely "he said" and "she said." Often he introduces a speaker simply with a colon. It produces something like a playscript. Here is an example of the effect from the story "Second Heart."

> In the morning, Junior:
> Gabe. Come on.
> What's up.
> We're getting Dad a load of wood.
> He's got lots of wood.
> Come on, Gabe. He's got bad feet. I got the saw in the truck. I got gas and oil. I even made you a little sandwich. Just half a load. We'll be done by one.
> Is Dad going?
> Dad can't be at that any more.
> I'm too stiff.
> Just you and me against some trees.
> They take the truck and go in Lady Slipper Road again.
> That deadfall stuff is rotten, June.
> Are you catching on?
> Junior parks where they were parked before. And get out. It's cold and low light. Grey rolling nimbus. Junior takes an axe from behind the seat.
> Okay.
> Junior: You can't guess?
> A sweat creeps into Gabe's armpits.
> There's a moose in there.

Along with this stripping down of the prose, Winter compresses too, using something like a prose "shorthand." Here's an example from the story "Lustral."

> At the end of summer I invited Femke to my parents' cabin. Get out of the city, see some woods. We hitchhiked and it's easy. People assumed we were a couple, which, secretly, excited both of us. We played cribbage and read Edgar Allan Poe. The flax and monkshood. A fire on the beach for hotdogs and a tin of beans.

The blue-flowering flax and monkshood are slipped in as shorthand for "idyll," "beauty," "romance."

Another Winter ploy is omission. Reviewers have described him as a minimalist and have linked him with Hemingway and Carver but his work looks and sounds like neither. It does, however, have things in common with Norman Levine and Winter has acknowledged Levine as an influence.

> His style is not one that appeals to a lot of people, but a lot of writers marvel at his talent . . . His economy of so little saying so much – when you try to write like that, you realise how hard it is to capture things accurately and truthfully with very few words. He was a writer's writer.

I would like to quote from my *Foreword* to Levine's *By a Frozen River* because what I had to say there casts considerable light on Michael Winter's practice.

> While Levine's writing always *seems* clear and simple, the stories themselves are far more complicated than the simplicity of language suggests. One might say that his work is as simple or as subtle as the people reading it. The stories usually function as an accretion of images – all of which contribute to the story's emotional current, adding tiny detail to what will be the finished shape. Levine refuses to explain or interpret his scenes for us, requiring us, in a sense, to *compose* the story for ourselves. It is that act of composition that turns these stories into such powerful emotional experiences.
>
> Consider 'Champagne Barn,' for instance. We are treated to a range of scenes and images: the Senior Citizens' Home where one of the residents, Mr. Tessier, has watched 68 corpses carried out over the years; the mindless chatter of the narrator's mother; a restaurant meal with the narrator's spinster cousin who is in her forties and still a virgin; a meeting with a childhood friend who has become a butcher; a tour of the decaying neighbourhood of the narrator's childhood. The story ends with the hack, hack, hack of the butchers' choppers in Reinhardt Foods. The last line: 'I would carry that sound with me long after I left.'
>
> As we will carry this story with us. Levine creates a world in this marvellous story – a world deftly suggested and then nailed with telling detail. He forces us to compose meaning from the seemingly random

encounters and events in five days of the narrator's life. Through the vividness of his detail (steely master that he is) he moves us to brood on the narrator's life, a brooding which overflows the story's bounds and compels us to confront our own direction and mortality.

This way of writing is essentially poetic and it is no great surprise that Levine's first two books were collections of poetry: *Myssium* (1948) and *The Tight-Rope Walker* (1950). [What *is*, perhaps, surprising is how prosy they are. Levine's verse, truth to tell, is fairly awful but so is the verse of James Joyce and Katherine Mansfield. Curious. Neither were Hemingway's poems anything to write home about.]

The lines that follow are from *I Walk by the Harbour* (1976):

> The beat and the still
> And the beat, caught, lift,
> Of the rook and the gull
> Over sea, roof, hill
> Disturb this place from sleep.

Levine wrote of these lines in *How Stories Mean*: 'It was the first line – describing the way the bird flew – that made me realize that the leaner the language the more ambiguous it becomes, and the more suggestive . . . The more you tell – the more you are keeping the reader out from bringing his or her experience in. So if you can reduce a thing to a minimum like 'The beat and the still' – then the reader brings his or her associations to that. So contrary to what people think, the more cryptic you are the more resonance there is.'

Another of the complexities of what Michael Winter does as a writer is his unconventional handling of time. Natalee Caple asked him about this in her interview in *The Notebooks*.

NC: Your timeline loops as if to suggest that memory and time are continuous and connected. How do you think about time when you are writing? What do the flashbacks and braided memories tell the reader about the narrator and the story?

MW: Okay, an example. In October, a brief snowfall. The hoods of all the cars covered in the snow. And suddenly we are thrown back into the previous winter. Or the previous winter hurtles forward to us. And then

> you see one bare hood, which must be due to a hot motor. And that hood connects to summer. In these moments, as in reflection, time seems to coil like a rope and touch at points and connect. So to be linear with events seems false to the practice of being conscious, and to be – what's the kind word? – to be elliptical is to be more accurate to how we look at the world.

Winter also shares that impulse to enshrine that I was writing about in the section on Mary Borsky – Alice Munro's "every last thing, every layer of speech and thought, stroke of light on bark or walls, every smell, pothole, pain, crack, delusion, held still and held together – radiant, everlasting." Though he'd probably be embarrassed to put it that way. But in a more muted way he's saying the same sort of thing to Natalee Caple in *The Notebooks* interview:

> I asked Norman Levine this question. About why his protagonists are always writers. And he said he's not interested in making things up. And I feel the same.

Scrupulous attention to the world and something of Hemingway's "making" instead of "describing" obviate the need for invention and lead to such glorious writing as the following paragraph from the story "Wormholes." I have read it dozens of times and am still slightly stunned by its strange power.

> The beer kept me from coming. You know how I come quickly. And she was pleased when she saw how hard an orgasm I had with her. She went to the toilet, which you can see from the bed. She came back to bed and we lay there for a few minutes. We listened to the people upstairs argue. She smoked. She said she had to go. I said you can stay. I can make you an egg. But she got up and all that nakedness.

Essential interviews with Michael Winter are to be found in *The Notebooks* and *Writers Talking*. Russell Smith rather brilliantly wrestles him to the ground in *Wild Writers*.

* * *

And here a concluding digression is called for. Caroline Adderson, Steven Heighton and Michael Winter are the only three Canadian writers I know who acknowledge the influence of another Canadian writer on their work. Caroline Adderson gives a nod to Michael Winter and Lisa Moore; Michael Winter to Norman Levine. Steven Heighton acknowledges the general influence on him of my 1982 anthology *Making It New* and mentions specifically that his lovely "Five Paintings of the New Japan" was modelled after my story "Gentle as Flowers Make the Stones" – both stories involving the ongoing translation of a poem.

It has been borne in on me during the last forty years that it is unusual to find Canadian writers who even *read* other Canadian writers. The only exception to this generality that I know of is T.F. Rigelhof. It is not at all unusual to find aspiring writers who have never read Leon Rooke, Clark Blaise, Norman Levine, Keath Fraser, Mavis Gallant . . . Similarly, older writers remain resolutely ignorant of Caroline Adderson, Michael Winter, K.D. Miller, Sharon English . . . while all of them seem to be cognizant of, say, W.G. Sebald.

If the country's *writers* do not read each other – an aesthetic and competitive necessity, one would have thought – why should we expect an audience to read us? If *writers* do not care, why should anyone else? And the anecdotal evidence of that collegial indifference is overwhelming. Is it that Canadian writers hold Canadian achievement in contempt?

I often find myself thinking of Michael Harris' words: "I cannot believe after many years of writing, editing, and collecting experience that there will ever be a Canadian literature."

It is difficult to suppress the thought that Canadian writers are the engineers of their own defeat.

* * *

Only seven years into the 21st century and important new writers are already treading on the heels of the writers on The Century List. I am enthusiastic about the work of Judith McCormack, Mary Swan, Madeleine Thien, Lynn Coady, Joan Alexander, Patricia Young, and Kathleen Winter. An obvious fixture on any future List will be Sharon English; her superb first collection of stories, *Uncomfortably Numb*, received two reviews and excited little interest.

Tinkering with and adjusting the List, extending its inclusionary dates, reconsidering omitted writers – all this is a part of what literary criticism should be doing. Evelyn Waugh objected to "... the abandonment of the hierarchic principle. It has hitherto been assumed that works of art exist in an order of precedence with the great masters, Virgil, Dante and their fellows, at the top and the popular novel of the season at the bottom. The critic's task has been primarily to preserve and adjust this classification ... This, I believe, is still the critic's essential task. ..."

In the Introduction to *The Sacred Wood* T.S. Eliot wrote: "It is the perpetual heresy of English culture to believe that only the first order mind, the Genius, the Great Man matters; that he is solitary and produced best by the least favourable environment."

Lesser writers, claims Eliot, in what might be a defence of the The Century List, are important because "... a great literature is more than the sum of a number of great writers. Secondary writers provide collectively, and individually in varying degrees, an important part of the environment of the great writer ... The continuity of a literature is essential to its greatness; it is very largely the function of secondary writers to preserve this continuity, and to provide a body of writings which is not necessarily read by posterity but which plays a great part in forming a link between those writers who continue to be read."

One might wish that some Canadian critics and readers might stray for a while through such books as Mathew Arnold's *Essays Literary and Critical*, Eliot's *The Use of Poetry and the Use of Criticism*, *The Sacred Wood*, *Notes towards the Definition of Culture*, and *What Is a Classic?* Through George Saintsbury's *A History of English Criticism*. Through T.E. Hulme's *Speculations*. Because we must at some point – beyond the inanities of *Survival* and the maunderings of postmodernists – give thought to Canadian literature's hierarchy.

* * *

The Century List Anthology

It is our intention at Biblioasis to produce an anthology based on the Century List to be called *The Century List Anthology*. This book will contain forty stories taken from the forty volumes on the Century List. Until such time as this is financially possible, I offer *The Century List Anthology* in the form of a List.

Caroline Adderson	"Shiners"
Margaret Atwood	"Poppies: Three Variations"
Mike Barnes	"Bitter Lake"
Clark Blaise	"A North American Education"
Mary Borsky	"Maps of the Known World"
Ann Copeland	"At Peace"
Libby Creelman	"Three Weeks"
Shirley Faessler	"Henye"
Cynthia Flood	"The Animals in Their Elements"
Keath Fraser	"Healing"
Mavis Gallant	"Luc and His Father"
Paul Glennon	"The Museum of the Decay of Our Love"
Douglas Glover	"Bad News of the Heart"
Terry Griggs	"Suddenly"
Steven Heighton	"Five Paintings of the New Japan"
Jack Hodgins	"The Lepers' Squint"
Hugh Hood	"Getting to Williamstown"
Isabel Huggan	"Jack of Hearts"
Mark Anthony Jarman	"Cowboys Inc."
Susan Kerslake	"Push-Me Pull-You"
Margaret Laurence	"The Perfume Sea"
Elise Levine	"Boy"
Norman Levine	"Champagne Barn"
Annabel Lyon	"Joe in the Afterlife"
Alistair MacLeod	"In the Fall"
K.D. Miller	"A Litany in Time of Plague"
Lisa Moore	"Ingrid Catching Snowflakes on Her Tongue"

Shut Up He Explained

Alice Munro	"Meneseteung"
Gayla Reid	"To Be There with You"
Patricia Robertson	"City of Orphans"
Leon Rooke	"The Deacon's Tale"
Robyn Sarah	"Looking for My Keys"
Diane Schoemperlen	"A Simple Story"
Carol Shields	"Good Manners"
Ray Smith	"Peril"
Russell Smith	"Dominic Is Dish"
Linda Svendsen	"The Edger Man"
Audrey Thomas	"The More Little Mummy in the World"
Guy Vanderhaeghe	"King Walsh"
Michael Winter	"Archibald the Arctic"

The Century List Anthology will, I hope, provide a starting point for a consideration of our achievement in the short story in Canada in the twentieth century.

ARMS, BOOKS, AND BIBLIOASIS RISING

In 2005 I became armigerous.

No, no . . . titter not! No, you can change overnight. As the Cheekie Chappie, Max Miller often said. The Music Halls. And that's another world I never knew but sorely miss.

I'm Gilbert the Filbert
The knut with a K
The Pride of Piccadilly
A blasé roué.

George Robey. Harry Champion. Dan Leno. George Leybourne. Basil Hallam . . .

Oh! Mr. Porter, what shall I do?
I want to go to Birmingham and they're taking me on to Crewe . . .

Miss Vesta Tilley. Bea Lillie . . .

She sang like a nightingale, twanged the guitar,
Danced the Cachuca, and smoked a cigar,
O! What a form! O! What a face!
And she did the Fandango all over the place.

Miss Marie Lloyd . . .

She sits among the cabbages and peas . . .

And all I ever saw or heard were vestiges of vestiges, occasional pantomimes, a few tinny records, and Olivier playing Archie Rice in Osborne's *The Entertainer.*

The old Music Hall trouper George Robey lived through and past the era of the Halls and long enough to play a bit part in Olivier's 1943-1944 film of *Henry V.* The film was financed by Filippo del Giudice and by the flour millionaire J. Arthur Rank. Del Giudice, an interned Italian citizen, was released on condition that he devote his talents and resources to making wartime propaganda and morale-boosting feature films. Del Giudice gave Olivier carte blanche. The famous battle scenes were shot in Ireland and came close to bankrupting the partnership. The battle lasted ten minutes in the film but took six weeks to choreograph, light, and shoot.

(What is likely to become *the* classic account of Agincourt has been recently published – a book by Juliet Barker called *Agincourt: The King, the Campaign, the Battle.*)

Kenneth Tynan said of *Henry V* to Thomas Kiernan, author of *Sir Larry*, "Larry didn't realize it at first because he was so close to it and so exhausted, but he had created what was perhaps the first true work of art that had ever been put on film."

Tynan nonsense, of course. Silent film in general had plenty of "true works of art" and in the realm of propaganda films Tynan was surely forgetting Sergei Eisenstein's *Potemkin* (1925) and *Alexander Nevsky* (1938). And one hesitates to bring her up but what about Leni Riefenstahl's *Triumph of the Will* (1934) and *Olympia* (1938).

Sir Laurence Olivier and Agincourt seem to crop up again and again throughout this book. Olivier interests me because apart from being the greatest actor of his age he was a man of great artistic authority and, to be frank, power. I admired his public life, his creation of the National Theatre and his directorship of it as I also admired Sir Kenneth Clark's career and involvement in so many important institutions, Director of the National Gallery, Keeper of Fine Arts at the Ashmolean, surveyor of the King's Pictures, chairman of the Arts Council, Trustee of the British Museum . . . I've always had rather a hankering after that sort of thing but fully realize I lack a temperament sufficiently calm.

And Agincourt keeps cropping up because . . . Let's go back to James Metcalfe, knighted in 1416 by Henry V for his part in the Battle of Agincourt. The coat of arms granted to James Metcalfe, known as the arms of Metcalfe of Nappa Hall in Wensleydale, make a canting reference to the family name. ("Canting" means joking, word-play, punning – a vice heralds seem much given to.) The arms were three calves passant Sable on a field Argent. The language of heraldry is French and this simply means three black bull calves on a silver background, or field, passing from right to left as seen in side view. The arms were worn on the surcoat over armour and served as an identifying badge in battle for a knight's followers.

When I was given the Order of Canada I was offered a coat of arms which would incorporate the Order and its motto. I would have felt that inventing a coat of arms from scratch in the 21st century was a pretentious and preposterous undertaking but the arms granted to James Metcalfe in 1416 were actually available as that branch of the family had died out in the eighteenth century. My brother has always been interested in genealogy and he had traced our family back as far as records survive. He had few doubts that we were connected to James in Wensleydale. I applied to the Canadian heralds and asked to be granted the Nappa arms hoping that, if successful, my brother would be pleased at re-establishing the link. I was granted the arms "differenced" by the addition of a red (Gules) chevron to make them uniquely mine. The arms are described as: *Argent a chevron Gules between three calves passant Sable.*

The Saguenay Herald of Arms, presumably jesting again, gave my battle helm a crest in the form of a porcupine, a reference to years of toil at the Porcupine's Quill. This casque is described as *a helmet mantled Gules doubled Argent within a wreath of these colours: a porcupine sejant Sable embellished Argent holding a sheaf of leaves Gules.* It is rather embarrassing to have a helmet. Even *more* embarrassing to have a helmet with a porcupine squatting on it. Too Monty Pythonesque. What sort of troops would rally behind a porcupine? What foot soldiers would charge shouting "For the Porcupine and St. George!"

I thought of a suitable motto to accompany the arms: *Servitium In Fide* – "Service in Faith." It *sounds* like a motto ought to sound. What kind of "Service," and "Faith" *in what* remain purposely vague though *I* know exactly what I meant.

After my death, the arms would descend to my daughter, Elizabeth. But Elizabeth has no children. Or is "without issue" as we armigerous say. My son, Daniel, has two sons but as he is adopted obstacles would be put in his way and he would have to make special application for a royal licence to use the arms and, if granted, the heralds would add to the arms "a mark of distinction" called a "Subordinary" to indicate adoption. The usual subordinary for adopted children is a pair of linked rings called "annulets."

But Dan's first language was Malayalam, the Dravidian language of the state of Kerala in South India and he is, quite reasonably, more interested in capentry and duct-work than he is in the toythings of late feudal Europe.

The research surrounding the arms, the calligraphy, the painting, the issuance of the Letters Patent, all this medieval tomfoolerie set me back something over $3000 and the Chief Herald of Canada and the Saguenay Herald of Arms and the Registrar of the Canadian Heraldic Authority managed to spell Wensleydale as "Wenselydale" throughout.

If the arms are unlikely to survive me, why did I bother? Partly for fun, but mainly because I have a need of the past. I feel it to be part of me. On my desk I keep a 17th-century British blue and white tile painted in the Delft manner depicting a running hare; I use it as a coaster for mugs and glasses. Beside it is a silver letter opener whose hallmarks translate as London, 1861; it is beautifully balanced in the hand. In front of me on the desk sits a piece of pantile picked up in the Frankish castle at Mystras north of Sparta, a castle built in 1249 after the knights in the Fourth Crusade had dismembered the Byzantine Empire. Beside it sits a piece of marble cladding picked up in Turkey at the temple to Athena in Assos, simple Doric columns beautiful against the blue sky, the blue of the sea far below. A couple of miles away the hazy shape of the island of Lesbos. Assos was once a home to Aristotle.

Whenever I go to England, as soon as I've dropped my bags I go out to walk in the old village, to touch stone that has stood for centuries, through the graveyard that surrounds the Norman church, through the ancient yew trees with their red berries, past the big 17th century house that once was a bakery, its outbuildings now a studio, past The Black Boy public house, patterned brickwork, cut stone lintels, window architraves, past a row of elegant 18th century houses, past a 19th century convent with a Pre-Raphaelite stained glass window. And that walk, that being again in history, that being again inside architecture, is as much a need as the thirst for draft ales or bitter.

Similarly, when we turn to literature, we should be able to wander through its architecture, through its streetscape, as it were, recognizing forms and styles, allusions, references, quotations, taking pleasure in decoration and detail. This is where we come from; this is what made us.

The past is not an oppressive, rigid constant but grows larger all the time as experiment and reaction and schism and innovation pass into history and become part of what we use to measure and to judge.

The past has to be our constant present; it is our yardstick.

T.S. Eliot writes in "Tradition and the Individual Talent" in *Selected Essays* that the tradition of the European poet ". . . involves, in the first place, the historical sense, which we may call nearly indispensable to anyone who would continue to be a poet beyond his twenty-fifth year; and the historical sense involves a perception, not only of the pastness of the past, but of its presence; the historical sense compels a man to write with not merely his own generation in his bones, but with a feeling that the whole literature of Europe from Homer, and within it the whole literature of his own country, has a simultaneous existence and composes a simultaneous order."

And *please*, earnest young thing, don't tell me that Eliot's critical thinking should be dismissed because he was vile to his wife, wore face powder, and espoused social views that wouldn't have gone down well with the lads at the pub.

Again, in "Tradition and the Individual Talent" he writes:

> Some can absorb Knowledge, the more tardy must sweat for it. Shakespeare acquired more essential history from Plutarch than most men could from the whole British Museum. What is to be insisted on is that the poet must develop or procure the consciousness of the past and that he should continue to develop this consciousness throughout his career.
>
> What happens is a continual surrender of himself as he is at the moment to something which is more valuable. The progress of an artist is a continual self-sacrifice, a continual extinction of personality.

Both quotations are pregnant with ideas for readers too.

Some of Eliot's preoccupations have become mine over the years. In *What Is a Canadian Literature?* I wrote:

> A literature is a relationship between books and readers. A tradition implies an audience. A tradition honours and bequeaths; it is a gift handed down from generation to generation. A literature is a living thing; it is the involvement of writers and readers, of publishers, printers, scholars, critics, reviewers, teachers, librarians, booksellers, book-collectors, antiquarians, bibliographers, and historians, in the cherishing of language.

And again from "Tradition and the Individual Talent" in *The Sacred Wood* (1920) Eliot writes: "Someone said: 'The dead writers are remote from us because we *know* so much more than they did.' Precisely, and they are that which we know."

* * *

The set-to with the sheila at McGill left me extremely angry and disturbed. It was not so much the financial loss that angered me but rather the mindless destruction of an idea. That it was casually destroyed by a woman entirely ignorant of Canadian literature made the situation all the more bitter.

I had envisaged earlier talking to an interested and sympathetic librarian and offering advice about how to keep the collection ticking over, what gaps to plug, offering introductions to private individuals who owned runs of *Midland* magazine under Knister's editorship, who owned the Alice issues of *The Montrealer* magazine, who owned the three University of Western Ontario's *Folio* magazines with Alice Munro appearing as Alice Laidlaw. I envisaged introducing this imagined librarian to talented and very connected dealers and bibliographers in England and the States who would nurture the collection. I envisaged suggesting outstanding young authors whose archival papers McGill might acquire as a complement to the books and manuscripts.

The books and the archives of the Porcupine's Quill could have been the nucleus of the best story collection in Canada. By refusing to complete the PQL archives and by refusing the 1700 books, McGill was not merely ceasing to acquire; it was negating the value of what it had already bought and was sending the message that it had no intention of using the collection in teaching or research. It was turning down the chance to enhance McGill's national and international reputation.

I had expected McGill to be a bastion of civility and civilization but I encountered nothing but bureaucratic hostility and a cold lack of charm. When I began having daydreams of burning the place to the ground and putting the Australian hag to the sword I realized that in the interests of my emotional health the matter was best regarded as part of life's rich pageant and expunged before it seriously festered.

The Porcupine's Quill archives easily found a home. Richard Landon of the University of Toronto's Fisher Rare Book Library accepted them with alacrity. Landon is not, thank God, a Cybrarian.

The 1700 books, a continuation of the first accession of 5200 volumes, made sense only in the context of the McGill collection. American and British first editions of story collections remained, of course, valuable as they were desired and collected in their countries of origin; Canadian books had no value whatsoever. Dealers to whom I offered them declined even to look.

So I cherry-picked, did a few disadvantageous deals, cancelled standing orders and magazine subscriptions, and saved from the accession the nucleus of a new library. Building this library, my fifth, will be the building of my last folly. Every single volume in it will have value in the international market. It will not contain a single Canadian book.

I resolved to put together a library of British and American stylists I enjoy. I am already beginning to see that my British interests lie more with novelists and my American interests more with story writers. I decided to adhere strictly to the policy of "following the flag," that is, collecting British writers only in British editions and the same for American writers.

Among the British writers I am acquiring are: Peter Ackroyd, Kingsley Amis, (I wouldn't give you chopped liver for Martin), Beryl Bainbridge, John Banville, Samuel Beckett, Malcolm Bradbury, Joyce Cary, Ivy Compton-Burnett, Ronald Firbank, Jim Crace, Roddy Doyle, William Golding, Kazuo Ishiguro, James Kelman, Saki, Ian McEwan, V.S. Naipaul, R.K. Narayan, Anthony Powell, Barbara Pym, Salman Rushdie, Graham Swift, Keith Waterhouse, Evelyn Waugh, A.N. Wilson – and a variety of quirks and oddities that appeal – Alfred Duggan, P.G. Wodehouse, Henry Green, Simon Raven, Alisdair Gray, Auberon Waugh, Alec Waugh . . . and even odder oddities . . . Henry Williamson's *Chronicles of Ancient Sunlight*, W.W. Jacobs . . .

Among the American writers: Eudora Welty, Raymond Carver, Flannery O'Connor, Sherwood Anderson, Richard Yates, Caroline Gordon, Peter Taylor, Jayne-Anne Philips, Barry Hannah, Rick Bass, Amy Hempel, Laurie Moore, Ethan Canin, James Salter. Ernest Hemingway is, of course, beyond the reach of all but the very, very rich.

For every author – Romanticism Rides Again – I'm aiming to have at least one title signed or signed and inscribed, a gathering-in and honouring of writers who have given pleasure.

* * *

Helping in the founding of another press also appealed to the Romantic in me. It also satisfied that hankering after a place in Canada's national cultural life. The idea of national cultural life no longer finds much favour with the Canada Council. Dan was more or less warned off his vision of the national when he applied for a grant for emerging publishers. Bureaucrats at the Canada Council advised him obliquely to play up the regional, the local. Community involvement was the flavour of the month. Outreach and Aboriginals. But with what knowledge and authority do these cultural bureaucrats presume to shape our cultural ends? They have as much knowledge of culture as shoe salesmen. A literature administered by a bureaucracy is an idea essentially comic. Dan and I felt no compulsion to reach out to Windsor, Ontario; we had bigger fish to fry.

In the Chapter "The Shapes We'll Be" I gave an account of the beginnings of Biblioasis. In an interview intended for *CNQ* Dan gave a somewhat different version of the genesis of the press.

> We invited John Metcalf, as a representative of the Porcupine's Quill, to the Windsor Festival of the Book in 2003. He had, at that time, just published a memoir, *An Aesthetic Underground*, and Thomas Allen sent a couple of copies along for the purpose of review.
>
> I knew, at the time, *of* John Metcalf, and could count myself among the legions of readers who had opinions about the man without ever having read much by him. He was a curmudgeon, a gadfly, a jaded shit-heel, a loud-mouthed Brit baying on and on about lord knows what. But he at least had entertainment value, and could be counted on to stir things up. I counted on him being ignorant, rude, loud, obnoxious, and at some point during the weekend, very drunk.
>
> I had, however, come to admire what he'd done with the Porcupine's Quill. Some of my favourite writers had come through Metcalf's hands, and a few of them, here and there, had more-than-kind things to say about him. Terry Griggs, Clark Blaise, K.D. Miller, all of whom I'd invited to the initial Windsor festival; Steven Heighton, Caroline Adderson, Leon Rooke, John Newlove, Libby Creelman. The Quill had a stellar list: I'd only rarely been disappointed with anything by them. So I resolved to give the man a chance.
>
> I tried to read something by everyone who came to the festival. One evening at 11:30, Alexis snoring softly in bed beside me, I picked up

John's *An Aesthetic Underground.* 'A Literary Memoir.' *Yawn.* That should do the trick.

Six hours later I'd finished it, and still I could not sleep.

I found the book brilliant, honest, candid, exhilarating, and very, very funny. Beautifully written. I also found it incredibly hopeful, if in a bit of a Sisyphean way: the rock is indeed heavy, but one keeps struggling. His thoughts on matters Canadian and literary in large measure mirrored my own: most of what was celebrated in Canadian literature – Margaret Atwood, Morley Callaghan, Robertson Davies, Timothy Findley, Rudy Wiebe – a long, long list – was middling at best, and often very bad. My experience was his: the best stuff was elsewhere.

The other thing that was immediately apparent: John was no mere curmudgeon or gadfly, he was not another bitter, mealy-mouthed critic. He was not jaded; somehow, against all odds, he remained an idealist who was excited about language and literature. He was generous to the point of self-sacrifice.

Also: in the early pages of *An Aesthetic Underground,* John wrote about the collecting impulse, and through the rest of the book showed how it had coloured his instincts as editor, writer and virtual-publisher. The importance of selective acquisition, of seeing the large picture. Trusting your gut. Collecting as act of creation. That is something I thought I could understand, and use as an ideal as I started my own press. My experiences as a used book seller – I used to think of myself as a minor nobleman in the literary aristocracy (though a more truthful metaphor in the Canadian context, I've since realized, might be: a minor functionary in the literary bureaucracy!) and enthusiastic book-collector might actually serve as a form of apprenticeship. There were Canadian precedents: William Hoffer, Hugh Anson-Cartwright.

We also both loved short fiction.

Despite the odds, the Metcalf of *An Aesthetic Underground* told me, this literature game was worth the leap. Also, that I might be able to take part in it after all.

The next day, I passed the book onto a good poet-friend of mine. 'You have to read this. It's wonderful stuff.' He, it seemed, knew all about Metcalf, and was quite sceptical. I persisted; he relented. A couple of days later, he brought it back. 'It was so depressing! It made me feel as if I should curl up in a ball and quit writing. I mean, why bother?'

How could it be that we had such entirely different reactions to *An Aesthetic Underground?* I found it exciting, positive, liberating; almost everyone else I've had read it felt it to be depressing and defeatist. I've reread it now a couple of times and nothing has changed for me. I have no idea how it is that most people – with the exception of a small coterie of Metcalfians, whether they are aware of their membership in this clan (and it is one) or not – seem incapable of getting it.

Three months later I'm waiting in the Windsor Airport for John to disembark. I've read almost everything by him. I'm now a convert. There's a bottle of Glenfiddich in a paper bag behind the passenger seat of my minivan with John's name on it.

He comes into the terminal with a coat over his arm and a thick Anthony Hyde paperback in his hand. *Anthony Hyde?* I don't ask.

He is polite, gentle and decorous, a touch tweedy. Soft-spoken and straight-shooting. I do not see him drunk.

He is, though, gladdened at the hotel by the sight of the scotch.

He does not know it, but he is a marked man. By the time he leaves on Monday I'll have cornered him about the idea of a chapbook series, some form of editorial mentorship. He'll, of course, think it is his own idea.

Well, well, the delusions from which the lad suffers.

Beckett, Samuel. *Proust.* London: Chatto and Windus, 1931. Top edge slightly foxed but an attractive and above average copy. Beckett's first regularly published book.

Biblioasis is beginning to firm up in exactly the way I'd hoped. We were lucky in getting books from Clark Blaise and Leon Rooke – Blaise's *Selected Essays* and a republication of some of Rooke's classic material under the title *Hitting the Charts.* This sees back into print such inspired performances as "The Deacon's Tale," "The Problem Shop," Mama Tuddi Done Over," and "Some People Will Tell You the Situation at Henny Penny Nursery Is Getting Intolerable."

I treasure a memory of Leon's delivering this last story at Fairleigh Dickinson University in New Jersey. We were on a mini-reading tour in the States. Hospitality flowed before the performance and by show time Leon was aglow. He worked himself deeper and deeper into Mr. Beacon's voice, gesticulating largely, until off flew his glasses, and unable to find them and therefore unable to read from the book, he simply improvised – a gravelly, unfaltering outpouring. He became so exercised in the role that at one point he started to climb the library shelves; the audience stared in silent tension.

We also published Eric Ormsby's selected poems *Time's Covenant*, *Little Eurekas: A Decade's Thoughts on Poetry* by Robyn Sarah, David Helwig's *Saltsea*, David Solway's *The Properties of Things*, Lorna Jackson's *Cold-cocked: On Hockey*, and Ray Smith's *The Flush of Victory: Jack Bottomly Among the Virgins.*

This last title was first written about twenty years ago. Ray always wanted me to publish it at the Porcupine's Quill and I had steadfastly refused. The book is a farcical military thriller – something like the George MacDonald Fraser Flashman novels – but grossly offensive to all possible genders, races, and nationalities. It is also, of course, very funny. I had refused it earlier because I had notions of maintaining the Porcupine's Quill's purity, nobility, and refinement. I had been, I realized, prissy and rather virginal. Dan was amused by the book, Ray brought its computer lore up to date, we diluted very lightly some archly disgusting dialogue and rendered less graphic the mile-high (statutory) rape of the drugged teenage daughter of General Bartlett, Chief of Defence Staff, by Captain Richard ("Iron Dick") Drabble.

I amused myself writing the back cover copy which I did in the form of "bullets" detailing some of the highpoints of Major Bottomly's "confession."

- The murder of the CIA agent in Ottawa known only as 'Hubble,' trampled to death by horses ridden by rogue RCMP officers.

- The unlawful confinement in Ottawa by officers of the Royal Canadian Navy of agents of SIS and their subjection to incessant buggery.

"Rogue" and "incessant" weren't bad, I thought.

Banville, John. *Beckett's Last Words.* Oxford: Joe McCann, 2006. Limited to 54 copies signed by the author. 12 copies bound in quarter goat skin. 42 copies bound in full cloth with 21 copies printed on Barcham Green Chester paper and numbered 13-33 and 21 copies printed on Hahnemuhle Old antique paper and numbered 34-54.

Some of these authors were of special significance to me, not only because they were among the country's best, but because they provided a link to the Porcupine's Quill. I wanted their publishing with Biblioasis to be seen as a sign that Biblioasis was becoming what the Porcupine's Quill had been.

Readers will notice that these writers are not exactly young. I wanted them in place because they gave the nascent press weight and gravitas. Their presence would signal to younger writers that Biblioasis offered a more-than-respectable home. But at the same time, so many older writers were making Dan slightly restive. He honoured them and understood that he needed them but was eager to find and publish new writers, writers closer to his own age. He was eager for the press to be entirely *his*. This gives rise, not to discord between us, but certainly to tension. I had, however, entered into the job with the aim of making myself redundant.

I do not think it will be long before Dan grows into total control. I have never before met anyone so brightly idealistic. I have rarely met such a quick study. His thinking is naturally on a large scale, big-screen. He differs from most Canadian publishers in that he has read widely and continues to read. He has a keen intelligence, excellent taste, and is not afraid to face depressing truths; all he lacked when we started out together was absolute confidence in judgement but the mounting stacks of typescripts will quickly foster that.

Waugh, Evelyn. *The Holy Places.* With wood engravings by Reynolds Stone. London: The Queen Anne press, 1952. Limited edition. Of this book 950 copies have been printed and numbered 1-950. This copy is number 63. A fine copy in dustjacket with minor wear. Inscribed by the author to Anne Ford in ink on the ffep. 'With Christmas greetings from Evelyn Waugh.' Anne Ford was the publicity director for Little, Brown, Waugh's publisher in the U.S.A.

When we were talking a couple of years ago about the idea of the press and the shape of the press Dan came up with the idea of translation as an important component. He had already published Goran Simic's *From Sarajevo with Sorrow* and *Yesterday's People.* I was interested in the idea for itself and also because it would probably lead to alliances and co-publication with presses outside Canada – alliances I'd always wanted for the Porcupine's Quill but had never been able to effect.

In the *CNQ* interview Dan wrote:

My own love affair with literature did not begin with Canadian books. Indeed, I came rather late to Canadian literature, in my second or third year of university, when a creative writing prof put into my hands Clark Blaise's *Tribal Justice* (pairing this with Ishiguro's *Artist of the Floating World*). A short period of literary nationalism followed, where I read Canadian writers voraciously, though I'm afraid a little too uncritically: Margaret Atwood, the rest of Blaise, Callaghan, Davies, Findley, Laurence, MacLeod, Munro, Ondaatje, Richler and company. Some of it was excellent (the Blaise, the MacLeod, the Munro, the Richler); some of it was middling (the Atwood, the Davies, the Ondaatje); and some of it was downright bad (the Callaghan, the Findley). Enough of the bad – which included all of the Canadian historical fiction then in vogue – cured me of the worst excesses of literary nationalism, and saved me from a career trying to teach it.

No, I became hooked as a more mature reader largely by works in translation. In high school Voltaire and Diderot and Camus; in university Rabelais (whom I was introduced to by Davies in that poor novel *The Rebel Angels*, enough of a gift that I will always remember Davies fondly by association), Sartre, Nietzsche, Kafka, Kundera, Dostoyevsky, Chekhov, Stendhal (especially Stendhal), Dante, Cervantes, and too many others to name. Most recently, the work of Patrick Chamoiseau, whose *Texaco* and *Solibo Magnificent* are two of the most thrilling, unsettling and playful novels I've read in recent memory (especially the latter, available on almost any remainder table in the land for under five bucks).

Kundera quotes Goethe: 'National literature no longer means much these days. We are entering the era of *Weltliteratur* – world literature – and it is up to each of us to hasten this development.' Not a plurality of national literatures, then, but one literature. Though now, nearly two hundred years later, we still seem too concerned with the national.

Publishing Goran Simic opened my eyes to the difficulties Canadian writers writing in languages other than English and French face trying to get published in Canada. There is no real money to help fund these translations. It is also a lot more work, so resource-shy publishers tend to shy away from these manuscripts. Even when Goran's books were finally published, there were difficulties. I submitted *From Sarajevo, with Sorrow* to the Governor General's Award for Poetry; a few weeks later a woman from the Canada Council called to question its validity: the award was only for books originally written in either English or French. I argued with her for a while, reminded her that Skvorecky had won the G.G. for fiction in 1984 for *The Engineer of Human Souls*, a novel originally written in Czech. She sounded sceptical, and said she'd look into it. I never heard back from her.

In the spring of 2006 we convinced Stephen Henighan to submit his latest critical book to Biblioasis, and after reading it, we decided on publication. Unlike his G.G. nominated *When Words Deny the World, A Report on the Afterlife of Culture*, focuses largely on world literature and literature in translation. The two of us got to talking, and I mentioned I'd been thinking of starting a translation series. Stephen offered to help organize it, and as he is perfectly placed to do so, I accepted and made him the General Editor of the series.

A couple of months later, a poetry manuscript by Ryszard Kapuscinski was sent to us. Translated by two Canadians, it had been rejected by other publishers, in large measure because it was not eligible for government funding. Ecstatic about the possibility of being able to associate a writer of the international reputation of Kapuscinski with our fledgling press, we accepted it. It will officially launch the Biblioasis translation series in the fall of 2007.

Salter, James *Dusk and Other Stories.* San Francisco: North Point Press, 1988. Cloth in dj. fine.

Dan's next invention was the Metcalf-Rooke Award. This annual award was "to uphold and celebrate the tradition of small press publishing in Canada and to champion the writing of new and up-and-coming Canadian writers." He joined forces with Max Maccari of Page and Turners fame who agreed to award a prize of $1500 and arrange a tour of Page and Turner stores for the winner. Dan guaranteed publication with Biblioasis.

Quill and Quire described the Page and Turners venture thus:

Page and Turners, Canada's newest book chain, is the brainchild of Max Maccari. He's got several ambitious ventures behind him already,

> including a reading series at Toronto Starbucks locations several years ago and a now-defunct micropublisher, Boheme Press. But these pale in comparison with his plans for Page and Turners. First and foremost, Maccari is bringing franchising to the trade . . . The franchise fee gets you a finished bookstore. 'It's called a turnkey operation,' Maccari says. He has contractors who will build the shelves and do all the work to set up the store. He has a contract with Van Houtte, a Montreal coffee company, to supply each of the stores. And the cafés come with tables and chairs emblazoned with the Page and Turners logo. The stores even come with books on the shelves: Maccari selects the initial complement of titles for each store.

The Award was announced and manuscripts began flooding in. It was not difficult to pick a winner. We selected a collection of stories by Patricia Young entitled *Airstream*. That excellent reviewer, Jim Bartley, opened his review in the *Globe and Mail*: "Are there lapses in Patricia Young's *Airstream*? Every book has them, but in the best they only prove the author's humanity. This collection of stories from Young, a prolific, award-winning B.C. poet, is a quietly assured wonder. It's a book of parts that integrate into an artistic whole, parts linked not by characters or plot but by a way of knowing and showing the world. Young gives us love and folly and pain and the unending mystery of women and men, boys and girls, with a nuance and balance suggesting Alice Munro, and with echoes of the same wisdom."

Jim Bartley also picked the book in his *Globe and Mail* Top Five Books of 2006.

Off to a rattling good start, one would have thought.

Max Maccari sent Dan a cheque for Patricia Young in the amount of $1500.

It bounced.

Quill and Quire reported: "A dispute between the founder of a chain of franchised bookstores and the franchisees has apparently driven the head office of Page and Turners out of business – and the founder out of reach. Most franchisees say they haven't heard from Max Maccari, who founded the Page and Turners chain, since late March or early April."

When I tried to tell Myrna about this I was laughing so much I couldn't get it out. There seemed to me something so comically incongruous about a solemn Literary Award given in the name of two venerable writers and a bouncing cheque. So unlike the Giller. More like taking-the-empties-back to scrounge up enough money for a postage stamp. The matter was resolved with the aid of a lawyer. Dan was not amused. I simply thought that, well, life was like that.

The situation made me giggle because it reminded me of an old BBC radio show starring the British comedian Peter Jones. He played a theatrical agent, a Cockney rogue all of whose deals were desperate fly-by-night scams. Lacking an office, he conducted his business from a phone booth. His conversations were peppered with such asides as "Gawd! It's 'ot in 'ere!"

Dan shouldered the load but we are still in search of a sponsor. And *some* dignity.

In the second year of the Award we received a wonderful manuscript from Kathleen Winter called *boYs*. I have been working on it with great pleasure and excitement. I've taken the book's opening story "You Can Take One Thing" for Oberon's *Best Canadian Stories* and Kim Jernigan has taken three stories for *The New Quarterly* and commissioned an interview. We are all excited.

There is a quality gulf between the small presses and the commercial houses. I know that I'm much happier judging the Metcalf-Rooke Award – disreputable origins, bouncing cheque and all – than I would be rewarding the efforts of such Giller Prize groaners as Vincent Lam and M.G. Vassanji.

Welty, Eudora. *The Golden Apples*. New York: Harcourt, Brace, 1949. Cloth and boards in dj. Fine. Signed on the title page.

Dan next began a series of reprints produced using print-on-demand technology. He called this series *Renditions*. In the *CNQ* interview he wrote:

> Renditions comes from render, one definition of which is to give back, to restore. Biblioasis Renditions, as a series, will give back what we feel are important books. The first title in the series was Ray Smith's *Cape Breton Is The Thought-Control Centre of Canada*; the second Smith's *A Night at the Opera*. The third is John Metcalf's very funny short novel *Going Down Slow* . . . The fourth title will be Ray Smith's *Century*, by far his best book, and deserving, as far as I'm concerned, of canonical status. Terry Grigg's *Quickening*, a fabulous short story collection, will be our fifth title . . .

> But I don't see any reason in keeping this to Canadian titles. As with my regular trade book publishing, I am less and less interested in being pigeon-holed as a Canadian literary publisher. I expect that we will publish books by non-Canadians in this series as well, and soon. What's the point of rendering anything not worth the rendering? And what does nationality have to do with it?

I'm not sure if Dan would entirely agree but for the moment I'm looking on Biblioasis Renditions as an aesthetic alternative to the monolithic New Canadian Library under the chauvinistic tutelage of the dread Professor Staines. Staines – if unchallenged – will produce a Canadian canon by default. The simple physical presence of the books, their availability, will define what Canadian literature is. The thought of a canon selected by Staines, a man who believes Callaghan a better writer than Hemingway . . .

With Dan's approval, I got underway another series called The Biblioasis Studies in Short Fiction. The first title is completed and awaiting publication: *God's Plenty: A Study of Hugh Hood's Short Fiction* by W.J. Keith. A second title *All the Heart Is in the Things* on the stories of Norman Levine with Cynthia Flood as principal contributor is under construction.

These and more general critical books by Terry Rigelhof, Stephen Henighan, Clark Blaise, and David O'Rourke present a problem. Jack David, publisher of ECW, told me years ago that sales figures for academic books had fallen to an estimated sale of 125 copies. Since then matters have probably degenerated further. Although the books I've mentioned are not academic and are scrupulously jargon-free they do demand of a reader seriousness and effort; this probably dooms them to comparable sales figures.

This ought to be an argument for abandoning the critical venture. But we cannot. If we do nothing to preserve the past, we cannot have a meaningful present. Without a past preserved, we are bereft of judgement. Without a past preserved, we wander lost in the world like patients suffering from amnesia.

We are forced to face financial loss on these titles. But we must ignore the reality. We must continue to act "as if." As if there are more than 125 people in 33 million who desire some knowledge of their literary inheritance. To not publish these books would be to concede that we are, in David Mamet's words, a nation of "savage shitheads in the wilderness."

These sales figures are painful *but not disabling.* In 2006 my Selected Essays *Freedom from Culture* sold one (1) copy. In 2006 my novella *Forde Abroad* sold zero (0) copies. This sales figure (or more accurately, sale figure) does not indicate the value of the contents of the book and does not negate them. Nor does it negate the effort that went into the writing of the book.

Our literary responsibilities are more complex than profit or loss.

We soldier on.

Yates, Richard. *Liars in Love: Stories.* New York: Delacorte Press/Seymour Lawrence, 1981. Cloth and boards in dj. Fine. A full page inscription on the ffep to Andrew Wylie, Yates' agent.

The limited edition chapbooks with which the press started continued with Patricia Robertson, Sharon English, and Guy Vanderhaeghe. After sitting on the limitation pages for over a year Mavis Gallant finally signed and returned the sheets for our edition of her great short story "Speck's Idea." I had particularly wanted to include her in the series as her reputation is international and I had plotted on using "Speck's Idea" as our bridgehead into the States, a calling card, as it were, which would help us secure a list of American writers for the chapbook series.

The purchase of *Canadian Notes & Queries* went through and Dan emphasized *CNQ* as the magazine's new name. The magazine more than doubled in size and became glossier. Michael Darling retired as Book Review editor and Zachariah Wells (no relative) took over. The magazine started pulling in energy from all over the country. We expanded into the visual arts. Liz Wylie curator of the University of Toronto's Art Centre, began writing for us. Roy MacSkimming agreed to publish in every issue transcribed interviews on which he had based his book on Canadian publishing *The Perilous Trade.* David O'Rourke contributed interviews with Irving Layton and F.R. Scott from his forthcoming book about the Montreal poets of the forties *Once There Were Giants.* We seemed to be developing an interest in photography. Dan and I wrote more than two hundred letters and easily doubled subscriptions. The magazine is beginning to hum. We hope to move to four issues a year. I look upon the intense activity around the magazine, the drawing-in of the best literary minds in Canada, as the building of what Hugh Kenner called The Elsewhere Community.

In his *CNQ* interview, Dan Wells mentioned that he had hoped from me some "editorial mentoring." Mentoring would be a pretty classy word for what he gets from me. I don't mentor him. I nag him. I pester him like a Dutch uncle and I'm sure it irritates the hell out of him.

From a recent letter I sent him:

> —— phoned me yesterday just to chat. He said he'd transmitted everything to you but had not received acknowledgement that you'd received them. He didn't *say* anything further but . . .
>
> He *is* working for you for free and his 'payment' should be that sense of belonging to an important venture, that sense of being one of a band of chosen few – 'we happy few.' It is – and forgive me the nagging – part of your job as a publisher to supply that magic of 'Harry in the night.' That personal touch is as important as the books you do – indeed, you're not going to *get* books without it. As a publisher you must realize that you have to appear to be All-Father, the All-Knowing, the All-Calm, the All-Soothing. You must absorb insults and tantrums and gross displays of egotism. You must realize that you're dealing with very strange and vulnerable people who aren't, at least some of the time, in their right minds. It's a circus and you're the ringmaster. You don't make the tigers jump through the hoop by brandishing a whip but by stroking them and whispering to them and slipping them gobbets as treats. And you must do all this even if your life is being chewed to ratshit, if in your caravan your wife is screwing the Daring Young Man on the Flying Trapeze and your son is again into *your* vodka and your piles are acting up.

I'm not really happy with the idea of mentoring. I can teach tricks-of-the-trade but aesthetic awareness is in large part innate; all a mentor can do is give the innate ability some exercise. There is little use in precepts. As in all forms of connoisseurship, one learns by handling beautiful examples and ugly examples. I'm happy really only to suggest that this or that example is desirable; all else will flow from that.

I point always to the particular. Handle this, I say. Heft that. Taste this. *Listen* to that. *Stop thinking!*

Luxuriate in this. A Lolita-like glimpse in Nabokov's 1948 story "Colette":

> Instantly she was off, tap-tapping her glinting hoop through light and shade, around and around a fountain choked with dead leaves, near which I stood. The leaves mingled in my memory with the leather of her shoes and gloves, and there was, I remember, some detail in her attire (perhaps a ribbon on her Scottish cap, or the pattern of her stockings) that reminded me then of the rainbow spiral in a glass marble. I still seem to be holding that wisp of iridescence, not knowing exactly where to fit it in, while she runs with her hoop ever faster around me and finally dissolves among the slender shadows cast on the gravelled path by the interlaced arches of its border.

All one can say is *yes*.
YES

Banville, John. *Nightspawn*. London: Secker and Warburg, 1971. Cloth in dj. Near fine.

In the *CNQ* interview Dan indicated future directions for Biblioasis. When I read his responses, I felt like cheering.

> I hope for nothing less than that Biblioasis becomes the best publishing house in the country. No: I want more than this. You ask if I have a national vision. I am less and less interested in seeing Biblioasis as a national press. Why limit it in such a fashion? And is it possible to be a truly great press if we set such a narrow limit to our aspirations and operations? I don't think it is. The presses I most admire: the Andre Deutsch of the 60s, the early Knopf, Faber and Faber. None of these presses would have considered limiting themselves in such a way. Andre Deutsch would have scoffed at being asked if he had a 'national vision;' so would Knopf or John Calder. I am beginning to think that we only harm ourselves as publishers by limiting ourselves in such a fashion.
>
> Literature has nothing to do with national boundaries. I'll bring up Goethe again and his idea of *Weltliteratur*. What Biblioasis is interested in is literature, and very little else. We are not interested in politics or community building. As a Canadian-based press, of course, we are interested in publishing the best Canadian writers we can get our

hands on. We'll look to both discover the next generation of great writers and celebrate the best of previous generations. Our focus on translation will, in fact, give writers the chance to be heard in Canada who might otherwise not get that chance. Whether it be Angola with Ondjaki's *Good Morning Comrades*, Toronto with Simic's *Yesterday's People* or the United States with American Joshua Glenn's *Idler's Glossary* we are interested only in putting out the best writers and most interesting books we can, regardless of where they come from.

So far, I think we've managed to do just that. I'm immensely pleased with our list and the writers we have been able to publish in a variety of formats. Michèle Adams, Caroline Adderson, Mike Barnes, Mavis Gallant, Adam Getty, Terry Griggs, David Helwig, David Hickey, Ryszard Kapuscinski, Annabel Lyon, John Metcalf, A.F. Moritz, Eric Ormsby, Patricia Robertson, Leon Rooke, Robyn Sarah, Goran Simic, Ray Smith, Russell Smith, Guy Vanderhaeghe, Kathleen Winter, Patricia Young . . . a partial list of those we will have published by the end of 2007, when Biblioasis will celebrate its Third Anniversary. What other prcss could boast a list this accomplished? I'm very proud and honoured to be associated with every single one of these writers and their books.

A new Quixote to ride with.
Windmills towering.
Vaster visions.
Servitium In Fide

BIBLIOGRAPHY

Books by John Metcalf

New Canadian Writing 1969. Clarke, Irwin. Toronto. 1969.
The Lady Who Sold Furniture. Clarke, Irwin. Toronto. 1970.
Going Down Slow. McClelland and Stewart. Toronto. 1972.
The Teeth of My Father. Oberon Press. Ottawa. 1975.
Girl in Gingham. Oberon Press. Ottawa. 1978.
General Ludd. ECW Press. Toronto. 1980.
Selected Stories. McClelland and Stewart. Toronto. 1982.
Kicking Against the Pricks. ECW Press. Toronto. 1982.
Adult Entertainment. Macmillan. Toronto. 1986.
Adult Entertainment. St. Martins. New York. 1990.
Adult Entertainment. Random House of Canada 1990. Paperback release.
What Is a Canadian Literature? Red Kite Press. Guelph. 1988.
Volleys. (with Sam Solecki & W.J. Keith) Porcupine's Quill. Erin. 1990.
Shooting the Stars. Porcupine's Quill. Erin. 1993.
Freedom from Culture. ECW Press. Toronto. 1994.
Acts of Kindness and of Love. (With Tony Calzetta) Presswerk Editions. 1995.
An Aesthetic Underground. Thomas Allen Publishers. Toronto. 2003.
Forde Abroad. Porcupine's Quill. Erin. 2003.
Standing Stones: The Best Stories of John Metcalf. Thomas Allen Publishers. Toronto. 2004.
Shut Up He Explained. Biblioasis. Emeryville. 2007.
Going Down Slow. Biblioasis. Emeryville. 2007.

BOOKS EDITED: Trade Books

Best Canadian Stories 1976. Oberon Press. Ottawa. (with Joan Harcourt)
Best Canadian Stories 1977. Oberon Press. Ottawa. (with Joan Harcourt)
Best Canadian Stories 1978. Oberon Press. Ottawa. (with Clark Blaise)
Best Canadian Stories 1979. Oberon Press. Ottawa. (with Clark Blaise)
Best Canadian Stories 1980. Oberon Press. Ottawa. (with Clark Blaise)

Best Canadian Stories 1981. Oberon Press. Ottawa. (with Leon Rooke)
Best Canadian Stories 1982. Oberon Press. Ottawa. (with Leon Rooke)
Here and Now: Canadian Stories. Oberon Press. Ottawa. 1977. (with Clark Blaise)
First Impressions. Oberon Press. Ottawa. 1980.
Second Impressions. Oberon Press. Ottawa. 1981.
Third Impressions. Oberon Press. Ottawa. 1982.
Making It New. Methuen Publishing. Toronto. 1982.
The New Press Anthology: Best Canadian Stories (Vol. I). General Publishing. Toronto. 1984. (with Leon Rooke)
The New Press Anthology: Best Canadian Stories (Vol. II). General Publishing. Toronto. 1985. (with Leon Rooke)
The Bumper Book. ECW Press. Toronto. 1987.
Carry on Bumping. ECW Press. Toronto. 1988.
Writers in Aspic. Vehicule Press. Montreal. 1988.
The Macmillan Anthology 1. Macmillan. Toronto. 1988. (with Leon Rooke)
The Macmillan Anthology 2. Macmillan. Toronto. 1989. (with Leon Rooke)
The Macmillan Anthology 3. Macmillan. Toronto. 1990. (with Kent Thompson)
How Stories Mean. (with J.R. 'Tim' Struthers) Porcupine's Quill Press. Erin. 1993.
The New Story Writers. Quarry Press. Kingston. 1992.
Cuento canadiense contemporáneo. John Metcalf (compilador), Traducción: Juan Carlos Rodriguez. Universidad Nacional Autonoma de México. Mexico. 1996.
Hugh Hood. Light Shining Out of Darkness and Other Stories. McClelland and Stewart. Toronto 2001.

BOOKS EDITED: Textbooks

Wordcraft (Books 1-5). J.M. Dent and Sons. Toronto. 1967-77. (Vocabulary and comprehension books. Grades 7-11.)
Rhyme and Reason. Ryerson Press. Toronto. 1969. (Poetry text book. Grades 8-10.)
Salutation. Ryerson Press. Toronto. 1970. (Anthology of world poetry. Grades 10-12.)
Sixteen by Twelve. McGraw-Hill. Toronto. 1971. (Canadian short stories. Grades 10-12.)
The Narrative Voice. McGraw-Hill. Toronto. 1971. (Canadian short stories. University text.)
Kaleidoscope. Van Nostrand Reinhold. Toronto. 1972. (Canadian short stories. Junior high school.)
The Speaking Earth. Van Rostrand Reinhold. Toronto. 1972. (Canadian poetry. Grades 9-11.)

Stories Plus. McGraw-Hill. Toronto. 1979. (Canadian stories. Grades 10-12.)
New Worlds. McGraw-Hill. Toronto. 1980. (Canadian stories. Grades 8-9.)
Making It New. Methuen. Toronto. 1982. (Trade and university text.)
Canadian Classics. McGraw-Hill Ryerson. Toronto. 1993.

BOOKS EDITED for Oberon Press

The Love Parlour. Leon Rooke. 1977.
At Peace. Ann Copeland. 1978.
I've Always Felt Sorry for Decimals. Robert Gibbs. Oberon. 1978.
Cry Evil. Leon Rooke. 1980.
Taking Cover. Keath Fraser. 1982.
The Elizabeth Stories. Isabel Huggan. 1984.

BOOKS EDITED for Quarry Press, Macmillan and ECW Press

Hockey Night in Canada and Other Stories. Diane Schoemperlen. 1991.
The Man of My Dreams. Diane Schoemperlen. 1990.
Death Suite. Leon Rooke. 1981.

BOOKS EDITED for The Porcupine's Quill Press

Cape Breton Is the Thought-Control Centre of Canada. Ray Smith. 1989.
The Improved Binoculars. Irving Layton. 1991.
Lunar Attractions. Clark Blaise. 1990.
Europe. Louis Dudek. 1991.
Endeared by Dark: The Collected Poems of George Johnston. 1990.
Victims of Gravity. Dayv James-French. 1990.
Volleys. Solecki, Metcalf, Keith. 1990.
Quickening. Terry Griggs. 1991.
Blue Husbands. Don Dickinson. 1991.
The Happiness of Others. Leon Rooke. 1991.
Portraits of Canadian Writers. Sam Tata. 1991.
An Independent Stance. W.J. Keith. 1991.
Flight Paths of the Emperor. Steven Heighton. 1992.
Dance with Desire. Irving Layton. 1992.
While Breath Persist. Gael Turnbull. 1992.

A Night at the Opera. Ray Smith. 1992.
Thank Your Mother for the Rabbits. John Mills. 1992.
Man and His World. Clark Blaise. 1992.
Forests of the Medieval World. Don Coles. 1993.
Bad Imaginings. Caroline Adderson. 1993.
How Stories Mean. John Metcalf and J.R. 'Tim' Struthers. 1993.
Apology for Absence. John Newlove. 1993.
Mogul Recollected. Richard Outram. 1993.
Shooting the Stars. John Metcalf. 1993.
From a Seaside Town. Norman Levine. 1993.
Canada Made Me. Norman Levine. 1993.
Onlyville. Cynthia Holz. 1994.
City of Orphans. Patricia Robertson. 1994.
Thrand of Gotu. George Johnston. 1994.
How Insensitive. Russell Smith. 1994.
A Litany in Time of Plague. K.D. Miller. 1994.
Lives of the Mind Slaves. Matt Cohen. 1994.
Popular Anatomy. Keath Fraser. 1995.
On earth as it is. Steven Heighton. 1995.
Driving Men Mad. Elise Levine. 1995.
The Lusty Man. Terry Griggs. 1995.
Influence of the Moon. Mary Borsky. 1995.
Help Me Jacques Cousteau. Gil Adamson. 1995.
Lovers and Other Strangers. Carol Malyon. 1996.
Sailor Man. Leo Simpson. 1996.
Telling My Love Lies. Keath Fraser. 1996.
The Garden of Earthly Delights. Meeka Walsh. 1996.
Kiss Me. Andrew Pyper. 1996.
The Porcupine's Quill Reader. Eds. Tim Inkster and John Metcalf. 1996.
Dancer. Shelley Peterson. 1996.
Buying on Time. Antanas Sileika. 1997.
If I Were Me. Clark Blaise. 1997.
Small Change. Elizabeth Hay. 1997.
Sleeping Weather. Cary Fagan. 1997.
Jacob's Ladder. Joel Yanofsky. 1997.
Promise of Shelter. Robyn Sarah. 1997.
Collected Poems (Vol. 1). P.K. Page. 1997.
Collected Poems (Vol. 2). P.K. Page. 1997.
The Schemers and Viga Glum. George Johnston. 1997.
Learning to Live Indoors. Alison Acheson. 1998.

Love in a Warm Climate. Kelley Aitken. 1998.
The Bubble Star. Lesley-Anne Bourne. 1998.
Belle of the Bayou. Joanne Goodman. 1998.
The King of Siam. Murray Logan. 1998.
Mixed-Up Grandmas. Carol Malyon. 1998.
Ripostes. Philip Marchand. 1998.
Noise. Russell Smith. 1998.
Aquarium. Mike Barnes. 1999.
Devil's Darning Needle. Linda Holeman. 1999.
Give Me Your Answer. K.D. Miller. 1999.
Old Flames. Kim Moritsugu. 1999.
Abby Malone. Shelley Peterson. 1999.
The Man Who Loved Jane Austen. Ray Smith. 1999.
One Last Good Look. Michael Winter. 1999.
Crossing the Salt Flats. Christopher Wiseman. 1999.
Southern Stories. Clark Blaise. 2000.
Kurgan. Don Coles. 2000.
Walking in Paradise. Libby Creelman. 2000.
How Did You Sleep? Paul Glennon. 2000.
Oxygen. Annabol Lyon. 2000.
Carnival. Harold Rhenisch. 2000.
This Is Our Writing. T.F. Rigelhof. 2000.
Great Expectations. Grant Robinson. 2000.
The One with the News. Sandra Sabatini. 2000.
Love Street. Susan Perly. 2001.
Facsimiles of Time. Eric Ormsby. 2001.
Gambler's Fallacy. Judith Cowan. 2001.
Dr. Swarthmore. Alexander Scala. 2001.
Pittsburgh Stories. Clark Blaise. 2001.
A Kind of Fiction. P.K. Page. 2001.
Dove Legend. Richard Outram. 2001.
Holy Writ. K.D. Miller. 2001.
The Lover's Progress. David Solway. 2001.
13. Mary-Lou Zeitoun. 2002.
When Words Deny the World. Stephen Henighan. 2002.
Seasoning Fever. Susan Kerlake. 2002.
A Tourist's Guide to Glengarry. Ian McGillis. 2002.
The Understanding. Jane Barker Wright. 2002.
The Stand-In. David Helwig. 2002.
The Deep. Mary Swan. 2002.

Uncomfortably Numb. Sharon English. 2002.
The Syllabus. Mike Barnes. 2002.
Montreal Stories. Clark Blaise. 2003.
After All! Hugh Hood. 2003.
A Game to Play on the Tracks. Lorna Jackson. 2003.
Forde Abroad. John Metcalf. 2003.
Director's Cut. David Solway. 2003.
Writers Talking. John Metcalf and Claire Wilkshire (Eds.). 2003.
Always Now (Vol. I). Margaret Avison. 2003.
Emma's Hands. Mary Swan. 2003.
So Beautiful. Ramona Dearing. 2004.
The Man Who Hated Emily Bronte. Ray Smith. 2004.
Contrary Angel. Mike Barnes. 2004.
Making Light of Tragedy. Jessica Grant. 2004.
Duet. David Helwig. 2004.
Always Now. (Vol. II). Margaret Avison. 2004.
Summat Else. Royston Tester. 2004.
A Lover's Quarrel. Carmine Starnino. 2004.
In John Updike's Room: Poems New and Selected. Chris Wiseman. 2005.
Dodecahedron. Paul Glennon. 2005.
Most Wanted. Vivette Kady. 2005.
Lines of Truth and Conversation. Joan Alexander. 2005.
Banana Kiss. Bonnie Rozanski. 2005.
Always Now. (Vol. 3). Margaret Avison. 2005.
The Names of Things. David Helwig. 2006.
Canadian Literature in English. (Revised). W.J. Keith. 2006.
Zero Gravity. Sharon English. 2006.
World Body. (Vol. 4). Clark Blaise. 2006.
Borderline. Bonnie Rozanski. 2007.
Bambina. Francesca Piredda. 2007.

BOOKS EDITED for Biblioasis

Catalogue Raisonné. Mike Barnes. 2005.
Bright Objects of Desire. Michèle Adams. 2005.
Airstream. Patricia Young. 2006.
Hitting the Charts: Selected Stories. Leon Rooke. 2006.
Saltsea. David Helwig. 2006.
Time's Covenant: Selected Poems. Eric Ormsby. 2007.

Little Eurekas. Robyn Sarah. 2007.
The Flush of Victory. Ray Smith. 2007.
boYs. Kathleen Winter. 2007.
The Goldfish Dancer. Patricia Robertson. 2007.
Cold-Cocked: On Hockey. Lorna Jackson. 2007.

Biblioasis Short Fiction Series

Balduchi's Who's Who. Leon Rooke. 2005.
Saturday Night Function. Annabel Lyon. 2005.
The Sociology of Love. Clark Blaise. 2005.
Mr. Justice. Caroline Adderson. 2005.
A Theory of Probablility. Judith McCormack. 2005.
Bigmouth. Terry Griggs. 2005.
Reynolds and the Theory of Dream. Russell Smith. 2006.
Graves of the Heroes. Patricia Robertson. 2006.
The Flying Woman. Sharon English. 2006.
1957 Chevy BelAir. Guy Vanderhaeghe. 2007.
Speck's Idea. Mavis Gallant. 2007.
Ceazer Salad. John Metcalf. 2007.

The Magnum Book Store Reading Series Publications

Acts of Kindness and of Love. John Metcalf.
Daddy Stump. Leon Rooke.
Sixty Billion Humans. Hugh Hood.
A Night at the Opera. Ray Smith.
Contacts. Dayv James-French.
Tag. Terry Griggs.
Trouble. Diane Schoemperlen.
Passages. Rohinton Mistry.
Extracts from *Works-in-Progress.* Joan MacLeod.
An Excerpt from *The Redeemer.* Doug Glover.
A Selection of Poems. Irving Layton.
Fragment of a *Novel-in-Progress.* Jane Urquhart.
An Excerpt from *In the Time of the Angry Queen.* Mark Frutkin.
An Excerpt from a *Novel-in-Progress.* Don Dickinson.
I Had a Father. Clark Blaise.

For Gods and Fathers. Steven Heighton.
From a Family Album. Norman Levine.
Keys. Carol Shields.
Dusters. Gael Turnbull.
Provençal Songs. George Elliott Clarke.
Waiting for Angel. Matt Cohen.
An Extract from *Graven Images.* Audrey Thomas.
Seven Stories. Yann Martel.
How I Got Started and Why I Can't Stop. Isabel Huggan.
Extract from *Black Nightingale.* John Mills.
Poems. John Newlove.

Food for Thought Reading Series Publications

The Lady and the Servant. Norman Levine.
Landscape with Poisoner. Caroline Adderson.
The Boy from Moogradi. Leon Rooke.
Lieutenant Lukac's Cat. John Metcalf.
Hiram and Jenny. Richard Outram.
Provence and *Mystery Stories.* David Helwig.
Delirium. Cynthia Holz.
Our People. Carol Shields.
Berry Season. Patricia Robinson.

MARQUIS
MEMBER OF SCABRINI GROUP
Québec, Canada
2007